How To Tie a Tie

Steven L. Denlinger

Dedication

To my wife, Laura, for being my love and my inspiration. Thank you for your constancy, and for offering this Cowardly Lion the courage he needed.

Abuse is an infection that surges through families,
begetting more abuse.

"Don't get above your raisin'."

~ Southern American Aphorism

"Why do some humans find the hero's journey of the heart irresistible, and leave home and all that is familiar to set out on a harrowing path of discovery, courage, truth-telling and healing? By telling his story, Steven empowers us all to find our voice and share his epiphany: a hand-me-down life isn't enough. The only life worth living is the one we lovingly build and learn to call our own."

~ Linford Detweiler, Over the Rhine

"Hear my cry, O God; attend unto my prayer. From the end of the earth will I cry unto Thee, when my heart is overwhelmed: lead me to the rock that is higher than I."

~ Psalm 61: 1-2, The Holy Bible, KJV, 1769

Table of Contents

Content Note

In this memoir, issues of abuse are addressed.

Note from the Author

I left the community I grew up in for myriad reasons, and this memoir has helped me come to terms with my departure. After experiencing and surviving the seven stages of grief, I was able to put my story to paper, looking for the answer to the following three questions:

- How do I disentangle myself from the cultural web of my childhood?
- How do I leave that culture and assimilate into the modern world?
- And, once I do, how do I maintain the friendships of those I love within my former community of faith?

Grief is messy, and thus, my life doesn't fit neatly into seven stages. It is a pattern among those who leave similar communities—few move through the stages of grief neatly. But as we look back over the vista of our lives, we can see a clear arc.

This memoir is about *my* journey through grief, my transition out of a hidden enclave into the modern world. It's about how I survived.

Foreword

Anabaptists and Anglicans hold in common the commitment to "amendment of life," a phrase found both in Article 6 of the Mennonite Dordrecht Confession of Faith and in the prayer of absolution from the daily prayer offices of the Episcopal Book of Common Prayer. My friend Steven Denlinger, whose life journey has taken him from the "Plain" religious habits of conservative Mennonites to the "fancy" liturgical rhythms of progressive Episcopalians, tells the penitential story of his difficult and dramatic "amendment of life" in this remarkable memoir.

To be sure, Steven's narrative does not at first feel like a tale of penitence. Instead, the reader encounters many commonplaces of the currently popular "deconstruction" genre: anger at the hypocrisies of faith communities, grief over the loss of old certainties and familiar relationships, and the crafting of a truthful selfhood beyond fear and trauma.

But readers anticipating the discovery of a new truth that replaces all the failed absolutes will search in vain. Instead, they will find a winding and sometimes risky path of faith that involves the anxious acceptance of a less certain world, the reluctant embrace of more ambiguous convictions, and the persistent haunting of the present by the ghosts of communities past.

As Steven confronts the hurt and harm he experienced at the hands of preachers and teachers and parents, he acknowledges that he himself participated in the abusive culture of his conservative Mennonite community; indeed, he recognizes that this abusive culture compromised his closest relationships long after he left the Plain people, motivating him to seek counsel and make changes. Steven's approach to coping with these difficult personal discoveries is to craft an art of life and love that redeems rather than repudiates his experiences of regret.

Indeed, Steven's memoir is as much a story about understanding the flawed family of faith that shaped his childhood as it is about discovering the self being born anew beyond the grip of controlling church and family systems. Steven realizes that those who hurt him the most—including especially his father—also loved him dearly and he returns this love with empathy and, eventually, a forgiveness that is not so frivolous as to forget.

The Plain people who populate the community of Steven's youth are conservative Mennonites who in the 1950's and 60's withdrew from assimilating Mennonite conferences to maintain separated nonconformist communities free

i

from the consumer culture and entertainment technologies of the late twentieth century. However, many of these conservative Mennonites had also been influenced by fundamentalist doctrines such as biblical inerrancy and normative patriarchy. It's this collision of controlling fundamentalism with nonresistant Anabaptism that contributes to some of the strangely contradictory compulsions of power amidst ostensibly peaceable people that Steven describes in this book.

Having been raised and baptized in the same isolated corner of the conservative Mennonite subculture that shaped Steven, I can attest that his characterization of this peculiar community rings true to my own experience, even if we pursued somewhat different pathways out. Like Steven, I experienced conservative Mennonites as contentious and creatively disruptive of their boundaries—including the confines of patriarchy that both of our mothers found ways to subvert. Like Steven, I had a wise teacher in my church school who encouraged critical and independent thinking and invited me to consider going to college. Like Steven, my experience of sexual desire and intimate relationships was awkwardly compromised by the invasively enforced purity culture of the conservative Mennonites. And although I did not personally experience the child abuse Steven describes, I certainly witnessed it.

Part of Steven's story is the immensely valuable gift of a liberal arts education at an evangelical Quaker college that we both attended, where new friends, consequential mentors, and cross-cultural experiences in large cities decisively changed the direction of our lives and made it possible for us to become something more than our communities of origin had planned for us. At the same time, our friends and mentors from Malone College helped us to also see what was good and beautiful in the flawed Mennonite communities from which we were running. Now that the value of a university education is described almost exclusively in terms of increased earnings capacity, this memoir reminds us of what has always been the greatest gift of a liberal arts education—the knowledge and resilience to craft a good life from the resources at hand—including those deriving from the accidents of birth.

Finally, as a lover of romances, I am delighted to pitch this memoir as a love story. It's a story of damaged love and lost love to be sure, but also the story of love found and love won. The work of love recalled here is unfinished, well past the happy ending and deep into the joys and sorrows of enduring covenant love—in both its divine and human forms. Because this memoir is first and finally a story of such persistent and enduring love, love that changes hearts and minds, we can be sure that it is a true story.

Gerald J. Mast, Ph.D.
Professor of Communication
Bluffton University

A Note about the Book's Construction

Because of the way memory works, it is impossible to recall exactly how things took place or what was said. Thus, I have embraced the conventions of creative nonfiction to find the truth. All dialogue is reconstructed to achieve this, rather than literally transcribed.

Except for those closest to me—most members of my family, and some close friends who loyally supported me across the eighteen years I took to finish this memoir—most names have been changed to protect the innocent, and perhaps the guilty. This is not a memoir of vengeance, but a journey of faith. My story shows the traumatic impact of physical abuse within a patriarchal community of faith, where many people I love still live.

Not every father in our community believed like mine did, and not every person in our community experienced the same physical abuse I did.

But some did, and some still do.

Preface

The day I left my Amish-Mennonite community in Ohio was the day my life began.

The decision was inspired several years before when I listened to Chaim Potok's novel, *My Name Is Asher Lev,* on the way home from college, tears rolling down my cheeks, absorbing the story of a child prodigy who grows up as an Hasidic Jew, driven to draw and paint the world as he saw it. The experience was gut-wrenching. I completely identified with the young boy as he struggled to escape his strict, insular culture to find his voice as an artist.

For the first time, I'd encountered in a novel someone who faced the same demons I had, who could not understand why he needed to leave to find his voice any more than I did. His family loved him every bit as much as mine had loved me. They fought him every step of the way out—just as mine had—for precisely that reason. Thanks to Potok, I knew I didn't belong there any longer and that I'd have to find my way out.

His story showed me the way.

Prologue

"Give sorrow words; the grief that does not speak
whispers the o'er-fraught heart and bids it break."

William Shakespeare
Macbeth, Act 4, Scene 3
First Folio, 1623

Secrets and Lies

Secrets are funny things. All families have them. Skeletons in the closet. Buried corpses you don't dig up in polite company.

Usually, those secrets involve sex.

In my childhood, I was fooled by my family's sincerity, which they wore as proudly as a Sunday suit. My father hated secrets. He'd felt them all around him as a child and had kept a few himself. He encouraged all of us to be open and honest.

I learned my father's lessons well, even when it meant fighting him tooth and nail. And thus, when I abandoned my family, I discovered the world was a confusing place.

The reality is, I learned too late, no one can be completely transparent.

As a child, I remember watching my Grandpa Denlinger wash his car. He loved taking care of that sleek, white Buick, loved waxing it 'til it shone. When he visited us in Ohio, he'd park it in front of our garage. He'd wash it, wash it again, then wipe it down with a chamois.

If I chose to help, Grandpa would reward me with a story, a gooey, ice-cream sundae of sweet, luscious words. Since he lived and worked among the streets and buildings of our nation's capital, I knew his stories were true because he was our grandpa and was to be respected. We admired President Nixon, who was conservative and didn't lie like the liberals. We knew even *he* had a close personal relationship with Grandpa. It wasn't that my grandfather ever told me or even implied such a thing; I just knew my grandpa was the biggest man in the world, and I couldn't imagine why the president wouldn't desire my grandpa's help and advice or want to hear one of his stories.

My grandfather also knew how to dress. His love for style showed in everything he wore, from his expensive suits and ties to his shined wingtip shoes, but especially in the way he used his expressive hands to tell his stories, with his gleaming gold watch.

He always dressed in a suit and tie. He'd once told me that he never wore jeans because, when he was young, he'd had to wear overalls to work on the farm. He'd left those ugly farm clothes behind when he fled the farm for his first professional job. At his funeral, I discovered from his neighbors in Chevy Chase, Maryland, that my grandfather was the only man on the block who washed his car and mowed his lawn in a suit and tie.

I think Grandpa was the first person I knew who first showed me it was

3

possible to leave the community of my birth and find a life outside. As a child, he was a mystery to me. It would be years before I realized why he seemed so distant with us, why my family talked about him behind his back, and why he ignored our whispers—they didn't bother him because our world owned nothing he wanted, and thus, held no power over him.

Each summer, my grandfather spent his vacation with us. Each summer, he taught me to paint, his fast-moving brush teaching my slower, more awkward hands how to add a glistening white finish to our patched-up cracker box of a house.

I idolized my grandfather's polished charm. I wanted to be just like him. He returned my affection. When I was six, he brought me a red Schwinn bicycle. I loved that bike.

My profound admiration for him kept me from understanding why my family distrusted my grandfather or gossiped about him. It blinded me to the discomfort my father showed when I asked him questions about Grandpa. It confused me when I first realized that he had a disreputable reputation. I couldn't figure out why.

I discerned the truth about my grandfather's mysterious past during family devotions one Saturday when my grandpa was visiting. He was there to paint the house again.

My father held this daily religious ritual in our living room, where couches and overstuffed chairs circled about the room. It started with someone reading the Bible, then Dad would make comments, and then we'd kneel and pray. We learned from infanthood how to listen quietly—those who didn't were corrected. Dad ran a tight ship, and he wanted to make sure each of his children knew the Bible, book by book, and verse by verse.

To keep us engaged, my father often asked one of his children to read from the Bible. That morning, it'd been my turn. When I learned this, I visited Grandpa outside, who was already up a ladder starting his task, his brush moving expertly, the white paint going on smooth and clean. When I told Grandpa that I would lead devotions, he smiled at me with affection. He'd be there to hear me read.

I was permitted to choose any Scripture passage I liked, so innocently, I chose to read the story of The Woman at the Well in John 4, where Jesus meets a "fallen" woman and requests that she call her husband.

To give my grandfather credit, he sat there and took it like a man; I'm sure he didn't think I was comparing him to the polyamorous woman. My father saw the situation differently. But because I was so focused on theatrically reciting the forty-two-verses in the tale, I failed to sense my father's growing dismay. When I dramatically arrived at the moment of Christ's startling revelation— "Thou hast had five husbands," said Jesus, "and he whom thou now hast is not thy husband"—my father took direct action, cutting into my stellar performance.

"There's an even better Biblical passage, Steve, that deals with the water of life." He cleared his throat. "So, ah, let's turn to…"

I was bewildered. How could my father cut short my moment in the sun? This was unforgivable. But, after reading the replacement passage, and offering an abrupt prayer, my father disappeared, saying he had lots of work to do that morning… out in the garage.

The family trailed out after him.

I sank back in tears, devastated by my father's rejection of the passage I had so carefully chosen. This had never happened to me before.

What did I do wrong?

My grandfather patted me on the shoulder. "I liked your passage," he said. "You're a good reader. That school of yours must be doing a good job teaching you." Then, picking up his paint bucket and brush, he wandered out.

Barely had the door closed when two of my older sisters thundered back into the room.

"What happened?" I wailed, hunching my shoulders in shame.

Outside, Grandpa descended the porch steps.

"You don't know about Grandpa's other woman?"

"What are you talking about?"

As my sisters smeared my grandpa's shining image, ladling on the family dirt, my mind sped over my grandparents' visits. The way Grandma and Aunt Betty always left for the Harleigh Inn in North Canton while Grandpa stayed at our house. The way Grandpa and Grandma never shared the same room.

Now I learned from my sisters that Grandpa had another woman in Washington, D.C., which is why he lived there. I suddenly recalled various snippets of conversation I'd overheard. There was also that odd formality between my grandparents that I noticed. I remembered my father's reactions when my mother would criticize him, or when they'd argue:

"At least I'm not unfaithful."

"At least I don't lie to my family."

And with a pop, the flashbulb of truth exploded.

My grandfather was not the man I thought he was. He'd been unfaithful to my grandmother, who was always gentle to me, and whom I adored for her ability to make such a good Thanksgiving meal, especially the mashed potatoes and gravy. I rubbed my eyes as my sisters continued talking excitedly among themselves. My vision of my grandfather was suddenly tarnished. Maybe I couldn't trust him after all. Was he even a Christian? Was he going to Heaven? Surely not if he was an "adulterer."

I needed to pray for Grandpa.

When I grew older, I discovered that my grandfather Paul Denlinger's problems with his marriage emerged after the birth of his fifth child, my aunt Lois. Frustrated by her many pregnancies, Anna (his wife and my grandmother)

5

announced to my grandfather that they would no longer share a bed. Like every other woman in America, my grandmother wasn't legally allowed to use birth control, but she didn't want more children, perhaps because, by then, her brothers had become suspicious that my grandfather wasn't being faithful. He had submitted to her wishes. For a while, he'd shared a room with my father, Earl, their only son, while Grandma had bunked with their oldest daughter, Betty.

When Paul won a lucrative sales position in Washington, D.C., he bought a house there, living in D.C. during the work week, and coming home only on the weekends. Which is when, it turns out, Grandpa began to have "memory" problems. You'd think a salesman who could rivet any audience with detailed stories wouldn't have this problem… but he did.

He somehow "forgot" to tell my grandmother he'd found a housekeeper named Florence (who had abandoned her vocation as a Catholic nun). Important details continued to slip his mind, like… oh, say… the way that ex-nun had given birth to three of his daughters.

Grandpa's memory problem only started to come to light when a heart attack struck him down while in D.C. When she heard the news, my grandmother called the hospital, only to be told his wife was already with him. My aunt, Betty, vividly remembered how her mother immediately reached for the Bible after putting the phone down.

The *coup de grace*, though, of his supposed memory loss was when, twenty years later, he brought that DC wife's three adult daughters to meet their "new" sisters—the ones he'd had with his original wife—then promptly left the entire group of siblings alone while he went to the drugstore for antacids. Stress probably, though why he'd brought them to meet the others, we could never figure out.

His children were left to get acquainted. At one point Betty—the eldest— fired a question at her new sisters they never forgot:

"How does it feel to be illegitimate?"

I remember being shocked when I first heard this story.

Today, divorce and remarriage are so common that this kind of passive-aggressive behavior seems naïve and rude—we expect children to get over themselves when families break apart. But within her Mennonite culture, Betty's response makes sense. She had been devastated by her father's behavior, and since she wasn't permitted to challenge her father, she decided to provoke her half-sisters.

I believe my father's life was an answer to my grandfather's example. Dad maintained a rock-solid commitment to my mother and us children. This gave us a profound feeling of security. Although my parents' marriage had its rough patches, I never wondered whether my father loved my mother. My father was determined to give his children what he never had.

The other part of the story I remember is Betty's reaction to my grandmother's submissive attitude to a husband who had essentially abandoned her. When Betty objected, my grandmother explained, "We shall continue to treat Papa respectfully. Always." From my grandmother's perspective, there was no other option for her at the time, not if she wished to remain within her Mennonite church or community.

My father must have felt the pain of his father's abandonment acutely since coming from a broken home in the 1940s was quite different than it is today. It eliminated my father's childhood. From the beginning, my father was forced to obey his mother, who had a will of iron. As the man of the family, he had to work a job while he was going to high school, getting up early each morning to do so. He had to discipline his younger sisters. Nor could my father tell their explosive secret to anyone outside the family. And so, he guarded it well, treating Papa respectfully and ignoring his frequent absences.

When Paul lived in Washington, D.C., he was known as the Mennonite father of three daughters and the husband of their Catholic mother. When Paul visited his people in Lancaster, he was known as the Mennonite father of four daughters and one son who worked during the week in the capital, two hours from home. Within their Mennonite community, my grandmother ensured that her husband's reputation—and thus her family's—would remain blameless.

It was a Devil's bargain.

How does a man guard a secret so gaping and vast? More to the point, what would cause him to create a life like that? One of my aunts once called my grandfather a pathological liar. I don't know about that, but I suspect he was good at it. During the week, he lived with his second family and worked in Washington, D.C. He made good money, drove a new Buick, and rarely provided my grandmother with financial help. He slept in a different bedroom when he was home, and although this must have appeared strange to his children, they didn't seem to understand the implications of this—except for Betty, after the heart attack. And every weekend, when Papa came home, he was treated like a king, no matter the pain and poverty he was causing them.

No disrespect to Grandmother, but one has to wonder what kind of lesson that policy taught her children. Perhaps she hoped her kindness would win him back.

It didn't.

I don't know what the men of my family have learned from this, but I know my female cousins have rejected this philosophy. One confided to me that, in our family, the men got away with everything.

"It's not fair," she told me, bitterly.

But patriarchal privilege was embedded in my family's culture. When one of my cousins was frustrated by the behavior of her husband, her aunt schooled her in the power of male privilege. "Men can't help themselves," she explained. "You've just got to forgive them."

This is the kind of toxic patriarchy they spoon-fed me as "normal," and it was because of this that I ultimately rebelled.

7

My grandfather's second family took care of him during the latter years of his life. One of Florence's children, Cathy, took it upon herself to move her father into a nursing home, and then she proceeded to clean up the house that her father had shared with her mother. As Cathy went through his papers, she discovered that she also needed to put her father's financial records in order. My grandfather had significant credit card debt, which Cathy paid off.

Both sides of the family struggled to know how to respond to my grandfather in his final years. At my grandmother's funeral, for example, Anna's children would not permit their father to sit too closely to their mother's casket or at the graveside service. A few years later, Florence also passed, and eventually... my grandfather followed his two wives.

I remember his funeral service vividly. It was there I learned that in the months before he died, Grandfather had attempted to mend his transgressions by reluctantly returning to the Mennonite church. Guided by his pastor, he had met with all his children to find reconciliation. They assured him of their forgiveness.

At the memorial service I attended, his siblings, his children, and his grandchildren were encouraged to tell stories about the impact our grandfather had had on us. The only thing I could remember was the time he saved my life.

So, I rose and told my story.

The story I told them occurred in August 1988 at the Washington-Dulles Airport amid my departure from the States. I was traveling to London, England for my final year of undergraduate work at Richmond College, and I was going against the wishes of my immediate family and my entire church community.

My way had been paid by a Rotary Foundation Scholarship. In my application, I had included a photo of myself in a Plain coat, which has no lapels and closes up the front with a series of buttons. It has no room for a tie, which is considered worldly, unneeded, and fancy—in other words, not Plain. The Amish version uses hooks and eyes instead of buttons. Otherwise, it's the same basic concept: both versions distinguish the wearer from the world through their Plainness.

I'm sure the Rotary Selection Committee was confused by that photo. The conservative Mennonites are a distinct subculture of Anabaptist faith that draws upon many elements of Amish culture—community, separation from the world, and simplicity of dress/style—yet it accepts some modern conveniences such as electricity, automobiles, and telephones. From the outside, it's easy to get confused.

But for me, that confusion was just fine if it gave me an edge in the competition. I was ready to take any advantage I could get, just to escape.

But here's where things get complicated.

When I'd first applied, I'd planned to continue wearing my Plain coat in England, probably because I never thought I'd win. *After* I won the scholarship,

I began to contemplate breaking away. I was twenty-four years old, and, for the first time, in charge of my own life. And I had come to believe I would be a better witness for Christ if I wore modern clothes.

But still I struggled.

The Plain coat, worn for any formal occasion, was an important symbol to us. My ancestors had endured persecution during the Reformation. Choosing *not* to wear the coat would be a major signal that I was becoming worldly, which was very bad.

I was on the edge, unsure what to do.

The turning point came when I first called my Rotary hosts, Richard and Joan Cook, who would board me when I wasn't in school.

Mr. Cook was a wealthy haberdasher who owned a store that outfitted men with high-end formal wear. When the subject of my clothing came up, I tried to explain our Plain coat tradition, but I might as well have been speaking High German because Mr. Cook didn't understand my rationale. Why would a proper young man, raised in a good home, not wear the appropriate suit and tie? I somehow couldn't get across to him that this was a religious custom. Across the ocean that separated Hartville and London, I could feel his stress rising.

"You won't wear a tie?" Mr. Cook was perplexed.

"We don't wear a tie with a Plain coat."

"No tie?" Impatience etched his voice.

"It's a cultural tradition."

"We encourage all the lads to wear a tie and jacket at every meeting." His voice was severe.

I'd lived all my life within our community, and I had never tied a tie around my neck. It dawned on me that Mr. Cook was giving me the perfect reason to change that. "I suppose I could wear a coat and tie."

"You're sure you can?" His voice was hopeful.

It was a crucial moment, that conversation. Suddenly, I saw a pathway open, a chance to break away. I could barely admit this desire to myself, so frightened was I, but the desire was there, beneath the surface. This was a signal from God.

I became sure.

"Oh, now, that's a good lad."

I could hear the relief in his voice. To my surprise my feelings echoed his. A weight had lifted. I had been fighting for this opportunity, ever since I had come to believe that the way my people were interacting with the world was wrong.

After hanging up, I took a deep breath. For the first time, I had a *bona fide* reason to buy my first suit and tie. Without consulting my parents, I went shopping at Sears, and when I came home with my new coat, I remember my mother's long face and the sadness with which she considered me. I'm sure she imagined I might start drinking or smoking while I was in England, or, worse, get a girl pregnant or marry a worldly woman not of our tribe.

She had reason to worry.

I was worried as well, although I didn't show it. But several weeks before I left for London, the tightness increasing in my chest, I wrote to my grandfather, telling him of my plans. I asked him if he'd please meet me during my long layover at the Washington-Dulles Airport.

He wrote back, agreeing to do so.

When I think back to that time in my life, I think of the dinner I had with him there. The parting gift of grace he offered gave me a lens through which I now view my year abroad.

When my grandfather greeted me at the airport, he treated me like a star. This was well before 9/11, so he was able to meet me at the gate. Although he was eighty-three at the time, he was still in full control of his mental faculties and his Buick, and he insisted on carrying one of my bags.

Grandpa had reserved a table at the nicest restaurant in the airport. He told me to order whatever I wanted. After carefully looking at the menu, I ordered a steak dinner. When it came, I consumed its deliciousness as I listened to Grandpa tell stories. The familiarity of his voice, the pride he showed as he introduced me to the waitress—"My grandson is going to London on a Rotary Scholarship to get a first-rate education"—reassured me.

During that meal, Grandpa told me he had once talked to a Rotarian about this scholarship, and he knew how much the scholarship was worth. "They don't choose just anyone. This is a big deal. It's going to change your life."

It was the first time anyone in my family had expressed pride in me for what I was doing. As far as they were concerned, I was slinking out the back door, intent on leaving the true faith. Now as I listened to my grandfather, I realized that he didn't believe that at all. He was proud that I was going to London.

But I didn't say this. At that point in my life, I didn't know how to thank him. My feelings about him were confused. He had lied to my father, had led a double life, and was not to be trusted. He was a person of the world, a sinner. Yet he was also the only one who was proud of me, who understood how much of a difference this would make in my life. I didn't know how to reconcile the cognitive dissonance that was battering the walls of my mind.

But our meal was coming to an end, and I suddenly dreaded losing the familiarity of my grandfather's presence. I glanced at my watch. In half an hour, I needed to be at the gate, ready to board the plane—completely on my own, bound for a life that would transform me in ways I couldn't yet imagine.

And then, during the last few minutes of that meal, my grandfather discovered that, not only had I never worn a necktie, but that I also didn't have a clue about how to tie one.

This was unacceptable to Grandpa. His favorite grandson, he told me, would not enter the world of Rotary unprepared. He told me to follow him, and we went to the men's restroom, with me still carrying my bags.

To someone who didn't understand our culture, tying a tie is not a big deal. But my people had rejected it because they valued purity above all else—thus, they maintained a strict separation from the world, especially in what we wore. In our Amish-Mennonite culture, a man's necktie was a symbol of all that was corrupt in the outside world. By wearing a tie, I was signaling my allegiance to the world, not to the people of God.

I was about to embrace this symbol.

I had rejected my family's warnings that I was becoming worldly, that I was on the broad road heading for Hell. If I went on this trip, God might punish me, probably by having my plane crash somewhere in the Atlantic.

A lifetime of conditioning is not easily overcome. Fear isn't a rational thing, and it simmered within my body. I was supposed to be a full-grown man, and I didn't understand why I couldn't overcome my fear.

My community knew how to control me, knew exactly what to say. "We cannot accept the changes you have made; we cannot accept what you are doing; we cannot accept you for who you are because no person doing what you are doing will make it to Heaven. We know this."

Only my secretive grandfather seemed to support me.

He alone seemed to understand what I was facing, an understanding that came from years of isolation, from a lifetime spent torn between the Mennonite family who condemned him for abandoning them, and the Catholic family who couldn't understand his religious background.

I was facing the same thing, leaving an Amish-Mennonite family behind who condemned me, and facing a world that wouldn't understand me. I was frightened to death of my future, sure that the world would eventually figure out my fraud and throw me back. During our conversation, he had somehow seen my fears. He had known instantly what I could not admit—that I was not ready to meet the world.

My grandfather had been there.

He knew that for me, learning how to tie a tie was a rite of passage essential to my goal of assimilating into modern culture. It was symbolic of the transition from the black-and-white morality of childhood to the more complex ethics of manhood.

My father's choice to withhold from me this moment represented the way my entire culture had hobbled me, teaching me that the outside world was a place I should fear, rather than an arena in which I could confidently negotiate. My grandfather had never criticized my father to me. But recognizing that I was unprepared to enter the world, my grandfather now stepped into the gap.

Today, I think back to that moment with wonder.

Taking out one of the inexpensive ties I had purchased, I handed it to my grandfather, and we turned to the mirror, my grandfather standing behind me. I breathed in his Old Spice cologne as his hands moved silently about my neck, guiding my hands as I tied my first tie. I stood there, my grandfather's arms around me, feeling the silence hover around me within that otherwise empty bathroom with its mirror, porcelain, and tile, aware of Grandpa's breath flavored by too many antacids as he gently helped me tie my first tie.

In the silence of that moment, my grandfather's actions offered more to me than any story he had ever shared. He bestowed on me a rite of initiation my father failed to offer me.

Now... here... by teaching me to tie a tie, he was preparing me to leave the world of my childhood, a world of secrets and lies. He was ushering me into a world in which I would have to identify those who told me the truth and those who offered me untruths. It would take me decades to understand how to do this.

But learning how to tie a tie was a start.

And then we were walking to the boarding gate, and then I was looking back at him as I entered security, and then I was alone in the empty hallway leading down to the plane, my boots echoing in the stillness.

Book I: Original Sin

Foolishness is bound in the heart of a child, but the rod of correction shall drive it far from him.

~ Proverbs 22: 15, *The Holy Bible,* KJV, 1769

Interpolation I: Playing House

Children have always played out adult rituals. Some dress up in their mother's makeup and high heels, and some wear the ball gowns of a Disney princess. Some play with trucks or act out Westerns with toy guns.

But in my neighborhood, my friends and I played "House" in an abandoned washhouse, located on the hill just above our home.

Playing house, often with dolls, is a fairly common game among most children. But in our case, perhaps because we lived in a very different world than most children, the rules of the game were a little different. Boys had to be in charge, and girls had to obey. And misbehavior was handled a little differently.

At six years old, I was the daddy—someone needed to be—and my favorite "daughter" was about a year younger. Everyone knows that a Daddy must spank disobedient children—in private, of course. My favorite daughter was especially naughty. Giggling, she would let me spank her.

This is not normal behavior among children who play together, but I suspect this idea came from our having observed siblings being punished this way. Or it's possible a sibling taught it to me. I cannot remember. Whatever the source, my memory is clear.

When I reached adolescence, I was reading a serial Western in the Grit newspaper I peddled around the neighborhood, when I came upon a scene in which a cowboy confronts the "spoiled" young heiress on the ranch where he'd just been hired.

Sparks flew between them—she told him he was rude, I recall—which in most romances leads to the requisite kiss. But this cowboy wasn't putting up with her attitude. He pulled her across his lap and spanked her. She flounced away, but he had gotten her attention, and soon after that, she fell in love with him.

It was at this point that my libido took charge, recalling my childhood game.

"What if spanking were part of sex?"

It was shocking, titillating.

As I reached my early teens, one of the older neighbor boys pointed me to a trailer in the woods behind our house, ostensibly abandoned. In reality, it contained an extensive library of hard-core porn magazines. I had not yet

15

reached puberty, but I was curious, and I loved to read. One day in a copy of Penthouse Forum, *I discovered a scene in which an angry wife spanks her husband. It supercharges their sex life.*

These moments of childhood play—combined with the severe corporal punishment I was receiving and watching both at home and at school—were disturbing. Perhaps they affected me more deeply than my peers. I am sure the adults in my life didn't imagine that my budding sexuality would fuse to these images during the most intimate and painful moments of my childhood.

One morning during devotions in our school chapel, we were asked to pray for two Christian Day School teachers who were arrested for beating a child in Pennsylvania. This was an example of the worldly "evil State" overreaching its rights, we were told. God had instructed parents and teachers not to "spare the rod," we were told. We should obediently bow our heads and pray that God would protect the teachers, we were told.

It's striking that no one seemed all that concerned about the child, who I recall was a special-needs student. Spanking a child was normal, we were taught. But none of our teachers asked the obvious question: "How could it be normal when these two teachers were arrested by the authorities?"

Only later did I realize the long-term psychological damage that can take place when an adult repeatedly strikes a child's buttocks, one of the body's most erogenous zones. Only later did I make the connection between the humiliation a person experiences when they are asked to bend over for discipline—a sexually submissive position—and a person's sexuality.

Even when it's a child.

Chapter 1: A Burning Desire

When I wonder, as I sometimes do, how it was that I fell in love with reading; when I consider why I have been God-haunted across the six decades of my life; when I contemplate what is the birthplace of my passion for the rhythms of the written word, I think about a welcoming classroom in Northeastern Ohio.

I was five years old, and the day approached when I would enter first grade. I bragged to my older sisters about how fast I was going to learn to read. Then, one day, my oldest sister sat me down and explained that the State of Ohio had a cutoff date. Because I was a September baby, I might not be old enough to go to school this year.

I was horrified, devastated, terrified. "Might not be old enough?" I was going to be six years old! Everyone that age went to school. Was she kidding me?

I went to my mother.

"We'll see, Steve." She sounded busy.

"We'll *see*?" What kind of answer was that? My life hung in the balance. If I didn't go to school this year, my life would be changed—no, my life would be over.

I decided that anything but admission into first grade this year was unacceptable. I wanted to learn how to read books, and I wanted to control when I entered and left my favorite stories.

How many conversations did I have with my mother? I don't know. But eventually, she talked to Sister Sommers, our school's first-grade teacher. My mother knew that Sister Sommers's students performed well on the Stanford Achievement Test because, using phonics, she taught them how to read and write, and she made arithmetic simple.

Sister Sommers was motivated by a faith that was shiny and clean, its structures undergirding her life like the cables and beams of a suspension bridge, and she could manage even the most stubborn of children by inspiring them to love learning. She could advise my mother about what to do with her tiny, firstborn son.

Several days later afterward, my mother informed me we had an important meeting with Sister Sommers at the school.

Finally, my mother was paying attention.

Several days later, on a hot day in August 1969, my mother brought me to my teacher so that I could take the first-grade readiness test.

Sister Sommers' face was pleasant. Her dark hair swept back and up into a white bonnet, framed by white strings that hung down on each side. There wasn't a hair out of place. Her green cape dress included an extra layer of cloth, concealing her bodice. She wore black hose and sturdy shoes.

She smiled at me, a tight adjustment of her thin lips that didn't reveal the mysterious teeth beneath. "Hello. I'm Sister Sommers."

"Hi."

"Your name is Steven, isn't it?" She used my birth name, not the cruder Steve that my family all used, or worse, Stevie.

I nodded. The tile floors looked freshly waxed.

"I teach first grade." Sister Sommers adjusted her lips again.

Inside the classroom, a long yardstick hung beside the chalkboard, and a row of books lined the front of her desk.

As I sat, Sister Sommers closed the door. She picked up an official test document from her desk, placing it before me, making sure it lined up with the edge of the table.

"Is the test hard?" My voice seemed small.

"You just do the best you can," she said. "Any questions, just ask, okay?" There was kindness in her eyes. Sister Sommers patted me on the shoulder.

Then she pulled back the first sheet and the test began. There were many shapes. Sister Sommers pointed to each of them, letting me choose, never pushing me to hurry, happy to wait for me, no matter how long I took.

I decided that, if I passed, I would learn to read the first day in case they changed their minds.

The test took forever, but when it was over, Sister Sommers began to grade it.

Her classroom was bright and cheerful. There were bulletin boards of colorful construction paper cut into orange pumpkins bursting open, a Horn of Plenty that poured out luscious fruit and fall vegetables, and turkey cutouts that clung to the classroom's wall of windows, set against the waving grass on the lawn outside.

My teacher interrupted my wide-eyed exploration. "I'm very pleased with your test," she said, smiling at me. She led me to the door. "I'm going to talk to your mother for a few minutes."

I nodded, pleased by her praise. But I was also worried. My mother could sink my plans.

Outside, Mom was staring into a magazine. She looked up quickly, searching the face of Sister Sommers, who told me I could take my mother's seat. They both went inside the classroom.

The hallway was quiet, and I could hear their murmuring voices. I thought about the test: the careful figures I had drawn, the choices I had made, the smiles Sister Sommers had given me. I couldn't tell how I had done, but I was sure I had pleased her. If only she could become my new teacher.

I heard a faint buzzing sound. A man floated in the air outside the windows at the end of the hall. I crept over. He wasn't floating—he was riding a mower.

Suddenly, the door to the classroom opened, and Sister Sommers was standing there with her big smile and kind eyes. I sat beside my mother while my teacher returned to her desk.

"Did I pass?" I asked, feeling moisture gather on my palms.

"You passed," Sister Sommers said. "You did well."

"Do I get to come to school?"

Sister Sommers glanced at my mother, then busied herself with papers on her desk. Mom sat as if in prayer. Her silence unnerved me—this battle was not over. My heart was about to burst from my chest.

Finally, my mother sighed.

How does a mother choose what is best for a child's future? More than anyone else, my mother must have worried about how much smaller and younger I was than the rest of my incoming class.

Our family did not attend the home church, where all my classmates attended, but a small mission church we drove to in nearby Canton, Ohio. How would I interact with the other students, who all attended our home church next to the school? Would I be able to make friends?

My actions must have given her hope. As I had scrambled to convince her that I needed to go to school *this* year, she had seen a determination already forged. In my arguments with her, I had revealed my passion for learning.

I was not a compliant child. Dragging my rolling wooden dog by its string, I argued with my sisters and often won. Now I wanted to start school, but I would be younger than anyone else in my class.

In the silence of the classroom, my mother picked up the test, leafing through it. I sat still, hoping against hope. I wanted to cry. I was sure she'd say no.

Finally, my mother turned to me. "Steve, you did a good job on the test. This means that you can enter school this fall, but…" She stopped, tears on her cheeks, her voice breaking.

I was suddenly hopeful, but I was also confused. *Why was she crying?*

My mother knelt in front of me. Behind her, Sister Sommers turned away. My mother tried to smooth my unruly hair, where my cowlick had sprung up again, despite the comb and water she had used.

"I'm worried about sending you this early… but I've decided to let you choose."

My mouth dropped open. This had to be a trick. How could this be? How could I decide something this important—whether or not I should come to Sister Sommer's classroom? Adults made decisions like this, a child was never permitted to decide something this important. But I wasn't going to give Mom time to change her mind.

"I want to go, I do," I said.

Sister Sommers turned back to me, smiling, little crinkles appearing under her eyes.

19

"You're going to love reading."

"Yes," I said. "I want to read."

Mom nodded, finally, to my teacher. Then she took me in her arms and hugged me tightly. Happiness suffused me as I felt her warmth, her understanding, her love.

Today, as I reflect on that moment, I am astonished by my mother's choice to let me make that decision. I have wondered since then if she ever regretted it, allowing me that much autonomy so early in my life. But it's also who my mother was. Someone less wise might have tried to control me. In that decision, my mother did not.

As I reflect on my pre-school days, I realize she had always encouraged me in my curiosity. As a child I had gained the nickname of Question Box from my family, probably because of the endless questions I asked everyone, especially adults. I didn't know at the time that this was the foundation of my profound love for learning, and my determined pursuit of it. The fact that my mother somehow recognized and encouraged this was the greatest gift she gave me. Perhaps she remembered what it was like to be the hard-working student her father pulled out of high school in her sophomore year to work on his vegetable farm. That decision had disappointed her deeply.

Was this the reason she ultimately agreed to let me start school early, even though I was emotionally and physically immature? In the days to come, I would be the student who stood at the doorway to the playground, crying because I was afraid to play with the other students, who all seemed larger than me, my teacher beside me trying to comfort me. How did Mom decide what was best for me as she sat there in that classroom, tears on her cheeks, looking down at my hopeful face?

Did she foresee what was coming?

Chapter 2: The Bishop's Diary

When I look back to my childhood, the memories of our church community dominate, especially our spiritual leader and church bishop, Brother Roman Miller. He was the first patriarch I ever knew, and he was remarkably effective. No one in our church dared to cross him. In fact, he was so influential that although we called ourselves conservative Mennonites, no one outside our church called us that.

Instead, they called us Romanites.

When I recall the church services of my childhood, I hear the sound of four-part *a cappella* music. Our church was large back then, over 400 strong. Everyone learned how to read music in our Christian school as children, so singing in the midst of the congregation felt like singing in the midst of a trained choir.

Those hymns still bloom within the rich and loamy soil of my memories, like leafy greens and white-gold cornstalks in my mother's garden. I hear the harmonies high and light, the women's voices cutting through the deep male rumble. I hear the middle voices filling in the spaces like water soaking into fresh-plowed earth.

Almost everyone in the church was related to each other, and thus the harmonies were enriched by a blend of close genetics, the lyrics flowing from what my tribe remembered as a bloodbath of persecution, beginning with the death and resurrection of Jesus Christ.

Oh, now I see the crimson wave,
The fountain deep and wide.
Jesus my Lord, mighty to save,
Points to his wounded side.

Our Sunday morning service always followed a standard ritual. Three congregational hymns brought us into the worship service, with a devotional talk, a long sermon, and finally, Sunday School. The service lasted for two-and-a-half hours. But twice a year, our ministers conducted a communion service. The service was very long, stretching well past noon, and it made me hungry.

I remember one communion morning when I was nine years old, old enough to be interested in what happened around me. I remember singing song after song about Jesus' love and blood. I remember instead of wine, the adults drinking grape juice from white coffee cups—the preacher wiping the lip with a pure white cloth—then eating small bites of bread, torn from a fresh-baked loaf. The warm and yeasty smell made my stomach growl.

Then came the foot washing, which was modeled after Jesus' example. To maintain modesty, the women washed each other's feet in a wing of the sanctuary, shielded from the main auditorium by curtains. The women filed in, then reappeared minutes later with relieved smiles. At the front benches on the men's side, church brothers knelt awkwardly at each other's feet, towels draped over their laps, washing each other's feet in clanking, galvanized buckets, then wiping them dry. Men, young and old, shook hands, brushed each other's lips in a Holy Kiss and muttered, "God bless you."

That Communion Sunday remains splotchy in my memory, a fuzzy home movie imperfectly filmed, but I do have spots of clarity.

A young minister, solemn in black suit and white collar, read the morning Scripture.

> *Then the soldiers of the governor took Jesus into the common hall and gathered unto him the whole band of soldiers.*

After the minister offered his thoughts, Brother Roman rose from his chair and limped to the plain wooden pulpit. Above him, both hands of the white clock pointed straight up against a wall of pale green. Plain and inornate, because, as conservative Mennonites, we frowned on fancy decoration.

In the audience on the men's side, I sat with my father. Before me, rows of men in black sat stiffly on varnished wooden benches, backs like walls between the pulpit and me. Beside me, my father kept his eyes glued to the front. Wearing a red beard with no mustache, as the Amish did, he watched as fervently as if he were about to witness the Second Coming.

Reading from St. Matthew in the King James Bible, Brother Roman painted a verbal portrait of Christ's passion. Occasionally, he paused to interpret, wiping his forehead with a white handkerchief. A shiver of awe danced up my spine. He made the story personal, as if we had all been there, participating in the crime of torturing and killing Christ.

"Brothers and sisters, they are spitting on our Savior's blessed face. The soldier uses a cat o' nine tails, a whip with tips of steel. It cuts the naked back of Christ, shredding it into torn flesh."

The auditorium stopped breathing. Like any good performer, Brother Roman knew how to command a room. Stern in demeanor, he was just and fair, and he knew the secrets of our community. He knew *my* secrets.

"By now, our Savior's back is like raw hamburger. The robe dries to his wounds. A crown of thorns is shoved down his brow, blinding his eyes with sweat and blood. Then, they rip the robe, oh my brothers and sisters, they rip that scarlet robe from off his sacred back. Again, the blood flows."

Against his black coat, Brother Roman's face gleamed, tears streaking down into the white strands of his scrawny goatee. He could not raise a full beard, I recalled my mother saying. Something about an accident that damaged his legs, something about him falling off a scaffold when he was a young man, something about God healing him through a miracle.

The stories about Brother Roman's compassion for the weak were legendary. Yes, he was severe with those who transgressed, but he was also kind to those who needed help. Both feared and beloved, he coaxed us along the narrow path to Heaven.

"But how can we condemn the soldiers, my dear ones? Each time we sin, we are guilty of the blood of Christ. Each of us has gouged that crown down upon his head."

A baby's cry pierced the bishop's focus. He ignored it, eyes darkening, reliving a moment he must have seen in his dreams.

On the women's side of the church, a field of bonnets glowed. This was always startling to those who visited—that the men and women were separated from each other. I didn't think this was odd at all because it's what I grew up with.

Odd was what I saw when we visited my father's family and went to their church, where women and men sat together. In fact, the first time I read Chaim Potok in my early twenties and saw how Hasidic Jews separated the men from the women, I knew exactly what he was describing. I felt connected to that world.

On this particular morning in April, with the rich scent of new-mown grass coming through the open windows, my mother suddenly caught my wandering eye, her head giving a slight nod toward the front. I may have been separated from Mom in church, with me sitting beside my absent-minded father, but I knew I'd better behave because my mother never missed a trick. Misbehaving in church meant severe consequences at home.

I focused again on Brother Roman.

"We are the guilty ones." Brother Roman hammered the air. "My hand is the hand that drove the nails into the blessed Savior's wrists. I plunged the spear into his side. The blood and water flowing from his side flows for me, my brothers and sisters. It flows for you. What prevents us now from asking pardon for our sins? Remember, 'He that eateth and drinketh unworthily, eateth and drinketh damnation to himself.'"

Brother Roman stared directly at me.

I avoided his gaze, studying the snag on my double-knit trousers. I was frightened by the bishop's warning, the idea that I could be damned if I drank the sacred bread and wine without confessing my sins first. I knew I sinned often. Just this morning, I had sinned by bickering with my sister over a piece of gum I coveted. I was glad I was too young to take communion.

In the silence which followed, there was only the faint sound of my heartbeat, the rustle of clothing, and the whisper of my father.

"Amen."

He was watching Brother Roman as if his life depended upon it. I wondered why he admired him so much, why he quoted him with such reverence.

"Confession is good for the soul." Brother Roman broke the silence. He nodded toward two young women, who rose. They were sisters, daughters of a short, jolly man who always patted me on the head. I liked him.

Dressed in gray dresses, the girls slipped past their peers to the center aisle. Their long hair was twisted up tight under their white bonnets. With eyes lowered, they approached the plain altar below the pulpit to make their public confessions, which people who had committed grievous sins were required to do before they could take communion.

Waiting, they stood in silence, the eyes of every congregant upon them. From the pulpit, Brother Roman's eyes clouded with disappointment. The papers before him rustled as he glanced through them. Then he set his jaw.

"Brothers and sisters, the Apostle Paul talks about one sin different than all others—the sin of fornication. It pollutes the body of Christ, hurting everyone, not just those who commit it. By not addressing it, we only encourage lustful behavior among our young brethren and allow our young sisters to lower their standards of purity."

I was old enough to know what the word *fornication* meant, a word learned in a brief, unfortunate moment. Only last year, my neighbor had taken me to his older brother's bedroom, which reeked of cigarettes. He'd showed me a playing card from his older brother's hidden stash. Posed on a bed of white fur, the nude bodies of a burly man and busty woman were intertwined. That tableau—along with the illuminating conversation my neighbor and I had had afterwards—increased my sexual education and vocabulary in one fell swoop.

Confused, I later asked one of my sisters, about the cards. Was this the way we were made into babies? Had Mom and Dad *fucked*?

I had never used that word before. Shocked, my sister put her hand to her mouth. "Mom," she called. "You need to hear what Steve said."

I don't remember the spanking I'm sure I received. I do remember I wasn't allowed to play with my neighbor for weeks.

Now before the congregation, two young women stood in submissive silence. One of them was pregnant. The other one had also committed fornication but hadn't gotten pregnant. Yet somehow, everyone knew. It may have been the first time I realized the inability of our people to keep secrets. Once one person knew, everyone did.

Brother Roman spoke slowly, biting into his words. "Brothers and sisters, two of our members request permission to confess." He nodded to the women.

The pregnant sister turned. Her wide face, framed neatly by black hair, was flushed. Tears streamed down her face. "I wish to ask for your forgiveness." Humiliation radiated from every pore. "I have committed fornication. I have had... I have lain with a man."

I wondered why she was crying. I studied the younger sister standing beside her. I still don't know how, in an auditorium that big, she looked out and found my eyes. Perhaps there was power in my curiosity.

For a moment, she held my gaze—furious, trapped, helpless.

Time stopped.

It was obvious the younger sister was anything but sorry. Instead, she reminded me of my older sister when she'd been caught doing something wrong and was waiting to be punished by our mother.

Perhaps realizing that people were watching her, the younger sister's face resolved once again into meekness, her expression becoming smooth and sorrowful.

Confused by her shift from anger to meekness, I thought about the playing card, the naked couple on the white-fur bed. I now knew it took two to make a baby. Before me were the two sisters, but where were the men? Would they be called up next?

The pregnant sister consulted a small white card. "I have brought disgrace and shame to the body of Christ, and to you, my brothers and sisters. For that, I beg your forgiveness."

She exhaled deeply as she knelt before us, hands covering her face. The wife of one of our younger ministers hurried to kneel beside her, comforting her as she cried.

Brother Roman nodded, satisfied. Then he turned to the younger girl.

Unlike her sister, the younger had no tears prepared. But she spoke fast and plain. "I'm sorry." No attempt to consult a white card. "I have sinned against God and you through the sin of fornication. I beg the church's forgiveness. I plead for your prayers that I might be pure." She fell silent. Face set, she stared straight ahead.

Beside her, the pregnant sister regained her feet. Together, the two young women waited awkwardly. The pastor's wife slipped back to her seat.

Brother Roman studied the silent congregation. "Because of their severe sin, we have put these sisters on probation. If they follow our counsel, they will be restored to full membership during our next communion service." The lines of his face turned rigid. "We encourage all of you, keep yourselves pure."

His face grew concerned.

"This sin, sexual sin, hurts us all," Brother Roman said. "'Every sin that a man doeth is without the body; but he that committeth fornication sinneth against his own body.' The impacts of this sin are eternal." He glanced down at the pregnant sister. "The child she bears may not... have a father. These are the lifelong consequences."

The older sister's shoulders hunched.

"Sin separates us from God." Brother Roman's voice dropped a register, becoming softer, warmer. "But there is hope. The Lord hates evil but loves the sinner. 'Wherefore, come out from among them, and be ye separate,' saith the Lord, 'and touch not the unclean thing.'"

The sisters made their way back to their seats. The tears had dried, the worst was over. The song leader blew into his pitch pipe, and the sound of familiar music swelled.

Praise God from whom all blessings flow
Praise Him all creatures here below

I stood there, singing, but I wondered again. Shouldn't the men have been up there, standing beside the women? What would happen to them? Surely, if Brother Roman could discover the women's sins, he could discover the men's.

Again, I wondered about the sisters, the humiliation they had faced when they confessed, our entire congregation gazing at them with disapproving eyes. They were helpless before their closest friends, vulnerable before their enemies.

And what would happen to the child born after such a public humiliation of its mother?

Rumor had it the bishop kept a diary of confessions—intended to fortify his memory in case anyone questioned his decisions—and he wasn't afraid to use his knowledge to maintain control. As I reflect on our community now, thirty-five years after I left, it makes sense why the community held Brother Roman in such awe. He did know the secrets of our community.

The diary's secrets are now inviolable. When a local historian requested to see the diary after the bishop passed, his family refused to let him see it.

I recall a conversation I had in 1990 with my Roman Catholic confessor—while teaching in Steubenville, OH—about how he handled people's confessions, since breaking the confessional seal is a sin so grave it requires absolution from the Pope himself. "I instantly forget anything shared in the confessional," my confessor said. "I think it's a gift God gave me."

As I listened to his words, reflecting on my own childhood with its forced public confessions, it was clear that our bishop did not treat private confessions with the same level of confidentiality. Whether or not a private confession became a public one lay in the hands of Brother Roman. His diary became a form of currency to ensure good behavior, a depository of power in our community, where guilt-fueled, private confessions morphed into a public weapon. He believed that the end result was a community that strove to keep itself pure.

Having endured trauma, I have often wondered whether our bishop understood the impact his ritual of humiliation and judgment had on the lives of those two young women. Being forced to confess publicly about sexual sin must have been traumatizing. People find public confessions about sex unforgettable, and any penitent forced to confess—especially a woman—would have been socially isolated. She could never recover her reputation or fully re-enter the community. God might be able to forget a sin, but people do not.

Half a century after it happened, that confession is seared into my memories. It was the moment when I first began to question my community, where social isolation was used to control those who stray. As my own need for control grew during my teens, I realized I could never remain in a world where I gave that kind of control to anyone.

And thus, my departure became inevitable.

Chapter 3: A Tsunami of Rage

By the time I was nine, I realized that our family was not like the others in our church. We rarely went out to eat, and few of my other friends had so many brothers and sisters. When we all barreled down the road in our Country Squire station wagon, it swayed from side to side.

Our aging cracker-box house was ragged, the tall weeds around the garage littered with spare tires and old automobiles. When he was home, Dad was always working on a car, often for someone who just wanted an inexpensive paint job. Dad was always looking for a way to make a quick buck, and he religiously filled out the "no purchase" entry form for the Publishers Clearing House sweepstakes.

Obsessed with his debts, Dad solicited loans from his wealthy friends in our church, or from my aunts when they visited from Pennsylvania, having intense conversations with them in his study. The youth group brought us Christmas baskets when they sang for the poor.

My mother had been reared by a stubborn Amish patriarch who ran a thriving vegetable farm. While rearing twelve children, he had *given* money to the poor—he had never had to ask for help. So, when Dad was finally forced to resort to government food stamps, my mother's humiliation boiled over. "Dad provided for his twelve children. Why can't you?"

They were in the kitchen, arguing again, and my father put up his hands, helpless against her anger. "I can only do so much, Maggie. God will provide."

Unfortunately, God wasn't providing enough.

Having borne her eight children, my mother felt she had done her part as a wife. Her family needed financial help. Acting decisively, she reached out to a childhood friend, asking if her husband needed another employee.

Shortly thereafter, my mother began to arrive each weekday afternoon at the Hartville Kitchen. It was housed in a long, simple brick building next to the village flea market, and it provided employment to scores of Amish and Mennonite women. There, amidst the bustling kitchen that created authentic Amish meals of fried chicken, mashed potatoes, and buttery biscuits, she stood at a low table, scrubbing filthy pans by hand.

My father appreciated my mother's paychecks, and those of my oldest sister Marcia, who also secured a job there. But in Dad's mind, a mother's place was to tend the family hearth. His wife's successful employment was an implicit criticism of his own failure to provide.

The situation stung Dad's pride. Now in his early forties, his life was controlled by a shrieking factory whistle that blasted across the town and surrounding farms every morning and evening, regimenting his work hours. Perhaps this brought on his migraines, monthly bouts of severe pain that ruled his life and crushed his spirit. It wasn't what he signed up for, he must have told himself, a life this grim. Even today, I can recall the blast of that damned whistle.

An outsider in our Amish-Mennonite community, he admired the success of small business owners in our church. Ever since he had worked for a successful autobody shop as a young man, Dad had dreamed of launching his own business, one that would pay the expenses of rearing a large family. He was an expert autobody craftsman, and word of mouth had spread about the quality work he did in his spare time.

My father was not one to think ahead. Although he had no business training, he did have an amazing God who promised to meet all of his needs. So, he had applied for a business license and zoning permit to work out of his home.

What could go wrong?

He could not imagine the havoc it would wreak on his finances. He could not imagine the emotional damage it would inflict on his family. He could not imagine the tornado of stress and rage he would create deep within the heart of his firstborn son.

One afternoon, Dad arrived home early and called a family meeting in the living room. He had an announcement to make. Sensing excitement, my brothers and I appropriated the sagging sofa, as with all family meetings. My mother held baby Heidi in the easy chair, and my sisters gathered around her. They looked concerned.

I now know that my oldest sisters had somehow learned about Dad's plans, and they had disagreed vociferously. As Marcia told me later, she had gone to Mom, wanting to dissuade Dad. Already in her late teens, Marcia had known Dad wasn't always practical. But Mom had restrained her. "He's my husband," Mom had said. "If I don't support him, who will?"

I had never seen Dad this excited. "I have quit my job. I'm starting my own auto body business. I just won the approval of the Lake Township Board to work out of our garage, and I've even come up with a name for our business." My father pronounced it like a man swirling wine, savoring the velvety mouthfeel: "Hi-Gloss Body Shop." His eyes twinkled. "I want to spend more time with my family because you boys are growing up."

As with All Things Dad at that point in my life, I thought this was a great idea. As his oldest and favorite son, I had followed my father everywhere over the past few years when he was home, even "helping" him in the evenings and on Saturdays. I knew it was normal for sons to learn their father's trade. It seemed natural Dad should start a family business.

Sitting before us, Dad explained the way things would work. "First, we're going to have to clean up the lawn and keep it free of old cars," he said.

I was all in favor of this. Much as I loved my father, I knew our front lawn looked like a junkyard, unlike my Uncle Ed's garage and lawn, which were impeccable. Getting everything organized was a great idea. Plus, we'd now have lots of money, so I wouldn't have listen to Dad and Mom argue about bills.

Because I didn't know about their earlier conversations, the reactions of my mom and older sisters bewildered me. Ann, tears streaming down her face, disappeared into the bedroom, and Marcia followed in silence. Elaine and my younger brothers had already dispersed, gone off to play. Mom sat holding my sleeping sister.

Finally, she rose quietly and retreated.

I didn't get it. Surely they understood the importance of Dad's new business. Our money problems would soon disappear. I was certain of this.

My father watched them go, seemingly as confused as I was. Then he shook off his worries, smiling brightly.

"Steve, you will be my foreman."

Pride flooded me. "It's a deal, Dad."

Until that moment, my father had been, at heart, a happy man. Smiling was second nature to him. One close friend from his days at the factory told me how Dad would whistle and sing. And why not? God cared for him and his family, just as He did the lowly sparrows. "Seek ye first the Kingdom of God and its righteousness," he often quoted to us, "and all these things shall be added unto you." Apparently, faith in God sufficed for a business plan.

But, in the following months, I wondered why God was doing such a piss-poor job. Rather than having more money, which I thought was the point of running your own business, we seemed to have less. Dad's understanding of business seemed akin to his understanding of our community's unwritten rules—everyone else seemed to know something Dad didn't.

For example, having daily devotions with his family was more important than putting in that extra hour of work. Dad got distracted easily, sometimes doing his accounting in the middle of the day when the shop needed his oversight to function. To keep his mind focused on Jesus, he liked to play recordings of sermons and evening church services that featured *a cappella* choirs and quartets.

But Dad's reel-to-reel tape recorder and eight-track tape player worked like his cars did, often breaking down. When a tape recorder broke, he'd go up to his office to fix it. While there, he'd get distracted by another task, or something that had broken, or a phone call… and since Dad wasn't around to keep my brothers and sisters on task, they would glance up, see that he was gone, and run off to play. I'd realize, suddenly, that I was the only one working.

31

One day after working in the garage, I lay in bed on my tummy, chin propped on my fists, reading *The Hound of the Baskervilles*, tracking criminals through London's streets with Sherlock Holmes. Downstairs, the basement door banged open and my father's voice exploded, fracturing the silence.

"Why doesn't Steve put stuff away when he's done?"

I knew what he was seeing; the basement was a mess. Yesterday, I had started building a rabbit hutch and had forgotten to put away the tools. A book— *this* book—pulled me into its seductive embrace.

His feet pounded up the steps.

I froze like a rabbit in that unfinished hutch.

The bedroom door flew open, and my father boiled into view. "Steven LaMar Denlinger." His voice quivered with rage. "How can you be reading when there is so much work to do?" His broad hand slammed down on my buttocks like an anvil, and I began to cry. But he wasn't satisfied. He dragged me to my feet and marched me off to the master bedroom.

Where the rubber hose awaited.

That's where I learned that it was *my* fault the business wasn't making money.

Until that moment, I'd adored my father. I'd loved his laughter, his jokes, his music. I'd helped him record audio letters on his 1960 reel-to-reel recorder to send to his sisters and mother in Pennsylvania. Sometimes, I'd sung solos for him in my high, unchanged voice.

But as the demands of business tightened, the unpaid bills mounting in piles on his office desk, my dad transmogrified into Mister Hyde, a tyrant who demanded perfection. Under his stern guidance, I learned to sand the cars, tape them, spray-paint them. When I didn't work hard enough, he spanked me.

My early adolescence disappeared into a fog of terror. I grew to know intimately the stings and bruises of paternal violence. Rubber hoses, rulers, sticks. The harshest punishments I ever received from my father took place during this time.

I began to fear and hate him.

During his better days—for example, when he received a particularly large payment for a well-painted car—my father flattered me, telling me how valuable I was to the business. But when the bills came crashing down, my father's suggestions began to sound manic depressive.

In fact, his suggestions frightened me. Why not quit school? I could work full time. After all, my Amish cousins left school after the eighth grade to help their parents on the farm. With me working full-time, the family business could finally turn a profit.

I knew all about my cousins, and I had no interest in living their life.

Quit school? School was the only place I could read without worrying about Dad getting mad at me. It was my only refuge from his rage.

For two years, I managed to navigate the days in which my father was ruled by irritation and explosive anger, contrasted with days of euphoria and happiness, when he seemed easily distracted. I never knew which Dad would show up. So, by the age of twelve, I'd become a master psychologist, an expert at assessing my father's mood, monitoring his actions with exquisite care to avoid falling victim to his wrath.

Everything I adored most about my father disappeared. For years, I believed my love was crushed under a mountain of debt, but that wasn't it at all. My love disappeared because my father hurt me. He hurt me because of the mountain of debt and his anxiety, and because he hurt me, I quit adoring him. My gentle, laughing dad had transmogrified into a monster who was ruled by sickness and despair.

I couldn't understand where my father had gone.

My conscience also began to torment me. Because I believed my father's failures were my responsibility, I believed I needed to work harder. Because I desperately wanted his approval, I worked harder. Worst of all, there was no end in sight—the bills just continued to mount. Where the money went was a mystery. The real problem was that my father didn't know how to track income and expenses, and he wasn't pricing his work accurately. So, as fast as the money came in, it went out.

In my father's shop, I had become a skilled worker, with my father placing more and more responsibility on my small shoulders. Play became something that made me feel guilty, because there was always work to do. Just because my younger brothers ran off to play didn't mean I could—I was the oldest son, and the most responsible.

In addition, my parents sometimes exchanged sharp words, and, as they flailed, I became their confidante. Each shared with me their frustrations with the other.

Surely, I could fix this.

Somehow.

But there was no place in my life where I had control.

What brought everything to a head was my body's reaction to the daily stress of a failing business. I had always suffered from dry skin, but now it was exacerbated. Patches of my skin dried out and began to itch. When I scratched, the skin began to bleed. My mother encouraged me to use hand lotion, but that did nothing. The toxic chemicals in my father's shop—lacquer thinner, solvent cleaner—dried out my skin like an overheated oven.

In school, sitting through boring classes, I would peel the dead skin off the tops of my fingers. At first, it gave me blissful relief, but then the bloody sub-skin oozed and itched even more painfully. My peers were grossed out.

33

Finally, my mother took me to see a skin specialist. He diagnosed me with eczema, a genetic skin disorder. When he learned about the chemicals my skin was being regularly exposed to in my father's shop, the specialist declared I could no longer work there. My father reluctantly agreed to release me. But I would need to find another job. Within our culture, every able member of the family pitched in.

There was one condition—two-thirds of my wages would go to my father. My sisters were already doing year-round work cleaning houses or baby-sitting, and they had made the same arrangement. I begrudgingly agreed.

Relieved that I was free of the autobody shop, I tried several summer jobs, even helping an uncle on his farm in Missouri, until finally, one of my cousins offered me a job as a mason's helper. In our tight-knit community, construction bosses preferred to hire from within our faith. Young men learned a trade by doing summer work, then accepted a full-time job after graduating high school, and eventually became skilled craftsmen.

I accepted the job. It was the summer after my freshman year, I was fourteen and small for my age, and it was the hardest work I'd ever done. One day faded into the next as I rose before dawn each morning. I gained physical power as I maneuvered wheelbarrows of mortar down ten-inch-wide planks and hauled heavy cinder blocks across basements—even when soaking rains left me slipping and sliding—and stacked them in rows for master bricklayers. I survived the fall of a chimney scaffold, scampering to the top as it swayed and tilted over, riding it down and then leaping to safety amidst the crash of metal. I loved the way I felt at the end of the day—sunburned and sore but completely relaxed, knowing that I would sleep soundly. I shot up six inches, and I gained a bronze tan under the blazing sun. Mysteriously, my skin issues also began to disappear.

It made me curious. So, in my sophomore year, I decided to write a paper on eczema for my Physical Science class. After researching what it was and exploring treatments ranging from fish oil to a salve extracted from coal, I discovered it responds best to infusions of vitamin D, which is found in sunshine. Thus, working outside in the sun had decreased my eczema.

It would be years before I also realized that eczema is exacerbated by extreme stress. It would be years before I made the connection between my complete lack of control working for my father, and my serious attack of eczema. It would be years before I realized I can measure my stress level by my skin's health.

As the end of my sophomore year approached, I thought about who I wanted to work for that summer. My previous boss had moved to Florida, and I was determined to continue building my body. I had gained a reputation as a hard worker (although a bit absent-minded). To my surprise, I was able to secure a job with the toughest construction boss in our community. He had a reputation for being a driver, and I sensed that if I survived him, no one would be able to mess with me again, especially my father.

My instincts were right.

By the end of that summer, my baby fat was gone, I had achieved my full height, and my muscles had bulked up due to the long hours and heavy construction work. To my father's surprise, he discovered that his small son had disappeared into the body of a muscular young man, tanned and lean.

We had always argued over meals, but as I had gained physical confidence, my tone had gotten sarcastic and sharp, almost contemptuous toward his religious ideas. It had been months since my father had spanked me, but he had always relied on the threat of a spanking to keep me in line. Now something had changed.

The fateful moment occurred on a Saturday morning at the end of the summer. Dad had just finished daily devotions with the family, and I was reading the newspaper while Mom sipped her coffee. The rest of the family had moved on with their day, perhaps sensing the coming conflict.

Dad had just explained that the only *true* faith was found in our little community.

"I doubt Jesus approves of the Romanites," I said, sarcastically. "What do you think you're going to do when you die and figure out you wasted your life going to the wrong church?"

My father had had it with my attitude. He stood to his feet, towering over my mother and me. "I am still your father, and you are still my child, and you still need to honor me," he said. "I deserve your respect."

"But you don't," I said, rising to face him, not willing to give in. "I've been working hard and giving you two-thirds of my wages. No one else in our church has to do that. You wouldn't be able to pay your bills without my help."

My words hit a nerve.

Suddenly, he exploded, coming around the table and grabbing me by the shoulders, dragging me towards the master bedroom.

"You're not too old for a spanking," he shouted.

Behind me, I glimpsed my mother, her jaw set. No help from her. I needed to submit. It would be easier if I obeyed my father. At first, guilt weakened my muscles, giving into my father's strength. But then, something snapped. Almost at the door of the bedroom, I suddenly fought back.

I pulled away from my father, escaping to the center of the living room. It was easier than I thought. My father charged after me, grabbing me, but it was useless. I wouldn't move. Guilt-ridden, I didn't fight him. I just stayed where I was, as if my legs were glued to the puke green carpet below me.

I'm disobeying God.

My father held on to me, but I wouldn't move. I had no intention of going with him to his bedroom where he kept that damned rubber hose. Shock flooded his eyes, our faces only a foot apart.

"No," I said. "You're not doing that to me anymore."

God can punish me. I don't care.

My father was breathing hard, pulling at me, not giving up.

"'Chasten thy son while there is hope.' The Bible says that. Proverbs 19:18."

"Then there's no hope," I said, jerking away. My father stumbled and fell as his hold broke. I turned toward my mother, perhaps for verbal support, but she had moved behind the table, her eyes wide.

My father recovered, getting to his feet, just outside his bedroom door. His rage, his frustration, filled the space. Breathing hard, I stood there in the center of the living room, unable to understand what had come over me. I had always submitted to his spankings.

I was done, I realized. I felt a rush of confidence, the adrenalin kicking in, the realization flooding me that I might even be… stronger than him. I didn't shout. Instead, I spoke in a low voice, my rage funneling toward him in my words.

"The Bible also says, 'Fathers, provoke not your children to anger, lest they be discouraged.' That's Colossians 3:21, Dad. I'm not a child anymore, and you're not going to spank me again."

I heard a sob, and I realized it was my mother.

I stood there, caught between the two of them, waiting for him to make another threatening move, or for my mother to try and bridge the gap between us. But my father turned and went into the bedroom, closing the door, perhaps to pray. My mother dropped into a chair at the table, her face wet with tears, her shoulders slumped.

The sight ripped into my heart like a serrated knife.

Several months later, my mother called me to the basement, where she was running a load of clothes through the ancient wringer. Dad was in the garage working, and I had been helping her clean the house, as I did every Saturday. But in the midst of our work, she wanted to talk.

I knew that Dad was pressuring Mom to talk to me, that she was concerned about the way his relationship with me had tilted. Her sweet face was distorted by her conflicting loyalties. She loved me, I knew this, but I was undermining my father's authority. As the firstborn son, I had a disproportionate amount of influence with my siblings.

"Your father deserves your respect," she said.

"I'm working to help him pay his bills. How is that not respectful?"

"Your refusal to recognize Dad's authority is hurting this family. Now your younger brother refuses to obey him."

I was aware of this. When I argued with Dad about religion at the dinner table, my siblings often joined my side, causing Dad frustration. I liked winning, but I also struggled with guilt. I knew the Bible said a son should honor his father, but I couldn't see anything honorable in the way he had treated me.

"What can I do?"

Behind my insolence, I was worried. I wanted to end the war. I didn't like the sense that I was displeasing my mother, or even my father. I wanted to fix things, I wanted to make everyone happy.

My mother leaned against the washer, the morass of swirling clothes thumping back and forth. She sighed. "You need to bend over, let him spank you," she said. "You need to submit to your father."

My stomach clenched as a rage I couldn't recognize... a rage I refused to recognize... overwhelmed me. I remembered the day, standing in the doorway of my parents' bedroom, watching Dad spank my younger brother. When he wouldn't cry, my father stopped the spanking, pulled down my brother's pants, and continued with the task. Eventually, my brother began to sob, ending the punishment.

"No way," I said, my heart pounding. "Never again. I'll respect him as my father, but not... like that."

I turned away from my mother and returned upstairs. I was done with being compliant, and I refused to bend. I didn't need to. My father no longer had the physical strength to subdue me.

I stood there, my hands fisting.

My father was wrong in his approach—thinking that he could gain my respect by spanking me, as he had when I was a child. Worse, my mother had agreed with him. She had refused to admit my impending adulthood—she had ordered me to allow my father to continue his abuse.

I felt betrayed.

I felt humiliated.

I felt enraged.

But that rage was also mixed with profound guilt. How could I disobey her? I had never stood up to her before, and my heart felt torn, seeing her disappointment. There was no one I wished to please as much as my mother, whose praise made me glow with pride. Yet there was no way I could look past the deep wound of her betrayal.

We were at a standoff.

Inevitably, my father's business folded. Thankfully, his boss at the factory gave him his old job back, and he returned to constructing screen doors.

Mister Hyde shambled back to his cave, but at first, I remained on edge, wondering if he had really gone. But it was true, I finally realized. The father I had once loved had returned. With no business to run, he had time again to play his instruments, and to tell his jokes.

My father and I had achieved a *détente*. Once I had stood up to him, he had quit trying to abuse me. It didn't hurt that he needed something from me—two-thirds of my weekly paycheck—which also motivated him to approach me with care.

I hated the long hours and hard labor of construction work, but I loved the impact it had had on my life. Thanks to the hours I spent in the blazing summer sun, my eczema had disappeared and my skin had tanned. The money I made had allowed me to set aside the dark brown glasses I'd hidden behind to get contacts, which highlighted my blue eyes. The hard labor had also forged a powerful body that would never allow my father or any other man to hurt me again.

But somewhere inside me, I realized that things were not the same. Mister Hyde had left me with a profound rage, for which I had no outlet. I had been taught that a child should honor his parents, no matter how much they choose to beat or humiliate him. I knew the emotion of anger was sinful, no matter what caused it. Good Christians forgave and forgot the offenses of those who hurt them, no matter what.

My mother's betrayal—pressuring me to let my father abuse me that afternoon by the wringer washing machine—had awakened a tsunami of rage against my parents. I had not given into it because I didn't know how, having spent a lifetime suppressing my emotions. So, I responded to the flood of cognitive dissonance I experienced with the only option I had left.

I numbed my rage.

I did not realize that you cannot choose which emotions you numb, or that when you numb one emotion, you numb them all. Nor could I have predicted that eventually after I found safety outside my community, that numbness would shatter, flooding my senses with post-traumatic stress disorder.

And the consequences would be devastating.

Chapter 4: A True Believer

When I was ten years old, my father and mother made plans to move to Lancaster, Pennsylvania, where we could live closer to Dad's family. My oldest sister, Marcia, was about to start high school, and my parents were worried that Hartville might not be the best place to raise children after all. They were concerned about the direction our church was going, spiritually.

Most of my mother's extended family had already left Ohio, due to the unfair way her cousin—a charismatic preacher who refused to be a team player—had been silenced by Brother Roman. Perhaps they felt disloyal staying there. It was time to cut their ties to this community in which after a decade Dad still felt like an outsider.

Whatever the reason, they didn't waste time. They put our house up for sale, and our Amish neighbor snapped it up. I announced to all my classmates that we were about to move to Pennsylvania. But when Mom and Dad went to Lancaster looking for a new church, they discovered that none of the churches out there had the godly mindset Dad wanted. The result was that my parents got cold feet… then changed their minds. I don't know how my father convinced our neighbor to cancel the sale, but he did, and we stayed put in our cracker-box house in Hartville.

I've always wondered how different my adolescence might have been had we left.

Our conservative Mennonite community believed that a Plain lifestyle was the godliest, the closest to that of the early church portrayed in the New Testament. I remember reading a letter that my mother's dying grandmother left to her heirs, which they found next to her kneeling body after she passed. "Above all, Dear Ones, keep to a Plain lifestyle," she pled. "Nothing is more important to your faith." She feared that worldliness would poison their love for God.

And so, I grew up with a fear of being called *worldly*, a catch-all term used to indicate that a person loved the world, rather than God. In fact, in our culture, having someone describe you as *worldly* could damage your reputation just as certainly as being called *racist* could cancel your reputation today.

It was a toxic label.

Dad believed that the best way to avoid worldliness was by following strictly the panoply of rules decided upon by our community. Each rule was based upon a literal command in the Bible. The problem was, not every biblical rule was followed, but only those that met the needs of our German culture. Dad never seemed to realize how carefully these rules had been cherry-picked, or how often they contradicted other parts of the Bible.

No one was allowed to drink alcohol because Proverbs forbade strong drink. Women were to wear white bonnets to cover their uncut hair in recognition of a man's spiritual authority. A woman's dress was to include an extra flap over their bodice, disguising its shape, because the Bible commanded women to be modest. No one was allowed to wear jewelry, not even a wedding band, because the New Testament stated that women should not adorn themselves. The list of rules went on, plucked helter-skelter.

And, of course, there were no contradictions. For example, if you brought up Jesus's command to pluck out your eye when it offends you, or any other body part, you would be hooted down. That command was obviously symbolic, we were told.

Dad was a true believer. He was convinced that practicing our community's lifestyle was the best way to follow Jesus in the modern world. If Jesus Christ were born in Hartville, my father believed, and had to choose a church to attend, he would have chosen to be a faithful member of Hartville Conservative Mennonite Church.

But there was one rule my father seemed to believe… *was* cherry-picked.

In their quest for Plainness, our community had concluded that musical instruments were worldly and distracting, probably because of the emotions the instruments aroused, emotions feared by our tight-lipped German community. As one of my outsider friends once said to me after watching me try to dance, "Your community bred all rhythm out of you."

This belief—that musical instruments are worldly—affected my father deeply. Other Mennonite churches—for example, those found in Lancaster, Pennsylvania near my father's family—followed the same Plain lifestyle that our community did. But in this one area, they differed.

The churches around Dad's hometown area as he was growing up thought using musical instruments, at least in the home, was quite acceptable. My father learned to play the piano as a boy—his family loved singing with it at home, and it bonded them tightly. But when Dad arrived in Hartville with my mother, joining the church just before they married, he discovered our community believed otherwise.

Decades before, our bishop, Brother Roman, had led our Hartville community in outlawing musical instruments completely. This was due in part to our Amish past—when congregational music sounded like the melodious chants of medieval worshipers. When the community converted from Amish to conservative Mennonite, our bishop permitted these melodious chants to evolve into four-part music through singing schools taught by twin brothers. There was no piano accompaniment, and the entire congregation could be conducted by any man who could wield a pitch pipe.

When conservative Mennonite bishops across the Midwest organized their communities into a fellowship in 1964, our bishop invited them to Hartville to rewrite their Confession of Faith. During that meeting, they decided that musical instruments were worldly. When they returned home, the decision startled many of their communities who had always allowed musical instruments in the home, regarding it as part of their humble lifestyle. They knew even the Amish played guitars and harmonicas.

Other conservative Mennonites may have been offended by the artistic pride we took in our music—as we fielded an *a cappella* choir that produced albums and toured abroad—but they soon followed our example, with other churches in our conference also touring the country and producing their own albums.

None rivaled us. We believed the unique quality of our community's music was undisputed. In fact, when one of my college friends first visited our church, decades later, he told me he was entranced by the "gorgeous sound" of these voices lifted in four-part harmony. Thus, unaccompanied vocal music became a sacrosanct element within our community's social fabric.

My father fiercely defended our community's rules about Plainness. He was a Romanite through and through, a zealous convert who had joined our church in order to marry my mother.

A true believer.

Except that he *wasn't*… not really. When there was no one to remind him of the rules about musical instruments, my father just seemed to… forget. It was as if, suddenly, he had never really believed them.

This occurred most often when we visited his family in Pennsylvania, or when we were visiting the home of, well… anyone who might have a piano. Then my father simply couldn't resist. He'd drift to the instrument, his hands gliding over the keys, teasing out the rich sound of a hymn, or even a Broadway tune he had heard on the radio as a boy—back when he played for his adoring mother and sisters, back before he fell in love with my mother, back before he decided he wanted to create a family where a son wasn't abandoned by his father… as he was.

So, when it came to the rules about musical instruments, Dad was—in the strictest sense of the word—a complete hypocrite. He was never very convincing when it came to defending the view that musical instruments were worldly.

This might be because my father had a God-given relationship to them that was unique. Give him any musical instrument (and I mean *any*), and five minutes later, he'd be playing a recognizable tune on it. In those moments, something in the disposition of his body transformed, his face relaxed into bliss, and joy came to earth.

Even in Hartville, Dad seemed to find a way to get around the rules about musical instruments. True, he couldn't play the piano or a guitar at home—because that was clearly stated in the rules—but then again, the harmonica didn't seem to be off-limits ("Come *on*, even the Amish played it!"), or, say... a handsaw.

I recall one Sunday night, when it was my parents' turn to host a "Young Folks Gathering," which included any singles who were sixteen years and above.

I was only fourteen. To avoid boredom, I had secluded myself in the corner of the living room, where I was reading J.R.R. Tolkien, who never bored me. Slowly, I realized the chatter had begun to die down. My mind emerged from Middle Earth as a haunting melody rose in the ensuing stillness, like the swollen and ghostly strains of a violin which had been left out in the rain.

Our entire living room was lined with young people sitting in benches and chairs brought from the church. Some leaned forward, watching my father, who was sitting on a folding chair. Even my mother and sisters had paused their work of serving coffee and bowls of Neapolitan ice cream to watch my father.

An old-fashioned hand saw was bent over my father's knee, the blade long, wide, flexible. In his hand was a wooden spoon, and he tapped the blade, first tentatively, and then more forcefully. My father leaned in, his ear close to the saw.

The room was silent, the trembling sounds of the saw wavering and whining. Finally, I caught the tune.

> *Mary had a little lamb,*
> *Little lamb, little lamb*
> *Mary had a little lamb*
> *Its fleece was white as snow.*

The sound of the saw was a high, drunken voice, unlike the hard, clean movements of a piano, but we could follow. The room breathed with my father.
How does he do that?

Perhaps in another world, in another lifetime, Dad's love for performance would have driven him to the local theater guild.

I realize this now as I reflect on a performance he gave for our church community, a monologue based on a short story by Grace Livingston Hill (1866-1947), a successful evangelical Christian writer of inspirational romance. I have worked in both amateur and professional theater productions, but I have seen few actors prepare as thoroughly as Dad did for his role.

He had been drawn to the story found in "The House Across the Hedge," but more importantly, he had come to embrace the story's theme—that

Christians are to separate themselves from worldly culture—in spite of what it costs them.

Hill's narrative imagines Miriam, a young Jewish girl living before the biblical Exodus. Miriam has become close friends with two outsiders, a charming Egyptian playmate and her gorgeous older brother. They epitomize the wealth and beauty of worldly culture. Between their families is a hedge separating the Israelite ghetto from a prosperous Egyptian society, one that has begun to tempt Miriam away from her people's faith.

My father decided to perform his adaptation of Hill's story as a way to inspire our community to believe in our separated culture.

He spent months memorizing the text. At night, he slept with a headphone set on, an eight-track tape recording of the story playing again and again, his unconscious mind nailing down each word, each syllable.

He practiced reciting it to us.

By the time he was ready, even I knew much of it by heart. Then my father poured out his performance in front of our skeptical community—all eleven, single-spaced pages of it.

He chose a Sunday evening church service. It was one of those old-fashioned events where anyone could get up and read a poem, share an anecdote of faith, or stage an impromptu Gospel quartet. Most performances were delivered modestly and humbly with a tentative air.

Not Dad's.

His dramatic monologue was enthusiastic, impassioned.

Eyes twinkling during the comedic moments, hands gesturing widely when emotions ran high, the most tragic moments of the piece bringing him to tears—my father was as dramatic as any Shakespearean actor playing on Masterpiece Theater. In an evening that was essentially an open mic, my father's performance is emblazoned on my memory.

It says something about my father's artistic nature that in a patriarchal community with such rigid gender lines, my father sought out a short story with a theme that spoke to him and used it to create a one-woman play (not letting the inconvenient fact that he was a man keep him from performing it).

My father said he performed the piece because he wanted to strengthen our belief in the conservative Mennonite faith, but what it really did was allow him to tap into his passion for theater, surreptitiously, within a community that believed theater was worldly.

I've often wondered what my father's life would have looked like outside our community. What if we had moved to a community that valued his artistic skills, one that didn't force him to sneak time playing music on odd instruments, like a schoolboy sneaking a cigarette in the bathroom? Perhaps my relationship with him would have been different if we had moved to Pennsylvania, where my father could have played any musical instrument he chose without guilt? Would he have joined a bluegrass or country music group that would have valued his creative gifts? Would his mental health have been different if he had been able to find emotional release through the strings of a guitar, or the keys of a piano?

How different would my own life have been?

I once asked my father why it was acceptable to play music on the saw, but not on the piano or guitar, and my father explained that the saw wasn't really a musical instrument. We both knew he was being hypocritical, but I didn't argue. Perhaps this was because I realized even then that playing music on anything brought him more joy than anything else he did.

Only as an adult did I make the connection between the creative gift that was buried within my father—a throbbing need to release his pain by creating eerie, haunting music—and the rage that exploded from him when that need was repressed by a religion that ruled his life, a religion he had embraced because he thought it would best allow him to serve Jesus, whom he loved with a profound fervor.

My father desperately needed the spiritual outlet that his creative gift gave him, but thanks to our community's irrational and self-serving argument that vocal music is somehow more godly than instrumental music, my father chose to repress his divine gift.

Yet the nuclear force of his creative gift could not be denied. By trying to tamp down that force, he lost control, creating chaos within our family.

If only he had harnessed that force and let it guide his life, he might have recognized that tamping down his creative force—the most powerful urge given by the Divine—is a blasphemy. I wish he had recognized the truth—one taught by the great myths—that when a hero blasphemes the divine, he is visited by a cruel and ironic fate.

A cruel and ironic fate that can bring... a spiritual Chernobyl... to everyone he loves.

Chapter 5: The Comic Book Rebellion

Our church was the center of our community. It was intended to be a source of spiritual comfort where we built a spiritual foundation for a meaningful life. It should have been a place where we were taught to love each other.

Instead, the church of my childhood hosed us down with raw fear. I took its teachings seriously. Convinced I was going to Hell, I was "born again" at the age of eight, receiving Jesus into my heart, hoping this would make me feel secure in Christ's love. But as a child with a sensitive conscience, the opposite happened. Fascinated by horror, I learned salvation could be easily lost. If I left even one sin unconfessed before I died, Hell awaited me. These teachings were strongly reinforced during annual revival meetings.

Thus, my sleepless nights were consumed by the belief that I was bound for a literal Hell where I would burn forever, tormented in a body that remained eternally conscious.

I was not the only one who suffered. One of the most dramatic series of events in our community began when a fiery and charismatic evangelist, Laverne Schwartz, began to turn our community upside down with vivid sermons about the darkness of evil. People flocked to his meetings.

Brother Schwartz's final service focused on demon possession. During the invitation, Brother Schwartz announced that he sensed there was one person who was "holding out" against the Holy Spirit's urgings to accept Christ. He urged that person to come forward when he gave the altar call and publicly commit to Christ.

The hold-out did not come forward.

But the next morning at our high school—when the teachers were leading students through a daily worship service—a young man, John, rose to give his testimony.

"I have been saved," he announced. His story was vivid, showing how he had given in after fighting God's Spirit for years.

The story of his conversion, which had happened during the long night before, was powerful, moving, and authentic. His peers could see that he was a changed man, and they listened raptly. It turned out a small group had been praying for him for months, and as they witnessed John's change of heart, they found themselves moved to tears.

After that testimony, the floodgates opened, and a spontaneous revival broke out at the high school. Students stood, publicly committing themselves to Christ. There were prayers, public confessions, more singing. It was a glorious day.

Swept up in the fervor, the teachers canceled all classes.

45

All day.

All week.

Then for another week.

Under the emotional impact of the revival, many students vowed they would keep themselves pure. With genuine and sincere vows, they determined they would never again go to movies or read comic strips from the newspapers.

Today, I have no doubt their intentions were pure and genuine, but, unfortunately, there are always unintended consequences to any decision. And based on my research, I know that the revival that started with such high hopes and changed many students' lives led to our warm, embracing community being split from top to bottom, creating divisions that appear to have never been fully healed.

It also led to a darkened room at the end of a hallway, and to a furious and humiliated teacher giving me the worst beating of my life.

I'd first heard the story of the revival from my older sisters, who attended the part of the building that contained the high school.

Since I was only a fifth-grade student, I was not directly involved in what happened. It would take me years to wrap my head around it—when, as a senior in college, I would write my senior thesis on the revival, interviewing some of the key players—and it would take even longer to connect it to my story.

I knew from the start how deeply it affected my family. My older sisters, sincere and impassioned, narrated to us each evening what was happening in school. They were deeply affected by the cathartic release they saw in themselves and in their classmates as one by one they committed their lives to God. My sisters shared with us about the emotional highs they were experiencing as they became vulnerable to each other, confessing every single sin publicly, and hearing others do the same. They bonded with their classmates during long sessions that included personal testimonies, Gospel songs, and prayer.

My experience, however, was a bit different.

In the adjoining elementary building, my cohort of fifth graders enjoyed a well-deserved reputation for being mouthy and hard to handle. With sixteen students in our class, we were one of the largest classes in our picayune school.

Smart and irreverent, we needed a highly skilled and savvy educator to gain our respect. Our first and second-grade teacher had handled us with ease because she'd had eyes in the back of her head. Our third and fourth-grade instructor had brought us to heel with the aid of her quick wit and consistent routines. Our fifth-grade teacher, however, struggled. Having recently returned from the mission field and having been weakened by a symptomatic blood condition, Brother Fisher found us difficult to handle.

We didn't listen, we didn't shut up. We were disrespectful to him and to each other. We didn't stay seated at our desks. We were every teacher's worst nightmare.

Eventually, Brother Fisher went looking for help.

We were in the midst of our devotional period when the door to the classroom flew open. In strode two men, one brawny and the other ramrod straight. One carried a large black Bible, the other carried The Oar.

Well acquainted by this time with the function of such implements, I stared at the paddle in abject terror. I thought about the stories I'd heard where male teachers, muscles hardened by summer construction, swung that three-foot oar like a golf club.

Normally, it hung on a nail in the principal's office. Now, that principal, Brother Yoder, stood before us: accuser, judge, and jury. He examined my classmates with clinical detachment, the way a scientist might observe a new strain of bacteria. Tall and severe in his dark Plain coat, he placed the paddle front and center on the teacher's desk.

"I've asked Brother Lapp to say a few words this morning. We're concerned about the fate of your souls."

I sat, barely breathing, eyes glued to the paddle, as did my classmates. Not a sound.

Brother Lapp stepped forward. He thumped down his Bible.

We all twitched.

"You all know the story about King Saul and his visit to the Witch of Endor," he rasped. "Saul's sin grieved the Holy Spirit, causing Him to turn away."

I knew where this was going, since this was the ultimate threat. Grieving the Holy Spirit was unpardonable. People who did this had no hope of forgiveness, no matter how they tried to repent. God turned them over to Satan, and the dread of Hell consumed their days.

I knew that healthy people died in their sleep so I worried that I too might die and find I had committed this sin by accident. So, I paid attention to what Brother Lapp was saying—the fate of my soul depended on it.

In the prime of life, Brother Lapp's broad shoulders were barely contained by his white shirt, buttoned tightly all the way from his protruding stomach to his bulging neck. We gaped at him with open apprehension.

No doubt which teacher would most enjoy wielding the paddle.

"And what was that sin?" Brother Lapp plowed ahead. "Anyone?"

We all flinched.

"Rebellion." His voice, hoarsely masculine, pitched to a shout. "Do you know what the prophet compared that sin to?"

No one breathed. The silence stretched as Brother Lapp scanned the class. It was then, trapped in that terrible silence, that I made my mistake—I sat up straight.

Brother Lapp's eyes locked onto me. "Steve."

I knew the answer because my father had read this passage to our family several weeks before. "Witchcraft," I muttered.

47

Brother Lapp closed in. "What did you say, Steve?"

"I said, *witchcraft*."

Brother Lapp bared his teeth. "That's right. Witchcraft. Listen to what the Bible says in I Samuel 15:23."

Brother Lapp thundered. He shook his Bible. His gestures, wide and powerful, paralyzed us.

On the desk, the Oar lay waiting.

Would the paddling happen in front of the entire class? With difficulty, I focused back in on what Brother Lapp was saying.

"Now listen to me, and you listen to me closely." He looked each of us in the eye. "Your class is the most stubborn class in school. We've heard everything about you. You don't listen. You do what you want. You think you're in charge. You disrespect Brother Fisher." He swiped a meaty fist over his mouth. "Well… We have had it. *Had* it. This rebellion, pure and simple, is over. We. Have. Had. Enough." With a white handkerchief, Brother Lapp turned back to the principal, mopping his flushed face.

Brother Yoder spoke into the stupefied silence, his voice oddly gentle. "I have been moved by the vows our high school students are making. They are turning their reading choices over to God. Some have even quit reading comic strips in the daily newspaper." Brother Yoder raised his voice and his preternatural white hair shook with intensity. "Comic books are of the Devil."

I looked away—I had a contraband comic book inside my desk. Thankfully, no one was paying attention to me; their eyes were locked on Brother Yoder.

"You may find Batman or Superman or Wonder Woman entertaining, but the images destroy lives. So, we have banned them. From now on, they are forbidden. Anyone who rebels will be dealt with most severely." With a fine sense of drama, he cracked the paddle against the desk.

This time, we all jumped.

The two men glanced meaningfully at our teacher, then strode out.

We regarded Brother Fisher with new respect.

In the classrooms down the hall, prayer warriors were on their knees, pleading for their classmates who had not yet yielded to God. Outside our windows, we watched two senior boys not yet aboard the revival train tossing a football back and forth. In the mornings, we sometimes filed into the high school chapel to listen to visiting speakers, while, in the back, our bishop, Brother Roman, observed the proceedings with a skeptical eye.

Our entire community was being torn asunder, with one side eager to encourage the ongoing revival, and the other side concerned the school was failing in its primary mission to educate its students.

Amid all this, I was just attempting to sneak in reading time. I did not intend to rebel—I was just anxious to finish my comic book. So, perhaps I fell prey to temporary insanity. What else would have made me decide to break the rules at a time when the entire campus felt like a high-security prison?

To be clear, I was a serious comic-book junkie, desperate to get my fix—every day. Fortunately, I had a neighbor who didn't belong to our community (who had earlier showed me his brother's pornographic playing cards) and with his massive collection of comic books scattered helter-skelter across his bedroom floor, he fed my addiction constantly.

No addiction is cured by a warning, no matter how dire.

Was this the reason I attended school the next day with more comic books hidden among my books? Or was it that, like any pre-adolescent, I didn't have the mental bandwidth to think ahead to the possible consequences?

I knew my peers were difficult to control, but I was quiet and scorned by them, so I usually flew under the radar. I didn't intend to bring down the wrath of the authorities upon my tiny body. I didn't see myself as a mover and shaker, and I certainly didn't see myself as a leader. But, at the age of eleven, few of us do.

I don't remember which comic books I brought to school that morning. Wonder Woman—enough of a woman for any man or boy—was probably among them. Another, my favorite, was the Two-Gun Kid because he was small but mighty.

I hated recess, preferring to stay in and read. That morning, I lingered inside with my illicit reading while my classmates played softball on the playground. At the end of recess, as my classmates streamed past me, my stocky classmate, Perry, snatched Wonder Woman up, crowing loudly.

My greatest enemy, Marlin Miller, then picked up the Two-Gun Kid, chuckling at the image of the small, masked gunfighter brandishing his gigantic Smith & Wesson.

Then Marlin froze, gaping.

Reflexively, I glanced at the classroom door, but it was too late. Brother Fisher was gliding down the aisle, his eyes riveted on the contraband comic books.

My boisterous peers fell silent, as methodically, he relieved us of the damning evidence, then gestured the three of us to the hall. Behind us, the room buzzed with horrified whispers.

Brother Fisher held up the comic books. "Who brought these?"

Silence. In guilty unison, we stared at our feet. Would my classmates rat me out?

"I'm waiting."

My fellow culprits shifted slightly.

"It's going to be worse for you if you don't answer because I'll have to call your parents."

"I brought them." The threat of dragging my father into this mess was the impetus I needed—because whatever Brother Fisher did to me couldn't match what my father would.

How wrong I was.

My classmates tried to protest in my defense, but I wouldn't stand for it. "No," I insisted. "It's my fault."

My classmates relaxed.

"I wouldn't have expected this of you, Steve." The hard clench of Brother Fisher's jaw assured me that my honesty had earned us nothing.

Behind Brother Fisher, Perry flashed me a quick, defiant grin. Clearly, he thought I'd gotten him and Marlin off the hook. I'd heard the rumors about his father, who'd once used a steel hanger to whip Perry's older brother. Severe corporal punishment was a known terror for Perry.

Marlin was the grandson of our powerful bishop. Until then, he'd always been the golden boy. I doubted he'd ever been paddled in school. That was about to change.

I'd been here before.

We stood clustered in a protective circle in this room at the end of the hallway that cut through our small elementary building. It was the place where boys and girls were taken who'd done something serious. The bookshelves on both sides closed in on us. The dry smell of aging books flooded my senses and spiked my fear.

Our stern principal arrived, handing Brother Fisher the paddle. It was eighteen inches long, two inches wide and two inches thick, and featured tiny, drilled holes down the business end. Our teacher carefully placed it on the table behind us.

Our principal frowned at us, his face rigid. "We're going to pray, boys. We hope each of you will show true repentance."

We all bowed our heads.

"Heavenly Father," our principal said, "we come to you this morning, concerned about the rebellion these boys have shown. Your Word teaches us this rebellion is of Satan. We ask that each boy might escape the Devil's fate through the punishment Brother Fisher will administer. In Jesus's name, Amen." And then he left us there, alone, with Brother Fisher.

Perhaps he wanted to distance himself from what was to come.

Marlin was the first to meet his fate. While Perry and I waited in the hall, we heard from inside the harsh, staccato cracks of wood on flesh. The blows came hard, fast.

I couldn't help but count.

Six cracks.

Beside me, Perry jumped. I fought the urge to cry.

The door opened. Marlin brushed by us, head down.

Brother Fisher loomed in the doorway. He gestured to Perry.

My insides were molten, fiery acid. I'd often been spanked at home, but at least, there, it happened immediately. This endless waiting was pure, sadistic torture.

The door closed. After a brief pause, though it'd seemed forever, the blows sounded again, solid wood against flesh.

Again, I couldn't help counting.

Six cracks.

This time, the blows sounded louder.

Thundering feet. Perry flung open the door. A glimpse of wet cheeks, Perry wiping his face with his sleeve, as he fled down the hall.

I turned.

Brother Fisher stood waiting. "It's your turn, Steve."

Feet dragging, I entered.

Brother Fisher faced me, gripping the paddle. It was stained darkly and covered by inky signatures cut into it by its numerous victims.

I stared at it, my brain a white wall of terror. I could barely hear his words.

"You're the leader here, Steve. Therefore, I'm going to have to spank you the hardest."

Burning terror snaked up my legs into the center of my tummy. I was short for my age, and skinny, easily the smallest kid in the class. I gawked up at him, the tears already starting.

But the time for negotiation was over. No plea bargain, no probation, no second chance. My teacher's angular face was all steel corners. He forced me, face down, over the table.

I began to struggle, but he held me casually, easily.

The air whistled through the paddle's tiny holes, then came the smash of wood hitting flesh, and my bottom burst into flames. I was wearing pants, but my bottom might as well have been bare.

No time to think. The cracks rained down. My legs collapsed, only the table holding me up. The paddle landed squarely on my buttocks, again and again and again.

I stayed inside myself during the first six cracks. But the paddling went on. Oddly, I found myself outside my body, drifting somewhere in the dark room, a consciousness somehow separate from the vengeful man and the anguished boy.

The man raised his hand, swung it again and again.

The boy sobbed, fought, wrestled to get away, but there was no getting away from that man, the one who only held him tighter, pinning his target squarely in place.

No pause.

No surcease.

No escape.

Just agony.

Going on and on and on.

Somehow, I kept counting. Fourteen cracks in all, a number still emblazoned on my brain.

Finally, the paddling ended and I fell back into my body.

That body fell to the floor.

It felt cold against my bottom, which burned with fiery bruises marching up and down my thighs that would later turn purple, then green and dark yellow.

Today, I am horrified by the calculated actions of those educators. That moment was about power, about forcing our class into submission. With our independent spirits, we had threatened a group of men who were trying to convince our community that we were in a spiritual battle, facing off against demonic spirits.

As a fifth-grade boy obsessed with reading, I was unaware of the comic book's power or that the core of this genre was its battle against tyranny. I did not know that the power of ideas could threaten a weak leader desperate to maintain patriarchal authority.

It would be decades before I realized that Wonder Woman's subversion of patriarchal corruption had made her a highly controversial character in the 1940s and 1950s, or that her kinky takedown of patriarchal power had inspired actual book burnings. To our authorities, her appearance was the irrefutable proof that the Devil was in our class's rebellion.

Wonder Woman had superhuman speed and preternatural senses. Wearing bullet-deflecting bracelets, she brandished a Golden Lasso of Truth that forced a man to reveal his true motivations, exposing him to the crowd's ridicule. Most telling of all, she could fly. Our revivalist teachers weren't wrong about the rebellion against tyranny lurking in comic books—any medieval churchman would have burned Wonder Woman at the stake as a witch.

My love of comic books revealed something about me that I didn't yet see. I simply loved their characters and storylines, not realizing how much this revealed about me. Like a lightning rod draws in lightning, my love for these rebel characters had drawn in the attention of my teacher, who was determined to force my cohort's submission. My choice to distribute my stash of comic books, which they had explicitly forbidden, had identified me as the leader of my class's rebellion.

My classmates and I were just a group of rowdy schoolchildren who did what all kids do when a teacher is unable to manage a class—homed in on his weaknesses and made his life Hell. But thanks to the revival taking place down the hall, an act of rebellion by elementary school children was now equal to the sin of witchcraft, which in earlier centuries resulted in a witch-burning.

Seeing themselves locked within a great battle against the Devil, the overwrought revivalists tyrannizing our school had decided, therefore, that our case had become a *casus belli*, an act of spiritual war. We needed to be crushed. And as the spiritual leader of this ragtag band of hoodlums—because why else would I have thrust a Wonder Woman comic book in their faces?—*I* needed to be crushed.

Deliberately or not, they had focused on the alien within our cohort. I was physically weaker than any other boy in the class, and I came from a family with no political power in the community. My father was an outsider. Yet in spite of this, they were determined to make me an example of what happens when a student rebels. As their executioner, they had chosen an angry and ineffective teacher—driven by rage for the disrespect shown to him by elementary students—and sent him alone into that darkened room with each of us.

They had handed him a paddle designed to maximize our pain.

They may not have been able to burn us, as the medieval church did to witches, but they had ensured that our teacher could put the fire of God into each swing of the paddle against our flesh.

My torturer watched me recover. When I could, I struggled to my feet. My sobs slowly turned into hiccups.

Finally, Brother Fisher walked to the door. "You may go to the restroom and clean your face."

I peered up at him.

Once again, his face wore a mask of kindness. "You can return to class when you're done crying." Then the door closed behind him, leaving me alone in the room, the damp and musty smell of the books embracing me.

I thought about my teacher and the two men who stormed our classrooms wielding that wooden symbol of absolute control. These adults claimed the power of God, the right to see into my soul, the God-given authority to humiliate and shame me.

If rebellion against *that* was the sin of witchcraft, then I was a witch.

That was when hatred for my entire culture took root in the dark, fertile soil of my pain, pushing into the crevices of my soul, twining through me. It found its way between the bruises, through the flush of fear that suffused my being.

In my mind's eye, the mouth of Hell opened before me. Its ghastly breath blasted the tender roots of my faith and seared them to cinders.

Chapter 6: Gifted Allies

After the Comic Book Rebellion, my battle with education moved from a direct challenge to my teachers to an intellectual rebellion. Burying myself even more deeply in the world of books, I stonewalled my teachers by doing as little homework as I could.

This caused my studying habits to atrophy, and I missed foundational lessons. Without repetitive practice, my skills in math and science dropped by the way. My parents couldn't provide support at home—they were focused on surviving financially and had no time to help a recalcitrant student learn study habits.

So, I fell behind my classmates, with my grades just scraping along. To my parents, it looked as if I hated school. To my classmates, it looked like I couldn't learn. To my teachers, it looked like I would never succeed in school.

The irony was... I was exhibiting the traits of a classic *gifted* student.

Today as a teacher, I would identify a student like this as at-risk. I would talk to his counselor and his dean, encourage them to test him and to look at the scope of challenges he faced as a learner. I might suspect abuse—due to the high poverty his family was experiencing—since the two are often connected. I would search for a way to help my student thrive. Of course, in 1976, support like that didn't exist in our little school.

But to my surprise, I soon drew in the attention of a novice teacher.

Brother Myrrl Byler was an idealistic young man hired by my school to teach my class. At first, he seemed like every other teacher. He was beginning his teaching career with only a high school diploma and an understanding with the school board that he would earn his four-year undergraduate degree while teaching us. As incredible as it sounds today, back then our school board hired teachers like this because they (mostly) couldn't afford to retain certified educators. Once teachers gained their certification, they were snapped up by public schools offering a living salary and benefits. In addition, any teachers the board hired had to follow the unique rules of our conservative Mennonite community. Finally, teachers were required to *indoctrinate* us, rather than teaching us how to think for ourselves.

My rowdy class quickly picked up on the fact that Brother Byler was different that anyone who had taught us before. A gifted teacher, Brother Byler read books to us, discussing them with us like we were adults, guiding our discussions with questions that didn't have pre-ordained answers, and listening to our reactions with respect, as if he could learn from *us*. Sometimes, he just asked us about our lives, expressing genuine curiosity, or remarked on our immature behavior with that slightly sarcastic voice we loved, effectively putting us in our place.

Brother Byler also confided in us about his college classes, which he was attending in the afternoons and evenings. He talked about why he had decided to go to college—about how he had gotten bored doing carpenter work, and about the way college would help him live a meaningful life.

Unlike other teachers, he was passionate about sports. In our community, attending professional sports events was considered worldly—like going to the movies or attending rock concerts. *Worldly* things took your mind off God, and *being* worldly meant you were destined for Hell. Although Brother Byler never broadcast the games he attended, we all knew he went. It proved he was a rebel, like us.

He was cool.

He was also the first teacher who truly believed in *me*. Until Brother Byler, I didn't believe I had a promising future. Although school was a refuge from home, it wasn't a place where I believed I could gain access to college and a better life. But my new teacher quickly showed he understood my passion for learning, which I expressed by reading rather than doing homework. He usually let me get away with reading while he lectured, but occasionally, when I was supposed to be doing work, he pulled my illicit book away and tapped me on the head with it, an ironic reprimand.

Somehow, he saw past my oppositional defiance. So, when I began failing my classes, he saw I was a rebel fighting the system, something he recognized in himself. Instead of reprimanding me or paddling me, which he had every right to do, he pulled me into the hall to start a dialogue, hoping to show me how the game of education is played.

"Why don't you study?"

"Don't you know homework is important?"

The way he approached me was unusual. Over the past few years, my teachers had believed I was "lazy" (because I constantly read books), or they had grown impatient with me (when I didn't turn in my homework), so it took time for me to grasp that Brother Byler was different. His belief in my intelligence, his attempts to help me see there was a reason for my education—but to take advantage of it, I would have to study and do my homework—couldn't register. I had never thought about the future, other than worrying about dying or being frightened by the end of the world. I didn't see a connection between my actions and the opportunities I could later grasp in life. So, I stonewalled Brother Byler.

Of *course*, I would improve.

Of *course*, I would do my homework.

Of course, I *didn't*.

I'd arrive home and set aside my schoolbooks, forgetting my latest promise. If my father didn't need me to work, I would bury myself in J.R.R. Tolkien's world of hobbits, or a Newbery Award book, or another Hardy Boys novel, where boys were heroes and no one abused them. Although I was listening to what Brother Byler said, I had a hard time believing that my homework had anything to do with escaping this claustrophobic world.

Is that why I never bothered studying?

Like my father, I had never been one to think ahead, and so I assumed that I would once again pull off passing grades at the end of eighth grade, just as I had in previous years. But as May approached, I realized something had changed. My grades were not improving.

The stakes had also risen. I was making friends, and I actually liked Brother Byler. He had a special relationship with our class, and he treated me with respect. Next year, he would be teaching only high school classes, he confided to us. If I didn't want to see Brother Byler and my cohort move on without me, I needed a miracle.

I turned for help to my friend, Verne Dashnaw, a talkative boy with white-blonde hair who had joined our class at the beginning of seventh grade. Like me, he had a weird family who were outsiders to our community. Both intellectually and athletically brilliant, he had no problem keeping up with his homework. Seeing my impending doom, Verne agreed to help.

I'd never been good at math, but he was. After averaging my grades multiple times, he offered me his blunt assessment. Too few assignments turned in meant too many zeroes in the gradebook. Even if I got perfect scores from now on, my earlier grades would now pull down my final grade. There was nothing I could do, Verne calculated. I was failing at least two subjects, and you couldn't be promoted to high school if you failed more than one subject.

It turned out my friend had *mis*calculated. When I got my report card at the end of the year, I had failed three classes—math, history, and English.

I would have to repeat eighth grade.

It was then that Brother Byler made his move. He invited my parents to meet him at the school to talk about my grades. My father put on his black Plain coat, and my mother, her best Sunday dress. I was not invited to this parent-teacher conference. Instead, I stayed home, unable to read a book, trying to work on my bike, pacing the garage, and trying to focus. It was difficult. Since I had failed the year, I figured Brother Byler was meeting with my parents to help them withdraw me from school. This meant my friends would soon know of my failure, and they would conclude I was not only poor, but stupid.

Social Hell was just ahead.

But when my parents arrived home, they had a surprise for me. Although I had failed three classes, I had gotten some of the highest scores in my cohort on the Stanford Achievement Test, perhaps thanks to all the reading I had done. Brother Byler had recognized that my problem wasn't my learning ability, but my lack of motivation to study. Thus, Brother Byler would pass me on to high school, but I would be on probation. In order to stay in high school, my first quarter's grades needed to reach at least a C in everything but math, since that was my weakest subject. In that, I had to get at least a D.

Today, I find it astonishing that a teacher had the power to make this decision, but back then, teachers in our small school had the final authority to pass or hold back a student. Brother Byler recognized my desperate need for autonomy, and he had the patience to play the long game. For the first time, I faced an adult who respected me and gave me a chance to earn my way into high school.

Relieved, I nodded. I had reached the end of my rebellion.

In the fall, I returned to school as a freshman, determined to pass my classes. I began to imitate Verne's homework habits, studying with him. I was determined to turn in every assignment. I did, and to my shock, I realized that when I worked hard, I could earn good grades. By the middle of the first quarter, my improved grades ended my probation, which lifted a great amount of stress. I would be able to stay with my cohort.

My determination also got the attention of my classmates. The first was my former enemy, Marlin Miller. A distant cousin, he was also the son of our choir director, John Henry Miller and throughout elementary school, he had everything I wished for: a father who taught him how to play ball, an extended family whose members were known for their musical abilities, and three gorgeous sisters—all of them blonde—who were considered cool within our youth group.

It was music that drew us together, from the first moment Marlin dragged me out of the school's typing lab into a rehearsal with an impromptu quartet. A few minutes later, we were singing a familiar hymn at the morning's chapel service. Our *a cappella* blend was magical. We were quickly asked to perform again, this time at a church service.

Marlin was the fair-haired boy in our world: talented, athletic, ebullient. I couldn't believe we had become friends. His dazzling tenor voice lit a performance with its rollicking warmth, and his charm commanded any room he entered.

With him directing our quartet, we did so well that we began receiving invitations to sing during church services and on choir tours. I was the smallest member of the group at four foot, ten inches tall, and ninety pounds, but I also had an exceptionally high voice, and my three popular peers needed me. We sang together often, with my determination driving us forward, and Marlin's talent and charm opening doors. Over the next four years, we became an item, featured each year on the choir tour. We called ourselves the School Quartet. Not a fancy name, but it stuck.

Although I had distrusted Marlin in elementary school, as we began spending time together, I quickly saw that he was as stubborn as I was, although he hid it behind a charismatic personality. During our first rehearsal, when his father came down to the basement and commandeered our rehearsal to teach us a song he liked, I saw Marlin's unhappiness. He didn't resist his father, but when we decided to practice again, Marlin suggested we meet somewhere else. It was a subtle move no one else may have noticed, but I recognized what he was doing. Marlin had stood up for our group's autonomy. No one else would run our show while he was around, not even his father, the most influential musician in church. With that move, Marlin earned my respect and trust.

Over the next two years, my relationship to sports also changed. Before, I had preferred to spend my free time reading, but as my body increased in strength and athleticism, thanks to my summer construction work, my friends pulled me into intramural games. In the spring, I decided I wanted to be a softball pitcher, and although I never made it past second string, Verne's encouragement gave me the courage to take more chances.

In the winters, I began going with him every Friday night to a local gym for pickup basketball games, which Brother Byler supervised. At the end of the evening—after I had mostly sat on the bench and Verne had made his mark on the scoreboard—we hung out in my room. We both ate ice cream and swilled root beer as he paced the small room, holding forth on intellectual theories, or on politics. He predicted Jimmy Carter would be re-elected, but I was doubtful, since my entire construction crew liked Ronald Reagan.

Having never turned in an assignment late, Verne was truly gifted, and one of the few students ahead of me in his reading. Thanks to a photographic memory, he could comprehend the literary aspects of any work far more rapidly. Most importantly, he understood the way that I thought.

He loved ideas and followed me effortlessly when I shifted from topic to topic—whipsaw fashion, a trait that I carry even today—and we bounced ideas back and forth like two players on an academic court. We could talk for hours. He was especially interested in my creative ideas. Reading the poetry and short stories I wrote, he told me again and again that I was brilliant.

"You don't fit into this community," he said.

I figured he should know, since he was an outsider himself, but I still didn't believe him.

By senior year, my grades had improved dramatically. Thanks to Verne's tutelage, I had learned to churn out the assignments I needed, but… learning still wasn't the point. I wasn't learning because I loved to learn; I was learning because it improved my grades, and good grades won me respect.

I had begun to build secure friendships outside of my immediate family. By then, having stood up to my father, I knew that I would never buy into his accretion of cultural beliefs. I was looking for a path out, and I knew that with my need to connect with people, I would need to create another "family" whose beliefs fit my own.

After rehearsals, or on the way to concerts, Marlin and I spent more time together, discovering that we were both searching for a way out of our community. This was complicated, since he was the grandson of Brother Roman, who had just passed. But we began to trust each other as we found honesty in each other's answers, and the time we spent in rehearsals and performance supercharged our growing bond. Since Marlin had charisma and his opinion was respected, his belief in me had the spillover effect of helping me build other friendships.

What I didn't understand was my unique ability to connect with people. I had gained this after reading Dale Carnegie's classic book *How to Win Friends and Influence People*, which taught that you could build trust by listening to other people, identifying their interests, and then asking questions based on those interests. Upon practicing Carnegie's suggestions, I had found, to my surprise, that they worked, not only with my classmates, but also with strangers. I quickly learned I could defeat shyness because—as Carnegie had taught me— if you match the other person's stories with brief tidbits about yourself, the other person will talk endlessly about themselves. More significantly, they will believe *you* are a fascinating conversationalist. For the first time, I was able to take the lead in conversations with others, and thus stumbled into one of my deepest passions, journalistic writing.

When I wasn't playing ping pong with Verne at lunch, I spent my lunches alone in our small library reading secular news magazines and newspapers Brother Byler now purchased each day for the school. One day, I realized we no longer had a school newspaper, and I decided I could lead it. By then, I had gained some confidence, having been named photo editor of the yearbook, joining a staff of classmates who were quickly becoming my friends, due to their respect for my work. So, I approached Brother Byler and asked if I could reboot the student newspaper, with him as the adviser.

I felt connected to the paper, I said, ever since the editor had published one of my poems in it my freshman year. Sitting across from Brother Byler in his office, once dominated by the men who compared our class to witches, I waited as Brother Byler considered my request.

In a small school like ours, teachers taught classes that included two grades at a time—which gave them sections of approximately twenty students—and Brother Byler had chosen to follow our class, continuing to teach us in English, Physical Education, and even US Government & Civics. Lately, he had become the school's principal, but he had still chosen to schedule his few teaching assignments with us, much to the annoyance of other cohorts, who envied our close relationship.

By then, I had gotten a poem published in a national collection of high school poetry, and perhaps that is what convinced Brother Byler I could reboot the newspaper staff… or perhaps it was because I was the only one interested. Either way, he named me editor-in-chief. As I reflect on this, I think this was the first time I really fought for a leadership position in school. Until then, I had believed things simply happened to me. Whatever the reason, it was the first time in my life that I was put in charge of any organization, and my decision to become a student journalist awakened a passion for writing that would shape the rest of my life.

Now, as we headed towards graduation, Brother Byler began to reveal to us that the way to discover Truth was by asking questions. Our lives should be ruled by this dictum. No question was too stupid, nothing was too sacred, and anyone who taught otherwise was not to be trusted.

Brother Byler's decision to show us this approach to learning, rather than indoctrinating us in our community's culture, garnered a great deal of criticism from our community. I heard him being discussed at family gatherings, sometimes with righteous fury. A highly verbal cohort in our community wanted to return the school to the bad old days, when the school followed a stricter regime, and when students were immediately paddled for disrespect and rebellion—not encouraged to question authority.

The fact that Brother Byler knew everyone was talking about him behind his back—criticisms he would occasionally share with us even as he stoically continued to lead our school—only made us admire him the more because it confirmed to us that he was a rebel like us. A decade later, when I watched the film *Dead Poets Society*, I recognized Mr. Keating, the teacher who was fired for teaching students to think for themselves. He was Brother Byler, only in a different setting.

Most senior classes run the school, but we dominated athletically, academically, and artistically, knowing that Brother Byler had our backs. Because he was a competent administrator and a vigorous recruiter of students outside our community, the school was now the largest it had ever been and the most financially successful. The board, led by a group of moderates who were horrified by what had happened when we were in elementary school, held firm and supported Brother Byler. They were disappointed when he decided to move on at the end of our senior year to begin a full-time master's program in English.

Brother Byler's approach to learning had been the key that had motivated me—finally—to throw myself into my studies. It had undergirded every decision I made in high school. For the first time, I had gained intellectual autonomy, and it had resonated with me deeply. It had helped me understand who I was. After all, I was still proud of the Question Box nickname I'd carried with me since childhood.

With the help of these gifted allies, I was also graduating high school. My family and friends were excited about my success with grades that placed me

Steven Denlinger

among the top half of my class, which was significant because Malone College, a local evangelical Quaker institution, now saw my little high school as very effective. Everyone who applied from our school was guaranteed a berth there.

The night of my high school commencement brought my options into sharp relief. All of my classmates and I were given a brief time to speak, since our valedictorian and salutatorian had generously decided that all fourteen of us in the senior class should share in their responsibilities. I have never seen this happen anywhere else, and it says something about the power of our senior class bond.

Speech class had taught me to enjoy speaking, and my training paid off that night. Using minimal notes that I jotted down just before filing into the auditorium, I recalled the moment I had begged my mother to start school early, describing briefly the entrance exam I passed under Sister Sommers' clear gaze. I described my mother and teacher allowing *me* to decide whether I wanted to join my cohort—and then imitated my excited answer: "Yes, yes, I want to go, I want to read." Caught up in my story, the audience was riveted. Glancing up from my notes, I wondered aloud, "I've always wondered whether I made the right decision."

They roared with laughter.

The feeling was delicious, and later, I replayed that moment again and again in my memory, imagining I might someday be a writer… or an actor. For the first time, I had held an audience spellbound through my words.

It was then, at that moment, that I began to consider how I could escape my past.

Book II: Shock

But ye *are* a chosen generation, a royal priesthood, an holy nation, a peculiar people; that ye should shew forth the praises of him who hath called you out of darkness into his marvelous light.

~ 1 Peter 2: 9, *The Holy Bible,* KJV, 1769

Interpolation II: The Beauty of Being a Patriarch

People make strange choices when they are afraid... when they feel they have no other options... when their world is unstable... and when they are desperate to feel safe.

Even if that means accepting authoritarian leadership.

My teaching mentor once told me people would do anything to feel safe, even if it meant giving up their personal freedoms. Our conversation took place three years before the Twin Towers collapsed, and I was amazed at his prescience. We gave up a lot of freedom in the following months.

Patriarchy is the oldest form of authoritarian leadership, and it is irresistible to men.

Since I am a man, I know this. As I left high school, I thought I wanted my autonomy—the ability to make my own decisions—but what I really wanted was to know how the game was played and how to secure a place at it.

In high school, Brother Byler had created a world in which I was given my autonomy.. and then some. Our senior class ran the school, and this kind of power also felt good. But now, out of school and facing a very confusing world, I had lost all power as I jumped to obey a construction boss who barked orders and shouted.

In addition, I am a bit of a hobbit, and I crave stability and order. I am drawn to a predictable world with clear rules, especially when faced with a crisis. Now, on the path ahead, I saw insurmountable obstacles blocking my dream life. I was determined to find a way to gain control in this unstable, post-high school world where my father was the dominant force. So, I considered my options.

I was a white, cisgender male.

If I accepted the patriarchal order, I would eventually achieve this power. And I had been taught the rules of the game... since childhood.

Chapter 7: Rejecting a Liberal Arts Education

The need to leave our restrictive community burned brighter than ever.

As I finished out the summer after high school, with some of my friends beginning their freshman year of college, I thought about my options. I could flee our community in order to fulfill my dreams. But I was tied too closely to my network of friends.

Unlike the memoirist Ira Wagler, who flees home in *Growing Up Amish*, our community didn't have a tradition of *Rumspringa*, a time when young people are encouraged to leave the community and explore the world. So, I didn't know if that would work.

What I did know is that I needed to escape the cycle of poverty that had trapped my father within this community. I needed to build a world in which *I* was in control.

Immediately after high school, I began my first year of full-time construction work. By November the damp Ohio winter was descending, crushing my spirits as I waded through mud and ice, learning the trade of laying block. I knew it could not be my future. I wanted to do more with my life than endure the trap of a blue-collar job, marry a conservative Mennonite girl, and produce a large family.

At home, the difficult years of my adolescence had created an impenetrable wall of hatred I could not surmount. In public, I honored my parents, but I could barely stand talking to Dad. This disturbed me greatly. As a Christian, I desperately tried to forgive my father, but my prayers hit a brass ceiling. Unable to live with the cognitive dissonance—I knew I should love my father, but in reality, I hated him—I began to deny my feelings. Good Christians didn't feel hatred, I was trying to be a good Christian, and thus, I didn't hate my father.

And so, I lived in a state of denial. Whenever I could, I avoided my father. I could tell he wanted to spend time with me, but when he sat down next to me, even during church functions, I would find a polite way to escape.

Part of this was the normal need to separate myself from my father, but it was more than that. At home at the dinner table, any conversation we had devolved into an argument, no matter what the subject. But afterward, I struggled with guilt. I knew I was a hypocrite, something I would never have tolerated in others.

What highlighted my dilemma was watching the way my friend Marlin interacted with his father. As I got to know them better, even spending a week in a cabin together in Southern Ohio hunting deer, I envied their cordial relationship. As they analyzed hunting strategies, or as they told amusing stories around the fire about hunting escapades gone awry, they laughed without inhibition.

When I visited their home, sometimes staying overnight, the three of us had long, comfortable conversations. There was none of the shouting that took place in our home. Instead of fighting for control, as my father and I did, the two of them listened to each other with respect.

Failing to understand the impact of a college education, I was confused by the differences I saw. Having been educated in child psychology, Marlin's father understood the stages of a child's development, and he strove to empower his children's individual personalities, rather than trying to control them. My father, on the other hand, focused on teaching obedience and respect: children were to obey their parents, and any rebellion resulted in a spanking. Thus, our relationship evolved into a battle for control, rather than a bond that nurtured my curiosity.

Maybe Dad's lack of education didn't allow him to piece the puzzle together. Maybe a better understanding of child development would have changed the arc of our relationship. But what came out of the Troubled Years—when my parents struggled to repair the harms done while Dad ran his business—devastated and confused me, sending me down a dark path.

When I was a child, Dad would awaken us every morning before he left for work in order to lead the family in devotions, then prayed for each of us individually. At the end of the day, as dusk fell on our crowded Ohio home, my mother would gather us for prayer, the family kneeling around the couch on our puke-green carpet. Her gentle voice led us in an evensong, always the same song.

Jesus, Tender Shepherd, hear me
Bless thy little lamb tonight
Through the darkness, be Thou near me
Keep me safe 'til morning light.

We'd all join in, harmonizing beautifully.

My mother's leadership during evening prayer demonstrated Dad's respect for her. He had always considered her a partner, rather than someone to dominate. Not that Mom would have accepted such nonsense—she had sought and found a husband who treated her with respect. Mom had a will of stainless steel, and no one—certainly not Dad—ignored her wishes. She was smarter than he was in practical matters, although she played the role of the sweet, submissive wife in public, like all good Mennonite wives. When my parents argued, Mom never lost.

Across my childhood, she had permitted my father to call himself Head of Household, but none of us was fooled. We knew who wore the pants, no matter how much my father blustered. Dad often teased Mom. "I'm the boss in this family," he would say, eyes twinkling as he glanced at my mother, "and I have my wife's permission to say so."

We laughed because it was true.

But now, as Dad adopted a regular work schedule, I saw that his relationship with my mother was at a low point. His business failure had left him with a raft of bills, and they sometimes exchanged sharp words.

Mom had always preferred the steady paycheck over business profits, and she valued the paid sick days his factory job offered when he came down with a migraine, which occurred about three days each month. But eager to make a fortune with his business, Dad had ignored her concerns. Now Mom's instincts had proved correct.

When Dad grew defensive, pointing out that perhaps the business had failed because she had never believed in his dreams, my mother stopped talking. The entire house simmered, and I learned what could happen when one strong partner loses respect for the other.

Not realizing what was going on, but sensing weakness, I argued with Dad constantly—usually about the ridiculous church rules Dad supported, or about his burgeoning credit card debt. To my surprise, I found an unlikely ally in my mother, who often joined my side, which startled me. When my father wilted under our joint attacks, my stomach churned. I felt like a pawn being used in some inexplicable battle.

Mom should be supporting Dad.

I realized how ridiculous this was—I had wanted to win, and Mom was supporting me—yet irrationally, I scorned her for taking my side, hating her disloyalty.

I could not comprehend the complexity of marital love.

My mother had married a strong, stubborn man that she loved profoundly. His financial struggles had made life very difficult, since money is one of the biggest stressors in a marriage.

Having carried his eight children, my mother had watched her husband launch a business with little chance of success. When the inevitable failure occurred, she had seen her formerly happy-go-lucky husband turn into an abusive Mister Hyde, taking his frustrations out on her oldest sons. She had felt torn between my need for autonomy and her belief that I needed to respect Dad.

Had she lived in a normal world, my mother might have walked out on my father. But she couldn't do that since she lived in a world in which divorce was a moral impossibility. So instead, she fought my father's worst impulses with every weapon she had, trying to get the family through a very difficult time.

As I watched my parents struggle, I drew conclusions about the way love worked. Before Mister Hyde had appeared, I had never questioned my mother, whose love for me had been unconditional. But now, as I saw her disloyalty to my father, I began to rethink my perspective. Although still sweet in public, Mom sometimes ridiculed Dad at home.

Is this the way all women were?

What if, like my father, I faced hard times in a marriage?

If I fell in love with a woman, and she got to know my weaknesses, she too might turn against me. I needed to become invulnerable, never giving up control, never putting myself in a situation in which a woman could mock me, as my father had done.

Sadly, I did not understand that love is a risk, that the depth of love you experience is equal to your level of trust and vulnerability. I equated true love with the loss of control. And that frightened me more than a lifetime spent alone.

It was at this point that my father revealed something about his relationship with my mother, which—had I taken the time to listen carefully, or had the maturity of experience to interpret what I saw—might have helped me avoid the dark path I was about to take.

One afternoon, my father was helping me change the engine oil and carburetor filter on the aging Chrysler he had bought for me. Suddenly, my mother appeared, asking him if there was enough money in the checking account for her to go grocery shopping.

"Not until payday," he said. "Can't you wait until then?"

She glanced at the new filter my father had purchased. The smile drained from her face, and she turned to leave, back to the kitchen where she was canning fruit.

My father watched her go, pain creasing his forehead. My stomach twisted as I stood there, holding the drop light above the engine, wishing I could be somewhere else. The spring-loaded door between the garage and basement slammed shut. Dad chuffed out a long breath. Then he turned back to the engine.

"She doesn't get it," he said, low and confiding. "But I can't stay angry at her. I get mad at her, and then when I climb into bed, and she moves in against me, I… I can't help myself. I love her so much."

What I didn't realize at that point was how much courage it took for my father to be vulnerable with me. Had I paid attention, I would have seen that under my parents' anger was a commitment to disagree without walking away from their marriage. The strength of their egalitarian relationship was due to my father's paradoxical attitude toward our community. Although a faithful church member, he refused to play the game of patriarchy. He treated my mother as his equal. He practiced the sacrificial model of love Jesus taught, and he tried to follow the Apostle Paul's instructions stating that the husband and wife were *both* to submit to each other in love. Yet because my father took the Bible literally, in which patriarchal leaders (not Jesus) demanded that women be silent, my father was unable to work out a biblical argument against the patriarchy.

As a teenager, I was observant, but not wise. Blinded by rage, my journal entries from the time reveal the way I misread my parents' relationship—believing that because my mother stood up for herself, she was manipulative, and my father was weak. I realize now that *weak* wasn't the right word—instead, my father had chosen to give up control. Only in later years did I recognize that my father had had the courage to marry a woman with a spine of steel who held him accountable, and that his willingness to be vulnerable revealed in my father an inner strength and confidence I could not yet comprehend.

And so, my need for control increased.

Only after high school did I turn from confiding my fears and dreams in my journal to becoming vulnerable with Marlin. It had taken years for him to win my confidence. Perhaps it happened because of our close musical partnership. The voice is your instrument, carrying emotion, and it is hard to hide within a vocal ensemble since each emotional thread becomes part of the weave of the group's sound. This is why *a cappella* music feels so intimate, and the tight-knit community built through it is unlike any other. When the fluctuating streams of talent and luck created magic within our School Quartet, it also created unbreakable bonds of friendship.

By now, we had chosen a new name, The Harvesters, and were beginning to perform full concerts in local churches regularly. Once we produced our first cassette album of songs, we became well known within conservative Mennonite communities in the Midwest, and I took the lead in organizing a tour to a series of churches on the East Coast. I was becoming a highly visible leader of our youth group.

In that first year after high school, Marlin and I did everything together. When not rehearsing or performing, we planned after-church activities and even organized youth camping trips in the summer to East Harbor State Park. I was never elected by the entire youth group during those years—instead, again and again, I would be chosen by the outgoing committee, who valued me for my steady dependability and hard work. In all our activities, Marlin played the front man, due to his charismatic personality. People loved and trusted him.

Our working partnership broke down our barriers. After youth activities, I found myself sharing with Marlin the personal details of my life on a level I had never enjoyed with anyone else. There was nothing we didn't talk about. Brother Byler had influenced us—just like the boys in *Dead Poets Society*—and we were determined to do something meaningful with our lives. It worried us that our peers were already dating steadily. Their dreams of a college degree and professional life were being put aside in favor of an early marriage, a steady blue-collar job, and eventually children. That was not the life for us, we determined, and so we refused to date any of the girls drawn to us.

Sometimes these conversations took place in his home, where we often hung out, sitting beside the fireplace. Sometimes his father joined us, offering unsolicited lectures on science or life, sharing stories from our community's history and its legendary leaders. A gifted teacher who recognized my leadership potential, he was giving me a course in how to wield influence within an egalitarian community.

71

Sometimes Marlin and I would sleep out under the stars, talking late into the night. During one sleepover in his family's treehouse overlooking the local flea market, part of which was located upon land his family owned, we tried to imagine what kind of girl we would eventually marry, talking quietly as peddlers wandered underneath, unaware of our presence. To my surprise, Marlin revealed that he believed whoever married me would have to be incredibly patient. My friend's observation worried me, but today I know how right he was.

There was a lot he didn't explain that night. I now know that he appreciated my growing willpower, but he was also worried about my instinctive reaction to anyone who tried to control me. Anyone who wanted my trust, he knew, would need to honor my autonomy

I had begun working my first full-time year as a bricklayer's apprentice, and Marlin was taking a gap year doing carpenter work, a trade his father believed he could fall back on during hard times. I knew Marlin would enter college next year to begin his bachelor's degree, and his father was encouraging me to follow the same path.

There was no place I felt safer during these years than in Marlin's home. Like Frodo entering Rivendell, when I entered Marlin's cozy home, I found a world of peace. Soft music from their powerful stereo washed over me like a comforting blanket, with no raucous arguments about theology. Voices were kept low. As Marlin's distant cousin, I was always welcomed like a family member. Marlin's three sisters adored him, and his mother doted on him.

His father was a benevolent force, someone who never worried about debts, as my father did. John Henry's master's degree ensured he was paid well as a public-school teacher, and it also demonstrated his belief in the value of a liberal arts education. He was the first truly educated person I knew. If I wanted to create an affluent home like his, I needed to get a college education.

But I considered that goal to be a stretch.

My father had originally promised that I could go to college when I turned twenty-one, which he considered the age of maturity. But now he was becoming more and more set against my going to college at all. The paychecks I brought home impressed him, and he couldn't understand why I would want to give up a career in construction. Proud of his own high school diploma, he was deeply suspicious of higher education, and worried college would draw me toward wealth—which he equated with worldliness. He feared that college would ruin the simple faith he had tried to impart within me.

I threw off Dad's worries. The most fascinating friends I had were attending college. One of them was Laban Coblentz, one of our youth leaders and the son of a legendary intellectual who had helped shape our community's separated lifestyle. In Laban, the apple had rolled far from the oak tree of our communal faith. Popular and charismatic, he was driven by an excitable energy.

I knew Laban was breaking the rules. When we hung out together, I often listened enviously to his summaries of the latest R-rated flick he had seen, and he often played Christian rock music at youth group events, or even secular rock and roll, which drew murmurs of concern from the faithful. Laban was also beginning to play leading roles in the theater at college, and I was drawn to the intellectuals and artists he introduced me to after his performances.

But Laban's activities had begun to draw reprimands from our ministers, and my close association with him concerned Dad. Although he loved talking to Laban, Dad worried that his worldly ideas would eventually lead him out of our community and possibly draw me after him. Even John Henry—who maintained a tolerant attitude toward college activities—occasionally expressed concerns about Laban.

My friend seemed to let all of this roll off his back, as if intent on breaking every rule in our community. Having lost his father as a child, Laban had few restrictions placed on him by his caring mother. Also, since Laban knew he was leaving, he couldn't be pressured to conform by anyone, not even the bishop himself.

I watched with envy, confused about how to create my own path forward. Unlike Laban, if I got into trouble, I would be a social outcast. In addition, Laban seemed to have a mysterious relationship to money, whereas I was sensitive to the possibility of financial failure. More than anything else, I wanted to avoid my father's path, which had left him impoverished and angry.

Today, as I consider my life at this juncture, it seems amazing that I did not just abandon my family and begin college. I was eighteen and legally allowed to make my own decisions. However, there were several considerations that haunted me.

First, I knew I hadn't put aside enough money to live on my own—I was giving two-thirds of my wages to my father, and I regularly spent the remainder. I doubted I'd survive financially. There was no organization that gave advice to conservative Mennonites who wanted to leave.

Second, although I argued with my father, I couldn't escape the fear that he might be right about the dangers of a college education: people who got a college education often left their faith behind. This fear was visceral, implanted within me across the years—verse upon verse, sermon upon sermon, warning upon warning. Yes, if I pursued a college education, I might be permitted to enjoy the pleasures of sin for a time, but eventually, that road would end in eternal darkness and pain.

Finally, I know now that I am a hobbit, someone who builds a solid home base, wherever I am, surrounding myself with a community of friends. This was true, even as a teenager. The idea that I would be a modern Huck Finn and "take off for the territories" by myself was a virtual impossibility. I didn't work that way.

The reality was, I deeply loved my family, and without my financial support, my father would struggle to make ends meet. The last time that happened... well, I didn't want Mister Hyde to return for my younger brothers and sisters.

I couldn't leave.

One of the most memorable conversations I had about my future took place about this time one evening after a youth group meeting. Laban and I continued talking after everyone went home, sitting inside his bright orange VW Karmann Ghia. Not just anyone could have driven a car with such an exotic appearance—we were supposed to be a community that aimed for simplicity in our automobiles—but the car fit Laban, somehow.

It was July, the window for my applying to college was closing, and Laban brought an intensity to our conversation that night, trying to convince me that I should go. He believed that I was right for college. I would never be satisfied staying in our community.

Facing him across the front seat of his car, I remember stonewalling him—agreeing that it was a good idea that I go to college—all the while knowing, deep inside, that there was no chance it would happen. Maybe people like Laban could go, but it wasn't in the cards for me. I had fully accepted the reality of my situation.

Even today, it's difficult to admit what I did.

I wish I could say that I simply applied to college, leaving home to pursue my dreams. It would have mirrored my struggle to attend first grade. It would have given me a more heroic story—the fighter who achieves independence, against all odds. But that's not what happened.

Forced to work with the cards I had been dealt, I realized that until I turned twenty-one, college was not an option. And so, I set that dream aside and looked at life realistically.

Desperate to gain my autonomy, and with no other way to relieve the ambition that churned in my belly like ground glass, I did the most logical thing. I turned my back on the bright and prosperous world of liberal arts that my best friend was choosing. Scanning the political landscape in our community, I reached for the ladder of patriarchal leadership.

And I began to climb.

Chapter 8: The Umbrella of Authority

My decision to embrace the world of patriarchy, and thus find a place within its power structure, makes no sense when you consider the difficult years of my adolescence. I had survived those years only because of a teacher who empowered me through his learning philosophy, one that was antithetical to patriarchal ideals.

He had taught me everything I loved about learning—being curious about the way things worked, asking difficult questions about people's motivations, developing egalitarian relationships with others, respecting other people's autonomy (no matter how young they are), being tolerant and empathetic toward people who are different, and even refusing to accept ideas just because they are promoted by those in authority. His ideas had found a home within the core of my soul.

So, the idea that I would accept the authoritarian principles of the patriarchy not only doesn't make sense, but it also went against everything I believed at the time. It was paradoxical.

Or perhaps not.

I recall my friend Marlin during this time reacting negatively to what he considered an unhealthy interest in power. He firmly believed that leadership needed to be collaborative, and he thought at times that I was "being rather pushy." I found this frustrating.

But when you announce your intention, the wise ones say, the Universe responds.

Several weeks later, at the beginning of August, I was invited to attend the annual Midwest Fellowship Youth Conference with a group of guys from our youth group. I leaped at the chance. It would be the social event of the year, I was told.

Most of the group were jocks, and they planned on spending a significant amount of time playing basketball. As we arrived at the sprawling conference grounds, with hundreds of young people in attendance, I discovered that we were meeting a small hip group of athletic young people my friends knew. I envied their easy camaraderie.

Eventually I discovered they had all attended Maranatha Bible School together, a winter boarding school located near the Twin Cities in Minnesota. Created to strengthen the faith of our young people, while also giving them a place where they could find suitable mates from outside their community, the school was protected, cloistered, and quiet with classes running from January through March, when farms were mostly in hibernation.

These alums looked important, and I wanted in. And so, I, as their tagalong, ate with all of them, played pickup basketball games on outdoor courts, and met cool, attractive girls, who welcomed my friends with enthusiastic hugs. This was the kind of popularity I wanted.

Something else happened that weekend. On Sunday afternoon, a powerfully built, middle-aged man from the woods of Wisconsin ascended the platform to preach.

Brother John Glick was all sharp edges and testosterone. As with many Amish-Mennonite ministers, he also ran a construction business. His image lingers in my mind: the rough-cut beard, the sunburned face, his eyes measuring the world about him with unsparing clarity.

He first read a passage from Matthew 8, describing the meeting between Jesus and a Roman Centurion, who comes to him asking him to heal his daughter. Just speak the words, he begs Jesus, and his daughter would be healed. As Jesus looks on amazed, the Centurion says,

> *For I am a man under authority, having soldiers under me: and I say*
> *to this man, Go, and he goeth; and to another, Come, and he cometh;*
> *and to my servant, Do this, and he doeth it.*

In other words, Jesus has power because He is under God's authority, the Centurion tells him. Thus, Jesus could command that his daughter be healed, just by speaking the words.

But rather than talking about the Centurion's great faith, Brother Glick extracted a different meaning from the text. He explained that the Centurion is describing the way authority should work within the family.

Under God, the father exercises the authority to command his wife and children's obedience. Most importantly, the only way for a son or daughter to know God's will is by listening to the father, since God primarily gives spiritual direction through him.

My mind moved rapidly through the logic of Brother Glick's argument. He was talking about power, and it made sense. Under this arrangement, a husband wielded a great deal of power, as did a father. God spoke to the wife and child through him.

But… this meant that for me to achieve this power, I would need to submit to my father. I flashed back to the conversation between me and my mother in the basement, when she told me I needed to submit to my father.

I have to submit to Dad? That's what this means?

As I listened to Brother Glick finish his sermon on authority, I finally recognized his source, a fundamentalist teacher named Bill Gothard who had gained a national following. I had heard about his teachings, since an entire bus load of our church members had attended his weeklong seminar in Cleveland. I had been invited to attend, but I had hesitated, only considering it seriously when I learned that my father disapproved of Gothard, since the man wore a tie (which meant he was worldly).

I was amused that Brother Glick was teaching material from a man my father considered worldly, and so I tried to write off the sermon as ridiculous. Marlin and I entertained ourselves for the rest of the service by passing sarcastic notes to each other.

But shortly before we were to leave for home, I spotted Laban talking to Brother Glick in the middle of the tent, and there was an odd intensity between the two men. I was curious, so I approached them. To my surprise, Laban seemed relieved to see me. He quickly introduced me to Brother Glick, and before I could blink, Laban was gone.

I suddenly recalled a story Laban had told me on the way up, finally putting two and two together. While attending Maranatha Bible School the previous winter, Laban had gotten into trouble with the administration, due to a theological argument he had had with one of his teachers, who considered him heretical. Ultimately, Laban had been asked not to return to the school. It dawned on me then. The pastor who had accused Laban of heresy was… Brother Glick.

Now, I realized that I was curious. It seemed so odd, the idea that this man had actually expelled Laban, who had always impressed me with his ability to escape trouble. I was also annoyed by Brother Glick's obsession with authority.

The man didn't do small talk, cutting right to the chase when he found out I was from Harville. Was I attending college as well? I fudged a bit, telling him I was planning to, very soon, since like Laban, I loved literature. I sensed increased tension in Brother Glick, but I wasn't worried. He had no power over me, and besides, I thought his ideas should be challenged.

"So, your sermon about authority—I'm guessing you got your interpretation from Bill Gothard?"

Brother Glick's face tightened. "I believe he does teach that, yes."

"Are you sure you're correct on that? That sounds pretty Catholic. I thought the Anabaptist and Protestant Reformers taught that God speaks to people individually." Brother Glick's eyes narrowed, but I plunged on. "We studied this during Bible class when I attended Hartville Christian High School."

There. That ought to show him.

Brother Glick's eyes narrowed. "The Bible supports Gothard's teaching," he snapped.

"But it doesn't exactly follow Anabaptist theology, does it?"

I was comfortable talking to church leaders, and Brother Byler had encouraged us to disagree with authority, eschewing indoctrination. Plus, I was on firm theological ground, so I was confident in my argument.

"Christians should talk directly to God," I said. "I'm sure of this. It's one of the basic tenants of the Amish and Mennonite faith. So, I'm not sure why I need my father to hear what God is saying to me."

For a moment, Brother Glick was silent. Precisely, he lined up the conference bulletin to rest inside his Bible, then snapped it shut. Ignoring my theological argument, he spoke like a reprimanding pastor, and his voice brooked no opposition. "I can sympathize with you." There was zero sympathy in his voice. "I suspect you're having problems obeying your father right now." His glance took in my Calvin Klein jeans and designer tee shirt.

I was glad I wasn't one of his sons. "What makes you think that?"

Brother Glick regarded me with scorn. "Perhaps you should begin your search for God's will by beginning to obey your father." I started to protest, but he raised his hand in dismissal. "Unless you wish to find yourself far outside God's will. It's not a place I'd want to be." He left me to chew on that gristly mouthful and strode away.

I watched him go, infuriated. Instead of responding to my argument that Christians have direct access to God without the help of a priest (a very basic belief among Anabaptists and Protestants), he had ignored my argument and changed the subject, making a personal judgment about my relationship with my father. According to him, by not submitting to my father, I was rebelling against God. His last statement, especially, made me see red. According to him, if I didn't obey my father, I was going to Hell.

What was I, a fifth grader again?

I slowly made my way back to our car, where my friends were getting ready to leave. In the excitement of goodbyes, I forgot the conversation I had had with Brother Glick. Laban didn't bring it up either, or perhaps he didn't want to talk about it.

But the next day at work, and in the weeks that followed, I often thought about that conversation. Brother Glick had touched a nerve because, in fact, I didn't feel good about my relationship with Dad. In fact, Brother Glick had cut to the heart of what I was experiencing.

Intuiting my discomfort with my father, Brother Glick had offered a solution to my problem. As a good patriarch, he believed that every father had a right to chastise their child, and a child's responsibility was to accept that punishment submissively—no matter how severe or invasive. In other words, like my administration in fifth grade, Brother Glick believed that my *rebellion* was the real problem, not my father's physical abuse.

Brother Glick didn't need to tell me he approved of corporal punishment. He was part of the patriarchal system that taught parents to chastise their children, so, he didn't need to spell this out.

What I didn't, what I couldn't accept, was his solution to my relationship with my father. Submission. Once I did that, my father would be pleased, my life would become easy, and God's blessings would pour down.

In a world in which therapy was not an option—because only insane people took therapy, and I wasn't insane—Brother Glick's solution made sense.

But I wasn't sure I could buy it. On the other hand, I wasn't sure I could live with my current situation. My anger toward my father was weighing me down.

Perhaps the problem *was* me.

Several months later, curious about Brother Glick's solution, I attended Bill Gothard's Institute in Basic Youth Conflicts, taking a bus loaded with many of our youth group to Cleveland. Everyone took notes in red spiral notebooks, the pages set up with bullet points.

Gothard kept things clean and simple, pointing us back to the era of the 1950s when patriarchy was the order of the day. He stood before us at a podium, a mild-mannered man in a conservative business suit, outlining his lectures on slides beamed up on a screen. His teachings were so popular that President Reagan once took the time to praise the institute in an official White House statement, which Gothard read to us triumphantly.

I could see that his ideas mattered to those in power, so I listened carefully as Gothard explained his Umbrella of Authority. Referring again to the Roman Centurion, Gothard used this model of military authority to show the way God intended relationships within the Kingdom of God to work.

Gothard showed a graphic image of this Umbrella. Under it was the father, under him, the mother, and under her, the child. The rain of evil bounces off the Umbrella of Authority, Gothard said. When people obey their religious authority, they are shielded from the Devil's influence. All very logical.

From childhood, I have been fascinated by organizational systems. Once in elementary school, while exploring trains, I created a model train club, spending hours creating leadership positions within a charter for the club. Although I was never able to interest my classmates in the club, it revealed how clearly organizational leadership appeals to me.

Now, as I listened to Gothard, I was fascinated by his interpretation of authority. It showed the pathway to patriarchal power, laid out neatly and logically. Within marriage and within the church, men serve as the leaders, and the women follow them.

At heart, I knew Brother Glick had put his finger on something when he intuited problems within my relationship with my father. Perhaps this was the reason our conversations turned into arguments, and why I struggled to accept the guidance of our ministers, especially when it came to my attending college. These were my spiritual authorities. If the problem was my inability to submit to my father, this might be why I felt so uncomfortable around him.

I found myself caught between my growing hatred for my father because of his abusive discipline that he refused to renounce and still practiced on my younger brothers, and the sneaking suspicion that Mr. Gothard was onto something, but... embracing any element of Mr. Gothard's teaching would entail profound personal consequences. Before I could earn my own patriarchal authority, I would have to submit to my father.

It was about this time that my sister Elaine fled our community. In recent years, I had realized her lifestyle was nothing our community would approve of. But she attended church and came to youth group activities, and for a time, she'd even dated a conservative Mennonite boy from Georgia... but that eventually ended.

As I had moved into youth leadership roles, Elaine had moved away from our youth group and community. She seemed familiar with television shows, which she watched while babysitting children from worldly families. She often quoted from them.

I was unable to empathize with my sister. I was still wrestling with my own identity, trying to decide where I fit into our community. To make it worse, as the firstborn within a patriarchal society, I had privileges that she could not access. She had pressures bearing down on her that were completely invisible to me, and so there was no way she could feel safe.

My sister was no fool. She often admired me openly as her brother, but as I began to take on more leadership roles, she began to put distance between us, calculating that I would not be an ally in her departure. She later shared with me that although she knew she could legally leave at the age of eighteen, she'd decided she hadn't wanted to take a chance that Dad would be able to force her to return home. So, she waited until she turned twenty-one, until even Dad had to recognize her adult status.

By that time, Elaine knew what she'd needed—someone to protect her— and she chose a Vietnam vet who could eviscerate Dad, literally, if he tried to come after her. She had known what Dad was capable of because she'd watched the way Dad had beaten me as a child.

When Dad got the news that his daughter had fled with a worldly man, he reacted strongly. At one point, he suggested that I help him do an intervention— physically restraining her from leaving while he convinced her of the dangers that she would face. I refused to help him.

"She's gone, Dad," I said. "There's nothing you can do."

"We can pray for her," he told me fiercely. "God will intervene."

Dad's grief was palpable, his anger and wish to control my sister intimidating. It seared itself into my memory like a stain that will not rub out.

In the next few months, my father struggled to confront his limits: he was powerless to bring Elaine back. She was gone. In fact, we learned, she'd left the state and had gone West. There was nothing he could do.

Or... was there?

Eventually, my father discovered in Hosea 2:6 a strategy to force Elaine to return home: a Hedge of Thorns. It was a bit like shunning, except a lot more intentional. As taught by Bill Gothard, a Christian father can use "prayer to bind Satan and build a hedge of thorns" around someone who has left to pursue a life of sin. My father reasoned that this hedge would protect my sister from evil by isolating her from her evil friends, eventually making her return home the only real option. And so, Dad began praying, asking God to build a Hedge of Protection around my sister. Day after day, week after week, he begged God to do this.

Although my father's strategy sounded positive on the surface—after all, who wouldn't want to "protect" my sister?—in reality, it worked as a tool of control. In fact, I read it today as nothing less than a magical spell that aimed to isolate my sister and force her toward a path of repentance leading her back to our patriarchal culture where only men had power. My father's spell—a way of ill-wishing my sister to force her to do *his* will—was intended to eliminate her autonomy.

Seeing my father pray this Biblical spell brought the emotional violence of my childhood into sharp focus because I was treated to a front-row seat to my father's grief and anger, which was now turned toward manipulation in both his prayers and in his actions when Elaine called home. Sometimes she asked him for financial help when she got into trouble, which he often sent her. I suspect she kept in touch because, deep down, she did love my father, but her requests for help gave my father his weapon, the chance to use his "love" to control her.

Sadly, I eventually realized that the only love my father understood was blind obedience. He didn't see God as a Father who loved unconditionally; instead, he saw God as an all-powerful Being who loved only those who obeyed Him. And my father, as God's chosen leader of our household, emulated this kind of conditional love.

Watching the entire conflict play out shook me. It made me think twice about leaving, as well, something I was considering on a regular basis as I attended plays with my friend Marlin. My friend Laban had essentially left and was producing his first original play at Malone College. But I didn't have the courage. I was too practical to flee into an unknown world without any real support, as my sister did. And I had everything to gain by staying.

As a youth group leader, my network of friends formed the foundation of my contentment. So, the thought of leaving and losing all of those relationships seemed impossible, no matter how appealing. There had to be a better way.

I was still trying to process my feelings about Elaine's departure when Brother Glick chose to visit our church. He preached another sermon on authority, and this time, I listened carefully. Having accepted the basics of how authority might serve *me*, I had begun to admire his absolute confidence.

When I approached him after the service, I could sense his skepticism. However, I was feeling vulnerable, torn by the mixed emotions brought on over my sister's departure. And so, I stood in the sanctuary well after church ended, sharing my frustrations.

My anecdotes about my abusive father got me no quarter from Brother Glick. "You'll have to obey your father." His square face was a brusque mask.

"Even when he's wrong?" I could hardly believe his words.

"Even when he's wrong."

"Sometimes, I think about leaving," I said quietly. "I'm eighteen. I'd like to go to college. I've even wondered whether I want to be a Christian."

Not far away, a few people stood talking in the sanctuary, and I didn't want them overhearing me. With my sister gone, I didn't need them thinking I might do the same thing.

But I knew that was a possibility, since leaving the faith could happen to anyone at any time. What makes you a Christian, our pastors told us, was your daily commitment to living for Christ. I could reject him at any time, and if I did that, I would no longer be considered a Christian, not by this crowd.

Brother Glick remained silent in the face of my doubts.

Perhaps he's heard this all before.

Have I said too much?

But for some reason—perhaps because he himself was so blunt—I thought Brother Glick might respect my honesty. I was also testing him, I know now, trying to see how he'd react to something outrageous. But oddly enough, whatever the reason, I trusted this brusque man. Perhaps his strength made it easy for me to be vulnerable with him.

Brother Glick knew I could leave at any time. For the first time, I saw in his eyes something... was it sympathy?

I realized, suddenly, that I had something he wanted. I was already a leader. If he could turn me into a soldier for the church, into a future pastor who was completely committed to Christ, his influence would be even greater than it was now.

"If I were to follow Christ, of course, I would commit completely." I felt my heart begin to pound, the adrenaline kicking in. "I'm sure God will be able to use me once I do commit."

Until then, my vulnerability had gotten his sympathy. But suddenly, his jaw jutted out.

"God doesn't need you, Steve. You need Him. But if you wait to commit to Christ, He may not be around to accept your offer."

I had not considered that God might not accept my offer. But I knew he was correct. From childhood, I had heard stories of people who committed the unpardonable sin and then tried to repent but then found that the doors of Heaven had been sealed against them, even though they begged for God's forgiveness.

Startled, I sat on a nearby bench in the now-empty sanctuary. Brother Glick sat beside me, his body muscular and intimidating from decades of brutal construction work. Unlike my father, this was a man who was used to taking charge.

"Steve, if you are going to be of any value to the Church, you'll have to commit to God."

I realized suddenly that he meant *submit* rather than commit. They were two different actions, but he had conflated them. In his mind, submission to authority was the only way to find salvation. My soul was suddenly on the line.

Glancing at me, Brother Glick opened his well-worn Bible to the Book of Ephesians. "'Children, obey your parents in the Lord, for this is right.'"

I stared at the verse, the words swimming. I had been prepared to resist this concept with every bone in my body, but now I wasn't sure. Would God reject me if I continued to treat my father with disrespect?

"Steve, God makes his wishes known to us through only one channel—our God-given authority."

"You mean my father."

"Yes, I mean your father."

I thought about my father, about the frustration I felt when I was with him. Brother Glick was arguing that I only had access to God through my spiritual authority—my father. According to Brother Glick, I had no choice but to obey him.

But this was the problem. How could I submit to Dad when I could barely stand being in the room with him? My father had little control in our household—my mother manipulated him, and even I was now stronger than he was. To make this Umbrella of Authority work, I needed someone I could respect.

But Brother Glick was offering me a card that I desperately wanted—the chance to eventually become a patriarch myself, like the strong fathers I admired in our community. To do that, I needed a more masculine mentor, and my oddball Dad wasn't it. I wanted more John Wayne and less Mahatma Gandhi.

Brother Glick might make a more fitting masculine role model. In his family, no one could doubt who was in charge. In addition, I knew our ministers respected Brother Glick, *and* he was taking a significant amount of time to talk to me. I needed to accept his help because, in him, I could see the spiritual leader—the patriarch—I could become.

"I need time to think about this," I told Brother Glick. But of course, I didn't.

Over the next week, desperate to reassert some control of my path in life, I embraced Brother Glick's belief system.

I started by going to my father and humbly asking his forgiveness for my disrespect. He greeted my decision with joy, giving me a hug. As he did, I struggled not to react, feeling almost nauseous, but afterward, when my father pulled away from me, his face beamed, and I felt a sense of relief. Perhaps I could do this.

I wrote to my new mentor, telling him I'd decided to submit my life to God, and thus to my father. Energized by my decision, I followed the advice he gave me by mail, getting up early to have personal devotions before work, reading my Bible and praying. I had always believed my quiet time with God was important, but I had never been able to do so consistently. I knew that if I wanted to be a leader, I needed to model what I believed.

When my father made statements during dinner that I disagreed with, I bit my tongue. Rather than disagreeing, I changed the subject, sometimes getting

Dad to tell his favorite jokes. I began to ask questions, curious about what Dad thought, and why. When Dad decided something, I tried to support him.

To my surprise, over the next few months, the mood lightened around the house. By now, my brother Dave had joined me in doing construction work, so I didn't worry about my father abusing him anymore. And to my surprise, I realized my father had become less severe with my three youngest siblings. Perhaps it was the lack of stress with my change in attitude, or perhaps my two youngest brothers and youngest sister were better behaved, but he seemed less strict with them.

At church, our ministers noticed the difference in my attitude. I was calmer, more serious, and I was now paying attention during church services, rather than passing notes to my friends. I began to distance myself from Marlin and Laban, choosing to spend time after church services talking to the older, most vocal leaders in our church, who loved critiquing the morning's sermon. At one point, when one of them asked me what kind of a relationship I had with my father, I shared about my interest in the ideas Gothard taught, and my decision to submit to my father as my spiritual authority. Their eyes lit up.

One of them was Brother Lapp, who had visited my fifth-grade classroom and threatened punishment just before the Comic Book Rebellion. Since then, he had paid little attention to me—he had lost his teaching position at the end of that year and had returned to trucking—but now he looked at me with interest as I asked questions about how to find God's will. He was happy to hold forth on the importance of authority and submission. I engaged with him, sometimes disagreeing on minor points, but agreeing on Gothard's core beliefs.

Having these new allies in my corner changed the way people looked at me. I could tell by the way the older people stopped me after services to ask me my thoughts on the sermon, or what I thought about various spiritual ideas. I was always able to give them a clear, respectful answer. Watching them listen to me respectfully gave me a rush of adrenalin. When I spoke up during discussions in Sunday School, people listened. My opinions finally mattered. I began to see the advantage of being aligned with my spiritual authority.

By deferring to my father, I was gaining a sense of control in my life. I no longer felt the need to argue. When I handed Dad two-thirds of my wages at the end of each week, and saw the grateful smile on his face, it felt good.

My father, of course, was overjoyed by my changes. He told me how much he appreciated my respect, and the way I supported him. The family was happier, he told me. I realized, of course, that this was because *he* was happier. He finally had his son under control, he believed.

As my second year of full-time construction work began, Marlin and my friends began making plans to attend Maranatha Bible School, starting in January and leading up to mid-February. I was excited by the idea. I loved meeting people, and I knew that the six weeks they'd spend there—although ostensibly studying the Bible—were actually a bit like a vacation. It was a good place to meet marriageable girls from other communities—some of the older youth group members had met their life partners there—and although I didn't intend to marry any time soon, I loved talking to attractive girls.

When I approached my father about going to Maranatha, asking for his approval, he looked crestfallen.

"I can't let you go," he said. "There are a lot of expenses, trying to raise a family. The family needs the money you're bringing in."

I was disappointed, and unexpectedly, I felt my blood boil. Why was I letting my father make this decision for me? Didn't I have the right to make this decision? Doubting my mentor's advice, I wrote him, explaining my frustrations. My mentor quickly responded.

"You can only discover God's will by submitting to your father's wishes," he said, "especially when it's difficult to obey. You need to stay home and follow your father's spiritual leadership."

I was in despair as my best friends climbed into vans to leave. But I sucked it up, continuing to go to work every day, working from dawn to dusk in the frigid Ohio winter.

When I went to visit my friends in Minnesota at the end of the semester, listening to the all-school choir perform, hearing Marlin perform in multiple ensembles, and seeing the way the girls worshiped him, I was hit by loneliness. I should have been there with him. I had missed out.

I began to doubt my choices, wondering if I'd committed to working for the rest of my life to support my father, thanks to Brother Glick's advice. I wondered if I would ever gain my own autonomy.

A year of work passed, and in the fall of 1982, Marlin began his first year of college. I assumed I would be working through the winter again. But then something wonderful happened. In October, my father pulled me aside.

"I've decided you should go to Bible School this winter," he said.

I blinked at him. "Really? I thought you... I mean, don't you need my paycheck?"

His eyes twinkled. "God works in mysterious ways. Someone in church has paid your tuition and reimbursed me for the money you would make during that time." He shook his head. "I can't believe it either."

I suddenly found my voice. "I'll go," I said.

My decision to attend Maranatha by myself proved fortuitous. When I arrived, I found that much had changed. I was now nineteen years old, a respected member of my church, and an emerging leader. My instructors all seemed to know who I was, and they knew about my powerful mentor. They spoke to me respectfully and listened to my ideas. My association with Brother Glick had given me credibility.

When it came to meeting other students, I was nervous. In Hartville, I was reserved, playing the organizational person working behind the scenes, letting Marlin be the front man. Now for the first time, I found myself alone with peers I didn't know. But within the first few days, I realized they all knew me—I was from Hartville, and they all listened to The Harvesters. Suddenly, I found myself the center of attention, sought after by the most popular young people, both guys *and* girls. As if by magic, the curtain had parted to reveal a new, extroverted Steve.

The most memorable class I took was my new mentor's. As I dutifully copied the bullet-point outlines provided by Brother Glick, I discovered his approach to learning contradicted what I'd learned in high school.

"God wants Christians to be ignorant about evil," Brother Glick stated with certainty, "and knowledgeable about good." His support for this theory came from a lone verse in Romans 16:19, in which the Apostle Paul wrote, "I would have you wise unto that which is good, and simple concerning evil."

My teacher interpreted this to mean we should reject all intellectual theories, and, therefore, since college professors taught intellectual theories, we should refuse to attend college because those who attended college lost their faith. "Since these teachers don't believe God has inspired every word in the Bible," Brother Glick said, "how can we believe anything they say? Better we remain ignorant."

Brother Glick explained that a Christian needed to follow the literal commands of the Bible without question. Reading critical analyses of the Bible could be dangerous. In addition, only one translation of scripture was accurate, the King James Version. Clearly, he sided with my father, who, when I tried to bring in different interpretations of Scripture, would throw up his hands and ask incredulously, "What's to interpret? Just read what it says."

My resulting cognitive dissonance was intense because, under the teaching of Brother Byler in high school, I had been taught that asking hard questions led to finding the Truth. I was encouraged to use critical thinking. Under that philosophy, I had thrived, experiencing real autonomy and the power to make my own decisions.

Over the last year, I had taken on a mentor whose worldview ran counter to this. Setting aside what I believed in my bones, I'd decided God's will was found by submitting to my spiritual authority, buying into Brother Glick's basic premise. Eventually, I pushed away Brother Byler's ideas, which caused me to doubt, and chose instead Brother Glick's certainty.

After all, I was happier than I'd been in years. My family was also happy, and my father was digging his way out of debt. I knew that eventually, I would embrace a patriarchal role. Rather than leaving our community—which was what I had planned to do when I first left high school—I had decided to stay. The path ahead was clear and certain.

I had left questions—and doubts—behind.

Shortly after I returned home from Maranatha, I had a crucial conversation with my sister, Ann, who was now teaching first grade at my *alma mater*. It was after dinner, and we were washing dishes.

A good listener, Ann asked how I liked construction work.

Her warm sympathetic ear caused me to drop my guard, and a flash flood of frustration I didn't even know I felt came pouring out. It had been a wet and snowy day outside and forgetting how happy I had felt several months before while at Maranatha Bible School, I told her how much I hated mason work. I told her I still wanted to go to college, but that dad would never approve. I told her I was afraid I would spend the rest of my life working outside, mixing concrete and laying blocks.

"Have you ever considered teaching?" she asked me.

Startled by the idea, my mind flashed back to the speech I gave at graduation. I had loved speaking that night. People had laughed. Yet I was confused by the idea of becoming a teacher. How could I when just six years ago, I'd been failing middle school? How could a person who had passed eighth grade on *probation* become a teacher?

Having been part of a raucous class who was difficult to teach, I knew handling a classroom took confidence, even bravado. That idea frightened me because I thought I had little of either. On the other hand, I *had* gained a lot of confidence in the past year. People respected me, telling me I now spoke with authority.

Ann's words had suddenly expanded my view.

"Are you serious?" I asked.

"Yes. I think you'd make a good teacher." She slipped another dish into the dirty water. "I've heard you speak. You love to learn. Young people admire you. Think about it."

I *did* think about it. Seven years before, I'd been a physically abused child. Now, I was considering becoming a teacher within the same type of school system that had stripped me of my autonomy and destroyed my love for learning. I was at an inflection point.

Chapter 9: How To Fail as A Patriarch

My sister's suggestion that I think about becoming a teacher—working in a conservative Mennonite school, of course—caused me to consider the teaching opportunities found within the network of communities like ours stretching across the United States and Canada.

My older sisters had already set a pattern for this. Having read and admired frontier fantasy books such as *Anne of Green Gables* and the *Little House* series, they had begun teaching in one-room schoolhouses in their teens as well—my oldest sister Marcia in our grandparent's farming community in Seymour, Missouri, and my second sister Ann at our *alma mater* here in Hartville, Ohio.

But I wasn't a young woman who could rely on her relatives or boyfriend to help her move out of state to take on a new job. As a male leader, I needed to own my own car, one that established my identity. I wasn't sure if Dad would let me do this, but since my father believed in serving God, I thought there was a chance he might let me leave home to teach, even before I was twenty-one.

As the Russians say, "Hope dies last."

So perhaps it wasn't a coincidence that I purchased a rusty, aging Datsun B-210 at the beginning of my journey into the patriarchy. In fact, I find it impossible to talk about this time in my life without considering what may be the worst big-item purchase I've ever made.

That is, if I were to simply judge the car.

But if I consider how the car's transformation and decline followed my journey into patriarchal leadership, I can see that it was more than just a car. My exposure to patriarchy, the power that came with it, and the abuse of power I observed around me, shifted my view of how men and women should interact with each other.

By this time, I was tired of the ancient Chrysler New Yorker my father had generously lent to me. It had a four-barrel carburetor, so it sucked down gas like a hungry boy with a chocolate milkshake, and it could reach ninety mph in sixty seconds.

I'd proved this, many times.

To be fair, the car served its karmic function—it had made me desperate to buy my own car. The color was the first problem. When my father had fixed it up and repainted it, preparing it for resale, he'd tried to save money by mixing all the left-over paint he had on the shelves.

Voilà! He created a shade of puke green (my father had a thing for that color) that was the visual equivalent of pulling fingernails down an ancient blackboard. That car was so ugly, it took therapy to eliminate the self-loathing it layered onto my identity as a teen. I hated that car.

From a practical perspective, the car did have its value. It was humongous, fitting four people in the front and four in the back. The bench seats were soft and luxurious, especially at night when the dash lights made the atmosphere almost romantic.

The car's four-barrel Holley carburetor gave it the speed of Wiley Coyote. And it was tank-like in size, giving me the brutish confidence to drive fearlessly. I earned myself a startling number of speeding tickets during that time in my life.

I should have gotten more.

But it was ugly, not something a teenager wants as their dream car, which was why I wanted an upgrade. I wanted something sleek and silvery.

When my father wouldn't co-sign my first loan, I got desperate. I would stick with the cash I had on hand, buying a car with my miniscule budget, and then fix it up, using the body-shop skills I had learned when working at my father's now-defunct shop.

It was about then that I found the car of my dreams.

I first learned about the 1974 Datsun B-210 from my brother Dave, who saw it while working at his first job with a local rubbish company, riding the back of a garbage truck. When he reported his find, I took a drive with him and spotted it in a field of weeds next to a decrepit house.

It was love at first sight—*not* that it looked like a dream to anyone else. It was a deep forest green and fiercely oxidized. When the door slammed, it produced only a tinny *clank*. The body—inside and out—was a sieve of rusty holes. On our test drive, as we bumped through the adjoining field, we could reach through the floor to grab the clover passing beneath us. Truly, this dream car lacked all redeeming qualities.

Perhaps it inspired pity. Perhaps it caused me to believe it represented me. Perhaps I decided it would bring my dream to life. But the $160 price seemed steep, so I decided to make the owner an offer.

I asked God for a sign, just to be sure. I needed to know this was exactly the right car. So, I offered the owner fifty percent of the hundred-and-sixty-dollar price tag he had scrawled on the windshield. Only a starving bluegill would have bitten at a price that measly.

Well, wouldn't you know? It took that bluegill only twenty-four hours to decide. When my parents' phone rang, I became the proud owner of the ugliest car in Stark County.

As my brother Dave and I drove my acquisition toward Market Avenue and home, I noticed a few things—the smell of ancient French fries rotting beneath the seat, a rust hole punched through the passenger door the size and shape of a fist, and a three-inch scratch engraved on the right lower side of the windshield. Plus, it wasn't a coup—it had four doors.

This made me question my decision, but instead of driving straight to the junkyard, and writing it all off as a learning experience, I ignored my doubts. Doggone it, this car was mine. I would make it into something of value, something finer than it ever thought it could be.

Dreams are powerful.

Through the dark months of the spring of 1983, after I'd returned from Maranatha Bible School, I began rebuilding the car. I put it up on blocks in my father's garage and threw myself into the task of deconstructing and then restoring it.

I first had to fill in the holes created by the salty slush that grows on the roads of Northeastern Ohio. This meant that I had to learn how to wield an acetylene torch. So, during all my spare time, when I wasn't outside in the bone-chilling cold mixing mud and carrying blocks, I was in my father's garage, welding sheets of scrap metal over the holes in my car.

There was one aspect to the car that was good when I bought it: the engine. It ran well and used no oil, but since the car had over a hundred-thousand miles on it, I decided to have the engine re-bored and rebuilt anyway, just to be safe.

That spring was a time of transformation, not just for the car, but also for me. Marlin was busy at college—a worldly life I had now rejected—and I recall a lot of time spent alone, working on my little Datsun. I also recall it being one of the happiest times of my life as I burned up the phone lines, building out the friendships I had made at Maranatha.

I was overwhelmed with the heady feeling of popularity. Many of my new friends came from fundamentalist Mennonite communities, and I was being pulled into that world, making friends with those who believed in patriarchal systems.

At first, as I got to know my new friends at Maranatha, I worried that they might find out the truth—that I came from a poor family with no social capital, and that I wasn't popular at all. But to my surprise, I discovered that was changing. My community had heard about my success at Maranatha, and although they were surprised, they also began to listen to me with more respect. For the first time, I was one of the two people elected by popular vote to help lead our youth group committee, rather than being one of the two people chosen by the outgoing committee, as had happened in the past.

I had become a leader in my own right.

I was fully grown, and an adult. I had a network of friends that stretched across the Midwest. The telephone was my friend, and the monthly bill began to expand. In the era before the internet, I could call long distance, and now, with my wages increasing, I had the money to pay the phone bills.

Leadership wasn't new to me; I just confused titles with leadership. As I look back on my teen years, I realize that I had been fulfilling leadership roles for years—I had edited my high school newspaper, served on our youth group committee, and managed The Harvesters—but had always worked behind the scenes.

91

Now, as my church offered me roles with more visibility, I spoke with much more confidence. My peers took direction from me. I had discovered my inner John Wayne, and I loved him.

Then something unexpected happened, something wonderful.

Every year, the Midwest Fellowship held its annual conference, which was a weekend of long services and sermons. In July of 1983, its conference was held at Hiland High School, in Millersburg, Ohio, in the overheated high school gym. I attended, seeing friends from Maranatha I hadn't seen in several months.

While I was there, one of my new friends, who had lived briefly in Arizona, told me that Sunnyview Christian School in Phoenix needed a principal. She didn't know me well, but she thought I'd be perfect for the job. She told me I should talk to Dan Yoder, the minister who was in charge of supervising the school. He was here at the conference.

By the time I ran into Dan, word had already been passed to him that I was interested.

"You'd be perfect for the job," he said. "I've heard great things about you from everyone I've talked to."

"God doesn't like it when you lie," I said. Dan burst into laughter, and I finally smiled.

"See, you have a sense of humor. The kids would love you."

I shook my head, doubtfully. "I'm not sure I'm right for the job. The chances of my moving all the way to Phoenix are slim. I'm busy leading the youth group—I'm not sure I'm ready to leave Hartville."

His face showed his disappointment, but he quickly recovered.

"Well, here's my number if you change your mind," he said, handing me his card. "I believe God wants you in Phoenix this coming year. No, seriously."

This guy certainly seems convinced.

As Dan walked away, glad-handing everyone in sight, I thought how ridiculous the idea of my going to Arizona to become a principal and teacher was. I had never lived away from home in my life, I had zero experience teaching in the classroom, and, until this past spring, my friends had regarded me as shy or, at best, reserved.

This job would demand that I take center stage. I would become a public figure in the church and school community. I would be responsible for approximately forty-five students and two older teachers. A lot of attention would be directed toward me. I had mixed feelings about this.

But I also knew that I enjoyed leading and working with people. And after my positive experience at Maranatha—coming to a place where I knew no one and walking away with a crowd of friends—I wasn't nearly as afraid to leave home.

This would be the perfect opportunity to prove myself—some in my home community still regarded me with skepticism. So, to gain real influence within our community, and influence it for the good, I needed to prove myself in a leadership position that was more visible. But I still wasn't sure I needed to leave to achieve this.

It was at this point that God stepped in.

In the middle of a blazing Ohio summer, I somehow came down with pneumonia. It hit me hard. It still makes no sense—I was as physically fit as I've ever been before or since, and it was the only time in my life that I've ever contracted it.

I found myself at home, lying flat in bed, with nothing to do but read and think, and read and think. I read books on leadership. I had conversations by phone, calling my new network of friends and asking their advice. I thought about what I wanted to do with my life.

I thought about Phoenix.

Because of my strong belief that God wanted to do something special with my life, I realized that this was God at work. The Master of the entire universe, with billions of people to care for, had taken the time to stop me in my tracks and guide me in a different direction—to Phoenix, it seemed.

It would allow me to have a positive influence on young people, just like Brother Byler had on me.

I took the job. In a rapid order of events, I called Dan, recovered from pneumonia, and decided that I had just enough time to finish renovating my Datsun and drive it to Phoenix to begin my new job as the principal of their Christian School.

Dan was happy and said he would expect me in Phoenix by the end of August.

It was July 15.

The situation boggles the mind: how could a young man with only a high school diploma, whose twentieth birthday fell on his first day of teaching, become the administrator of an entire school, grades one through twelve?

The answer is patriarchy—the most important qualification I possessed for being Sunnyview Christian School's new principal was that I was male.

Practically speaking, this meant that I would oversee teachers older than I, and one of them had years of teaching experience and a university education. I don't remember if she had a teaching degree, but it didn't matter. The school board wouldn't hire a female principal, no matter how many degrees or how much college education she had. In fact, a college degree would have caused people to regard her with suspicion, thinking that she had feminist tendencies, which were unacceptable within a patriarchal system.

So, I was the natural choice to lead Sunnyview Christian School.

I set to work. I painted the car and mounted the newly renovated engine (rebuilt by my childhood buddy) under the gleaming hood of my now-silver dream car. I cleaned up the upholstery and put in new carpet. I shined the gauges and the gearshift and the steering wheel. I restored my car to the flush of its first beauty... but there was a problem.

No matter how I dressed it up, the car was still a Datsun B-210, 1974 edition of a penny-ante car that clinked instead of clunked when I shut the door, sang tenor rather than bass when I goosed the engine, and shifted gently when I leaned against it.

My Datsun, I realized, would never become my dream.

During the last few weeks I was at home, my church made a big deal about my departure. It shocked me that, suddenly, everyone was telling me what a significant leader I had been to the church youth; how could I leave?

That was a bit rich. They could have told me that sooner. But I quietly played my part in their dramatic sendoff, happy to believe the youth group couldn't go on without me.

The Sunday before I left, I was invited to give a speech, explaining what I was going to be doing in Phoenix. Everyone promised to pray for me. My parents looked at me with new respect. Like my father before me, I was leaving home to serve God in a far, distant country.

It took me until the day before I left for Phoenix to finish putting my little Datsun B-210 back together. I didn't even have time to try it out on the road. Over forty hours of travel lay before me in a car that was completely untested.

That evening, while my mother finished washing and packing my suitcase, I took my brother's car and drove over to see Marlin one more time, who was now in his second year of college. In the last few weeks, we had had long conversations about my choice to leave, and although he had a lot of questions, he was generally admiring of my decision.

Marlin was hanging out with his father and mother on the back deck. Marlin asked me whether I was ready. I wasn't sure. At that point, his father jumped into the conversation.

As an experienced middle school teacher, John Henry gave me a "Pull-Up-Your-Socks" speech. "Don't smile until Christmas." His secret to getting his classes in line? He'd arrive at his classroom late on the first day, stand in the doorway, and eye his new students up and down. "Let them know you are in charge," he said.

Good advice, I thought. Then I was off.

Four days later, I slipped down Superstition Mountain during the wee hours of the morning. Ahead of me, far below in the valley, the lights of Phoenix glittered. Beside me, eighteen-wheelers honked their horns, trying to avoid the little silver Datsun slipping between and ahead of them, struggling to keep up with the speed limit, even while going downhill.

When I arrived in the city, I pulled into the first motel I could find.

I had a hard time sleeping that night, due to my nerves and excitement. In the morning, I ate breakfast at a Waffle House and then went to meet my new employers.

When I arrived at the home of the school board chairman, his cheerful wife greeted me with pleasure, and she fed me a second breakfast. They had heard everything about me, they said, and they were happy to meet me. I met her first-grade son, who would be one of the elementary students in my new school.

As I met the rest of the community, I basked in their warmth.

Indeed, my new community had thought of everything, including housing. Since I was single, I was housed with a young couple—the bishop's son and his wife, who had just returned from their honeymoon.

I have never heard a cultural value expressed more clearly than the one my host shared with me just before our first meal. We were relaxing in the living room, waiting for dinner. His new wife would teach first grade under my supervision, and she was busy preparing our meal.

The Man of the House kicked back on an easy chair and watched me leafing through a *Rod and Staff* magazine, one of the periodicals supported by the conservative Mennonite establishment. I assumed he was trying to figure out why I hadn't gotten married yet.

I wasn't wrong.

But he was a diplomatic fellow, and he didn't want to be too obvious, so he talked about himself. "You know," he said, "I'd never want to be single. Look at me. My wife cleans the house, washes my clothes, cooks my meals—why would anyone want to be single?"

This conversation challenged the freedom I had always had. Until then, I had not had a serious relationship with any conservative Mennonite girl, choosing to deliberately remain single. My community didn't date casually—if you dated, you were on a short track leading to marriage and parenthood.

I still considered marriage to be a trap. My friends who dated quickly got married and, once they were married, they had babies; any talk of college education fell into a black hole.

No, I would remain single, I determined.

Arriving in Phoenix and taking on my new position was like walking into a peaceful world straight out of *Anne of Green Gables*. Life was simple, and people dropped by each other's homes for a meal after Sunday morning service with no more than a friendly invitation.

There was one major difference, however. Cars. Really fast cars and trucks. Members of the youth group worked in the construction and service industries, and the type of truck or car you drove established your status. Occasionally, they drag-raced. I quickly saw that my little silver dream was not going to place me in the cool crowd of young people.

Nonetheless, I was welcomed enthusiastically by my students, and I quickly made friends within the youth group. I was, after all, just a few years older than most of them, which meant that I taught some of them during the day, and then hung out in the evenings with them in the youth group.

I discovered that my predecessor had not been overly social. For some weird reason, he'd thought a principal should have gravitas, should take his job seriously, and should spend time with adults rather than with the most rebellious youth in Paradise Valley. He had been backed by one of the ministers across the valley, an influential leader who still resented the way the School Board had fired my predecessor.

This would eventually cause me grief.

But as the hot, dry weather of Phoenix moderated into a temperate winter, I grew to love the bright world of the West. I grew to appreciate this warm-hearted community of conservative Mennonite transplants from Pennsylvania. I had rarely felt so loved.

I found a great deal of satisfaction in my new role. By imitating the teaching style of Brother Byler, I was building relationships. I often had discussions in which I posed questions for my students, listening carefully as I perched on my teacher desk, asking them follow-up questions. Our Socratic dialogues helped me form a close bond with my class. In return, Dan Yoder (who was now my direct supervisor) and the school board gave me plenty of positive feedback.

Granted, the job was a bit of a babysitting gig. I didn't directly teach any of the academic subjects. Instead, students spent class time filling out workbooks, and then I graded them—just like a trained monkey.

Okay, that's not quite accurate. It would have taken a very special monkey to lead the chapel service each day. Here, I followed the example of my father, who had led our family in devotions each morning since I was born—though, of course, I made changes.

Rather than reading from the Bible each day, and then discussing it—I was sure they'd had plenty of that—I chose to do what Brother Byler had done to my seventh-grade class in vacation Bible school the summer before he started teaching us—he'd read us a book, *The Gospel Blimp,* a satire about a church that decides to evangelize by using a blimp to drop tracts, rather than building relationships with their neighbors. The book had made us all skeptical about preaching *at* people, rather than showing them how much you care by helping them through genuine friendships and neighborly behavior.

So, during class devotions in the morning, I read to my students from a memoir I enjoyed, *Wonder O' the Wind*, written by an actual shepherd, W. Phillip Keller, who reflects on how the Holy Spirit shepherded his turbulent, rebellious life toward a deeper relationship with the Great Shepherd. Like my mother, I was already drawn to memoir, and I was stirred by stories taken from real life. Like my father, I loved the rhythms of language—I was drawn to performing the spoken word.

I was beginning to find my own teaching style, one based on relationships.

Realistically, I was as successful as any young man with only a high school diploma and no classroom experience could be when asked to teach seventeen high school students and supervise two experienced educators teaching twenty-eight elementary students.

The only thing missing from the picture was a real education: challenging reading, rigorous expectations, curiosity, questions, discussion, reflection.

Ironically, I thought I had changed since converting under Brother Glick's guidance. But what I'd failed to grasp was how powerful my real beliefs about education were. In spite of my attempts to become a patriarch, I couldn't do it. I couldn't bring myself to indoctrinate my students. Instead, I was teaching them to question authority and think for themselves, just as Brother Byler had taught us to do.

On the surface, though, my goal was clear: I wanted to please God. I had joined the leadership ranks of the patriarchy and intended to use the privileges it gave me for the good. Thus, I had taken on a leadership position where I was the male authority in a community that believed that God intended men to lead, and that women were supposed to follow—in fact, they weren't allowed to have a voice during church services.

Sadly, it didn't dawn on me that by doing this, I was attempting to become the very thing I had resisted as a child, the very thing that had almost destroyed my faith in God, and the very thing I'd spent my high school years plotting to escape.

But I suspect people didn't actually buy the role I was playing. Just like my father, I may have said that the men should be in charge. But in reality, my approach to teaching showed that I didn't really believe that. Thanks to the small things, the truth of what I really believed was becoming clear to the community.

This was especially evident in my newsletter I titled "Notes from the Principal's Desk," which I sent home to the parents regularly. I labored carefully over these, trying to sound godly and wise (at the ripe old age of twenty). Today, I realize that I was actually promoting a liberal arts education in which I told the parents that I was teaching their children how to think critically.

This was the first time I had such a large podium upon which to speak my mind, and I thought that by writing home regularly, I could establish myself as an influential leader, just as Brother Byler had. While I didn't know much about education, I replicated the approach my high school teacher had used with passion—and, of course, it caused controversy.

This didn't surprise me. I coveted Brother Byler's controversial approach in our community, the way he had challenged ideas and entertained uncomfortable questions. Like him, I was allergic to indoctrination, and so, I ignored the raised eyebrows.

My non-patriarchal approach also came through clearly in my choice of friends. Rather than hanging out with the sober young men who also planned to be patriarchs, or with older patriarchs who could mentor me, I quickly became close friends with a young man my age, Glendon Yoder. He was both the son of Dan Yoder (the pastor who recruited me) and Sunnyview's biggest rebel.

Glendon and his two brothers were known for their fast trucks, muscle cars, and pretty girlfriends. Like me, he embraced oppositional defiance, especially when it came to heavy-handed pastors. He told me his stories about the ministers who'd tried to reprimand him and I told him mine.

When I first met him, Glendon had begun to settle down, but his reputation was still that of a rabble rouser. I quickly discovered that behind his brash and confident smile was a young man who owned a thoughtful, questioning nature and a deep faith. He was going steady with a polished young woman who skirted the dress code in ways that regularly drew stares and reprimands from the ministers. She didn't have a problem with body image, and she wasn't about to submissively follow the dictates of the ministers.

She had her own stories of doing everything she could to piss off the ministers, and I liked her immediately. I liked the fact that Glendon was her boyfriend.

"They all think I have her in the sack," Glendon said to me privately, laughing uproariously.

I suspected their relationship was far more traditional than Glendon let on.

As I made friends and helped lead the youth group in my new community, I worried at times that my highly social behavior might be hurting my reputation as a school leader, especially since I was sure Brother Glick, for example, would not approve. My actions were definitely not consistent with his fairly distant approach to people, and certainly not patriarchal in any sense of the word.

But I had learned something important from my time at Maranatha Bible School, when I'd first experienced popularity. I had been pulled into a very exclusive group of students who enjoyed being "popular," and one of the new friends I'd made—an earnest young man with whom I had quickly become friends but didn't fit with the new popular crowd I now "led"—found himself excluded from our social events. He could not understand how I could exclude him from the social excursions we took to the Twin Cities. He wanted in, and my friends told me that he just didn't fit in.

Instead of choosing to spend time with the people I actually liked, I found myself choosing to hang out with the popular students *because* they were popular. Most of them were also wealthy, and my excluded friend was not. I should have been more sensitive, in view of my own family's circumstances, but I was in actuality afraid of being excluded myself.

I have often cursed that damaging choice—the young man I excluded from my "in-group" was an original thinker who wasn't afraid to say what he thought, and in many ways, far more interesting than my popular friends. When he challenged me several times about why I wasn't inviting him to join some of the activities, I was disturbed... because I knew he was right. It was the first time I had been given that much social power, and I handled it badly. Excluding people wasn't in my nature.

This is the one area in my social life that I have found is non-negotiable. I am drawn to intelligent, determined individuals who don't fit any mold. They are eclectic, loyal, and brilliant. They are the rebels who embrace oppositional defiance. They are the ones who ask all the difficult questions—the most interesting people in the room. These relationships feed me.

Thus, I continued my friendship with Glendon, but within the wider community in Phoenix, our friendship raised eyebrows. A principal and teacher should embrace gravitas, follow the rules, *and* choose the right friends, some people believed. But having learned through my mistakes at the social hothouse of Maranatha, I decided I was not going to kowtow to others' expectations when it came to my friends.

I'm also sure the community expected their new patriarchal leader to be serious and sober, a model prayer warrior. Instead, they got a popular young man whom the students liked, and who hung out with the "wild" young people, rather than spending time in prayer meetings.

To be fair, being "wild" within a Mennonite community wasn't like being wild in the outside world. My questionable behavior primarily revolved around the fact that I stayed up late Sunday nights playing Rook (a harmless card game) with Glendon and his brothers over multiple glasses of soda. All quite legal within the church, of course, but not something one might expect the school principal to do on Sunday evenings. To some community members, this was troubling. But the idea that I should go home to pray and prepare for my teaching tasks the next day bored me.

Besides, I knew the right people liked me. The previous principal, as far as I could tell, had been fired because he hadn't been popular enough. I wasn't about to follow his example. I loved the fact that I was socially popular among the cool students and young people.

All of this led to one of the strangest meetings I've ever encountered in the history of my teaching career.

Chapter 10: Eating Dinner with a Wolf

I received a note from Brother Tim Stutzman, a pastor at a local church, who handled his congregation with an iron grip. This was a minister who'd once reprimanded church members for laughing in the sanctuary. He was a powerful member who provided spiritual advice to the School Board. Since I couldn't imagine him being anything but outspoken, this meant no decisions were made without *his* input.

I already knew quite a bit about Brother Stutzman. The Board believed he had tried to run the school through my predecessor, who had quickly gravitated toward Brother Stutzman after he arrived, joining his church. Naturally, Brother Stutzman had taken him under his wing. This caused deep resentment from the Board, since Sunnyview owned the school. In fact, when I was hired, my supervisor had specifically told me that the Board expected me to make Sunnyview my home church. I had agreed, and since everyone there had made me feel welcome, I was happy with the arrangement.

But as time went on, I had become curious about Brother Stutzman. I wondered whether he would reach out. Now he had.

The invitation put me on edge because Brother Stutzman was a friend of *my* spiritual mentor, Brother Glick. Months earlier, when I'd informed Brother Glick by letter of my hiring, my mentor had shot back a kind note. "You can trust Tim's wisdom and judgment," he said.

I wondered what Brother Stutzman would think of me. Was he inviting me as a way to "feel me out," to see if I was similar to my predecessor in spirit? Perhaps he wanted to lure me to his side.

At lunch, I picked up the phone and gave Brother Stutzman a call. Of course, I'd be happy to visit.

Brother Stutzman was glad to hear from me, and he promised me a good meal.

"My wife's a very good cook. Then perhaps afterward, we could chat in my study?"

"Sure," I said, cautiously. His manner was welcoming and friendly, but there was also steel in his voice. For some reason, I was worried.

When I mentioned the upcoming dinner to Glendon, a strange expression flitted across his face. "Okay, give it up," I said.

"I can't stand Tim," he said, not using the honorific. I was surprised. I hadn't realized how much he disliked the man. "I don't like the way the man operates. He *really* likes being in charge, way too much, in my opinion. We've had a few… he might call them clashes; I'd call them fundamental disagreements."

As I listened, I realized what was bothering me. I would be facing a pastor whose methods of control were like those of the bishop within whose church I had grown up. I knew that type and was *dead* sure Brother Stutzman would not offer me apple pie and joyful praises.

But I was actually wrong—there *was* apple pie.

Mrs. Stutzman offered me a delightful dinner, a custom most Mennonite women share. I sat at the end of the table opposite my host. Between us were his children and one of my junior students, Kristina. She was well-mannered and suitably awed by the presence of the school principal.

I quickly surmised that Brother Stutzman wasn't interested in hearing from anyone else at the table. As far as he was concerned, this was a conversation between two patriarchs, one mature and the other in need of mentoring. The rest of the people in the room were just decoration.

My host grilled me, conversationally of course, asking questions about my family and the Hartville youth group, referring to his friendship with my mentor several times. The rest of the table sat silently, presumably listening attentively, or at least doing a reasonable enough facsimile so as not to bring the wrath of their spiritual leader down upon them.

But then the meal was over, and my host escorted me to his spotless study. Licking his thin lips, Brother Stutzman sat back in his seat behind his enormous desk. After asking me some questions about how I was hired, which I tried to answer in detail, his smile disappeared.

"I expressed my concern to John about you being hired. You're very young. I don't mean in terms of age. I mean in terms of spiritual maturity."

My jaw dropped. I hadn't expected him to be quite so blunt. My heart began to race.

"Brother Glick has been very supportive of me working here."

He offered me a condescending smile.

"I have nothing against you, Steve. You seem reasonably intelligent. But I would have expected Brother Yoder to hire someone with more experience."

He licked his lips, and I waited. Clearly, he had more to say. I kept my face neutral as he told me that he'd given my mentor a call after discovering I'd been hired, wanting to know everything about me.

"John and I have been close for years, and I trust him completely." This was the same thing Brother Glick had told me about Brother Stutzman, so I leaned forward, curiously. "When I discovered the facts about you, I became understandably… concerned."

I started to respond, but Brother Stutzman raised his hand.

"But what really surprised me… was when he told me he too had serious reservations about the Board's choice to hire you as the spiritual leader at our school."

There was a slight ringing in my ears as I took this in. I tried to line up the facts. I was sure Brother Glick had been supportive about me taking on this job. Yet here in this study, I was hearing the opposite... supposedly from one of his best friends in the ministry. I couldn't believe my ears. This was a *huge* breach of trust. I didn't want to accuse my mentor of lying, but... wow!

Brother Stutzman licked his lips again, like a wolf salivating over his prey. My stomach suddenly dropped, like I was in an elevator dropping too quickly. This was the moment I was sure he'd pull out the sordid details of my past.

But he didn't. It turned out that Brother Glick had not told him any real details, merely the fact that, under his guidance, I had recently recommitted my life to Christ.

Apparently, this was transgression enough.

"Brother Glick is worried," Brother Stutzman said, "that when you find out what happens within the upper echelons of church leadership, it will embitter you. To put it candidly, Brother Glick believes you're too young to lead alone."

I couldn't say anything. Why would Brother Glick turn against me? He'd told me he believed in me, that he trusted me. His letter of advice had been nothing but supportive.

And what was I supposed to say to Brother Stutzman? Was he hoping I would beg for advice? Was he trying to scare me? Was he hoping I would resign? Was he trying to suggest that Brother Glick needed help mentoring me, and that *he* should assist Brother Glick by serving as my mentor here in Phoenix?

Brother Stutzman kept hammering away. "Steve, hard decisions must be made, and things aren't always black-and-white. Being a leader is difficult, and it will take a great deal of wisdom to make these decisions." He licked his thin lips again.

I remained silent. What could I possibly say to that?

"I just wanted you to be aware of that." He kept licking his lips.

That isn't normal. Is something wrong with him?

Brother Stutzman stopped talking and stared at me. He probably wanted to intimidate me but I realized something. The only power he had lay in his friendship with my mentor, whom I now distrusted, and while I *felt* as though this was an interrogation where I, the student, had been hauled into the principal's office, *he* was not the principal. I was.

That gave me my power. My confidence.

"I'm really sorry that you are disappointed by my hiring. I hope I'll be able to win your trust over the next year. Brother Yoder has been a big support to me as I've been settling in, and the Board also has been incredible in supporting my decisions."

"Oh, Steve, I didn't mean to say—"

This time I held up my hand and I continued on.

"No, no. I'm grateful for the conversation you had with Brother Glick. It's been really… enlightening." I rose to my feet. "I'm sure you're busy, so the fact that you took an entire evening like this to share your thoughts was really generous. Please tell your wife how much I enjoyed her delicious dinner."

He rose and shook my hand, warmly. "It was no problem, Steve."

We stood for a moment in silence, both of us measuring up the other, and then I turned to go.

"I should probably head back home. It's going to be an early morning."

"I'm sure you have a lot of grading to do."

I didn't, actually, but I was planning to meet Glendon and his brothers for a Rook game.

"Well, you know how it is." I offered him a sincere look, taking a deep breath—no sense in letting him know how betrayed I felt. "Thank you, as well, for your wise guidance, which Brother Glick promised you would offer." I could be polite; I could play the game because, when it came down to it, that's what it was. Him posturing to retain some sort of hold over me that he thought he had.

I'd let him think that.

But I'd run my school the way I saw fit.

I also would not tell him that my mentor didn't deserve his confidence, or that I no longer trusted either of them, because that knowledge was not for their consumption. It was my power over them.

As I reflect on that dinner and the conversation that happened afterward, I realize that it was a turning point for me. Not that I realized this at the time, but the impact of Brother Stutzman's revelation that he and Brother Glick had talked about my future as a leader within the church was that I realized the way power really works in the "upper echelons" of church leadership.

It was then that I saw the oppositional divide between their leadership philosophy and my own, which had been carefully inculcated by my high school teacher, Brother Byler.

I was moving toward a relationship-driven teaching style that was collaborative in nature and empowered my students to take charge. I wasn't there yet, but the significance of that conversation with Brother Stutzman was that I saw what I *didn't* want to be during that conversation.

I saw at that moment that my mentor and his friend absolutely believed that God spoke through them. But rather than using this divine influence to empower me, they were afraid that if I moved up too quickly, I would see the corruption in the leadership structure of the church. This is why Brother Glick didn't want his students (or me) asking questions. The most important thing was maintaining and exercising his authority, rather than searching for the truth through questions, rather than being vulnerable and open to those you serve.

I didn't realize this at the time. But what I did remember seeing, as I was heading home in my little silver Datsun that night, was the canary in the coal mine.

I had noticed Kristina.

There had been something *off* about her.

Perhaps I put two and two together, what I saw in school and what I saw in her home, but somewhere inside me, an alarm had been blaring as I sat there talking to Brother Stutzman, his family sitting silently and submissively while the two of us had chatted about important matters in the community.

Back then, I didn't know that much about my student, one of Brother Stutzman's close family members. I had noticed that she was the only female student I had who wore light touches of makeup, and whose blonde hair didn't fit neatly into the required white covering she wore over it. At school, she also reacted oddly to me, especially when I grew stern. She was… jumpy around me, in a way my other students weren't.

Over dinner, I had observed her careful, subservient reactions to the patriarch of the house.

It was the same attitude I'd seen in class toward… *me*.

I suspect now it had something to do with the way I enjoyed the power that came with being called a principal, even of a school this small. Back then, rather than seeing myself as a servant to the students I was teaching, I saw myself as their authority figure, someone they needed to obey. Concerned that I remain in control—both standing in the classroom and sitting across from this power-hungry pastor—I didn't offer my students a vulnerable, humble spirit.

Instead, I saw myself as a rising patriarchal leader.

I hadn't bothered to take the time to get to know Kristina as my student or as a person, nor tried to find out how I could empower her as a student and young leader. As far as she was concerned, there was nothing she could trust in me.

Years later, Kristina and I connected again, first through Facebook and then by Zoom. She had left the conservative Mennonites by then, and I discovered we had a lot in common as Kristina shared with me about the abuse and shame and trauma she had gone through as a teenager, attending Brother Stutzman's church.

As we discussed our work together during my first year of teaching, Kristina looked happy. She was in therapy, and she was proud of how far she had come since my year in Phoenix. She told me about the abuse she had experienced. She talked about the judgment she had experienced as a young woman within the church's purity culture. Having seen the same behavior in my own community, I was saddened by her story.

I was especially disturbed by my hesitance to intervene. As I reflected on my work with her, I recalled that all the abuse signs were there. Although I was a very young teacher, my abuse detector was dead accurate. Unfortunately, I didn't trust myself, and more importantly, I was never given the training as a teacher to help students like Kristina.

I have since come to trust my gut, which is now a familiar and trusted guide, or *detector*, for me. I am now fully trained, and I can also intuit—and trust that intuition—when someone has been, or is being, physically abused. Sadly, I am not alone in this intuition; it is common among those of us in the tribe of abuse.

"Do you remember that dinner conversation?" I asked Kristina during our Zoom call.

"I don't," she said. "That doesn't mean it didn't happen. I just don't remember."

We talked about what it was like in my classroom, which was made up of chairs and cubicles facing the wall with a table of resources in the center. My teacher's desk was at the end of the room. Each of my seventeen students worked privately, each completing workbooks at their level at their own speed. When they would finish each workbook, I would grade it. When students had questions, they put up a red flag or raised their hand.

I asked Kristina what she remembered about me as a teacher, perhaps hoping she saw my potential. But Kristina was blunt, her comments fueled by strong feelings. "I found you frustrating," she said. "I wanted to learn, and you didn't take the time to help me. Other students would raise their hands, and you would help them, but not me."

Kristina's reactions helped me understand, viscerally, how ineffective I was as a young teacher, and why I was unable to help her or gain the trust she would have needed to come to me for help.

Not that it would have helped.

Brother Stutzman was someone who had manipulated and dominated my predecessor, and I desperately needed to keep my distance from him. Second, I didn't know how to respond to a 17-year-old teenage girl who was attractive, intelligent, and more mature than her years.

After all, I was only 20 years old.

That moment over dinner, I believe, was when I began to reject the patriarchy. By then, I'd known that there was no way I could align the two philosophies of leadership and teaching because there was something wrong with Brother Glick's philosophy of education, which depended upon instilling "the fear of the Lord" (through corporal punishment) rather than building trusting relationships.

What my year of teaching taught me was that I wanted a philosophy of teaching that was relationship-driven—not one that used fear to frighten my students into submission. I wanted to empower my students, giving them increasing levels of autonomy, just as Brother Byler had offered me, so that they then became motivated to learn.

One thing Brother Glick *was* right about, though, was that I hadn't been ready to move into "the upper echelons of church leadership" and interact with leaders like Brother Stutzman. I never would be.

And that was why I knew that—if I remained a leader in this world, having power meals with the wolves who guided our communities—it would corrupt me.

Of course, the most important result of my year in Phoenix was my father's change of heart when it came to the subject of college. I'd come home for a visit in February and had passionately described to my father how much I enjoyed teaching.

This brought him joy. He told me again about his sister Martha, who had decided to become a teacher and had gotten her college degree to teach in a public school. The result had been a career with a good salary.

I listened patiently as my father reminisced because his memories set him up for the news I had to share. When he was done, I told him that the Board Chairman of Hartville Christian School had offered me a part-time teaching position in English... but I would need to begin college if I were going to accept the position. I tempered this possible conflict with the good news that this job offer meant I could return to Ohio.

A smile broadened my father's face. He wanted me to return home—he said he'd missed me. I knew, though, that this also fed his ego. The offer from the Board paid a high compliment to his parenting. "You need to come home and go to college to get your teaching degree," he said.

It was a blessing my father would later deny, but at that moment, it was exactly what I needed to satisfy the patriarchal beliefs I still held. Like the young patriarch Jacob, I had obtained my father's blessing for my future, slyly but successfully, and could, therefore, claim I was in submission to his wishes.

God works in mysterious ways.

When I flew back to Phoenix to finish out the year, I met with the school board to inform them I'd be returning home to take a job teaching at my *alma mater*. They expressed deep disappointment, and, while I had grown to appreciate their warm personalities, and the decision was difficult, my desire to attend college and teach at the school I had once attended helped me push through my regrets.

I was accepted at Malone College, an evangelical Quaker college supported by a network of evangelical Friends churches, with federal grants, thanks to my father's low income. The first three years of college cost me nothing.

I attended full-time while teaching part-time.

Ultimately, my father withdrew his blessing, plagued with questions. He had seen other young people begin college. Too many had left the True Faith after getting an education, often leaving the conservative Mennonites. He feared I might follow the same path. His older children followed suit. It didn't matter that I was an adult, twenty-one years old.

Ann, especially, seemed haunted by her fears. "I worry you might lose your faith," she told me during another conversation over dishes in my parents' worn kitchen. It was a hot summer evening just before the school year began. I could hear the voices of my younger siblings outside, still playing a game with their neighborhood friends. I dried a dish.

"I'm not Laban," I said, referring to my close friend who had gone to college and left our community. My voice had grown stronger, more confident in the past year. "I don't intend to let college change me. I'm going because I need the degree to teach."

In the resulting silence, the dishes clinked as Ann carefully washed them. She shook her head. "I've seen what happens to people when they go to college, and I'm afraid…"

I tried to mollify her. "Why don't we do this? If you ever worry my beliefs might be changing, just talk to me. I promise I'll listen."

How little I knew about education, and how experience changes what you believe.

Book III: Denial

Wandering between two worlds, one dead,
The other powerless to be born,
With nowhere yet to rest my head,
Like these, on earth I wait forlorn.

~ Matthew Arnold
"Stanzas from the Grande Chartreuse," 1855

Interpolation III: The Upper Room

The young men in our church were taught, very explicitly, that masturbation was sinful. To remind us of this, when we had revival meetings, the unmarried boys and men sometimes had a secret prayer meeting with the evangelist in the "upper room" of our church, where the older women sewed quilts during weekday afternoons. During this super-special session, the evangelist explained that "unclean thoughts" (about sex) were wrong. Apparently, the truly Christian male had only pure (non-sexual) thoughts. He never thought about sex until suddenly, on the night of his wedding, it all became... good.

Just to hammer home the point, during one of these sessions, a visiting pastor warned that there were lifetime consequences for boys who masturbated too much. First, your (eventual) wife would only have daughters, and second, you would go blind.

This frightened me.

I was about to go blind.

During my early teen years as I approached puberty, my sexual fantasies began to center on female submission. I didn't know that fantasies are shaped by experience, often traced to a person's first sexual arousal. I don't remember being aroused when punished by adults, but the similarities between my childhood discipline and my fetish are eerily familiar.

I was deeply ashamed of this fantasy.

Loving parents spanked their children on the bottom, I was taught. God had created it for this precise purpose. Since my parents always spanked in private, this meant that an adult physically struck one of the most erogenous parts of my body during every spanking. Although I don't remember this happening to me, I did see my father pull down my brother's underwear when he was twelve and didn't cry hard enough.

Although my father sometimes disciplined in anger, the punishments I received were usually ritualistic——a parent led me to a private place, I was forced to bend over, the parent used a "rod" on my buttocks, and the spanking continued until I cried, demonstrating repentance. Then I was comforted and often hugged.

In our house, this happened so often that I thought it was normal... that all mommies and daddies did this. It took me decades of hearing from others outside fundamentalist communities... who didn't experience this... to realize it was not normal.

111

I was not the only child in America who was beaten this way. And based on the conversations I've had with fellow travelers, many other children were also confused by awakening sexual feelings that fetishized intimate moments of punishment. Sadly, their parents also had no idea that they were transgressing boundaries.

As time went on, my fantasy strengthened. Soon it was the only one I had, although I was never okay with it. After each release, guilt would overwhelm me.

I would excoriate myself.

I would beg God for forgiveness.

I would promise Him never to think those evil thoughts again.

But that determination never lasted. I was a healthy male, and testosterone flooded my body every day. The impulse to seek release was overwhelming. The fact that I was made this way felt… familiar. Just like God creating a tree with delicious fruit, putting Adam and Eve in that garden, pointing it out to them, and then forbidding them to eat it.

Yes… it totally made sense.

About as much sense as stuffing a boy full of hormones and telling him he was supposed to think only pure thoughts. Not a paradox, at all. But then again, I didn't know how sexual desire worked back then.

Apparently, neither did any of the adults.

Chapter 11: Finding a Guide

In one of my father's favorite jokes, a Baptist dies and goes to Heaven. St. Peter meets him and begins to show him the wonders of Heaven: tree of life, streets of gold, his own personal mansion, and a special pew in the heavenly choir. But something odd happens as they turn a corner. Before them, the Baptist sees a small compound surrounded by high walls. Curious, he starts to ask a question, but St. Peter puts his finger to his lips, and gestures dramatically. They tiptoe around the compound, and, once past, the Baptist looks back. "What was that?" he asks. "Who's in there?"

"Oh," St. Peter says, shoving his hands deep into the pockets of his fluffy white robe. "That's where the conservative Mennonites hang out. They think they're the only ones here."

My father rolled on the floor, laughing, when he first heard this joke. But in actuality, it captured his situation perfectly. Everyone who visited our church and met Dad thought that he was kind and tolerant and accepting of them. They believed he showed unconditional love.

But I knew better. Based on his comments across the years, I *knew* that he believed in his heart of hearts that our little conservative Mennonite church was the only church in 2,000 years of history to practice the pure Christian lifestyle that Jesus had taught his disciples. And in my heart of hearts, I think *I* believed the same thing.

Now as I entered college in the fall of 1984 at the age of twenty-one, I was truly happy with my newfound power and influence. Although I had doubts about the Umbrella of Authority, my following it had worked out just fine. By submitting to my father, I'd become an influential leader in our church.

I was teaching at my *alma mater* during the mornings and taking college classes in the afternoons and evenings. My students appreciated me. My brothers were following in my footsteps, doing construction work and supporting our family. With increased financial security, my father had begun to mellow. This made me happy.

I attributed all this to my acceptance of Brother Glick's patriarchal philosophy, although, to be fair, *he* didn't approve of me going to college. But I wasn't about to ask him for his advice. The corrupt authority of Brother Stutzman—whom Brother Glick had recommended—had planted seeds of doubt in any spiritual authority who tried to tell me what to do.

This skepticism was now exacerbated when I entered Malone's campus and discovered a shocking truth—people who weren't conservative Mennonite *also* thought they were Christians.

It got worse.

The young people in the college choir who came from other churches seemed to believe theirs was the only True Faith. *And...* there was a kicker... if you didn't attend their denomination, you probably weren't going to Heaven.

Our church youth had often questioned whether our conservative Mennonite church was *legalistic*, which meant that people believed that your salvation depended upon your following certain rules. Some of them argued that since Christ had died for our sins, and salvation was unconditional, when you accepted salvation, you were free to do whatever you wanted. A true Christian had a new heart, so he or she would *only* do what is godly. Thus, there was no need for rules, like the ones our church had. For example, a woman's dress needed to reach four inches below the knees, and people weren't supposed to go to professional baseball games, since they were *worldly* entertainments.

This was a very big deal to my new friends. Our community's rules proved to them that my church was legalistic, whereas their faith offered them freedom in Christ. I caught a glimpse of pity in their eyes when they found where I came from:

Poor schmuck, he doesn't even know how legalistic his church is.

This got my attention. My father had always taught us that our denomination was the purest form of Christian faith there was. Now I was discovering that other people thought the same thing about theirs. Did this mean there could be *more* than one true faith? Or worse, that ours wasn't the one true faith? Did this mean that there was a chance our faith was wrong?

I was confused.

My confusion only worsened when I attended my first class in Introduction to Sociology. The class sounded suspiciously liberal. So did my professor's hyphenated name, Jane Hoyt-Oliver.

Janie, as her students fondly called her, was in her thirties, and she glowed with an evanescent joy as she introduced the first book of the course, written by Willard Swartley: *Slavery, Sabbath, War, and Women*.

I took the book home and began reading, but once I read Willard's argument that the Bible's argument for slavery is just as logical as its argument for patriarchy, I grew angry. When he went on to explain that the same thinking is used to argue men must be leaders, and that women must submit to their authority, I slammed the book shut.

I can't read this.

I worriedly recalled Brother Glick's insights about the way worldly professors deceive their students. "I would have you ignorant concerning evil," he had quoted the Apostle Paul. The words boomed through my skull.

I opened the book back up, found the slavery passage again, and reread it more carefully.

How do they let a woman like this teach at this school?

Suspicious of my professor's leanings, I began to research Janie. Although she "claimed" to be a Christian, she had earned her B.A. and M.S.W. at Syracuse University's School of Social Work in New York and had a master's degree in social work. She had also taken courses at Duke Divinity School while her husband was completing his MDiv. All of this aligned her with the liberal State, I thought, which often invaded homes and accused godly parents of child abuse.

I suspected she also rejected the belief that every word of the Bible was inerrant (as in, no errors in the original version) and inspired. Her worldly professors would have had every reason to lie to her. Worst of all, her research in domestic violence and homelessness meant she approved of welfare, which our community believed encouraged laziness and interfered in Christian marriages.

It would be years before I realized the impact of my indoctrination by Brother Glick and my father. What I didn't realize at the time is that Janie *did* believe that the Bible is inspired and God-breathed, but that she also recognized that "inerrancy is, however, up for cultural interpretation and had been throughout the centuries," as she clarified in an email to me years later. That kind of nuance was something I couldn't begin to comprehend at that point in my life.

Arriving early before class began, I met with my counselor, telling her I wanted to drop Janie's class. My counselor said I needed it to graduate. Seeing my concern, she tried to calm me.

"Just give her time," she said, kindly. "I think you'll like Janie."

Frustrated, I headed across campus to class, a September chill in the air. I wondered whether I had made a mistake leaving Phoenix to return home. Already, I was having questions about what I was learning.

Have I sold my soul for a college degree?

During class discussion that day, Janie answered our questions about what we were reading. No, Willard wasn't saying the Bible is wrong, she explained. The writers saw their world through a specific cultural lens. The Bible is a translated document containing universal Truths, not specific cultural codes.

As Janie unpacked Swartley's arguments, I began to squirm. Here was a woman teaching false doctrine. This was simply wrong. Did she not understand the Umbrella of Authority? Yet she exuded quiet confidence and power. Often when I'd glance up from furiously scribbling notes, I'd catch her smiling at me.

This woman needed a *man* to correct her thinking because she lacked a true understanding of Scripture. I decided I would do this after class.

When the discussion ended, I approached Janie who was standing amid an eager crowd of students, answering a question.

When she turned to me, I began confidently, "If what you say is true, how do you explain Scripture that says wives are supposed to submit to their husbands?"

"Here we go again," someone said.

Another girl giggled.

I flushed but held my ground.

Janie didn't argue, just listened.

I pushed on. "How can you teach that men and women are equal? Isn't the entire Bible based on the Umbrella of Authority?"

Janie still didn't answer—Aha! I'd caught her!

But then her trademark smile appeared. "Steve, right?"

I nodded.

She gestured. "Yes, I agree with Gothard. Women are to submit to their husbands."

I gaped—she *agreed*. But how did she know about Gothard? I was sure that she had never heard of him. I was so looking forward to explaining the truth to her.

Janie's smile turned wry. "But, Steve, several verses later, Paul makes another remark that Gothard never mentions in his Institute for Basic Youth Conflicts. Husbands are to 'submit to their wives.' What are we to make of that? Which command do we obey?"

I instantly recognized the verse. How could I have forgotten it?

There were more mutterings behind me, another giggle.

My face grew red.

Janie nodded. "I was surprised by that, too, when I first read it." She nodded again. "The central issue at play here, Steve, isn't whether the Bible can be used to support a patriarchal system. It can. But the Bible can also be used to support slavery. 'Slaves, submit to your masters.' It can support genocide. 'Kill every man, woman, child, and beast in the city. Leave not one of them alive.'" She glanced around at the group. "Are we to argue, therefore, that slavery or genocide is right?"

I was already shaking my head, and, around me, other students did the same. I'd never thought of this before.

"You're Mennonite, right?"

I nodded.

"Then you know the Anabaptist reformers believe every believer is her own high priest—that we can communicate directly with God. That free will is crucial in allowing a person to make an authentic decision. The whole point of the story of the Garden of Eden is not to explain the Creation. It's that Adam and Eve, Satan and God… they are all part of a drama about freedom. The Creation story shows that every person must make their own decision. No authority can—nor should—decide what you can or can't do. The point is that all of us are equal in the sight of God, and the Devil tried to take that away from us."

I was stunned by her comment—she had upended my basic belief system. For the first time, she had said something that explained *everyone's* belief system in a Universal Truth. Her explanation of the Garden of Eden story was simple, obvious, and yet I had never considered it in quite this way. It threw everything I had been taught into question.

For the first time, I saw clearly why I could no longer subscribe to Brother Glick's philosophy of authoritarian leadership, and why I had bonded so powerfully to Brother Byler's philosophy that we needed to search for truth through questions, rather than simply accepting what an authority figure said. This is why I had been unable to indoctrinate my students—even while I *thought* I was attempting to do so.

It was the most powerful inflection point in my life.

I walked away from that class with my patriarchal philosophy—which had guided me for the past three years—shattered on the floor in front of me. According to Janie's interpretation, if free will made us human, how could it be taken from a woman without making her less than human? If I followed every commandment in Scripture literally, I'd be approving of violence: stoning, beheading, eye-gouging. Patriarchy required that women follow men, yet that didn't seem to sync up with the egalitarian power structure I now saw as central to my faith.

I realized at that moment that Janie was someone I could absolutely trust.

Years later, over the course of several conversations, as I interviewed her for both my Soul Teachers blog and later for this book, I realized how uniquely prepared Janie was to guide me during that very difficult time. As "a very happily married professional woman," the mother of a one-year-old daughter, and the wife of a United Methodist pastor, her faith "was at the heart of all" she did.

"We had both prayed about me taking the job [of professor at Malone]," she wrote to me in an email after one of our phone conversations. "Several people of faith had advised me not to take it (some even telling me it was a temptation and not from God) since our daughter was so young."

I remember the shock of visiting her church and seeing her work with her husband. Her face shone with genuine joy as she interacted with their parishioners. Although I didn't understand at that point how a woman could serve in such a visible role, I knew I felt safe with her—she was a deeply committed Christian who understood where I was coming from, and perhaps, where I was going.

And so, I began to drop by Janie's office when I encountered a problem. My anger at my father for his ridiculous worries about college. My worries about another guy on campus who was "more liberal" than I was. A negative reaction I got to a music review I wrote in which I ridiculed a student for revealing that her love for God made her want to "dance on the toilets with Jesus." Dealing with an unstable visitor to our youth group who first seemed suicidal, and then began to stalk me, literally chasing me in her car as I headed off to college the next morning.

In each case, Janie would always ask me first how *I* felt about things. She recommended that I provide mental health resources for my stalker, that I might want to use empathy when reviewing students for the newspaper, that perhaps I should get to know the guy and hear his reasoning behind his "liberal" positions, and that perhaps I should try to understand where my father was coming from.

Janie made me feel visible by listening carefully to what I said, by disagreeing with me when something didn't make sense, and by refusing to sugar-coat her comments. More than anyone else I had met, she wanted to know my feelings and emotional reactions to situations I confronted, knowing this was important to my understanding what *I* believed. Like Brother Byler, she wanted me to think for myself.

Although she could have taken the position of a mentor, with its hierarchical role, she chose to set that aside in favor of a friendship, which was more egalitarian. She was one of the few professors who seemed to understand the culture in which I had been raised. Yet instead of dismissing it as legalistic, she was careful to point me toward the positive aspects of our simple life. She never offered easy answers to me, instead, asking thought-provoking questions that allowed me to discover my own answers.

By respecting where I came from, she didn't trigger my oppositional defiance, and I was finally able to realize that I needed to decide what I really believed about my home culture's patriarchal structure.

Janie's affirmation of my autonomy also gave me the courage to begin making my own decisions, rather than feeling the need to get my father's "permission" for my decisions. I was becoming an adult, she reminded me. This prepared me to attend a life-changing opportunity.

According to the letter I received from the English Department in May, my "outstanding academic work" had earned me a scholarship to attend Malone's annual summer theater trip to Stratford, Ontario, free of charge. My favorite professor, Mr. Dale King, was leading the trip.

I wanted so badly to go, but my parents would never give their blessing.

I'd grown to love reading and discussing literature over the past two years, and the chance to explore theater was irresistible. I was attending local productions, and I was surprised by how these experiences reached deep inside me, using story and strong characters to create a powerful experience of empathy, all through the sensuous rhythm of language.

I did not realize until much later in life that it was my father who had taught me to love the spoken word by the way he dramatically recited Bible stories to us as a child, and through that dramatic monologue he had memorized and performed in church. How could I *not* go?

When I told my father about the opportunity, he was not on board with my decision. Theater was worldly. "The word *actor* means *hypocrite*. Haven't you listened to your cousin Joe Overholt?"

Of course I had. My older cousin, an eccentric bachelor, often took over the pulpit at the end of church on Sunday mornings, carrying a stack of theological tomes. He lifted his chin, stuck his hand into the front of his Plain coat, like the Emperor Napoleon, and began to proclaim his latest obsession—the evils of theater, young women who dressed immodestly, or the importance of spending the night in prayer. We groaned inwardly—Sunday dinner would now be late—but he sure knew how to hold an audience. He was my father's closest friend.

"Joe's studied all about theater, you know," my father said. "He's researched it. He'll tell you that theater comes from the Greeks."

My father didn't need to repeat Cousin Joe's underlying premise about hypocrisy—we had argued about this premise many times. Clearly, no Christian who wanted to go to heaven could be involved in the theater.

I glanced at my mother, who was quietly cleaning up after dinner. She didn't try to argue with me, intellectually. Until that spring, to know that she disapproved of me would have brought me to heel, but not anymore. I no longer held to my father's strict code of Separation. I was making friends with "worldly" girls from college, and sometimes they visited our church, meeting my parents with great interest. My mother was friendly as always, but she told me often that she suspected they wanted to date me, even marry me. My mother's disapproval was hard to manage, emotionally. I struggled to remember that although she was my mother, I was an adult with the power to make my own choices. This often came up when I dropped by to see Janie, who would listen quietly, and then ask me what I believed I should do. She reminded me often that, although I needed to treat my parents respectfully, I also needed to own my decisions *and* their consequences.

I thought about my offer to my sister Ann as I'd entered college. "Come talk to me if I begin to change." How naïve I'd been to believe I could go to college without being changed. But I had not yet been changed irrevocably… or so I thought.

Thanks to Janie's perspective on autonomy, I was beginning to confront the use of authority and power. I hadn't yet come to terms with how decisively my father's use of severe corporal punishment had been normalized in my mind.

Now, as a young man who was teaching part-time at our Christian school, I was growing uncomfortable with the way our culture inculcated respect and obedience, teaching us that we had to crush the will of the child so that they would learn to submit to God. Our only option, according to this view, was to use corporal punishment.

I was beginning to think that parents and teachers *did* have other options.

This came through to me one evening when I dropped by Janie's place to submit a late research paper. She invited me into her homey living room for a moment, curious about my most recent piece in the newspaper—I was now the News & Features Editor. Were there any further developments?

As we talked, her four-year-old daughter, whom Janie had sent to bed earlier, interrupted. She was stubborn, insisting she had the right to stay up late.

Janie quietly insisted she go back to bed.

It was a standoff.

My father's solution would have been simple—a spanking, using raw punishment, to demonstrate the adult's authority. He had once spanked all four of us boys simply because we hadn't gotten to bed on time.

But Janie's approach was different.

She knelt, patient and attentive to her child's needs. Without appealing to authority, without raising her voice, she helped her daughter see what was best for her.

Eventually, the child chose to go upstairs.

The little form disappeared. I listened to the sound of happy feet above us for a moment, then I turned to Janie, my eyebrows raised.

"A person should always be given the dignity of choice," she said.

"Even a child?"

"Yes." Janie closed her eyes.

That battle of wills with her child must have demanded a lot of strength and restraint.

She reached over to gather a stack of essays, with mine on the top. It was getting late, and she still had grading to do, I realized.

"I have to go," I said. "I'm redoing a story for the newspaper—one of my reporters dropped the ball."

As I left Janie that evening, heading back to campus, I compared her approach with her daughter to what I had seen growing up. "Children obey your parents in the Lord, for this is right" was a verse I knew by heart. It had been repeated to me, again and again, both at home and in school, where my teachers (most of German ethnicity) had hammered home this foundational belief. Children must learn to obey their authorities, first and foremost, and adults had the responsibility to ensure this.

Now, as an adult in my early twenties, I was shocked by Janie's parenting method. I was still struggling to grasp a belief that is foundational to my teaching today: a person's freedom of choice is central to their humanity. It's what I had seen in the parent/child relationships I had envied—for example, the way my best friend's father had treated him, seeking to understand and empower him, rather than focusing on eliciting respectful obedience. It's why slavery is wrong, and it's why a woman's choice is essential.

It's also why I believe in relationship-based teaching, because unless I see each student as an individual—rather than as just a "spoiled child" or "highly enabled"—I will never be able to win their respect and ultimately influence them in a positive way for life.

What I didn't realize as I made my way to the newspaper office to deal with a reporter's poor choices, was that this would be crucial to my own thinking process as I faced a choice of my own, one that would take me one step further on my way out of our community.

My choice would involve a young woman... who wasn't conservative Mennonite.

Chapter 12: Technically Virgins

The first scholarship I had ever won, which would now pay my college theater trip to Stratford, Ontario, supercharged my sense of confidence. In addition to exposing me to a world where intellectual Christians lived and interacted with art, it also allowed me to spend time with my favorite professor, Dale King, who had recommended me for the scholarship.

Growing up, I had thought myself an introvert, but my teaching experiences at both Maranatha and then Phoenix had encouraged my extraverted personality to explode into view. Now, on a bus with adults who loved Shakespeare, I found myself again surrounded by people who seemed interested in my thoughts and views of the world. The feeling was exhilarating, and it took me a while to sit down.

When I finally did, my professor joined me. With his rumbling bass voice and opulent vocabulary, I soon found myself undergoing a leisurely tutorial on Shakespearean drama. Mr. King shared stories from other theater trips, and we discussed the readings I had completed. Having won this scholarship, I knew that he and his colleagues considered me special, and I reveled in that.

At the Queen's Inn in Stratford, awed by the vintage Victorian architecture, I discovered I had a roommate.

"I'm Mark," he said. He was a church organist, and his primary goal, he told me, was getting the attention of the doe-eyed brunette he had noticed sitting with her mother on the way up. Mark was sure she was interested in him.

"Do you know her name?" he asked.

"Let's find out," I said. He looked at me with gratitude. I had no intentions of dating a girl outside the conservative Mennonite community, and I had seen her worldly clothes, so I knew I couldn't date her. Like a modern Cyrano de Bergerac, I might as well help him.

The first show we saw was a bawdy musical, *The Boys from Syracuse*, which was a remake of Shakespeare's *A Comedy of Errors*. The stage was luxurious, and the working girls scantily clad. I was shocked by the lead actress's familiarity with sex—I just knew she had no morals whatsoever. Riveted, I was barely able to drag my eyes away from the stage, which embarrassed me, but when I glanced around, everyone else in the party was laughing uproariously, and I decided maybe the problem was my dirty mind. Since the trip was for college credit, I had to write several papers, so I focused on specific things I could write about. I wondered if our conservative Christian college was aware of what we were seeing.

When I wasn't watching the show, I was assessing my roommate's chances, sizing up the girl we both found fascinating. She was way out of his league, perfectly made up with long dark hair. Her blue skirt and cream blouse looked elegant and expensive. As if feeling my eyes on her, she glanced over, and we exchanged smiles. Then I returned to viewing the musical, but my thoughts were going a million miles an hour.

I thought about the girl my parents expected me to marry—someone who wore the right clothes and followed our church's standards. She would never come on a trip like this. For a moment, a flash of resentment flooded my body, thinking of my mother's reactions to the girls from Malone who came to church with me. I pushed those feelings down. This trip wasn't the time to deal with that.

The next morning, Mark and I wandered through the town. By then, I knew the girl's name was Diana, and seeing Mark's continued interest, I decided to help him out. I wasn't afraid to talk to anyone, certainly not a girl that I had no chance of dating anyway.

As we came through the center of town, I saw Diana and her mother up ahead. I moved confidently toward them, introducing myself, but when I turned to Mark, he was gone. I caught a glimpse of him slipping into a nearby bookstore, leaving me stranded with the two women. Diana seemed shy, but her mother lavishly introduced me to her daughter, and I was soon wondering who was meeting whom. Diana was attending a Bible college in the Midwest, her mother told me, and she was attending this trip for college arts credit.

Just like me.

The mother didn't mince words, asking me if I loved Jesus. I was used to this behavior—all good evangelical Christians witness to people they meet—and so I knew what to say. I told her I attended a conservative Mennonite church. She seemed confused, but not Diana.

"I think Steve comes from a church like the Amish." She turned to me, smiling. "Did I get that right?"

"Something like that," I said. I was floored. This girl either knew a lot about religion, or she had already asked about me.

"I'm studying psychology, and we did a unit on the Amish and Mennonite subcultures," she said, in explanation.

Out of the corner of my eye, I could see Mark pretending to read a magazine. When the women weren't looking, I gestured to him, but he shook his head, ducking behind his magazine.

As we approached a bakery, Diana asked me what kind of croissants I liked best. When I admitted I didn't know, her mother jumped in.

"Steve, you've never had a croissant?"

"Oh, Steve, you must try one." Diana's enthusiasm was genuine. "Mother, why don't we buy Steve a cup of cappuccino and a croissant?"

"I think that's a splendid idea." Diana's mother grabbed my arm and steered me toward the bakery, as Diana drifted along beside me. Being with the girl made my heart race, but there was also a tinge of guilt. I was supposed to be helping Mark. But then again, he didn't seem all that interested. I decided this was Mark's problem. Diana was interesting. Even if I couldn't date her, there was no harm in enjoying her companionship.

Once we sat down, Diana's mother began firing questions at me about my faith. I answered them as best I could, thinking the conversation a bit strange. I'd sometimes get a question in for Diana, and I loved listening to her answers, but then Mom took over the moment things began to slow down. It dawned on me that they were working as a tag team.

Is she vetting me to see if I am worthy of her daughter? Seriously? They should be interviewing Mark.

Once I figured out their game, I relaxed, even growing amused. I liked the way Diana was looking at me. When Diana's mother began asking me about my spiritual journey, I told her about the moment I had been born again, when I had gone to my father at the age of eight, and he had prayed with me.

Diana was listening intently. Actually, they both were. When I began to describe my church community, about the way my father had not been crazy about me going to college, but that I had gone anyway, Diana's mother interrupted.

"What a story, Steve. You should write a spiritual memoir. I can already see the title—*Between Two Worlds*." We were interrupted by a waiter, who was carrying a tray loaded with the three buttery pastries and tiny cups of espresso.

"You really think I have a book in me?" I sipped my espresso, finding it very bitter. "My mother thinks most writers only have one book in them."

"Your mother sounds like a wise woman," Diana's mother said. "Does she read a lot of books?"

The hem of Diana's bright red skirt had crept up above her knees. I glanced up, and Diana raised her eyebrows:

Caught you.

I was instantly flustered. Suddenly, I realized Diana's mother was waiting for my answer.

"Oh, yes. Both of my parents like to read." Diana slipped me a sly grin, which only flustered me more. If any of the girls in our church had caught me checking them out, my reputation would have been destroyed. Yet Diana had... liked the way I was looking at her.

"I don't know that much about the Amish," Diana's mother said. "Are they Christian?" My mind was pulled back into the present, and I was thankful for my high school class in Mennonite History.

"Oh, yes," I said. "It's another branch of the Christian faith, neither Protestant nor Catholic. Theologians call it the Third Way. Or Anabaptist." I was surprised that as a Bible teacher, she seemed to know so little. But before we could say anymore, I noticed Mark strolling toward us. I had forgotten him, and I guiltily leaped up to wave him over.

"Hey, Mark," I said. "We were just talking about you. Diana, did I mention he's an organist at a church?"

The three of us listened as Mark talked about the music of Johann Sebastian Bach. He hoped to do his Ph.D. on the importance of theology in hymns.

The two women listened politely, but at one point, I saw the two women exchange a look, and Diana gave a slight shake of her head. Mark didn't notice. But I noticed Diana's mother didn't ask him a single question, so I asked him several questions to keep the conversation going. I thought he was a natural teacher, and his stories were interesting. But I also knew Cyrano wouldn't have had any better luck with Mark than I did.

She's really not interested in him.

Eventually, the women politely got up to leave, and then suddenly, Diana seemed to trip. I instinctively reached, catching her by the arms. She recovered and gave me a grateful smile.

As they left, she glanced back at me one last time, and I realized my heart was pounding.

I kept forgetting that I wasn't supposed to date a woman like Diana. Instead, as I realized that Diana seemed interested in me, the entire trip came alive, and I entered the theater the second night hoping to catch another glimpse of her. Within moments, I smelled her perfume as she sat down with her mother behind Mark and me.

A few moments later, the stage went dark, and I was pulled into what has since become my favorite of Shakespeare's plays, *A Winter's Tale.* Until that trip, I had never attended a professional theater production, and I was astonished at the intensity of the experience. I began to understand why Cousin Joe hated theater so much—it mesmerized me. Not just the lighting and stage design, which were minimalist and complemented the actors' costumes, but also the performances. For the first time, I saw professional actors whose lives and careers were consumed by the theater. The cast was relatively small, so to my surprise, I saw several actors playing completely different characters with just a few changes in costume

Shakespeare's story of a virtuous queen accused of adultery captured my attention. I was almost brought to tears by the lead actress, by her elegant outfit, her obvious purity, and her humble pleas to the king. She was obviously innocent—how could the king not see that?

But the biggest shock happened at intermission, when I realized where I was, and turned to see Diana and her mother. Diana had a mischievous smile on her face.

"Hey Steve, I noticed you couldn't take your eyes off the queen." As I looked at her in confusion, she raised an eyebrow. "Maybe you preferred her last night with less clothes on?"

I gaped, embarrassed, until suddenly it hit me.

"Wait, that was…?" I glanced back at the empty stage. "Are you saying the same woman played both parts?"

The entire group laughed.

That's when I realized what real acting was. The elegant and pure-minded queen that I had just empathized with so deeply was the same scantily clad working girl who the night before had shocked and titillated me. Diana was just teasing, but for me, that moment transformed the way I viewed theater from then on. It was at that point, as well, when I really understood the power of illusion— that what you see is not necessarily obvious.

After the show, several of us went out for ice cream. Mark and I quickly joined Diana and her mother, and my professor's wife joined us. As we ate, I found that by now, everyone was curious about my background. Suddenly, Diana asked me a question.

"Steve, I'm so fascinated by your world. But is it true that you're not allowed to date worldly girls?"

Everyone turned to me.

"You mean, girls like you?" I shot back.

She grinned. "I didn't say that, but let's say for the sake of argument, yes, me. For the sake of… argument."

The older women chuckled, and I caught Mark's grin. I was trying to think fast. It was pretty clear that Mark and Diana weren't hitting it off.

"Well," I said. "I don't think my parents would much like it. I might get excommunicated from the church, which would be bad. But then again, my mother went to New York City to be a missionary, and she fell in love with a guy much more worldly than her. And hey, they had eight kids."

"Interesting story," Diana said, glancing at her mother. "My parents were also missionaries, only they went to India. I was born there. So, I think they win on the spiritual front. But, then again, I'll take a pass on the eight kids. Other than that, perhaps a missionary kid like me might be spiritual enough after all to satisfy your mother."

"Of course, Dad had to change to marry my mother," I said. "He became almost Amish."

"Well, that's not my plan," Diana said. "And based on what I'm seeing"— she gestured toward my jeans—"any Amish guy wearing Calvins isn't exactly planning to stay Amish."

I put up my hands in defeat, and the group laughed.

"I think she might have your number, Steve," my professor's wife said.

"Not yet, I don't," Diana said, acerbically. She mock-punched me in the arm as we split up, Mark and I heading back to our room. I couldn't quit grinning, until I suddenly realized how quiet Mark had become. I remembered my plan to help Mark win her, and I felt bad. He didn't mention Diana as we got ready for bed, telling me instead about his plan to be a composer just like Bach, focusing only on hymns for the church.

But clearly, he had been thinking about Diana. Over breakfast the next morning, he confirmed what I'd been feeling.

"I think Diana wants you." He shrugged his shoulders. "We didn't really have that much to talk about. And she clearly hit on you last night."

I played dumb. "Really?"

Mark punched me in the arm the same place Diana had, only his punch actually hurt. "That's for stealing my girl." Then he laughed. "I think you guys were made for each other."

"Whatever," I said, acting as if I didn't care. I was glad he was okay with me going after Diana, but the fact that I now admitted to this both excited and terrified me. I wasn't on this trip to find a girlfriend. I was here to study literature and theater. What would my parents say? This was exactly what they were afraid of. I was breaking *so* many rules on this trip.

And I looking forward to breaking even more.

After that, things moved like lightning.

The next evening after another Shakespeare production—this time one of Shakespeare's histories—the same group went out for ice cream, and before I knew it, Diana had asked me if I had ever seen Stratford Lake in the moonlight.

We'd barely left the shop when Diana grabbed my hand for the first time, any pretense of shyness gone. We talked the entire way, and, by the time we reached a park bench overlooking the lake, I thought I had discovered my soulmate. I was in deep.

The air was sweet with the smell of honeysuckle, the moonlit expanse of water before us silent and still. Faced with Diana's laughing eyes, and the smiles we both couldn't wipe off our faces, I wanted to spend the night talking. I wanted to sacrifice my life to make her proud of me. Above us stretched a deep blue sky spattered with stars.

We wouldn't be going in anytime soon.

The best part? Diana and her family only lived a half hour's drive from my home.

We spent the rest of the trip home together in a pleasant blur of excitement, sitting together on the bus, and eating at the restaurant overlooking Niagara Falls. We never seemed to run out of things to talk about. Her mother took pictures.

And it turned out Diana didn't need to get my phone number. I got hers.

I never believed Diana would meet my mother's expectations, and I was right. When I returned from my trip and showed my mother the pictures I'd taken of Diana, hoping Mom would understand, I saw her brow furrow in concern. It didn't help when I explained that she was a sophomore at a Christian college and the daughter of a high school Bible teacher. I thought Mom would realize that Diana was about as Christian as it was possible to get. But instead of focusing on Diana's character, my mother zeroed in on the physical.

"Diana wears a lot of makeup."

I bristled, angry to the core of my being that my mother could only see the outside and not the pure heart of this girl that I loved.

I gathered the pictures from Niagara Falls and stormed out.

I was not about to let my mother keep me from the best thing that had ever happened to me. As far as I was concerned, Diana was a perfect match.

But my mother's reactions stayed with me because they pointed to a deeper problem—what my community's reaction would be when they discovered I was dating a worldly girl who wore makeup, jewelry, and short red skirts.

Within a few days, I drove to Kent to meet Diana's family: her sister, brother, and father. They lived in a simple ranch house, and after a dinner of pizza ordered in, the family settled in to show me *Witness*, a film about a cop who rescues an Amish child and his widowed mother starring Harrison Ford and Kelly McGillis.

By then, I had begun watching VHS tapes of movies in the evenings with some of my guy friends, and R-rated films weren't new to me. But I hadn't yet gone to a movie theater—this seemed a step too far. I was very curious about *Witness*—not because it was about the Amish, but because I had heard some of my college buddies discussing its famous nude scene. This wasn't the night I got to see it, however, since Diana's older brother fast-forwarded the video past that scene in order to protect the eyes of Diana's new Amish boyfriend, a perception which both amused and annoyed me.

Fascinated by my background, the brother wanted to know how similar our church was to the Amish community. I explained to him that I wasn't Amish, but I had Amish cousins, and *they* were annoyed when they heard the Amish in the film wear buttons—very few Amish would ever do this, since the Amish think buttons are worldly, choosing instead to wear old-fashioned hooks and eyes on their clothes. Other than that, I told them the film portrayed the Amish fairly accurately, including the way they spoke German.

Eventually, Diana pried me away for a trip to a popular youth hangout. I was quiet over coffee and ice cream, and Diana wanted to know what was wrong. I finally broke down and told her what was bothering me—I didn't know if my parents would ever approve of us dating. I expected Diana to be upset, but she took a surprisingly upbeat view of the fact that we couldn't date publicly. In fact, when I told her about my mother's reactions, she only became more fascinated, to my surprise. My unavailability made me even more of a catch.

She suggested we date secretly. She could visit my church as "a friend."

Relieved by her decision, I agreed. Ours was a star-crossed love, we decided, laughing. We were Romeo and Juliet, the children of two warring religious denominations.

When Diana and her brother attended our youth group activity as "friends of mine," no one but my mother suspected the truth, since I regularly invited friends from college. In return, I visited the church her family attended several weeks later, and unwittingly, I found myself in the world of fundamentalist— or, *born again*—Christianity. It was very different than my church.

First, there were no decorations in our church, as there were here. In my church, the men sat on one side, and the women on the other side, but here, entire families sat together. Our women wore modest dresses that were homemade, and the men were expected to wear their Plain coat and suits, but here the women wore clothes that might be called immodest, and the men wore suits and ties.

Our church was also spare and simple with no decorations or varnished wooden objects, whereas Diana's church had a decorated sanctuary with stained glass windows. Our wooden benches were hard—when we prayed, rather than kneeling on the soft kneeling bench in front of us, we all turned around and knelt on the hard, tiled floor, facing the even harder benches. For communion, rather than being served grape juice in tiny cups with a little wafer, we drank from white coffee cups (to make sure no one thought it was actually wine).

The most significant difference was in the way they handled music. Instead of *a cappella* hymns, the congregation all sang melody with a band accompanying them. The size of the sanctuary, too, was different. Like their faith, it was gigantic with multiple wide aisles, rather than the single narrow aisle in our church. Apparently, the way to heaven was not a straight-and-narrow path that only a few people could squeeze into. Instead, their faith was a six-lane freeway, conveying a massive, born-again crowd to Jesus.

They also seemed very confident they were going to the Pearly Gates, depending on a doctrine called "eternal security." Unlike my father, who believed that one sin would send you to Hell, they believed once you are saved, you are guaranteed a mansion in Heaven, no matter what you did from then on.

I was stunned by how sure they were about this.

Perhaps because they didn't worry about their salvation, they also didn't seem worried about being worldly, as my father was. Based on what I saw, they seemed to live life to the full, and they had a lot more fun. Television, radio, theater, fashion.

And then there was our relationship, the speed of which had me worried. When we were alone, Diana kept… *distracting* me. We might be dating secretly, but, in her mind, we *were* dating, which meant that I needed to fulfill certain… expectations.

My mother's instincts were dead-on. Diana was anything but the "good girl" she pretended to be for her parents and community. She had been dating since middle school and knew the way boys thought. By continuing to date me, Diana was betting on her instincts. She had concluded that, as the son of Amish parents, I had a lot more worldly experience than I was letting on.

She couldn't have been more wrong.

Toward sundown, Diana and I slipped out for a late-night sundae after another evening with the family.

In a booth at our favorite ice cream shop, Diana sat across from me, shining dark curls framing her peaches-and-cream complexion. We were talking about the differences between the Bible college she attended and my Christian college here.

"So." Her eyes danced. "I have a personal question for you."

"Yeah?" I took a sip of coffee.

"Do you believe sex is always... just sex?"

I choked, spilling my coffee.

She giggled, wiping the table with a napkin.

I was flustered. Where was this going? We hadn't even kissed yet. "What did you say?"

She composed herself. "I asked if you believe sex is always just sex." This time she stared at me, full on. She was the confident young heroine in *The Karate Kid*, the movie we'd just watched a week ago, and she knew what she wanted.

But that was a *movie*—now suddenly, here we were, talking about sex. My Amish-Mennonite mind was spinning.

She reached for me. Her hand was warm. "It's a discussion some of us are having at school."

I took a deep breath. She'd just transformed my view of her college. I'd seen photos of chapel services in the brochures from her college. Photos of young women just like her, stretching up their hands in prayer. Were they all like... her?

She shifted, amused at my reactions. "Are you saying you've never had this conversation at Malone?"

"Not really." I couldn't get the words out. "At least, not with girls. You mean... students believe...?"

"Well, no."

I held my breath, unable to believe we were having this conversation.

"I believe we should be virgins on our wedding night." She brought her coffee cup to her mouth and talked around it. "Technically."

"*Technically* virgins?" The words burst out of me, and she grinned. She had me now.

"Yeah, you know. Like, a blow job—is it actually sex according to the Bible?"

129

Oh, my God. Did she just say that?

"Uhm, I don't know." Actually, I knew exactly what I thought—it was sinful and forbidden—and that made it tantalizing.

"Are you saying Christians can do... *that*... without sinning?"

"I'm asking what *you* think?" Diana was no fool. She knew how to dance, verbally, and she wasn't about to perform this ballet alone.

"I think it's... interesting."

Diana's lip curled. "Joseph thought it was wrong."

Ah... her previous boyfriend hadn't forsaken his beliefs for her, and she hadn't liked that. Was I strong enough to risk her dislike? Did I want to?

"We had arguments. He even told my mother."

"He told your *mother*?"

"Yeah, what a jerk, huh? He should have figured Mom out long ago. But that's Mom. They think she's their spiritual counselor, and before I know it, they're confessing everything to her. Then *I* hear... Well." A moue of annoyance crossed her face.

I decided I was not going to be one of "them."

"Well, you needn't worry about me." Whatever we did, I had no intention on sharing *anything* with her mother.

She offered me a trusting smile. Her certainty warmed my chest.

"Good." She grabbed her purse and stood. "Come on, let's go to Riverwalk. I can't wait to... show it to you." She winked.

I jumped up. I wasn't sure what was going to happen next, but I wasn't going to pass up the chance to find out.

I'd never been to the Riverwalk. Diana loved its romance, the privacy it offered, the benches placed strategically. Getting out of my car, she pulled me toward the walkways glowing under the lights, with music drifting from nearby bars.

I was in a fog, worried but also excited. I had never kissed a woman romantically. My parents believed that moral and sexual purity were the same thing, and they expected me to save my first kiss until my engagement.

Diana had no intention of waiting that long.

Chapter 13: Between Two Worlds

We went, then, to a boardwalk along the river, Diana pulling me along, excited to have found a man she could trust. Me playing it cool, yet with my heart beating fast, unsure about what was coming next.

After we found a bench and settled in, Diana pushed her back into me, and I wrapped my arms around her. It was my move. After a moment, she held up her right hand, showing off her long, polished nails, examining them. The golden light caught their brilliance.

"Look."

I admired them. Around us, the gentle sounds of the river blended with Diana's scent to form an earthly paradise of quiet joy. Diana had told me all about her nails. They were her fashion fetish, something she loved about herself. My mother had hated them when they showed up in the photos I had taken from the theater trip.

"You like them?" she asked.

"Yes."

"Did I mention what fingernails like these can do?"

I froze. Her words oozed sexual energy, and after our conversation in the ice cream shop, my guard was up. But I was also drawn to her, seduced by her confidence. I kissed her on the neck.

"Perhaps you should tell *me* what they can do."

Diana turned and reached behind me, laying her fingers lightly on my upper back. "This." Her breath flooded one ear, then the other. "They can do this."

Through my thin cotton shirt, I felt the light tickle of her fingernails, a light scratch down the back. Until that moment, I had not realized how sensitive my skin was back there. Pleasure spread throughout my body as she skillfully activated my skin.

I was so on board with this. I wanted more. As she continued, she looked up into my eyes, her nails drifting down my back. She was definitely driving the train. I moved my mouth toward hers, my body alive. I wanted to kiss her red lips as deeply and passionately as any romance hero.

And then, suddenly, I heard it… in the back of my mind… my memory bringing it all to life again: the sound of a bus roaring down the highway, and the cheers of my classmates.

I pulled away from her, standing uncertainly.

Diana remained seated, upset and confused. "What's wrong?"

131

The Cuyahoga River raced beside us, the sound matching my rush of embarrassment. "I can't kiss you."

"Why not?"

I didn't answer. The temperature had changed. I no longer felt the heat of a July night. Waves of cold washed over me. I sat down beside her, shivering.

Her voice softened.

"When did it happen, Steve?"

How did she know?

"In choir."

"At Malone?" I could hear her disbelief.

"Yeah."

It had happened a year before at the end of my first choir tour with Malone. There was an initiation ceremony on the last trip home. After curtaining off the front of the bus, herding all of the novices there, they began an unforgettable ceremony. In front of the cheering choir members as the bus roared toward home, each new member was pulled out from behind the curtain, and one after another, dramatically kissed by one of the veteran choir members.

It was intended to be a harmless and fun activity, a playful twist on the childhood game "Doctor." We needed to be cured, we were each told in turn, and only a kiss from the right person would do the trick. Every novice enjoyed the experience, it seemed.

Except me.

To be fair, I was warned (vaguely) by a friend. And because the girls liked me (they told me later), they saved me until the end... when the three most popular girls in the choir proceeded to kiss me, dramatically and enjoyably, one after another.

Finally, the first one returned—a sophomore girl on whom I had a massive crush, but whose alpha personality scared the shit out of me—and she gave me one *more* kiss. "You so deserve this," she said, delivering a deep-throated kiss that left me breathless.

It also left me nauseous and emotionally distraught. Not that any of them knew this, of course, other than the friend who had warned me, who now sat beside me on the bus, concerned with my reactions, as we roared back to campus.

It had been my first kiss... or should I say, my first *three* kisses. That's right. I was tightly wound, I took my faith seriously, and yes... before that night, I had never been kissed. Not quite the forty-year-old virgin, but pretty darn close.

I was a twenty-one-year-old man who came from a conservative Mennonite family where my parents told us stories about their pure courtship. They were engaged in three months, they didn't even hold hands until they became engaged and they didn't kiss until their wedding day, six months after being introduced to each other by their pastor. They taught us that our body was a temple of the Holy Ghost and should not be defiled by lust.

Today I know it wasn't the kissing that bothered me. The girls were sweet and delivered kisses that were warm and intimate, each providing me a moment in time as the crowd outside our little bubble cheered. The intimacy of the moment set my heart racing.

What distressed me afterwards, I believe now, was something I didn't count on.

I wasn't in control.

The invasive nature of the kisses (as delicious as they were) sent me back to my childhood days when adults abused me physically. My mind wanted it, but it scared the shit out of my body, which couldn't forget.

When we arrived back at the campus, I left my friend and headed to the school to work, but I couldn't focus. I was having a hard time breathing, and my mind was racing in circles. I knew I should have been the happiest guy in the choir—my friend had told me afterward that every guy in the bus wanted to be *me*. Clearly, I was strange. Why would I react so strongly to three of the most beautiful women in the choir kissing me?

Now, sitting with an attentive Diana, the chills were gone, and my heart was once again calm as I finished my story. She grabbed my arm, squeezing it.

"Oh, Steve, of course they wanted to kiss you. I do, too."

I took a deep breath.

"You felt nauseous," Diana said.

"Yes. And I don't know why."

"But they liked you, they wanted you. You must have felt flattered."

"Uhm…"

"But that didn't give them the right to… to kiss-rape you."

I had never thought of it that way.

"I couldn't let it go," I said. "After the trip, I talked to each of those girls. I tried to show them how I felt."

What I couldn't quite explain to them—or even Diana, now, even though I wanted to—was that there was another layer that felt even more ridiculous. In my community, even if a girl wanted to kiss a boy publicly, she would *never* take the initiative, unless they were already dating. Men were in charge, and no girl would be that bold. Now, as I processed those kisses, especially the last one, I realized that I had been flirting with my crush for months. No wonder she had taken the initiative. Clearly, she believed, *I* never would.

"Did it help? Talking to them?" Diana asked.

I shook my head. "They were horrified by what I told them. They had wanted to show how much they liked me. It was intended to be a great compliment. I believe them. Why did I have to feel so guilty? Why couldn't I just let it go? Perhaps I would have eventually forgotten about it. But I couldn't."

Diana wrapped her arms around me. She didn't try to initiate another kiss… just held on. The warmth of her understanding burned through me, bringing me alive again. By now, I'd decided my feelings for Diana were real, and I wanted more than a secret romance.

But I didn't know how to deal with her expectations. If she only knew how much I wanted to give her everything she wanted, to do what her former boyfriend wouldn't do. But I also knew that I wasn't ready to go there.

The ensuring sexual frustration kept me on edge.

Even today, I am stunned at my ability to that summer to keep from becoming physically intimate with Diana. She was willing, and I found her entrancing, but my parents' belief system was too deeply instilled within me— and so I found myself unable to even kiss Diana.

I'm even more impressed with Diana's patience in continuing to see me. Perhaps she respected my "dating standards," as my parents would have described them. Perhaps she thought that if she had patience, I would eventually come around—she was quite determined. Perhaps she was truly in love with me, and therefore, worth waiting for.

I spent my days that summer in the blazing sun doing mason work. In the evenings, when there were no youth group activities, I snuck off to Kent to visit my secret girlfriend. We spent time with her family, talked and held each other close at the Riverwalk, and talked through the differences between our worlds.

Eventually, Diana's mother came up with an idea. Perhaps I should take a Bible course focused on the one belief that seemed central to the differences between our cultures?

After a phone call to Malone, I discovered I could fulfill one of my religion credits through a college extension course taken at a nearby conservative Bible college. The class just happened to focus on the book of I Corinthians.

I jumped at the chance. Finally, I would be able to research and conclude why the conservative Mennonite church—unlike all the other Christian churches I knew—translated literally the biblical command about a woman needing to cover her hair: "But every woman that prayeth or prophesieth with her head uncovered dishonoureth her head" (I Corinthians 11: 5). According to the Apostle Paul, the covering was a symbol of a woman's submission to the patriarchal order, in which the head of the woman was the man, and the head of the man was God.

As I saw it, this was the one area in which my community truly disagreed with Diana's—the covering that our women wore, what most outsiders called a *bonnet*, which was a spiritual symbol. By wearing this symbol, a woman signaled that she was in submission to her male spiritual authority (either her father or her husband), and thus, to God.

As Diana began to question me about the covering, I realized that although her family was conservative and took the Bible literally, they did not see the need to practice it. I found this odd.

Yet, to be honest, the restrictions placed on women within our culture really bothered me. We as men could wear modern, store-bought clothes, whereas women had to make their own clothes to ensure they were "modest" and "plain" to demonstrate their "separation" from the world. It didn't seem fair.

I also couldn't understand why other evangelical denominations didn't follow the Apostle Paul's instructions in I Corinthians 11 that women were not to speak publicly in church—and that they were to cover their heads. If we followed the same Bible, how did they avoid this clear and literal command?

I decided that it was time for me to figure out why most evangelical Christians—who proudly stated that they followed the Bible literally—had tossed aside this command. If they could ignore this rule, why couldn't I?

I wanted a real relationship with Diana, and her willingness to have an intimate relationship—with both of us still remaining "technically virgins"— was appealing. She was the most beautiful woman I had ever known, and I believed we had a future together. I wasn't ready to ask her to marry me, in spite of my parents' speedy courtship, but I hoped we could at least move toward an engagement.

Being around her was exciting.

If indeed my community was wrong, I could leave and join Diana's church. I hoped they were wrong, because I knew Diana would never join mine. But if my community was right, I would have to break up, no matter how I felt.

The thought of losing Diana made it hard for me to breathe.

The covering worn in our culture was very confusing to people on the outside. We interpreted this rule with great specificity. Every woman in our subculture wore a covering on her head starting in her adolescent years after she accepted Christ. It was unlike the worldly bridal veiling, which was long and flowing, and made with lace or a diaphanous chiffon. Those materials would have been impractical for everyday use, and, not Plain enough for our community.

As interpreted by our church, a woman's covering needed to cover all of her uncut hair, which was done up in a bun. Only the woman's family saw her uncut hair. In fact, my father once explained to me that he had to convince my mother to take off her covering and let her hair down on their wedding night because she had never let a man see it before. As I was growing up, my sisters were comfortable letting their hair down around the home, but in public, that would have been inappropriate.

To a lay person, this covering worn by women looked like it was made of white cotton, but the approved material used to create the covering was actually a heavy nylon netting, which was white, opaque, and carefully ironed into a circular shape. The crown at the top was perfectly flat, fully covering the woman's bun, and circling around that crown was a pleated brim. On each side of the covering, hanging down, was a thin white polyester ribbon, carefully ironed, that we called a string looping from one side to the other. In the most conservative Amish-Mennonite or Beachy churches, the string did not loop but hung down on each side.

Knowing Diana would never wear the covering, I took my extension course on I Corinthians seriously. Over the next few weeks, I read every commentary I could find, trying to understand I Corinthians 11. After class, I sometimes discussed what I was finding with my teacher, a local Baptist pastor. He admitted that when you took the Bible literally, the Apostle Paul had indeed commanded women to cover their heads.

"Most pastors have come to the conclusion that it's a cultural thing," he said. "There's no way they are going to be able to support making their women wear a veiling—it is a Middle East custom, one that Muslim women follow today. I respect your church for at least being consistent in taking the Bible literally."

By now, Diana had returned to college for the fall semester, and in her letters and our phone calls, I sensed disapproval when I talked about my quest. One night, as we talked by phone, she snapped.

"So, Steve, you think your community might be right, asking women to wear the covering?"

"I don't know," I said. "My professor told me he respects what my community believes."

There was a long silence. "Really? I'm surprised. My mother admired his biblical scholarship a lot."

Based on Diana's reaction, it was clear her mother's respect for this pastor would soon end. It was also clear that things with me were not going as she had planned. My professor was supposed to give me a rationale for *leaving* my community, not *respecting* its beliefs.

Meanwhile, a different side of Diana was emerging. Although she was still the sweet young woman I had met and fallen in love with over the past summer, she no longer deferred to me. In fact, she reminded me of her mother, who had put me off with her opinionated ways.

I thought about the way Diana's father always let her mom lead in family prayers. He was mostly silent, and *not* the spiritual leader in their family. Was that the way a marriage between me and Diana would work? I feared that when a real crisis hit, Diana would take charge, whether I liked it or not.

I was having second thoughts about our being compatible.

Diana had inherited her strength from her mother, and I realized now she had no intention on marrying a man who would expect her to defer... or submit... or whatever I wanted to call it. She wanted to be a full partner in a marriage. Theoretically, I agreed with this. But in reality, I hadn't made up my mind.

This was clear in my conflicted feelings about the covering. Having only recently rejected the patriarchy, I was still uncertain about what a woman's role should be in society. I had not yet escaped a core patriarchal belief—men are to lead, and women are to follow—that I had so enthusiastically embraced not four years ago.

Diana sensed this.

She was not one to wait around. She intended to force me to decide what I thought, and so, in our letters and phone calls, our conversations became more focused. Secure at her college, surrounded by eligible males, Diana was growing impatient. She was hungry for a normal romance that allowed room for passion, like the ones her girlfriends had. She longed for snuggles by the fire, and, eventually, an engagement ring.

If I wanted to keep Diana, I was going to have to change what I believed.

This worried me. I saw the potential consequences if I began dating Diana openly. I had risen from an impoverished family to someone who was respected as a teacher and leader in our community. If I moved forward with Diana, all of this was at risk, a proposition that worried me. Yes, I wanted Diana, but I also wanted to keep what I had worked so hard to build.

If I left, I would lose all of my friends.

But in this, sadly, I was lying to myself. There were plenty of people who had left our community and maintained their friendships. People like my friend Laban. People still answered his phone calls and read his letters and welcomed him when he returned home to visit. He would have been able to repent and return anytime he wished. What really worried me was that people had also spread rumors about him, voicing strong opinions about his eternal future.

That was the heart of the problem. I didn't think I could handle the negative judgments of my community—the gossip that stuck to anyone who left. I enjoyed my popularity. If I left, my reputation in our community would be toast.

I was also frustrated by the pressure I felt from Diana. I knew, vaguely, that I would eventually leave... *sometime*... but I was not going to let Diana force me to decide. If I left, it would be on my own terms.

When Diana came home for Thanksgiving, we returned to the Riverwalk, but this time, we argued. She was tired of my indecision. If I wanted to keep our relationship secret, that was my problem.

"If you want to go to a theological class and argue about an ugly white bonnet, fine." She stood before me, her arms crossed. "I won't be wearing one... ever."

I froze, anger gripping my chest.

Diana's eyes were blazing—there was not an ounce of give. Usually, her gaze was soft and supportive and empathetic, so I wasn't used to this side of her. For the first time, I realized she was the proud daughter of her confident mother.

I tried to defend myself. "I would never force you to wear a covering—"

"But you certainly wouldn't marry a woman who doesn't." She bit off the words, the color high in her cheeks.

I dropped my eyes, unable to respond.

She had me there. I wasn't giving her a choice either, and she knew it. I was letting our culture get between us, rather than following my heart.

The problem was... I didn't understand how to love. The only person I was thinking about in this situation was myself... my reputation as a leader in my community... the influence I had. Romance had been fun for both of us, but I didn't have a clue about what true love was, which would have required me to focus on what *Diana* needed.

"Why can't you leave?" she asked, softly. "I know you want to."

It is clear to me now that what Diana had wanted was a man who could love her, who wasn't afraid of giving affection, and who would be able to support the strong woman she was. At that point in my life, I wasn't that man. I wasn't willing to give her the freedom she needed to grow into the person she wanted to be. Instead, in spite of everything we had in common, I chose to obsess over a symbol that ran contrary to everything she believed about freedom and autonomy.

To top it off, at the age of twenty-two, I seemed unwilling to make tough life decisions, and to show her who I was as a man—which included my emotions and sexuality—and thus, she didn't feel safe committing to a relationship with me. I seemed far more concerned about my mother's feelings than Diana's.

My indecisive responses were not what she needed.

Today, I am not surprised by my emotional paralysis. I was still in the grip of trauma, to which I had responded by trying to control every aspect of my world, suppressing my emotional urges. I was desperate to take charge of my life.

I came from a family that had no power in our community, a family that struggled to stay afloat financially. What had allowed me to access power was my reputation. Desperate to protect it, I didn't have the bandwidth to consider Diana's needs. I was stuck in my world. This had at first appeared exotic to Diana, but as she saw its toxic effects on my life, she had come to realize that if she joined it to be with me, it would destroy her autonomy.

There was no chance this would happen.

I, on the other hand, was torn by the choice she was forcing on me, and angry at her for putting such conditions on our relationship. I simply wasn't free to leave, I thought. When I first met her, I was fascinated by the freedom in her world. Now I realized I couldn't satisfy her demands—not without giving up everything I had worked so hard to earn.

So, at Christmas, I took the safe way out. I retreated behind the rigid strictures of my community and told Diana that any woman I married would need to wear a covering.

And just like that... our summer romance was over.

I didn't realize it at the time, but my problem was very simple. I had only one lens through which I viewed the Bible: my father's literalist one. I didn't yet understand that there were different lenses that were necessary to make sense of the contradictory teachings across Scripture. Until I gained the use of those lenses, nothing about my world would ever make sense.

Thus, I concluded that my community must be right, even if it frustrated me.

I had decided to break up with Diana after following a methodical, decision-making process, first writing a research paper analyzing our lifestyle, and then doing a cost-benefit analysis of our relationship. I had weighed the advantages of staying with a woman I loved against the possibility of losing an entire network of friends, and I had made a brutally logical decision. Even though my heart had wanted Diana, I had chosen my community.

The decision was logical—and utterly wrong.

Today, I grieve the hurt I caused Diana. She had taken a risk in dating me and had done everything she could to support me. Very much in touch with her emotions, she had tried to be understanding and give me the space I needed to decide. Ultimately, for her efforts, she had gotten only pain.

Fearing what I didn't understand, afraid that my community might be right, I was the Cowardly Lion who lacked the courage to follow my heart, choosing instead to stay safely inside my community. Diana's mother had been dead-on accurate:

I *was* caught between two worlds.

Chapter 14: A Way Out

"Congratulations."

This first word of the letter I received in January 1988 changed my life. Mr. Alan Coleman, the District Foundation Chairman in Essex, England, was awarding me a Rotary Foundation Scholarship to attend Richmond College in Kensington, London. Of the five college choices I had listed in my scholarship application, this was my first choice. It was a big deal. Out of the four hundred scholars they'd chosen to study in the British Isles, only sixteen would be sent to London—and I was one of them.

I burst into the house and excitedly read the congratulatory letter to my family. My siblings were happy for me, even proud. But they eyed my parents nervously, and for good reason. Neither was about to offer me their blessing.

My father reacted by leaving the room, heading down to the garage to work on one of our cars. I knew he didn't approve because he was never good at keeping his feelings to himself. He expressed his anger in various ways. When I was a child, he had used his hand or a stick to get me to comply with his directives. Now that I was stronger than my father, he could only blow frustration at me, and since I was no longer afraid of him, that didn't work either. I simply blew up at him in return.

My mother was a different story.

Even before I entered first grade, my mother had learned how stubborn I could be. I had her determined nature. But since childhood, she had used her warm attention to shape my behavior. This had fed my self-worth, making me dependent upon her approval. Since she was the most powerful presence in any room—usually cheerful and friendly to everyone, the parent everyone adored— I loved it when she confided in me. Enjoying her trust inspired me to be the best person I could be, and a compliment from her had me floating on air.

But my mother knew how to control me, as well. When I was a child, she had quickly learned that by withdrawing the warmth of her pride in me—using "the silent treatment"—she could let me know without saying a word that she disapproved of whatever I was about to do. She hated arguing with anyone. Since unlike my father, she had never had much success through physical punishment, remaining silent was now the only way to get my attention.

But we would eventually talk about the scholarship I had won. I knew that as surely as I knew the sun would rise. And when we did, I needed to know why I was going. Otherwise, I would fold... and my plans to leave would come to naught.

My mother took her time—time while I watched her reactions to see how I could mitigate her disapproval. I might be a man, but even a man cares about what his mother thinks about any life-altering decision he makes. I had learned the hard way not to underestimate her influence. When she finally approached me, I hoped I could explain what this trip meant for me.

To me.

On Saturday, several days after the letter arrived, I was reading the paper… or was pretending to. My mother couldn't be rushed, and I patiently waited until she placed two slices of apple pie between us, along with two cups of coffee, then lowered herself into a chair.

"This scholarship—are you sure you should go?"

I suddenly lost my appetite.

I believed my mother and I shared a closer relationship than any of my other siblings. The times I treated my mother disrespectfully are some of my most painful memories from childhood. Refusing to obey—being disrespectful—to the woman who had birthed me and loved me unconditionally seemed almost blasphemous.

"You're over twenty-one, Steve. I can't stop you from going, but I can worry about you." Mom heaved a sigh. "I'm worried about you being that far away from home, surrounded by young people who live wickedly. They will drink and smoke and dance. Who will encourage you to maintain your purity? The time you spend with worldly girls from your college… it worries me."

I found myself growing defensive, in spite of my determination to keep this conversation focused on the advantages my year abroad would offer me.

"I'm not going abroad to party, Mom," I said. "This year will strengthen my resume. It will allow me to represent Rotary and our country. I'm going to be studying English and history. My favorite authors are British, men like James Herriot and J.R.R. Tolkien and C.S. Lewis. I'll be studying within their world."

I didn't know what else to say. I was trying to give her a reason to support me, but behind her words lay the tears she had shed when Diana and I were dating, the nights when she couldn't sleep while waiting for me to return home. I knew what she wanted for me—marriage to a nice, conservative Mennonite girl. Once that happened, nature and inertia would take their course.

"You may not plan to follow the wrong path, Steve, but I know the way women think. I know how much you enjoy spending time with them. And until you are married, I worry that you will make mistakes that will hurt your reputation."

I knew why she was worried. My mother had begun to see a pattern in my relationships. Diana had turned out to be just a starter romance, and afterward, it was hard to admit that my mother might have been right about her. I had followed that by briefly dating a conservative Mennonite girl—someone who was extremely popular among our young people—but even that romance went south when her parents objected, and I, in anger, decided to end it. Since then, the only women who hung out with me were college classmates, none of whom met my mother's approval.

"I don't think it's possible to please you when it comes to the kind of woman I marry," I said. "You've never approved of anyone I've dated."

"That's not quite true," my mother said, sadly. "When you began seeing that nice girl from our church, I thought you'd found your feet. Even today, I see the way our young people admire and follow you. I think you might eventually be chosen to be a minister... but that will only happen if you settle down with the right woman, someone who will encourage you to love and follow Jesus, rather than the things of this world."

"But don't you see what a great opportunity this is, how it will build my career as a teacher... or whatever I choose to do?" I asked.

"I know all of this," she huffed out her frustration. "I've read the brochures, and you've told me. They're paying for everything. And please know, Dad and I... we are so proud of what you've done as a teacher, as a youth group leader. We don't want you to lose all that. You've worked... so hard... to prove yourself to our community."

She knows I'm breaking away.

There was no way around it. She would never be happy with my decision to leave. Yet I had no choice. If I wished to find my freedom, this trip was necessary, and thus I needed to come to terms with the reality that I was about to disappoint my mother... deeply. I didn't know how to avoid it.

She rose to her feet, giving me an obligatory smile, then returned to her work, cleaning and polishing the kitchen counter. She couldn't hide the concern, her forehead tightening, battening down all the worry inside.

The pie lay untouched on both of our plates.

In spite of my mother's worries, I was genuinely excited about the Rotary Foundation Scholarship I had won. But having never won an academic award before, I needed a roadmap that would allow me to process my success. I swung between the low expectations my community had for me, and the high emotions and flattering attention I was receiving from my professors and peers, who recognized what I had accomplished.

And so, I went through a roller coaster of emotions. When I was feeling emotionally down, I couldn't believe I had won. When my emotions were running high, I was certain the people in my community would be impressed, once they heard about it.

When the word finally got out, it turned out both expectations were right. Within my college community, my peers and professors commended me. But back in my home community, most of the community viewed it as my parents did, with deep suspicion: Why would Steve want to spend a year abroad? Surely nothing good would come of that.

One person's reaction to my success, in particular—a caring youth leader named Freida—encapsulated these feelings. Our conversation occurred at the annual school sale, a community event that raised money for my *alma mater*, where I was still teaching English, part-time, to support myself in college. To my surprise, when I "casually mentioned" the award I had won, Freida didn't even know I had won it.

Standing together at a display table where she was working as a volunteer, sorting clothes, I worked hard to bring her up to speed, explaining why I had been chosen for this prestigious award.

She soon changed the subject. "How is your sister Elaine doing?"

"Oh, fine. We occasionally hear from her."

"Well, please know that I am praying for her. You must find it difficult, all your worries for her. I always thought she had such a nice soprano voice."

It dawned on me then that Freida might be sending me a subtle message. Here I was mentioning my great academic conquest, when in reality I should be worried about my sister Elaine. Clearly, Freida must think me a self-centered fool.

But Freida had done more than remind me of my shortcomings. By bringing up my sister's name—who had brought such shame to our family in the eyes of our community—Freida had also reminded me of the tenuous nature of my own reputation.

I suddenly realized why Freida was unimpressed. She was a fine scholar herself—being named valedictorian of her high school class, having graduated *summa cum laude* from the architectural school of a local university—and yet she had remained a humble leader who volunteered for the school sale. Instead of bragging about her accomplishments, she was thinking about my sister.

Like Freida, my community saw my excitement about winning that scholarship as evidence of pride—the same fatal flaw that caused the angel Lucifer to fall to Hell. For the first time, I appreciated the stretch between my community's expectations and the complexity of pursuing my ambitions. There was no role model I could emulate.

I began to realize how alone I was.

Several months later, I came fully awake in the early morning hours, my breathing short and vicious. Around me, in my dorm room at Malone College, there was silence.

The dreaded nightmare had returned.

I threw off the covers and made my way to the window, staring out at the gleaming track that stretched around the athletic field. The situation between the Soviet Union and the United States was at its most tense, everyone frightened and convinced that nuclear war might be minutes away.

At least I was.

The digital readout on my alarm clock blinked red. 5:12 AM.

Outside my window, bullets of rain shot down. I had not been getting much sleep. Standing there, looking out into the cold, gray dawn, I thought about my absurd dream, the flock of Intercontinental Missiles (ICBMs) heading toward my dorm, the individual missiles burying themselves in the field just outside my window, the brightness of detonation, nuclear Armageddon, my world at its epicenter… destroyed. The dream had brought me awake in a flash.

It makes no sense. I wouldn't even see the missiles coming.

Wide awake, I tried to re-anchor myself.

Sustained breathing came from my roommate, who was dead asleep. He was a star athlete who traveled a lot. At first, I loved the fact that I had my dorm room mostly to myself because I needed time to study and work. But I quickly found that I didn't like living or working alone because the silence was loud and lonely.

Occasionally, late at night, we occupied the same space. When we did, we exchanged stories, me talking about my Amish-Mennonite childhood, which fascinated him, and him describing the drinking parties he and the other jocks were attending off campus. His language was laced with the profane and the obscene, words like *fuck, shit, Jesus Christ, damn.*

My roommate never worried about Heaven or Hell, never woke up frightened when he slept in our dorm, never had nightmares—or if he did, he knew how to ignore them.

I couldn't.

I would awaken, panicked breath tearing aside the veil of sleep, abruptly yanked back into the world of consciousness. I would pad to the window, peering outside, my heart pounding.

They were my first real panic attacks as an adult. At the time, I didn't understand the nightmares. But as I look back on this time in my life—having taken the first step outside my community—I find nothing surprising about this pounding on the basement door of my subconscious.

My crisis was existential. I believed that by leaving, I was abandoning my faith. I was torn by my fears. Was I right to leave? Was I right to accept this scholarship to London? Might this cause me to end up after death in a literal flaming Hell?

Thanks to my classes in psychology and sociology, I had begun to recognize that the overwhelming fear I had had in childhood—causing me to run screaming to my parents for help, telling them "I can't breathe, I can't breathe"—might have been panic attacks. Now I was experiencing nightmares about the end of the world, which made me react in a similar way, spiking my blood pressure. I had begun to wonder if they were all symptoms of the same root fear: by leaving home, I was rejecting God.

Arguing with my father was a form of trauma itself as I was never going to change his mind, and he would never change mine. Once, while walking on

145

campus, I ran into a professor and within our conversation, I ended up opening up to him about my struggles with my father. It was the best thing that could have happened to me at the time. He suggested I find a therapist to help me work through these issues.

I considered it, but I knew it would never work. I tried to imagine such a thing, tried to wrap my mind around the idea. Psychologists helped insane people, and I knew I wasn't insane. And so, I spiritualized what were symptoms of emotional and mental distress, telling myself I just needed spiritual counsel for the journey of faith I was about to take.

I needed to know how I could survive as a Christian while living on a London campus filled with students who were nothing like me. I wanted reassurance that I was strong enough to do it and maintain my faith. And I was looking for someone who could tell me it would be okay, but there was no one who saw or would understand the existential crisis I was facing.

Except, perhaps, one other person…

"I don't know how to deal with my mother." I was back in Janie's office. "I don't know how to fight her."

"Do you need to?"

I did. I had to fight my mother because if I didn't, I'd be giving up and I couldn't do that. I'd never be in control of my own decisions—my own life—if I didn't stand up for myself. What I didn't realize at the time was what this conversation was about.

I was struggling with my parents for control over what I wanted to do in my life (finish my education with a year at a secular college, traveling abroad on this prestigious scholarship), but in actuality, I was fighting to be *in* control of everything around me.

"I suspect your mother has already put you in God's hands, but you're also her firstborn son. You can't unplug that connection easily." Janie set her teacup down. "Your mother sees the world as a fearful place, Steve, but remember, when she was young, she *also* left home. Now, you, too, are refusing to hide within your safe, little community. You're following in her footsteps. She just doesn't realize it yet. Have you thought about keeping the disciplines I discussed with you?"

I remembered the book she had suggested, *Celebration of Discipline: The Path to Spiritual Growth* (HarperSanFrancisco, 1978), by evangelical pastor and teacher Richard Foster. I had scanned through it, taking in its argument that the traditional disciplines of faith, like prayer and meditation, were essential to spiritual growth.

"I'm keeping a journal." I shrugged. "That's kind of like talking to God, right?"

"You might want to consider a more classic form of prayer," Janie said, and I realized she was amused. "You need more than just your own thoughts, Steve. You need a relationship with God, one that only comes through time spent with Him, in order to get through your year away from home. You don't have any control over what you are about to face. You never have. That's how a journey of faith—the one that you are about to take—works."

I realized that she wasn't talking about the trip I was going to take to London. Janie, more than anyone, saw my desires because she had created a safe space in her office where I could be vulnerable with her, and she realized the journey I was about to take—moving out into the secular world where I would be a very small fish in a very large pond—was a spiritual and emotional one, rather than intellectual. Perhaps she knew that I was ultimately looking for a way out of my insular community, although I don't think I ever told her.

Most importantly, Janie knew that I would struggle with having *no* control over my surroundings in London among people who were unlike anyone I had grown up with. And although she was worried about me, the arc of our conversation across the years tells me that she was also confident I would find my way.

Only after I left my family behind, only after I met my grandfather at the airport and allowed him to show me how to tie a tie, only after I headed down the passageway into the plane, did I realize how alone I was. The sudden absence of any familiar voice left me in a vacuum.

It hit me then like a dam breaking, terror flooding over me. I paused for a moment, frozen, other people moving past me.

No one I knew would see me for the next nine months.

Over the last year, I had thought such freedom would be energizing. I had always dreamed of how wonderful it would be to be on my own, with no one looking over my shoulder. Now, having left my community behind, I expected to revel in the ensuing rush of freedom, to feel pure joy washing over me, to realize in full that I could do whatever I wished and be whatever I wanted to be.

But no.

Instead of being empowered by that feeling, paralysis gripped me. I stood alone in the passageway leading to the plane, scared that I'd get on the first plane back because I might find the world too big. Too loud. The people too sinful.

I breathed, slowly, mentally talking myself down off the ledge, just as I had in those mornings when I came out of my nightmares, overwhelmed by terror. I had planned for this, I had prayed for this. I heard in my head Janie's calming words: "God is with you, Steve."

I was not turning back.

I forced my legs to begin moving again, joining the line of people heading down the passageway toward the plane door. I was sure they could read my mind, but apparently, they couldn't. No one looked at me twice.

As I entered the plane, an efficient stewardess welcomed me, a smile on her face.

"Welcome." She touched my arm. "Enjoy your flight."

Her voice came to me as though under water. I stumbled up the aisle, peering at the seat numbers. The cabin around me slowly filled, dissipating her floral scent.

A short time later, I sat in my seat, the belt tightly cutting into my stomach. Nausea moved up my throat. Sounds of a child's sharp cry, a woman's low voice hushing it, compartment doors slamming closed. Smells of the aging vinyl seats, bright lights in the cabin flickering on and off, the airplane's engines rumbling to life.

There was the sound of the captain's voice over the intercom. The wheels bumped along as I gripped the arms of my seat, frightened out of my mind. I hoped I was making the right decision. I prayed to God, not the Angry God of my father, but Someone I was only beginning to see through the past year's fog of fear. I prayed that I might have the strength to transform into what I knew I needed to become in the next year. I prayed as I fled the community I now deeply distrusted.

I was heading off on a journey of faith, trusting that somehow my view of God and the world was somehow correct. I struggled with guilt.

In the past few years, as I had led my community through music and teaching, I had grown to appreciate their kindness, their strong support for me, which showed in the kind remarks they made to me after my speech in church laying out my vision of myself as an ambassador for Christ for the upcoming year.

I was making this journey alone, and as Janie had pointed out, I was literally going by faith, finding it impossible to predict where my path would lead. Perhaps I would find that the world was a dark and scary place and would wish to return. Perhaps I would be sucked into the world's temptations and reject my faith in God. Or perhaps—and this was my hope—I would find a way to maintain my faith while living within the dark and scary world I was about to enter, ultimately deciding to leave my community and embrace a lifestyle that allowed me to practice a more authentic faith within that world.

Had I been dishonest by not telling them this?

All of these scenarios were real possibilities, yet when I talked about the upcoming year to my family and community, I hadn't shared these crucial doubts, probably because I didn't want them to worry about whether I would survive.

I had confidently announced that I intended to be an ambassador for Christ to the outside world. I didn't mention that this might mean I would be leaving our culture, entirely, never to return.

But in fact, that's exactly what I hoped to do.

Book IV: Anger

Bring me my bow of burning gold:
Bring me my arrows of desire:
Bring me my spear: O clouds unfold!
Bring me my chariot of fire!

~ William Blake
"Jerusalem," from *Preface to Milton: A Poem*," 1810

Interpolation IV: The Body Remembers

In 2011, the psychologist Marlene Winell argued that religious abuse can manifest as a type of Post-Traumatic Stress Disorder (PTSD). This occurs when religious abuse is acute, chronic, and complex, creating Religious Trauma Syndrome (RTS).

The body remembers.

My experience with corporal punishment—which my father believed the Bible required of parents—was not a one-off. I experienced it again and again, both at home and at school. I observed it used on others, again and again. There was no place in my world where I felt safe from it, except perhaps in the library. The abuse was acute, chronic, and complex.

The shame attached to this type of discipline is a close cousin to the shame people feel about being sexually molested. In both cases, the victim—unless they have been taught otherwise—believes that it is their fault, and that they brought it on themselves.

They don't realize that no one has the right to abuse them... ever.

Fortunately, the laws have changed. Educators are trained to be mandatory reporters, and trauma counselors help victims process their shame and protect their privacy. But because this kind of shame is complicated and sticky, it still takes exceptional courage to seek out help.

As I was growing up, this shame generally kept me and my peers from talking to each other about it. After all, when we were older and more mature, we would see the value of such discipline. The memories of our pain and humiliation would fade, leaving only the moral lessons.

Sorry to disagree, Unnamed Relative, but it isn't that simple. Ask your own children.

The body remembers.

As I left for London, I was determined to forget the abuse I had experienced. But I didn't reckon on the trauma, which is defined as the body's reaction to the abuse. It cannot be wished away. I was about to turn twenty-five, and many of my peers were raising children of their own, using on them the same parenting techniques they had experienced. That's just what you did.

I couldn't bring myself to take that route. But that didn't mean I would escape the past. The memories of humiliation, the memories of pain, were locked within the cells of my body. These memories fused with my growing need for control, my reading, and my imagination, shaping my most powerful sexual fantasies.

151

I didn't realize this was a manifestation of the trauma now simmering within me, which was building into a classic case of RTS. No one in my world had any knowledge of this, nor did they recognize its symptoms. I didn't even dream of seeking therapeutic help. The only information I could glean was found in the raciest romance novels or in boutique porn magazines that catered to BDSM, an acronym that refers to the world of Bondage & Discipline, Dominance & Submission, and Sadism & Masochism—all forms of power exchange within sex.

I was completely unaware of the long-term consequences of my abuse.

Chapter 15: The Gift of Yourself

When I think back over my year abroad, there's a moment that encapsulates the challenge I faced in attempting to assimilate into the outside world. It happened on a night when friends took me dancing at a club for the first time. I was not yet drinking alcohol, so I couldn't count on it for courage, but eventually, I ventured out alone onto the dance floor.

As I stood there with music pounding through my body, the foreign smells of sweat and cheap perfume and cigarettes surrounding me, I wondered how to move. Completely exposed, I just *knew* everyone was watching me, even laughing at me.

How am I supposed to act?

Is this dance move okay?

Is that one?

As I stood there paralyzed with self-consciousness, trying to decide what to do, I realized the truth: the people around me were drinking, talking, and flirting—lost in their own agendas—barely seeing me. When I arrived back at my group, I found no one there had noticed my uncertain dancing either.

No one gave a shit.

Part of my reaction occurred because I was coming out of a community where vulnerability was discouraged. Part of it was me trying to deal with trauma I didn't even recognize. Part of it was because I was so self-absorbed that I didn't have the mental bandwidth to see other people around me. Like a child in a cradle, all I could see was myself—my feet, my hands—what *I* was experiencing.

The result was social isolation. Friendship, never mind romance, requires the courage to reach out, to have the courage to be vulnerable, and I had withdrawn into a shell, trying to protect myself. Worst of all, I was so self-absorbed that I couldn't see that everyone else had the same fears. One of my peers, who eventually became one of my closest friends in London, said to me recently, "I was just as scared and out of my depth as you were, Steven. None of us had it figured out."

When I arrived at Richmond College, I found out that my peers spoke an entirely different *cultural* language. All the social rules I'd followed carefully in my conservative Mennonite community didn't work in London; I couldn't fit in. Even though I'd abandoned the Plain coat and dressed like everyone else, people saw me as different.

Part of my problem was that my college wasn't made up of British students—it was dominated by American exchange students who came from

East Coast colleges for their requisite semester abroad. While I took my studies seriously, they used their time outside of class to party across Europe since none of their grades transferred—just the credits. They also lived in a different universe, one shaped by Hollywood values. I had little experience with film or television. I hadn't seen *Star Wars*, I didn't know how to moonwalk, and I believed Madonna was someone Catholics prayed to.

I didn't want to be an outsider. I was determined to find a place in the modern world where I, as a Christian, could influence society. Remaining on the fringes was not for me. I just needed to find the path.

I found that path after listening to a lecture in Drama as Literature. Professor Michael Richard was a riveting speaker with a genuine passion for teaching and a charismatic smile that made you feel you were the most important person in the room. With his authentic British accent, Michael told such incredible stories of his life as an actor that I felt compelled to stop and talk to him.

"I really enjoyed your lecture. I directed a short play for middle school students a year ago, and they... I mean I... really loved it," I said.

As the drama director, Michael was always on the hunt for male actors.

"You should sign up for my directing class," he said, smiling warmly. "We're doing the coolest French play this semester, *La Machine Infernale*. I think there's a role that might be right for you. Go see your counselor."

My heart skipped a beat because I had never dreamed I would have a chance to act on stage in London. That seemed way too exotic for me—I had been planning to study English and history. But my counselor was efficient. By late afternoon, I was entering the studio down the street where Michael would be teaching the class and directing the fall show.

In the first week, he held auditions for the fall play, an adaptation of the Oedipus myth. Everyone in the class would audition.

To my surprise, Michael cast me as Oedipus, the romantic lead.

This was *major*. Clearly, Michael thought I had talent. Over the next few days, my entire vision for the year shifted. Originally, I had planned to study English and history, but now I saw my future differently. Here in London, I had a chance to get involved in the theater scene.

I had fallen in love with the theater during that exciting week in Stratford with Diana, and now, watching a professional at work, I realized there was nothing I wanted more than to be a director. I was born for the theater, I concluded. If nothing else, as a high school English teacher, I could direct as an extracurricular activity. This year would give me the experience I needed.

And so, I agreed to play the lead.

As the cast began their work on the play, Michael explained that he intended to explore the decadence of our society, which shows up in the way power corrupts leaders, especially religious ones.

Over the next few weeks, as part of our character work, I shared with my director about the fundamentalist world of my childhood. Michael began to question what my religious leaders were like, and upon hearing my answers, he told me he saw me as a young man in full rebellion against my religious culture, and their corrupt leaders. I should be able to easily relate to Oedipus, because in the play, he faces the exact same struggle.

"You're the perfect Oedipus," he said. "You're playing an innocent, naïve young man facing unparalleled corruption."

As Michael and I continued to work together, he began to share with me about his own past. Our first conversation about this occurred one night after rehearsal, when the cast ended up in the warm, yeasty world of one of the local pubs, and I joined Michael at his table, where several of the cast were drinking with him. As our conversation shifted to religion, they disappeared.

I was curious about something he had said in class about his background, so, I asked him what his experience with religion had been like as a child. He told me about his own world, vividly sketching out the South African community where he had first tasted the bitterness of religion, an evangelical and Anglican version of faith. It promoted apartheid and white supremacy.

Michael hated everything his religion chanted. With the world of theater, Michael had found a glittering pathway out. He had embraced a powerful belief in equality and fairness and had rejected segregation and racial intolerance. Now, to his surprise, he had run into me, someone who shared a similar religious past, someone also eager to escape his home community.

"I just don't know how," I said.

Michael lit a cigarette. "I came to the conclusion, years ago, that there is no God."

"But how did you come to that conclusion?" I asked. "How did you leave your community?"

"I just left. The minute I turned eighteen, I was gone. That's what you're doing over here as well, right?"

"I think I'm in a different place," I said. "I think... I'm leaving my culture—but I don't intend to toss out my faith."

An ironic look came into his eyes. "So, you're going to be a preacher, Steven? Am I going to be your first convert?"

I laughed. "No. You have every right to your own beliefs. I hate the way my community shoves religion down other people's throats."

"Well, on that we can agree."

"But I'm still curious," I said. "How did you feel when you escaped? Did you feel guilty?" He gave me a suspicious look, so I hastened to reassure him. "I have mixed feelings about leaving *my* community. I'm not saying I feel guilty... I just don't know how to deal with the changes I'm going through."

Michael stubbed out his cigarette in the ash tray.

"I've never felt guilt. It's a waste of energy. This life you have... here...

right here?" Michael tapped the table with his car keys. "'This is it,' I decided. And it was a fuckin' relief to know that. I was glad to get rid of something I couldn't believe, anyway."

Moments later, I stood outside the pub, watching Michael fold his lanky form into his black Fiero. He gave me his signature wave and roared away. I stared after him, envying him for his assurance.

Michael seemed happy here in London. He wasn't that much older than me—maybe ten years—but he was fulfilling the kind of life I was beginning to think I wanted: teaching students and directing shows. Most importantly, I could tell he was passionate about what he did. Spending time with him was inspiring.

How do I tap into that same passion?

Wouldn't it be easier just to let it all go—what I've been taught?

All my life, people had been telling me what to do and who I should be. When was I going to quit doing what my community wanted me to do and go after what I wanted? It suddenly became clear, something that had been hovering on the edge of my consciousness.

For the first time, here in London, I had the freedom to figure out who I was. Did I truly believe what my parents, my community, my college had taught me? Did I want to follow their life plan?

I need to figure out what I really want out of life.

Knowing that would allow me to plan the rest of my life. If I knew what I wanted, and if I could find the courage to ignore what my community thought, this year would be worth it.

Outside of the theater, however, I was experiencing great frustration since I seemed unable to make real friends, especially guys I could spend time with. I missed my wide network of close friends, any of whom I could call on the phone and just… talk.

Here in London, that wasn't an option. The cost of calling people in the States was high, approximately three dollars a minute. So, I began writing letters. In addition, I began a monthly newsletter, approximately five or six pages, single-spaced, that I sent to the mother of my construction boss, who had become a supportive friend. After making copies, she would send them out by mail to almost 150 people each month. My London address was in the heading, and I soon received lots of mail, with people that I barely knew responding as the letters were passed around conservative Mennonite communities across the States.

Those letters didn't help me integrate with my peers in London—instead, the time I spent reading and responding to them, sitting alone in my room, kept me from spending time making *new* friends who could have given me needed support with empathy and a listening ear.

I could have found them in places like the Common Room, where a range of students hung out, playing games and even watching movies. I could have wandered down to one of the local pubs. I could have struck up conversations with anyone, something I excelled at doing. I might have even attended a local evangelical church similar to my community (without the Plain rules I didn't like), making friends there.

But that's not what I did. Absorbed in my feelings, I went to my classes alone, not bothering to talk to people. I went out to the theater in the evenings. When I returned, I wrote letters home, letting my worried friends know once again how unhappy I was. Climbing into bed alone, I put on my headphones and turned into my pillow, tears streaming down my cheeks, listening to soulful Christian artists.

At one point, I wrote in my journal:

The world is so big and doesn't care about its inhabitants. For an individual accustomed to being surrounded by loving, caring friends, facing a world like this can be very traumatic. I was warned about culture shock, but no warnings can really prepare anyone for this. I am so frustrated by my loneliness and inability to relate to the world.

I failed to realize that I didn't need to get lost inside my head at that critical point in my life—I needed friends who were physically present to fuel and balance me. Since mine were at home, I needed to get out and make new ones, as I had always done before. But the voices of my community were still trapped inside my head, telling me how wicked the people around me must be. And by withdrawing into isolation, those were the only voices I was hearing.

Never had I felt this alone.

My isolation had begun to affect my work in the theater. Knowing my inexperience, Michael encouraged me to work more collaboratively with the cast. He encouraged me to become more vulnerable.

"Truth can only be found and played when the actor has the courage and confidence to be vulnerable. Being afraid to try things shuts down creativity. The purpose of rehearsal is to take risks and try new ideas. You must be willing to make mistakes."

For the first time, I was being exposed to the creative process, which forces an artist to confront their fears head-on. I needed to quit worrying about *what people thought*, Michael taught me. I needed to embrace mistakes, without embarrassment, as a way to grow. It was essential to make one mistake after another in rehearsals, because only then I could eventually fumble my way to the most truthful way of playing a scene, which would create a moment that was transformative.

This was a new concept.

I had grown up in a community where mistakes were considered sin. As a leader in my community, I had learned to be very careful about what I did, even breaking up with Diana. I worried constantly about what people thought, since at home I had believed that having a spotless reputation was the source of my power.

Now Michael was asking me to change my approach.

It was at this point when our director had us play a game during rehearsal. It was intended to help us get to know the character we were playing. One by one, Michael had us take a turn in the hot seat in the center of a circle, and fellow cast members could ask us any question they wanted about our character. We were to answer in the voice of that character.

When it was my turn, the cast fired questions at me about my character, but then—perhaps because I was a brand-new actor who had a hard time differentiating between me and my character—the questions shifted.

How does your Amish family feel about you living here? Do they talk to you about the clothes you are wearing? Do they have problems with you kissing girls on stage? Do they worry you might not come back?

I struggled to respond. These were exactly the questions I feared. Michael could have stepped in and redirected them, but he let me struggle, perhaps realizing that this was exactly what I really wanted to talk about. He also knew that I desperately needed to connect with my castmates.

And then, in the midst of their questions—suddenly, I snapped. I didn't care that I might hurt their feelings, since obviously, I thought, they didn't give a shit about mine. "Most of you assume you know all about my world—you think I'm Amish, for example. I'm not."

As I explained to them about my world—about the way we were separated from society—they sat listening raptly, as if watching an exotic creature in a zoo, fascinated by a world that was commonplace to me.

"I'm fairly sure my community is praying that I will *not* succeed here," I told the cast. "They want me to come home with my tail between my legs. Yeah… my mother sends me letters all the time filled with Bible verses, reminding me to keep myself pure, sexually. I'm sure my father believes I am going to Hell."

But as I explained this to the cast, in my head, I was struggling with the real issue: letting go of the past and living in the present. With all the skills I had in talking to people, I was clueless about how to connect with them… here.

Yes, people were friendly to me here in London. But by the time I'd finish my first conversation with someone… usually a desperate, confusing ramble about my faith journey… any chance of a friendship was gone. People didn't see me as someone cool they'd like to get to know better. I was a boutique specimen, not a potential friend… or even a lover.

None of my peers were interested in the spiritual storm I was experiencing. They were on a party semester in London and just wanted to get on with having a good time. They turned to talk to people who were interested in *them*.

But I too wanted to live the normal life of an exchange student—I just couldn't figure out how. Why did I keep choosing that line of conversation when the same result occurred every time? Why couldn't I just *change* and focus on having a good time?

"I'm twenty-five years old," I told the cast, having gotten into the weeds of my community, yet *again*. I wondered if I had lost them, but they were strangely attentive. "I can't seem to figure out my life—I don't know what I'm going to do when I return home to Ohio in June."

I stopped, finally. I was all out.

Michael was sitting beside me. "If you don't like the community you've come from, why can't you just leave, Steven?"

"I don't know."

But I did know. I was scared to death of my community's judgment.

Michael put a warm hand on mine.

"Steven, if there is one gift I hope to give you this year, it will be the gift of yourself. To be what you are—not what your parents or community wants you to be—but what you are, and *who* you are."

He had been saying this to me, in one way or another, all semester. Yet, that night was the first time I truly heard what he was trying to say to me.

After that conversation, I returned to rehearsals with a freedom I had never felt before. And the cast responded. I had already shown I could be trusted to deliver on the role I had been cast to do, and they respected my hard work: I had spent all of our fall break working on my role.

I had come through for the cast.

But it took the first night of the show for me to realize how much things had changed. During our first performance, with a full house including my professors and college peers, there was a moment when I got distracted and totally forgot my lines. It happened during the Wedding Night scene, and my blood pressure spiked as I turned to face my Queen.

I know now this is bound to happen to a new actor, but at that point, I had no experience on stage, and I had never experienced anything so frightening as my mind going completely blank, the silence growing in the intensity of a packed theater.

But my fellow actor handled it like a pro. Seeing the fear in my eyes, she skillfully fed me just enough lines to get me past the rough patch. When I thanked her afterward, she had tossed it off as just business.

"It happens to everyone," she said.

For her, it might have been just another night in the theater, but for me, it was everything: I realized I could trust my cast mates.

What next happened, I couldn't have predicted. Thanks to the openness I had showed, and perhaps my improved performance, my castmates responded. Any time I went offstage, preparing for my next scene, I found one of my castmates waiting.

"You're kicking ass," one of the guys said, giving me a friendly slap on the back.

One of the girls hugged me. "You're rocking this."

Each time I exited, I'd find another castmate giving me an affirmative touch or compliment. I began to relax, charged by the attention I was getting, and suddenly, I realized that I really was, as Michael had described, "inhabiting" my role.

And at the end of our last performance, for the first time, the audience gave us a standing ovation, my castmates clapping as I came out for my final bow, with me cheering them in response. But at that point, I didn't know why.

What just happened?

It took me years to understand that the shift had occurred when I finally had the courage to open up to the group. For the first time, I had dropped my emotional barriers, which had allowed me to connect with my peers.

This had had everything to do with the trauma that was driving my life. Until then, I thought I was going through culture shock, but in reality, I was doing what I had been doing for years in an emotional crisis—numbing my emotions. That worked well in our restrictive community where few men showed emotion, thanks to our German background, an ethnicity known for emotional coldness toward strangers.

But in our theater cast, in which emotional openness is valued, my inability to express my true emotions came off as arrogance and standoffishness. As people responded negatively to this, it became a vicious cycle, keeping me from interacting empathetically with my cast mates. As one of them told me years later, she saw me that semester as *sincere* and *serious*. This is a polite description of someone who is not emotionally available.

To top it off, I had not yet begun to drink alcohol, which meant there was *never* a time when I let down my guard. Thus, no one got to know me well.

And so, when I first entered the theater, I trusted no one. Thanks to the fears my community had implanted, I saw everyone else as non-Christian and worldly. I was suspicious of male authority figures because of my experience with abuse. I was suspicious of those I saw as non-Christian, even though—as I discovered later—most of them would have described themselves as Christians (although not fundamentalist). I was especially suspicious of my director, probably because I wasn't used to teachers who used praise and affirmation to work with talent. Thus, I put deliberate distance between me and the entire company.

All of this had changed when I shared with the cast what I was really thinking, cracking the emotional barrier between us.

It is ironic that I walked into the theater believing that acting was hypocritical. In reality, my experience that semester taught me that actors need to be completely in touch with their emotions so that they are able to use them— like a painter uses color in creating an image on canvas—to help the audience feel the emotions their character is feeling. You cannot do that unless you are able to be utterly vulnerable with an audience.

But I would not make this connection for years.

I had also learned something important. In sharing with the cast, I had given up control, I had trusted other people, and I had found support. I felt safe with my castmates. It helped me realize that I might be ready to take the next step, a choice that would force me to confront my greatest fear.

Drinking alcohol.

Chapter 16: The Most Basic Rule

In London, I discovered one of the secrets to connecting with people lay in the lowly cigarette. It was a conversation opener. People smoked in pubs, in the Tube, even in the hallways of the dorm. If you chose to smoke, it was considered good courtesy to offer a cigarette to others. The act of smoking was sacramental, a physical manifestation of communion in London's modern, urban culture. It created instant intimacy.

The other secular sacrament was alcohol.

Unlike my father, I had long believed drinking was not a sin. I'd often pointed out to my father that Jesus had no problem drinking wine and hanging out with people who drank. Now I also saw, during Rotary events, that alcohol also allowed you to connect with others.

But I didn't know if my body was cut out to handle alcohol. So, for the first three months, I paid extra to purchase nonalcoholic drinks, even when I went on pub crawls intended to help students connect with their peers.

On one of these events, I was walking in a crowd between pubs when I became aware of Mia, a young woman whose blue eyes and seductive face were framed by a rich mane of golden hair. I had been charmed with her languid New Orleans drawl, several pubs back, when we had introduced ourselves. Now, she had joined me as the entire herd migrated through a backstreet.

What impressed me most about Mia was her ability to smoke. It took me a good five minutes to even realize she was doing this, holding her cigarette down at her side with two perfectly manicured fingers, blowing a shapely funnel of smoke from the far corner of her mouth.

It was downright sexy.

Mia's sophistication proved her to be a creature of the World. I was particularly fascinated by her background. Like me she had grown up in a conservative world, but unlike me, she hailed from a wealthy home in New Orleans.

She was familiar with rules, and she must have known what it was like to struggle against a rigid, unreasoning culture. We had that in common, I thought. But unlike me, Mia appeared to have no hesitation in dumping her home-town restraints, and clearly, no concerns about drinking alcohol. As we talked and walked across the next two pubs, she managed to put down two pints.

When I walked her to her room, she giggled at one of my silliest jokes. She seemed to be everything I wanted in a girl. But when we arrived at her room, she didn't invite me in, and I didn't have the courage to move in for a kiss.

I don't want to spoil what we have by rushing things.

Afterward, I walked home in a daze.

A few days later, my Rotary host, Richard Cook, called to let me know our Rotary Club in Harrow was planning their fall dinner and dance. It would be a formal event, and I should bring a date.

I asked a friend, but she couldn't make it, suggesting I take Mia, instead. I was more than happy when Mia agreed to go. When I next ran into my friend, she mentioned that Mia had gone all-out, spending a small fortune on a little black dress.

Message received. This date was a *big deal* for Mia.

On the night of the dance, I waited for Mia at the entrance to Richmond College. Moments later, she appeared, a vision in blonde hair, black velvet, and sparkling blue eyes. As we took the cab to the tube station, I admired her earrings: black roses with a hanging pearl suspended in a delicate gold wire basket. Her elegant fragrance veiled the acrid scent of cigarette smoke.

When we arrived, Mia met my hosts, charming them with her beauty and intelligence. Having her beside me made me proud. As we danced, Mia's fingers lightly touched my arms, her body working with mine to improve my dancing.

During dinner, older couples kept dropping by our table to meet her. When I went to the bar to pick up a drink for her, the men who knew me best made a point of telling me how much they admired my taste in women. Afterward, as she kissed Richard and Joan Cook goodbye, I wondered what it would take to win her. The night was perfect.

On the train ride back to college, Mia confided in me that she was trying to choose her father's birthday gift. Her mother had given him a yacht last year, and she wanted my advice on what to get someone who had everything he wanted.

"Why don't you buy him something simple?" I asked.

"What do you mean?"

"I don't think it's the cost that matters," I said. "Your gift just needs to demonstrate that you are thinking about him, and that you love him."

Her eyes lit up. "You're right. I can't believe I didn't realize that." She grabbed my hand and squeezed it, and it made my heart skip a beat.

She moved in against me, there in the crowded subway car, and I found myself dazed by her trust in me, the potential we had for a relationship. But it was the last meaningful conversation we had.

That night, when I dropped her off at her dorm room, she smiled, reaching for me with both hands, but at the last moment—our entire conversation about her father's wealth flashed through my mind—I turned the moment into a quick hug, then turned and left.

Afraid to take a chance, I choked.

Our conversation about her father had been the moment when the power of my past slammed into me. It was one thing to leave home with the support of your family and all its resources backing you, like Mia; it was another to leave with no resources to lean on.

Unlike Mia, I was entirely on my own. She had the power to make a phone call and have enough cash wired to her to buy an expensive dress for a formal dance with a guy she had just met. My family, on the other hand, was struggling just to get by.

Mia's world of wealth and privilege was foreign to me. Even if Mia fell in love with me, I would never fit into her world. Although I carried myself confidently, and appeared to come from affluence, in reality, I was simply a chameleon. Once Mia and her family realized I was an imposter, she would discard me.

That was the moment when I quit attending pub crawls. I didn't enjoy partying, I told myself, since that meant watching people have fun (since I couldn't seem to relax and just be). All I seemed to think about at events like this was the fact that I *wasn't* drinking. My ability to connect with people—to make people feel comfortable through attentive questions that made them open up to me—had disappeared, perhaps because their lives seemed so different.

What I didn't realize was that my social conditioning was formed within Christian youth group meetings, which are relatively quiet, and where conversation skills are valued. Here in England, I was mostly hanging out with American students from the East Coast, who brought the noise and chaos of their college bar culture with them. Learning how to flirt—meaning, not taking anything seriously—was essential, and for a guy, being quick to buy a girl a drink was important. In other words, being able to dominate socially was the key to getting what you wanted. Having a wing man, or even a group of buddies to watch your back and support you, was crucial to having fun.

I didn't understand any of this.

What eventually separated me from the pack is that I had so little in common when it came to our values. Most of the exchange students at Richmond seemed to be there for a party semester, whereas I was there to study and to learn. They seemed to have the express purpose of getting trashed and getting laid—they weren't interested in real conversation, I concluded. In addition, the fact that I was obviously *not* a drinker made me feel uncomfortable with them, and since I'm not good at hiding my feelings, that made them uncomfortable.

Because of this, I turned to a less expensive option that I loved—attending theater productions, often shows Michael recommended in our drama class. On any day of the week, I could purchase an excellent ticket for about five quid, and, for two or three hours, lose myself in the best theater of the Western World. But sitting alone, surrounded by people I didn't know, wasn't the same as spending time with friends who could practically read my mind, and after the show, I'd return to my dorm alone, listening wistfully to the sounds of fun going on around me, wondering why I couldn't seem to connect with my peers.

But to do that, you need to find shared values, which I thought was impossible, since I divided the world into Christians and *non*-Christians. You also need to like people around you, which I didn't think I could do, since I had been taught since childhood that people who drank were *drunks*.

What I desperately needed was a peer mentor, who could help me understand the world around me and help me change to meet its cultural expectations.

Occasionally, I ran into Mia, who had integrated effortlessly into the campus culture. We hadn't really done anything together since the night of the formal dance, but she seemed happy and was always surrounded by friends. I envied her popularity and ability to leave her world behind.

I might have eventually tried to connect with her at some point, perhaps even tried to become friends with her, except for a story I heard about her.

I was at breakfast in our communal dining hall when I overheard some jocks at a nearby table talking.

"Have you heard about Mia?"

The guy talking had been out on a pub crawl the night before, when he ran into her. She had been drinking a lot and needed help getting home. By the time he got Mia back to her dorm, she'd been too drunk to stand. So, he undressed her, put her to bed, copped a feel, and then left.

Or so he said.

I sat there, shocked by his casual recitation of sexual molestation (and possibly rape), listening with increasing disgust to his story about a young woman who several weeks ago had seemed perfect, a young woman who was now an object of humiliation to his two buddies, and, although I was at the next table, me.

The guys finished breakfast and left. I remained hunched over the remains of my fake eggs and sausage, my brain spinning. I had held this beautiful young woman in awe.

How could I have been impressed with her? How could she have been so stupid? How could she have fallen to this?

Our patriarchal world put all the responsibility for rape on the woman—it was the *woman's* responsibility to dress modestly so that men wouldn't be tempted by lustful thoughts, rather than the *man's* responsibility to act in a way that is always appropriate and respectful of a woman's freedom to choose.

Thus, instead of focusing my anger at the guy who reported "copping a feel"—but had most likely done far more—I chose to blame Mia.

Today, I am appalled by this victim-blaming. It revealed with crystal clarity the fact that I was still viewing the world through a patriarchal lens, seeing the world as a place where women are the weaker vessel, where women are the cause of man's original sin. In my world, it was no surprise that things happened the way they did: Mia wore provocative clothes, Mia got too drunk to stand, Mia had to be taken home drunk, and thus *Mia* laid herself open to molestation. Of course it was her fault.

Today I know it is *never* the victim's fault. I also understand, sadly, that my reactions revealed the patriarchal lens I still used to view the world. And thus, I'm not surprised by my shortcoming. At the time, I couldn't foresee how much I needed to change.

That night, I wrote to Janie, sharing with her the story of Mia. "How can I even think about dating a girl who chooses to humiliate herself in this way?"

As someone who had guided me away from patriarchal thinking, she must have been horrified by my first reactions in a letter to her. She quickly responded.

You seem distressed by your friend who is becoming drunk often. My first reaction is clinical—this young woman is probably alcoholic and may not have known it because of her background. Her troubles are only beginning unless she looks seriously at the choices she is making. She needs a supportive friend—I hope you'll try to talk to her and be a friend who won't exploit her.

But I couldn't take Janie's advice to show empathy to Mia. My arrogant reactions—honed by years of listening to preachers condemning the *sin* of alcoholism, rather than showing us how to support someone who is struggling with something that is both a disease and is exacerbated by genetic tendencies—were too powerful. And yet, as I read Janie's letter today, I realize that she gave me the right advice, which I refused to take.

Life is not all black-and-white, Steven. People are not all good or all bad, although some are more so than others. This young lady is both a victim and a person who is choosing unwisely. I think you're sad to see the situation because you're seeing exploitation up close. I believe God is saddened by this also.

Today, as I reflect on that time in my life, I realize Janie's letter revealed something else. I couldn't empathize with Mia because I had too little experience living in the world.

I'd been cocooned in my insular culture. Arrogantly, I thought I knew how to follow the community rulebook, but I was new to risk-taking. And my black-and-white approach wasn't working.

I wish I'd done the noble thing and talked to Mia, but I didn't. Instead, I ghosted her. Flat-out ghosted her, knowing—in my ignorance—that she'd been at fault. Today, I cringe at this patriarchal—or, if I call it what it really is: misogynistic—view. I should have been better. Perhaps if I'd had the conviction of my faith, I would have acted like a Christian in this situation. Instead, I blamed her and felt her unworthy to be my friend. The Lord himself only knows what kind of friendship I missed out by doing so.

Back then, I couldn't get past Mia's "sin"—becoming a spectacle, losing control of herself in public, humiliating herself, and, worst of all, I thought, letting a man "take advantage" of her. I didn't recognize that this phrase alone puts the blame for the molestation on the *victim*, rather than the perpetrator.

In spite of my idealistic dreams of trying to be an ambassador for Christ, my actions toward Mia showed that I was anything but that. I wanted a romance that would make me look good, not one based on a genuine friendship. I didn't have the courage—and certainly not the wisdom—to care about someone else who seemed even more confused than I was.

I quickly forgot about Mia—*and* I forgot the most basic rule of the universe—the shit you throw out flies back in your face.

I would quickly remember.

Chapter 17: Stumbling around London

By November, I began to realize that the idea of drinking had become a problem for me. Until then, I had believed that drinking alcohol would only exacerbate my culture shock. But I eventually realized that it was the opposite way around. My disdain for alcohol had become a social barrier, isolating me from my peers. I thought it also might be keeping me from pursuing any kind of romance.

At the heart of my disdain was fear of the unknown. I feared that if I began drinking, I wouldn't be able to stop, turning into an alcoholic. I was like the little kid at a birthday party with a fear of clowns—unable to keep my eyes off the clown. Since all social functions, both in college and during Rotary events, included alcohol, I was unable to relax and socialize with my peers. All I could think about was the clown… er, alcohol.

To top it off, since going out and meeting girls seemed to involve alcohol, it usually led to me having to explain my decision not to drink, which was a real downer. I was torn by the entire situation. My social life, which until then had always been defined by my relationships, simply wasn't working.

Out of this time of emotional turmoil and powerful hormones, I wrote and published a deeply allegorical poem at the end of my October newsletter. In it, the speaker falls in love with a woman, but struggles to act, too intimidated by the sexual marketplace. Like Narcissus, the speaker is overwhelmed by his own pain, too self-absorbed to look beyond himself.

My goal was to use images to unpack a romance that had ultimately failed, causing me great pain. In this allegorical and unrequited romance, the speaker gets drunk on the wine offered but ultimately spills the last of it on the ground outside a flower shop. The romance is loveless.

Unless I intended to destroy my carefully burnished reputation back in the States—and my unconscious clearly intended to do exactly that—I probably should have used a metaphor other than alcohol.

Melted ice cream?

Crushed chocolate?

Wilted flowers?

Any of those would have been sturdy choices. But no, I had to choose *alcohol* as the central image of the poem, which I titled "Spilled Wine."

I stagger drunkenly up the wasted street
Dead leaves kick from my hunched figure

Swirl in stream-like eddies and skip over gaping manholes
Dance with gusts of wind that murmur wild, tuneless love songs.

The most powerful image and phrases in the poem—the "hunched figure" who "staggers drunkenly" up the "wasted street" were gigantic red flags to my community, in their eyes an obvious cry for help. My audience of conservative Mennonites had no interest in my metaphors. I may have intended the speaker to be seen as Narcissus drunk on love, but no one else did. They all read the poem as a confession: Steve is getting drunk and stumbling around London.

A literal interpretation made far more sense—and far juicier gossip.

At home, my mother discussed my poem with our family. She was no literary critic, but she could judge my purple poetry. To her, it was irrefutable proof that her firstborn son had become an alcoholic, wandering the streets of London, having abandoned the faith.

I soon began receiving letters from my readers, and it was clear they believed what my father had taught me as I was growing up: drinking alcohol would cause me to sin, lose control, and lose my salvation, which meant I would go to Hell after I died. My readers clearly agreed with my father, writing to remind me of the apocalyptic consequences of drinking.

I was somewhat amused by these letters, since I hadn't yet begun to drink. I told myself that my readers had simply misread the poem. It wasn't intended to be a confession of sin, but a poem… about unrequited love. And so, I wrote off their concern and condemnation, although their reactions would have crushed me several months prior.

I was no longer listening to readers who wrote to tell me they were "praying for" me. If they wanted to think badly of me, that was their problem. I was six thousand miles away on the other side of the Atlantic Ocean.

As November approached, I reached my goal of waiting three months to drink alcohol. I was mostly through culture shock. Thanks to the friends I had made in the theater, I no longer felt so alone. I doubted I was an alcoholic, since I was able to walk into a pub without craving liquor.

I had also gained confidence. I had adjusted to living in London, I had played the lead in a play, people on campus knew who I was, and my professors loved my work, probably because I rarely did anything but study, since, unlike my peers, I had no money to party across Europe. Now I was curious, perhaps obsessively so, about how my body would respond to alcohol.

Perhaps I should finally try drinking.

It was about that time when Michael invited our directing class to go on a field trip to Stratford-on-Avon, the birthplace of Shakespeare. I thought back to the theater trip I took to Stratford, Ontario, when I fell in love with Diana. That romance still bathed that memory in a rosy glow. Maybe Stratford-on-Avon in *England* was the place to have my first drink.

In addition, my castmates made me feel safe. By then, I had figured out that drinking with a group of friends—in case I got drunk—was far preferable than trying it alone.

So, on the evening of our first day there, after seeing the first show and going out with my group for dinner to a Greek restaurant, I ordered a glass of champagne, making a declaration of independence from my community. I didn't make a big deal of it—after the waitress brought me the glass, I just sipped it curiously. Michael, sitting not far away, looked on with delight, but allowed me to make the experience a private one.

The crisp, bubbly liquid was pleasant, but not as sweet as I expected. It trickled down my throat with a slight burn. I waited for the inevitable craziness that my father had warned me about, but that's not what happened. I had another glass... still no insanity. Then dinner was over, and my friends and I wandered back to our bed-and-breakfast, pleasantly buzzed.

The next time, I drank more. Soon, I was more than matching my friends. At one point, Michael even joked that I had become "a lush." The resulting hangovers were a sort of penance, but once I recovered, I always convinced myself that I would be more careful the next time.

Which, of course, I never was.

What I didn't realize was that drinking alcohol can be done skillfully, without hangovers. But because I grew up in a culture that preached total abstinence (or you become an alcoholic), I didn't realize that you have to *learn* how to drink—not mixing drinks, drinking water between drinks, and learning how food (or the lack thereof) interacts with alcohol.

One night, I found myself lying on a bed that spun in circles. My stomach was nauseous, and my father's warnings echoed in my ears like the strident bells of the sinking *Titanic*. It's one thing to be warned about Hell, it's another thing to feel like you've arrived.

Several weeks after I had begun drinking, I received a letter from a friend of my mother's. "Steve, your mother is afraid you are getting drunk and wandering the streets of London. I'm sure your poem was metaphorical, but perhaps you should let *her* know that."

Shocked, I realized that I hadn't gotten a letter from my mother in weeks. I knew her use of the silent treatment to bring me into line, and my chest tightened with anger. She could play the silent game all she wanted—I was an adult, living in London, and I wasn't about to let her manipulate me into giving up alcohol, just because *she* didn't think Christians should drink. I tried to calm myself, but I couldn't let it go.

I finally called my mother. I told her that yes, I'd begun drinking, and that I was old enough to make my own decisions. My mother didn't say much, but, for weeks, I could not forget the tears in her voice.

After that, I received no letters from her, which filled me with a nagging sense of guilt. But I also felt relief because I no longer had to read her letters that quoted Bible verses and exhorted me to remember who I was as a child of God. They filled me with shame, knowing there was no way I could ever satisfy her.

As I look back on that moment with the distance of time, I wish I had taken a better path in letting my mother know about my changes. My angry phone call hurt her deeply, and I deeply regret my thoughtless words.

During my most difficult moments, I survived by pouring out my heart to my old friend Marlin Miller. In high school, he'd had my back, and here in London, I missed having him as my wingman. Together, we could have figured out my questions. Together, we could have effortlessly built a new friend group.

For this reason, when Marlin called at Thanksgiving to tell me he'd purchased a plane ticket to visit over Christmas, I was ecstatic. Finally, we'd have time to process what had happened over the past four months. I desperately needed a baseline reset.

When I met Marlin at the airport, I relaxed into his hug. Talking with him was like settling beside the warmth of a fireplace I knew. For the first time in months, the world felt right.

As we talked over a meal in a London pub, I ordered a bitter (and then one more). I had wondered at first what Marlin would think of my drinking, but he just joked about how much I had changed. But I noticed he never ordered alcohol, choosing a glass of non-alcoholic cider.

The next two weeks passed quickly as we explored England and Scotland together. We took in several shows, and I introduced him to the friends I'd met, letting him see my world. I was surprised by their complimentary comments about me. I didn't realize they knew me so well.

Marlin affirmed what they said. "I'm not surprised by the way people respond to you," he said. "Clearly, you've been successful here in London."

But there was something Marlin hadn't told me. He had a reason for visiting me.

"A lot of people back home are worried about you," he said, not looking me in the eye, several days before he was scheduled to fly out.

"You mean about my drinking?" I snorted. "Yeah, I got the letters."

"No, it's more than that." His concerned gaze finally landed on me. "They think you should… return home."

"They think I should come home?"

"People are worried."

I wanted to get up, to leave and escape this conversation. "I can't believe you are telling me this," I said. But we were talking past each other.

"It's the changes you've been making," Marlin said. There was a long beat. Then, "They've even purchased your ticket."

My mind reeled, unable to process it all. I'd misread his intentions. The pain hit me then, like a dancer missing a step and stubbing his toe, the pain shooting through my body.

"I'm not going home," I said.

Marlin roughly ran his hands through his hair. "I'm also worried about the changes. You're moving too fast, leaving your friends behind. I don't know how to say this." He chuffed out his frustration. "Do you realize how self-absorbed you've become?"

I shook my head.

How could I explain? Why should I have to? No shit, I was self-absorbed; I was desperately trying to figure out where I fit into this strange new world. My best friend had just told me how successful I had become, and his conclusion was to tell me I should return home?

"It's like all you're focused on is your own changes," Marlin said. "Don't you realize how much listening I've done, and how few questions you've asked about *my* difficulties?"

My mouth dropped open. He was right. I *had* done too much of the talking, *had* taken up all the oxygen. But he should have figured out why I wasn't paying attention to his struggles—the stakes I was facing were existential.

Without looking at my friend, I got up to get another pint of bitter. The pub was almost empty. As I stood at the bar, the afternoon light throwing shadows across the ancient, polished bar, I tried to shove down my anger. Marlin and I had always been so open with each other. Now I felt as if my friend had taken advantage of that vulnerability.

My stubborn belief that I could do this thing, that I could survive on my own out in the world, that I could forge a new identity… all of it had collapsed under the weight of his words.

He was right—I was self-absorbed. I was struggling to process my homesickness. I was missing my friends and fighting to bond with the people. And although I'd survived culture shock, I still had a long way to go before I could integrate into the outside world. It may be that I was making a last-ditch attempt to reconcile with my past.

Today, I know how difficult it was for my best friend to watch me struggle through the grief and pain of leaving our community. He had been pressured to serve as an ambassador from my community, and at that point, he thought the best solution was to encourage me to come home. Perhaps he thought that was my wish. But what neither of us suspected was the powerful reaction I would have.

As I stood there at the bar, waiting for my drink to be poured, I felt a flood of certainty pour through my veins. For the first time, I knew where I belonged, and it wasn't back home in my community.

It was a turning point.

When I returned to the table where Marlin was waiting, the topic was closed. Thanks to our deep friendship, we knew each other well enough that we didn't have to talk about how we felt. I knew he had unhappily accepted my decision, and he knew I was frustrated by his lack of support. We also trusted each other enough that we never questioned whether or not we were still friends. So, when I finally took him to the airport, we hugged goodbye. As he strode through the gate, part of me left with him, perhaps the last remnants of my latent adolescence.

Within a year, Marlin himself had left our community, and we were able to talk about that experience. It was then that I realized how deeply we had both needed each other at that point, and I now regret not being in a place where I could give Marlin the support *he* needed. Because in spite of his doubts, symbolized by the plane ticket, he had also affirmed who I was becoming through his admiring comments, helping me move forward with my life.

Marlin's visit was also crucial because it shattered any illusions I had about my community. By ruthlessly using my closest friend to manipulate me, the leaders of our church had taken an irreversible step and were now the enemy. Their actions revealed the extent they would go to trap me within their thorny hedges. More than anything, his visit showed me I needed to learn how to find a community of fellow travelers.

I was about to find that community.

Chapter 18: Breaking away from the Farm

My first clue that I had permanently changed came about halfway through my spring semester when I applied for and secured an internship at the Vincent Shaw Talent Agency. There I did mailings, answered the phone, and ran errands. The owner of the small agency, Mr. Vincent Shaw, and his assistant, Cherie, were curious about my background. They asked questions and listened avidly to my stories.

My role also gave me opportunities to see shows and report on potential talent. As I interacted with theater professionals, both at the agency and during and after shows, I began to realize that theater was a place where I could potentially combine my love for words and music and art. It was an art form that connected directly to my emotions, allowing me to express what I believed in a way that affected others. Theater was not just entertainment, but something I loved.

Because Mr. Shaw's role demanded unstinting and ruthless evaluation of artists—who all sought for his approval and advocacy as a talent agent—he understood the value of judging a thing on its merits. He understood human complexities, and how these play into making hard decisions. And thus, he'd read me like a book from the day I'd entered his agency. He knew exactly what I needed to do to carve out the life I needed, and he didn't let my feelings get in the way of teaching me this. The most powerful lesson he taught me occurred when I had the temerity to show off my writing.

Before I met Mr. Shaw, I'd considered myself a talented writer. I was proud of the newsletter I wrote each month, which had previously gotten me into trouble with my community. But I had come to peace with their criticism because the point was, I believed, they were paying attention. That was worth something.

I considered my latest newsletter, full of travel anecdotes, my attempts at poetry, and what I was learning from my travels abroad. Perhaps if he read it, my writing would impress him. He might appreciate my talent—maybe even take me on as a client. So, when I wrote my March edition, I mailed him a copy of the letter.

The following Monday when I arrived at work, Mr. Shaw was alone. He glanced up and put his work aside. "I gave Cherie the morning off. We need to talk."

My stomach turned. This didn't sound good.

He considered me for a moment, then broke into song, dramatically sung in his baritone voice:

How you gonna keep him down on the farm
After he's seen Paree?

I gaped at him.

After a moment, he quit singing. "You've never heard that song, have you?"

"No."

"That's what I thought." He picked up my newsletter from his desk. "You wrote this?"

"Yes."

"It's pompous shit." He crumpled it, then tossed it into the wastebasket. I thought of the hours I had spent at the campus lab, typing and revising it to artistic perfection.

Mr. Shaw measured me. "You want to go back to your community? You think you can still fit in?" He shook his head. "If I had my way, I'd give you £500 sterling and cut you loose in this city. I'd force you to survive on your own. You don't belong to your community anymore, and you need to figure that out."

I stared at him, heat rising into my face. He didn't understand the complexity of my leaving. How could I leave all my friends? How could I just cut them off? They knew me. They were at least reading what I wrote. He didn't know what *he* was talking about—probably because he didn't and couldn't understand my community.

But of course, he did.

My monthly newsletter was an attempt to remain connected to my community. Had I really wanted to cut ties to my community, I would have spent the year quietly doing whatever I wanted, rather than looking back over my shoulder at my network of friends. Rather than following my heart and cutting strings to my community, I was somehow hoping to maintain my friendships, even though I must have realized that was going to cause me eventual pain.

Mr. Shaw knew I needed to make a clean break, but I couldn't yet admit to that. I couldn't bear to admit the obvious: that I didn't fit in anymore. The prospect of losing my entire social network filled me with tremendous turmoil.

It might have saved me a lot of pain had I only taken his advice.

As the spring semester continued, I realized my world had shifted.

I had begun to listen, and I had slowly become aware of a world of potential friendships on campus. Comfortable in my relationships with those I had gotten to know in the theater, I had gained the confidence to open up to the flood of new exchange students, which was most of the student body, since very few British citizens actually attended there. In fact, I don't remember meeting a single student who wasn't either an American or a foreign student, many of them from the Middle East. Thus, my only social connections to England came through Rotary events.

Thus, the new cohort of exchange students saw a friendly, well-adjusted upperclassman who confidently made his way around campus. By now, having faced down the dragon of our community by refusing to return home, I was no longer worried about what my community thought of my choices. Since I was comfortable with drinking alcohol, I had begun regularly chatting up strangers in pubs, which I no longer saw as the foyer to Hell, but instead, as a place of community where alcohol helped people relax with each other. In my classes, I became outspoken and engaged. The world around me became a fascinating place once again, where I could make real friends and enjoy life.

My Rotary hosts had respected my decision when I'd first arrived and told them I didn't drink alcohol. About once a month, I'd take the tube out to Harrow station, where Richard would pick me up and drive me to their home for a pleasant evening of conversation and food. Over dinner, they would ensure that my glass was kept full of non-alcoholic wine, even though they drank regular wine themselves.

In November, when I told them I had begun to drink alcohol, they were concerned. They wanted to know why. Over our monthly meal, I explained my evolution. Once they understood why I had refrained at the beginning (I didn't want to try too many new things at once), and why I ultimately chose to begin drinking (because it was a way of connecting with people), they were relieved and supportive. From then on, our meals became even more interesting, as they took me through an entire series of drinks across each meal, Richard offering me a dry sherry as an apéritif when I first arrived, then moving us on to white wine for the first course, red for the main course, and finally Baileys Irish Cream with our dessert.

As I reflect now on my decision to drink, I realize something I could not have known at that point. Alcohol can be dangerous, yes, but there's a reason it was chosen as a symbol of communion between God and people. When people drink alcohol, they find it easier to become vulnerable, and it helps them connect with others. This is especially important when it comes to the awkwardness of meeting people. Not everyone has the ability to turn off and on socially.

During my first few months in London, I endured a perfect storm I could have avoided, had I only learned how to handle alcohol under the guidance of adult mentors. I was an adult, and yet, because I had grown up in a culture where drinking itself is considered a sin, I learned to drink as many high school and college students do today, learning from other students whose only goal was to get drunk, rather than to use alcohol as a social grace.

I was someone who needed friends in order to be happy. I loved conversation, and so I enjoyed eating out with friends or talking on the phone. I knew that what is required for any friendship is absolute authenticity. Now as I began drinking, I realized that if alcohol is used correctly—meaning, if you can avoid getting hammered—it can be a delightful enhancement to social situations. The old Latin phrase puts it best: *in vino veritas*, or "in wine there is truth," because alcohol can break down barriers.

My refusal to drink alcohol when I had first arrived in London had actually hurt my ability to form relationships. By not allowing myself to drink in social situations, and feeling extremely awkward about it, I had lost my confidence. Like in middle school, I had felt like an outsider, unable to fit in, primarily because I was afraid of drinking.

At first, I took refuge in a sense of righteousness—*I can stay sober while my friends make stupid decisions due to alcohol.* But this didn't work for me. I had always empathized with people, which is what drew them to me. My judgmental attitude—which I simply couldn't hide in social situations—had made me uncomfortable and pushed people away.

This made it impossible for me to form friendships with others, which I need to be happy. It had become a vicious cycle. I had begun to withdraw from the rest of the world, hiding in my room, writing letters home, and fearing to interact with the world. I had embraced my father's fear of being worldly. The more I did this, the more I pushed people away.

I entered the world of drinking culture because I thought it might help me relax and build relationships with other people. To a large extent, this is what happened. The cycle of mistrust reversed itself. I made mistakes, yes, but I found a community of friends who were empathetic and who taught me how to drink. In addition, as I dropped the mask of distrust, I became gregarious and friendly once again. As I emerged from my shell, people began to trust me.

When I reflect on what my drinking experiences were like, I realize that the negative impacts were low. Yes, I got drunk on occasion, but since I wasn't driving in London, there was no danger that I might be unsafe. Nor did I ever hook up with anyone, probably because I am a Virgo, and too cautious to take many risks sexually. The times I got drunk occurred because I mixed drinks or drank too long.

What I also didn't realize at the time is that my need for control never really let me go wild as a college student, which was both an advantage (I kept safe), and a disadvantage (I missed out on some experiences that someone who was more of a risk-taker might have enjoyed). However, because I drank and smoked—something that was forbidden in my culture—it felt like I was having an incredibly wild experience, which was not the case.

There were unexpected rewards for joining the drinking culture in London. In addition to making friends, I quit judging the lifestyles of other students. Curious and open-minded once again, I began to listen to others, rather than wasting my energy judging them for doing things I wouldn't do—like getting shitfaced or having sex.

I also expanded my vocabulary, rather than being limited to the biblical allusions I used when I first arrived, which so confused my peers. I realized that the value of using common cliches and swear words wasn't to shock people, but to instead express familiar emotions that allowed my peers to empathize with me. This unlocked new relationships, as well. Learning the language of my peers also energized me because it allowed me to communicate clearly.

For example, I began to get the jokes I'd missed before (because most drinking jokes involve getting drunk and hooking up). I began to realize that being a sexual prude makes no one happy except those who don't give a shit about other people's happiness. As I followed the secret rules of college culture, I began to feel as if I had finally stepped out of the black-and-white world of the hidden enclave of my past into the colorful new world of my future.

My inhibitions were dropping. Each night, I walked down to The Builder's Arms for a few pints of Guinness and a smoke. I moved beyond naïve, for better or for worse. It is hard to feel holier-than-thou when you are kneeling in a filthy WC, hurling your guts out. And none of my friends judged me when this happened because they'd all been there.

Yes, I was way beyond culture shock.

But even though I'd assimilated somewhat at that point, I didn't entirely leave the practices of faith behind. Even with a hangover, I would often shower and get dressed on Sunday mornings, and creep down the street to St. Stephen's parish church, where I would reflect on the mistakes I had made the night before, chanting a general confession, and receiving absolution.

Was I becoming an alcoholic? This frightened me before I started drinking. And it is true, there are times I went overboard, at one point being called a lush by one of my friends. But after the initial mistakes, I learned to pace myself. I concluded my body wasn't genetically disposed toward alcoholism—once I got past a couple of drinks, I was either hurling in the restroom or falling asleep… neither of which made me a very interesting companion.

So, I learned my lessons. Given the choice between alcohol or a favorite dessert—like ice cream or cheesecake—I would take the dessert any time. Mixing drinks ensured that I woke up with a wicked hangover—and plenty of retching. I could avoid a hangover, not by drinking less, but by drinking *smarter*. Before hitting the sack, if I took an aspirin and eight ounces of water for every drink I consumed, I could avoid a hangover.

But most importantly, I learned from my friends that my view of the world was wrong. When I arrived in London, I somehow believed that most Amish-Mennonite people are essentially good, and most worldly people are essentially bad. Now I saw that people were people, no matter what religion they belonged to. I knew kind people in my home community, and now I was meeting kind people out in the world. I knew people in my home community who were abusive and cruel, and now I met people in the world who were abusive and cruel.

In terms of bad or good people, there was *no* advantage to living in our separated community. God's grace and forgiveness was needed in both.

I first confided my thoughts about leaving in Janie, my sociology professor, who had consistently responded to my letters of homesickness and pain during the first semester. She had provided a supportive and listening ear during key moments, helping me process what I was experiencing, giving me her insights about why people might be responding to me. She was able to draw upon her knowledge of the outside world, since she had attended prestigious schools such as Duke and Syracuse before becoming a professor at Malone College.

Now our conversation had percolated to the point where I felt I could give her my decision about what came next in my life. Since I felt she knew me better than anyone else, I wanted her insights.

"I don't think I fit into the conservative Mennonite world anymore," I wrote. "I'm still a Christian, but I think Christians need to live in the world, not behind sheltered walls in virtual monasteries."

I wondered what Janie would think. More than anyone else, she seemed best positioned to advise me on whether I should leave my community, since she had been educated at worldly schools before coming to teach at a small Christian college in Northeastern Ohio.

Janie's letter was kind and thoughtful, reminding me that being a person of faith in the outside world clashes dramatically with people who don't make the same choice:

> *God calls us to be generous, to be servants to others, to turn the other cheek, to find times of solitude and listening, to set ourselves apart, and to live simply. This is at odds with the majority culture; that culture expects us to be working to grab what we can, to fight others to keep them from getting "what's ours," to not worry about others much, and to delight in whatever pleases our personal taste.*

I was relieved by her words, her willingness to accept the idea that I might not want to remain within my world. And yes, I knew I was definitely going to conflict with the majority of people—I knew myself well enough to know that I would never fit in anywhere. But she used the word *God*, and I was struggling to understand who that person was. Did Janie see God the same way I did—a grandfatherly man with a long beard in some heavenly throne room, watching over me to make sure I didn't sin, ready to send me to Hell if I did?

Living here in London, with an ocean between my home community and me, I had begun to realize that my community did not always understand who

God was, and for that reason, I could not trust them. My community's God had determined that real Christians (i.e., conservative Mennonites) needed to sing only *a cappella* music. My community's God had decided that people must wear the clothing styles of sixteenth-century Europeans. My community's God had put men in charge and had taken away a woman's autonomy, when I knew that without personal autonomy, a creature is not human.

My community's God... no longer made sense.

But I wasn't sure I had the courage to actually leave. To do that, I needed to have an air-tight reason. Otherwise, the many friends I had—people that I really liked, and some I even loved—might convince me to stay. What was driving me to leave?

Yes, there were the beatings I had received... both from my father and from my teachers at school. I had begun to feel the anger in my core, but that wasn't the reason I was leaving. Not everyone in my community treated their children the way Dad did. In fact, I had begun to suspect that my literalist father and my sadistic teachers were in the minority. I didn't need to imitate their behavior in forming my own family.

This wasn't what was driving me to leave.

No, it was because I was beginning to change my view of the Bible. This had started during my years at college. Once an admirer of the patriarchal system, I had been dramatically affected by the way Brother Glick had broken my trust, admitting to his close friend the corruption he saw in the church's leadership. Add to that his belief that Christians were to remain ignorant— which went entirely against my Question Box personality—and he had completely lost my trust. Once I began to see the contradictions in the Bible— realizing, for example, that the patriarchal model was based on the same Scriptural principles as the belief that slavery is proper, I had realized that the Bible could not be read as a literal text. There had to be a different way.

I needed to break away in order to find a way of living that would allow me to fulfill the one imperative I recognized—finding a way to live like Jesus would live within the world. I needed to find a lifestyle that I could defend based on a common-sense reading of the Scripture. I needed to be part of a community that would draw people in, and make them feel safe, rather than one whose rules were literalistic and allowed authority figures to hurt children. I didn't know where that community was, but I did know that it wasn't my home community.

Therein lay the rub.

If I left, I would abandon the network of friends I had built up so carefully within conservative Mennonite communities across the nation. Having watched my sister leave and having seen people who were once her friends gossip maliciously about her—all under the guise of "praying" for her—I knew what would happen to that network of friends. Thanks to my newsletter, I had already gotten a taste of this in the letters of "prayerful concern" about my actions.

Once again, I was faced with the reality of my choices. Whatever decision I made, I was going to hurt someone. If I stayed, my family might be happy, but I would be miserable. If I left, I *might* find happiness and fulfillment, but I would also increase the shame my family had endured after my sister Elaine left. There simply was no easy way out.

And that's where things stood when one of my drinking buddies asked if we could do breakfast so we could talk about *his* faith.

Chapter 19: Just A Different Scripture

One of my drinking buddies who was quite close to me was Pat, a senior from a New England college who was spending a semester abroad. We had connected at a party when he had told me that he had been raised as a strict Catholic but was now lapsed. However, he could identify with me, he went on to say, since he knew (like everyone else now seemed to know) that I was "on leave" from my own strict Mennonite community. One Saturday evening at another party, Pat confided in me that he was having serious questions about his faith.

"Your faith is so strong," he said. "I'd love to talk about it."

Caught up in my own doubts and uncertainties about my future, I was amazed that anyone who knew me as well as Pat did would think I had a strong faith. Curious as to what he wanted, I agreed to meet him for breakfast.

A year ago, I would have viewed this as an invitation to "witness" for Christ, a term we used to describe how we advocated our brand of Christian culture. Our community took this task seriously, with small groups sometimes performing *a cappella* Gospel music and preaching on the streets of nearby cities, stopping passersby and thrusting "Gospel tracts" at them. I had mostly avoided these trips—they made me feel like a used car salesman trying to foist off a lemon—so I wasn't going to practice their techniques on Pat.

The next morning, over shepherd's pie and Guinness at our favorite pub, he didn't waste time. As a biology major, he approached things methodically, he explained to me, and so he'd renounced his faith, just like most of his peers. Until we became friends, he had been through with faith, thinking it was bullshit. His future included laboratory research. But lately, as we talked, he'd begun to have questions.

Although I wasn't going into science, I could identify with him. "What made you question your faith in the first place?"

"Evolution. It doesn't sync up with the Bible, and I don't do blind faith."

"I know what you mean," I said. "But I don't believe that faith equals blindness, intellectually. The person who influenced me most on this was my high school English teacher, who taught me the only way to find the truth is by asking questions, not by simply obeying an authority figure."

Pat was nodding. "I wish I had had your English teacher. The nuns and priests at our high school weren't interested much in hearing our questions, especially mine. "I was a little... argumentative."

I laughed. "I was a bit that way myself, especially with my dad. But I'm curious… not that I disagree with you… why do you think evolution doesn't sync up with the Bible?"

Pat gestured impatiently. "Well, how do you defend Genesis as 'inspired' when it shows God creating the earth in six days? That's magic, not science. There's so much evidence that disproves the account. The Bible was originally a collection of stories told around the fire by wandering tribes, then finally written down, yet I'm supposed to treat it like a… science textbook? If that's what I'm forced to defend, how can I take my faith seriously? How do you?"

Last night, he had admired my faith—now I felt attacked. I took a sip of Guinness, trying to collect my thoughts. "Okay, to be fair, I've never taken a course in evolutionary theory, so I probably can't answer your questions about *how* God created the world."

Pat looked startled. "Wait, you're questioning the Bible's depiction of creation? I thought all Christians believed every word was inspired by God."

"Fundamentalists do… and I disagree with them. To be clear, I believe the Bible is divinely inspired—but not literally, word for word, as they do."

"What does that mean, exactly?" Pat asked.

"I have a general theory that makes sense to me about the Creation story. It may not make sense to you."

"Try me," he said. "To be fair, I'm not trying to denigrate what you believe. I'm just trying to figure things out."

"No, I get you. I'm also struggling to figure all this out."

"Which is why I wanted us to do breakfast."

I shrugged. "You mentioned treating the Bible as a science textbook—and that the creation story should be taken literally."

He nodded, annoyed. "Yup. In fact, some of my religion teachers argued that all the scientific evidence was created by God to give the earth 'an appearance of age.' I got into trouble when I disagreed. I told them if you believe that, then God is by nature deceptive."

I laughed. "I can see why they were pissed off. But I agree. If that's what God did, you have every right to mistrust Him."

Pat picked up his box of cigarettes, shook it down, and then lit for both of us, handing one to me as I continued.

"I've also heard some biblical scholars say they believe the word *day* in the Bible is symbolic—you know, 'a day to the Lord is as a thousand years, and a thousand years is as a day'—so in actuality, they argue, God created the world, but he just took millions of years to do it."

"So, what's the difference between that and the theory of evolution?"

"My point exactly."

"So, what do *you* believe?" Pat asked.

I took another sip of Guinness. This was the real question, I was beginning to realize, the heart of our discussion.

"I'm not sure I understand this, entirely, but I think it has to do with literary genres. If you believe that the Bible is written in different genres, like history and poetry, then Genesis is mythology."

"Meaning… not true."

"No, myths aren't false. Myths *contain* truth, but you don't take the details literally. I mean, when Genesis was written, science didn't exist. As you said, it's a collection of stories told around the fire. It's like trying to explain why the sky is blue to a kid—you don't break it down into a scientific explanation. You just tell the kid that God painted the sky blue, and the kid gets it. The point of the myth is not *how* the world was created; the point is that it was created by God. From what I've read, a lot of scientists don't think faith and science necessarily clash—they just answer different questions."

"So, let me see if I got you right," Pat said. "Evolution may be the *how*, but behind evolution, there's a divine Being at work?"

"Yes," I said. I could see him struggling to wrap his head around what I was saying. "The myth was never intended to explain creation—it was written long before science existed. So, treating the Bible as a science textbook makes no sense."

"That's fair." Pat was listening closely.

"I think a lot of religious leaders… for me it was fundamentalists, but it sounds like for you, it was priests and nuns… have tried to use the Bible as a weapon to eliminate doubt and uncertainty."

Pat chuckled. "Yes, my Catholic teachers were all about eliminating that. They thought doubt was a sin."

"Same here. I think most of my Mennonite teachers and ministers—except for Brother Byler—were afraid that if I doubted, I would leave. They felt extremely threatened by the questions my classmates and I were asking."

Pat jumped in. "It's ironic. As a scientist… okay, one that hopes to be one… that's the whole point of learning. You only discover new ideas by questioning what is known."

For the first time this year, things were becoming clear. I was beginning to realize that the reason I had somehow hung on to my faith… although I questioned everything about the rigidity of our culture… was because Brother Byler had taught me that true faith isn't threatened by questions. The Bible isn't a magic box that pops out answers.

I tried to put this into words Pat might understand as a scientist.

"I don't think the Bible answers all our questions," I said. "But I do think it offers me stories of devoted people who demonstrated that by faith, they were able to confront the issues of their day. Perhaps I'm comfortable with uncertainty… because when I read the Bible, I see that the ones God loves the most—like Job or Abraham or David—ask the most questions."

"So, what does the Creation myth tell you?" he asked.

I pulled on my cigarette. "I believe it shows there is a divine imagination behind the evolutionary process, beginning long before The Big Bang. I'm accepting that belief by faith—which means that when I consider my own personal story, it makes the most sense to me.

"But that's the choice I've made. I could just as easily believe there is *no* divine presence within the process, and that all things happen by chance. But if I believe that, I believe that everything in my life happens by chance."

"Which is where I've been sitting," he said, speaking the words through the plume of smoke as he exhaled.

"And I'm at the first."

He frowned. "Are you saying evidence doesn't matter?"

"No. I think it matters. We all look at the way our life has worked out. Some of us, like me, think they see the hand of God in our lives. Others see their lives as a random sequence of events. You can't prove or disprove either, but you tend to choose the one that makes the best story. I think that's what faith is—choosing to believe in God, even when the evidence isn't absolute."

Pat stared at me. "Most Christians I've met think they know all the answers. It's as if they're afraid of *not* knowing the answers. But you, you're different. You don't seem to need to know. In fact, you seem to be more comfortable *not* knowing. Your faith is… strange."

We laughed.

I thought about whether or not Brother Byler stepping into my life when he did, or the fact that he had empowered me by providing a safe space where me and my classmates could ask tough questions… were random incidents.

"I think life… growing up in a community that takes the Bible literally… has taught me to be skeptical of certainty," I said. "I've known too many Christians who are very certain of their faith, and that attracted me, until it scared the shit out of me.

"What did?"

"The fact that a person could be so sure, and yet so wrong," I said, looking at my empty pint. "I'll be back."

I got up to go to the bar. As I did, I thought back to the moment when I graduated from high school, with uncertainty staring me in the face. I thought about the way I had run into Brother Glick, who offered me that certainty, the way he had taught me to indoctrinate my students in Phoenix, and the way I couldn't do it. I thought about the way I had tried to defend the Umbrella of Authority to Janie, and her kindness in helping me see that the Bible could be used by people like Brother Glick to manipulate those he led. I thought about the way I came to see that his belief in the value of remaining ignorant wasn't a useful guide to living my life. I simply couldn't buy Brother Glick's certainty. And so, I had become deeply suspicious of people who were sure.

I had arrived back at our table, where Pat was finishing up another smoke.

"You asked me how I could be so comfortable with uncertainty. Whether it was through evolution, or a literal six-day creation—God standing there waving his hands and the world blinking into existence—or God doing it over millions of years, with each day symbolizing a million years, I really don't care. *That* doesn't make me doubt whether God created the world. It just means I don't know how He did it."

"So, in other words, you're okay with God being a total mystery. You have faith in… a God you don't totally… understand. Is that fair?"

"Yes," I replied. "At least… I think so."

We both laughed.

"I think both of us have been knocked off our feet by this year," he said. "I saw what you went through when we both arrived. It took you awhile to adapt—you didn't talk to anyone at first—but you've changed. You seem to know what you're doing. People listen to you when you talk. But it seems we've come to a different conclusion about why it all took place."

I nodded. "I mean, it's funny. Perhaps the only reason I still believe in God is because… and this is where my faith comes in… one of the best explanations of mystery came to me from someone who doesn't even believe in God."

"Okay, I'm listening."

"Do you know my theater teacher, Michael Richard?" Pat nodded. "The other day, he was telling our class about the time he met Pope John Paul, and how moved he was by the man's charisma and spiritual power. Utterly moved. Then he said, 'I don't have the gift of faith. I admire it, I appreciate those who do, but I don't have it.' That was months ago, and I still haven't been able to forget his words."

"So, you think you've been given the gift of faith?" Pat probed.

"I don't know if *I* would describe it that way. But I do know that even with all the doubts I've faced, here in London, even with my utter frustration about the way my community practices their faith, I still believe in God."

Pat stubbed out his cigarette and rose to leave.

"I still don't understand *why* you believe in God," he said. "Maybe it is just a gift. But if you don't mind me saying something personal?" I nodded, still sitting. "I think your greatest strength is your confidence as a person. You may not know what the Hell you believe, but no one talking to you would realize this. I certainly didn't. You seem to have, deep within you, a strong belief in God. That comes through clearly. It's why I wanted to talk to you."

I didn't forget that conversation.

Pat's problem was my problem—having to make up my mind about whether I wanted to return to my community. In spite of what I had done, I knew they would take me back. Sure, I'd have to repent for the stuff I'd been doing in London, but forgiveness, after all, is what Christianity does best. The past wasn't the problem.

The real problem was *my* inability to forgive my community's past—and what I thought about them. This year had been amazing because for a brief time, I'd been able to forget about them. Now, with my departure looming, I needed to know if I *could* fit back in. I had found happiness here in London, building a new community of friends who accepted me for who I really was, but now, as I thought about returning to a past that contained so much pain, the tension was rising within me.

Today, I know why I was dreading my return. But at that point, I was far from realizing why the thought of my return home flooded me with such foreboding. I didn't yet understand the source of my anger, nor was I able to link the current of palpitating anger—lurking just under my consciousness—to the abuse I had been through.

Several weeks before I left for home, two Egyptian women taking a Chaucer class with me asked if they could introduce me to a friend. "She wants to meet you—she heard you're Amish."

These two classmates often whispered to each other during class, and they were clearly bored with the class, which annoyed me, especially since I liked our earnest professor. So, I dodged their repeated suggestions, but they persisted. Their friend knew what a "fine scholar" I was, and she "insisted."

Finally, in the week before I left, I agreed. This sent them into peals of laughter, which confused me, but it was too late. Grabbing my arms companionably, they steered me to the Common Room, where a beautiful young woman, dressed in an elegant red skirt and silver blouse, rose from a couch, setting aside her textbook and notebook. I caught a glimpse of her writing, graceful and fine.

"This is Isis," they chorused, then wandered a short distance away. She eyed me curiously, taking in my black jeans, trendy boots, and herringbone jacket as I stood facing her uncomfortably.

"I wanted to meet you," she said softly. "I hear many stories." She didn't clarify whether they were college rumors, or anecdotes from her friends. "I hear you have to return to your Amish people. What do you plan to do?"

Her manner was polite and attentive. I had expected someone different. Unlike her friends, Isis was clearly intelligent, and genuinely curious.

"I'm not sure," I said, uncertain about how much I wanted to tell a stranger, but she pushed me.

"Will you put on the clothes of your parents' religion again?"

I wondered why she was so obsessed with what I wore, but that became clear when our discussion circled around to religion, and I discovered her father was a "fundamentalist Muslim." When I tried to explain that I was not Amish, but conservative Mennonite, defining a few subtleties—electricity, but no TV; non-ostentatious cars instead of buggies—she quickly understood the difference.

"So, your family dresses differently, they are separated by their religious garb, but they live among modern Americans." When I nodded, she said. "And they let you come here alone?"

"Not exactly, but—"

"You're a man… so you can do what you want."

My eyebrows rose. She had captured my dilemma so easily. "Yes. I can do what I want, that's true. But…"

"You're torn by your choice. Between your family… and your desire for freedom."

It felt like she was reading my mind. My expression must have shown my shock because she smiled sympathetically, then reached out and cupped my chin in a warm hand for just a moment, like a mother comforting a worried child.

"I am facing the same choice," she said. "My father is very wealthy, very powerful. He knows how I dress here, in this modern city, but he knows I fear to leave, and he has sent my friends to watch over me."

She glanced back at the other women, who were watching us, smiling encouragingly at her. But when she turned back, there was no smile in her eyes, only a strange intensity.

"My father knows that when I return, I will put on the traditional clothes of Egyptian women. I will wear hijab, I will be his dutiful daughter. I will marry the man he has chosen."

"And you're okay doing that? You don't mind… giving up your freedom?"

"I'm not okay with doing that. I do mind." She glanced back at her friends, who offered us fresh smiles of encouragement, then lowered her voice. "Your family is quite strict, too?"

"Yes."

Her eyes flashed in anger. "You can leave, though. If you are willing to lose your family, you can leave and start another. I know this because I understand the heart of your culture."

Here I stood in the Richmond College Commons, talking to a Muslim woman. Wearing expensive and modern clothes, she could have passed for any sophisticated woman in London. Yet, because of her fundamentalist religion and her father's influence, she had few choices—her father held absolute power over her future.

I thought about my sister Heidi, the conversation I had had with her before I left. She had come back from taking Bill Gothard's Institute in Basic Youth Conflicts, and inspired by his model of patriarchal leadership, she had promised my father that—just as Gothard taught—she would not marry a man unless Dad approved.

I couldn't live with that. I refused to buy into the patriarchal system, letting my father dictate my future. But was that because I was a man, as Isis had concluded?

My older sister Elaine had left, but she kept calling Dad, asking him for help. She seemed unable to find success in the outside world. The biblical spell my father had cast—the Hedge of Thorns taught by Gothard—appeared to be working brilliantly.

Would my experience be the same… after I left? Like my sister, I could leave. Would my father cast a spell on me, too? And then there was my family, warm and loud. I loved them, just as Isis did hers. Would I struggle to deal with the loss of my family… if I left? Did my being a man have anything to do with it? And that's when the truth hit me.

"Fundamentalism." I shook my head. "Our worlds are a lot alike; Muslim or Amish-Mennonite, the impulse is the same—the need for control by male, religious authorities."

She smiled, her eyes sad and distant. "They are, and that's why I wanted to meet you."

"You're not going to stay here?" I asked.

"I'm not. I don't understand everything about my faith, but I am who I am because of it. And I can't leave it."

Abruptly, Isis turned and walked away, toward her friends, whose faces leaped into focus. The three young women left the room together, her two friends glancing back curiously.

I sank into a nearby couch, my mind racing back over my conversation with Isis. Her family was not unlike mine. Her father's literal approach to the Quran was the same as my father's. It was just a different Scripture.

Yes, Isis had decided to return to her Muslim world, just as I had decided to return to mine. Our worlds were similar—and we were both torn by them. Her choice to wear hijab would fulfill the same purpose as my sisters' hand-sewn dresses, both styles of clothing designed to hide their bodies, as if they were objects of shame. Just like my sisters, Isis had little autonomy within her fundamentalist religious society.

I thought back to a comment made by one of my close friends a year before, standing in the parking lot of our church sanctuary in Hartville, Ohio. For several years, as we taught together, he had listened to me struggle through my frustrations with "our faith," as I put it.

"You don't have a problem with faith," he told me that evening. "You have a problem with your community's culture. It doesn't work for you."

And that's when the flash of insight hit me. My conflict with this type of society had little to do with my faith in God, but instead with a literalistic thought process that destroyed the spiritual freedom God offered every human being. My conflict was far larger than a woman's lack of autonomy—thanks to the spiritual control that my patriarchal society demanded of everyone—whether man *or* a woman. My conflict had emerged years ago because this type of society directly opposed my vision of a community where I could thrive, a community that worked in sync with the kind of God I had come to believe in and had chosen to trust.

My friend was right—after a year in London, I didn't believe I fit into my Amish-Mennonite community. That world no longer called to me as a sanctuary.

The tectonic plates of my internal landscape had irrevocably shifted. I now saw the people outside my community as potential friends and allies, not as "the World." I now saw people as people, not dividing them between two tribes of Mennonites and *non*-Mennonites. This understanding, while freeing, was also a transition from the known to the unknown.

Although I thought I was returning home from a year of traveling abroad, I was actually beginning a spiritual journey that would take decades as I searched for a place that would allow me to shed my powerful need to control, a place that would recognize the autonomy God had given me, a place that would empower me. Until I could find that place, I would have to make my journey alone.

And that terrified me.

Book V: Bargaining

Charity suffereth long, *and* is kind; charity envieth not;
charity vaunteth not itself, is not puffed up,
Doth not behave itself unseemly, seeketh not her own,
is not easily provoked, thinketh no evil;
Rejoiceth not in iniquity, but rejoiceth in the truth;
Beareth all things, believeth all things, hopeth all things,
endureth all things.

~ I Corinthians 13: 4-6, *The Holy Bible,* KJV, 1769

Interpolation V: An Imitation of Love

As I returned from Europe, having come of age there within the college bar culture, I saw that flirting worked best when you kept your guard up, treating an attractive woman as an object rather than as a person with feelings. I didn't realize that for a romantic relationship to evolve toward friendship and love, both partners need to become vulnerable with each other.

Instead, I knew—based on the "wisdom" of my drinking buddies in London, that women didn't date their friends. So, as I returned and began to date, I drew a distinct line between the women I fell in love with, and the women who were my friends

In addition, in order to deal with my PTSD, I was continuing to numb my feelings. Becoming the Top in a relationship based on dominance and submission ensured that I didn't need to be vulnerable, although I wanted my partner to be. Unaware of my true emotions, I kept telling myself that we only played these roles in the bedroom.

In reality, I never let down my guard.

Objectifying a woman, focusing on her external qualities, and remaining indifferent to her feelings felt masculine and powerful. To be fair, some women find it intensely flattering (which is why it worked for me), but objectification is the selfish version of love, an imitation that kills vulnerability. In contrast, true love is by nature egalitarian. It requires vulnerability. It requires that you give up control. It's why the Apostle Paul encourages husbands and wives to submit to each other (Eph. 5:21).

One of the best descriptions of love I know occurs when psychologist Sean Maguire (Robin Williams) explains this to Will Hunting (Matt Damon) in the film Good Will Hunting (Miramax, 1997). You can't really understand what love means until you're willing to be "totally vulnerable" with the person you love, Maguire says. You need to care about something else more than you care about yourself.

I was far from this. Struggling to deal with PTSD, I thought I needed more control, not less. When I objectified my partner during our play, and she gave up control to me, I found the experience intensely satisfying. But I was like the Ringwraiths in J.R.R. Tolkien's world, who didn't understand the corrosive power of their rings of power—I failed to consider the cost.

I thought the control offered by my partners would keep me protected, emotionally. I failed to realize that this control was killing off my ability to be vulnerable. Each time we entered the world of my fetish, where our actions were ruled by my memories of abuse, I lost more of my ability to truly love a woman. And thus, any chance I had to find the kind of relationship I wanted... and a happy marriage... kept moving farther and farther away.

Chapter 20: Flood of Guilt

Buoyed by the bright freedom I had enjoyed all semester, I decided to return home early so I could graduate with my class and walk for commencement. I was ready to move on with my life.

I wrote a final letter to my readers, letting them know I was coming home. When my classmates at Malone discovered I would attend graduation, I got a flood of letters expressing their excitement about seeing me again. I replied to each one.

I was ready to launch my new life *outside* of our community. I looked forward to beginning a teaching career, preferably as a drama teacher. But a teaching position wouldn't start until fall, so, until then, I needed to earn money. Communicating by mail, my old construction boss had offered to give me summer work when I arrived home.

But a small kink appeared in my departure plans: I wasn't much of a saver and hadn't budgeted my finances carefully, so my stipend had disappeared during the trip I'd taken to Greece. I had eaten lavishly and spent more money than I should have on souvenirs. Rather than waiting to develop the many rolls of film until I'd gotten home, I'd spent the money on slides and had produced a slide show for my friends.

Like my father, I was fearless about borrowing money. People tended to trust me, so when I ran short of money, friends who believed in me would send loans or gifts by mail. But now, just before I left for home, I ran short of spending money... and money back then didn't transfer easily across the ocean by way of an ATM.

I realized a few more pounds would be helpful. After all, friends wanted to go out with me for drinks and dinner, and I wanted to buy gifts for my family. When I got home, I would easily pay down my debts by doing summertime work, I told myself. And once I started a salaried teaching position—which I was sure I would quickly secure—money wouldn't be a problem.

Until then, I had not tapped my host family for funds, but I thought that since I was leaving, they might be generous. My host was wealthy, and I would promise to return the money by mail once I returned home. So, a few days before I left, I called Richard to say goodbye. As we were about to end the conversation, I told him I had a favor to ask—could I borrow a few pounds to tide me over?

There was a brief silence, perhaps because of the shock. "So sorry," Richard finally said, his discomfort radiating through the phone line.

The ancient red phone booth where I stood suddenly felt cramped.

I wanted to hang up the phone, but my fear of being stranded battled my sense of politeness. Desperate, I allowed the silence to hang.

"Rotary has a policy," Richard continued, his voice as even as a bank president's. "Host families are forbidden to lend money to our Foundation Scholars. I'm sure you understand."

Embarrassed by my financial helplessness, I decided to act as if I hadn't just asked that question. "It's okay, Richard. No problem, I completely understand. Give Joan all my love. I'll call you from the States."

"Oh, yes, you must," he hastened to say. "You're a family member now, truly, and we'll expect to hear a report each Christmas."

He chuckled, relieved.

That conversation forced me to confront a reality, one that many who leave fundamentalist communities must face: I didn't know how to manage money. It is a common problem for those who leave. Over the next few decades as I have met and read about other escapees, I have realized that learning how to handle money is a symbol of independence. For those of us who do not understand this, the leaving becomes that much more difficult.

In fact, one of the primary reasons those who leave return to their communities is financial. It is for this reason that organizations such as Footsteps in NYC have been created for ultra-Orthodox Jews, and the Amish Heritage Organization has supported those who leave the Amish. They provide career advice, education, and therapeutic support. But, of course, those hadn't existed when I was leaving, and I wouldn't have known where to look for them if they had.

As the date to return home to Hartville from London loomed, I began to rethink my plan of departure from my community. I was torn by uncertainty. I needed to survive, yet, to remain in Ohio meant re-integrating into a culture I'd rejected. But to leave for parts unknown meant losing an entire support network of friends and family.

Fortunately, the financial lesson with Richard, while a hard lesson to learn, was not insurmountable. I wasn't stranded in London—I had enough money to purchase a Tube pass to the airport, and Rotary had provided a return ticket by way of LaGuardia Airport. I would even be able to buy a burger and fries at McDonalds during the layover in NYC.

But Richard's words had made me reconsider the future. I had glimpsed the wolf at the door—a scary moment. How would I survive outside our community? How did one leave? I knew I wanted to, but I hadn't really thought about where I would go, nor the logistics in actually doing so. Until the last year, I had always lived at home—or, at least, within a supportive community—and, thus, I didn't know anything about getting an apartment.

And I had even sold my car to raise money for my trip, leaving me no reserve funds. The truth was… I was not financially prepared to leave. That's what Richard's lesson taught me.

Unfortunately, it hadn't taught me *how* to rectify that situation. That, I was going to have to figure out on my own.

I did know that I needed to act fast to secure a teaching position outside my community in order to secure my independence. Until then, I'd be stranded at home, subject to the whims—and rules—of my family.

The public school where I had student-taught the year before wasn't looking for an English teacher, but one of my college buddies was actively advocating for me to consider teaching at a Mennonite high school about an hour from home, a school that was more "liberal." My friend had agreed me to take me on a tour and introduce me to the principal.

I was hesitant, not really liking that option. I had been thinking of only applying to secular school districts, so the fact that this was a Mennonite school, even a "liberal" one, made me pause. If the administration had heard the rumors from my community about my year in London, it might make them pause before hiring me to teach their children.

This feeling of uncertainty made my stomach twist. My plans to leave my childhood world—so clear in London—looked far more complicated when I faced the financial and practical realities of surviving on my own.

What now?

Despite my mother's worries and questions about what I had done in London, she did her best to welcome me home. She celebrated my success the day after commencement by throwing me a graduation party at the Christian school where I had attended first grade and eventually graduated high school.

She was proud of my accomplishments in college and wanted to support me as best as she could. After all, she had had to quit high school in her sophomore year, deeply resenting her father for that. She was especially excited about the fact that I was graduating with two B.A. degrees, one in English, the other in history. She loved history.

But by the time I reached the building where I had gone to school—and had been physically abused—I had lost my appetite. As I walked through the double doors into the foyer, what should have been a triumph was overshadowed in my mind by the bad memories of this place.

I entered the long chapel where our school had daily devotions. Like our church, it had no religious icons or decorations since simplicity was valued. I gazed out over the room, well-lit by the windows letting in the May sunshine, and I remembered the various evangelists who had preached to us there on those grey Ohio school days. The rows of chairs filled with my restless classmates were gone—replaced with tables beautifully set with white tablecloths, decorative ribbons, grape juice, and hors d'oeuvres.

People had started to arrive. With her trademark smile, my mother was welcoming my friends and college professors, while my siblings served the guests.

I shifted, feeling the weight of my Plain coat, but it chafed on me, both literally and figuratively. I didn't know how to deal with the mental bifurcation the moment demanded. This was where the abuse had happened, yet you wouldn't know it, looking about me at the friendly faces greeting each other, and me.

No one else seems to have a problem with their past. Others received the same treatment I did. Why couldn't I just get over it all?

But I knew then, as if God had spoken to me in thunderous tones, that I never would. I needed to find a way to exorcise my past—not just physically, but also mentally. Unless I could, I would never be able to find peace, never be able to find happiness in the outside world where I knew I belonged. I needed to put my sentimental and nostalgic feelings aside.

There was no returning to this world.

A week later, I attended church with my parents. As I stepped into the auditorium, people I knew well greeted me in a friendly way, telling me how glad they were to have me home, but their eyes slid around me as they then moved on.

A few minutes later, I found my way to an empty bench on the men's side of the auditorium and sat down, surrounded by the men who knew me. Sitting with my legs crossed, my arm casually stretched over the back of the empty bench, I smiled confidently.

What no one saw was my panoply of worries, the uncertainty flooding my nervous system as I struggled to figure out what to do next. What I wanted here in Ohio was someone who had been through the same dark night, someone who could reassure me and direct me to the right departure gate… but there was no one like that here.

I recalled my last Sunday in London—having a late breakfast with a friend in an ancient English pub and the lazy conversation with someone who was about to return home to a welcoming family, the warmth of empathy rather than judgment. On that glorious morning, my chosen family, a diverse collection of people I had gathered across the year, had still been together… and they'd believed in me.

Now that support group was gone, scattered around the world, while I had landed back here in my simple church sanctuary, surrounded by childhood friends and my blood relatives. I felt lonelier than I had on my first day in London, not knowing anyone.

As I sat there in my home church on that ancient wooden pew, I felt every fiber of my home community not having my back. I had been a rising and highly visible leader in this very church; everyone had read and discussed my monthly letters. They'd taken note of what was between the lines, ferreting out the sins I had committed: drinking alcohol, dating worldly women, going to the theater, and even acting in a play. In addition, due to my loneliness, I had shared specific details with those who'd written and questioned me, some whom I barely knew, details I should have kept to myself. While I'd ensured my public letters were relatively discreet, only hinting at my changes, that other correspondence wasn't as circumspect—and people talked.

They were able to connect the dots.

By the time I'd arrived home, thanks to my close friends, I'd been informed about the rumors that had circulating—that I had begun to drink and smoke (true), that I had been "impure" (not true, I was still a virgin), and that I attended parties (true). Conservative Mennonite communities across the country were discussing all my exploits, both those I had admitted to, and, even more salacious, those they'd imagined. The tightly knit community of conservative Mennonites used "prayer requests" to keep people up on what was going on, both in church services and on the telephone. I had watched this happen with my sister, Elaine. I definitely knew how things worked—what had possessed me to be that in-their-face?

As I reflect on it now, decades later, I realize the answer to this is complicated. Perhaps I'd been more like my father than I'd realized, unwilling to learn and follow the invisible conversational boundaries by which modern society operated.

But I wasn't—and am not—the only one. Those who grow up in highly restrictive environments and then leave struggle to recognize what is appropriate to share. Their reality is fascinating to those on the outside, but in moderate doses. I saw this again and again in London. People were fascinated by my background... until I wouldn't stop talking about it. It's why I struggled to connect with people in London, why girls were put off by my rambling attempts to process my past. I needed therapy for the culture shock I was experiencing, a shock that went far beyond British vs. American.

I just didn't realize it.

Saddest of all, few escapees from insular cultures read people well since people within the modern world have been trained from birth *not* to be transparent. It, therefore, is not surprising that I shared too much, both through my newsletters and the stories I told my community.

There was one net positive: my oversharing signaled something important that I would not realize until years later. Those newsletters were my first attempt at writing memoir. Only now do I see my letter-writing for what it was—an oil lamp lit within the deepest cavern of my soul, its flame sputtering. By writing those letters, I'd unwittingly discovered memoir's power to transform any writer who is willing to strip-mine the ragged gullies and rocky hilltops of his soul.

What I was missing was a therapist who could help me process the steps of my departure so obviously spelled out in the experiences I'd shared in my letters. I've often wondered how different my life might have turned out had I been able to access a therapist during my journey away from my community. Because, without this processing step, you end up sharing raw stories that make readers feel uncomfortable.

I know that first-hand.

Today, I wish I'd done it differently, I wish I'd shouted it louder, I wish I'd shouted it sooner. I wish I hadn't let my fears and my desire to please people silence my voice. During those moments when I let my fears stop me, it didn't just halt my progress. My refusal to be authentic, to speak truth to power, left me paralyzed, unable to feel true joy or sorrow, unable to look ahead and find direction.

It blocked my deepest passions.

It took me years to understand the crushing feeling of paralysis that would overwhelm me when I spent any significant time with my family, especially during these first few months after returning home, before I left the place for good. It overwhelmed me. My home community described it as guilt—something meant to drive me back home, as repentant as the Prodigal Son.

Yet… what I was feeling on that varnished church pew was *not* guilt—it was something else entirely. Guilt, I had learned as a child at my father's knee, came from God, a feeling of emotional pain and oppression, warning me that I was traveling down the wrong path. Guilt signals you've done something wrong—you've hurt someone, you've broken a moral law—and it guides you toward penitence and healing.

When I think back over my time in London, I realize that after I rejected my community's manipulative invitation to return home at Christmas, my "guilt" disappeared. I realize now it wasn't guilt that I was feeling—instead, it was a sort of peer pressure that overwhelmed me, a sense that I was being watched by my community. I was free of that feeling because I was there, finally, on my own. I began to build friendships with classmates. And the feeling I translated as "guilt" stayed away until I returned home, when it returned like a gale force.

But back then, I didn't understand this. I wasn't able to differentiate between guilt and peer pressure. Thus, its disappearance—and then reappearance—confused the Hell out of me. Why would I feel guilty in Ohio, but not in London? Wasn't I the same person?

I began to suspect a dark truth, one that I couldn't even comprehend because the idea seemed so blasphemous. Was it possible that the guilt I was feeling—because of my society's rules which I'd broken in London—might not come from God?

I mean, well… not unless… God only lived in the Midwest.

Today, those feelings make sense. I wasn't experiencing guilt, and my feelings hadn't come from God. What I'd *thought* was guilt had been societal rejection. My community's rejection—their attempt to cancel me in their gossipy prayers and those letters expressing concern for refusing to follow their rules—equaled rejection by God *in their minds*. They wanted me to believe this rejection by God meant being consigned to eternally conscious torment in the afterlife.

Which, based on my upbringing, scared the shit out of me.

My close-knit community knew exactly how to hit me, right where it would do the most damage, and they were right. It was yet another layer of leaving this community I'd have to navigate around.

I needed to reject the peer pressure to which I was so sensitive and begin to make my own decisions. I needed to find a community where I could feel free to be myself. I needed to learn how to build a community where people felt free to make difficult choices without being afraid of feeling ostracized.

I didn't yet understand the deep and powerful need I had to create this kind of community. That need would define all the choices I would make in my life and would ultimately define the essence of my faith.

So, where, amid this gale force, did I find the courage to leave? What convinced me that the guilt I was feeling wasn't real? What allowed me to turn my back on my culture and walk away?

I didn't realize it at the time, but as I sat there on that church pew in May 1989, I'd held within myself a weapon that protected me as I left our community, and that was my theater teacher's gift to me. Until then, I had been the Cowardly Lion standing before the great and mighty Wizard who my community claimed they were serving. They claimed He was God, but how could that be when He only seemed to exist here in the Midwest?

That conversation in the theater had been crucial because that was when Michael had given me the weapon—the gift—of understanding. He was the only teacher I'd known until then who had taken the time to draw me out, to assure me that I had the freedom to make my own choices.

In all our work together, Michael had helped me understand I was not alone. His childhood stories from South Africa had helped me understand that the Wizard my community worshipped was not the God I wished to follow. Thanks to Michael, I had seen behind the curtain, had caught a glimpse of the vicious Being who demanded that children be beaten. Thanks to Michael's wisdom, I grew to understand that there was a pathway of escape. Despite his own rejection of any faith, he had respected mine—yet also helped me understand that those who abused me were not men of God.

I hadn't had the courage to work this out back then—or even admit it to myself—but I believe, today, that it was at that moment, sitting there on the varnished bench in church, that the power of my family's culture lost its hold. You can only control someone when you have something they want, and I no longer wanted to fit into that culture. Thus, I could no longer be controlled.

This knowledge, this understanding, had destroyed the Wizard's power.

Chapter 21: Out of Sync

Although I left my Amish-Mennonite community, I determined to remain within the larger Mennonite world, perhaps because it felt safer, and I quickly landed a teaching position at Central Christian School in Kidron, Ohio. This was due to my college buddy Gerald Mast, who seemed to know everyone within the more liberal Mennonite world.

For those on the outside, these communities appeared to be the same, but they weren't. They seldom mixed. Within my home church, there was strict regulation of what you wore, where you went, how you dressed. Within the larger Mennonite community, education was encouraged, but there was little regulation of dress. Moderate drinking and dancing were permitted, and there was much more personal freedom—the focus being on building community and holding to the pacifist tradition.

This new Mennonite community was much more in line with what I wanted in the outside world, and it was a safer choice than simply leaving. Within this more liberal world, people were highly educated, and much more tolerant. Almost no one knew me, so few knew about my wild year abroad, other than what I recorded on my resume, which highlighted my year abroad. Thanks to my outstanding references from Malone College, and the fact that I was a Rotary Foundation Scholar, my new principal enthusiastically welcomed me.

However, I failed to understand that although this school was more liberal, it expected its teachers to carry themselves with humility. I had just survived a tough year in a secular culture where self-assurance was key. Now, I found myself in a community whose values ran directly counter to that. Forgetting that a little humility went a long way, I approached every task with overconfidence.

London had been a shock to the system, a dog-eat-dog world with a clear power structure. Rejecting most hierarchical structures, Central Christian was a community where teachers treated their students like friends, and where students called teachers by their first names. At first, I thought this was a great idea. But having been raised and taught in a patriarchal world, I discovered that I had not really left that structure behind. Although I thought I believed in equality—in reality, I still operated with a patriarchal frame of mind. And my students quickly came to understand this.

I expected unqualified respect from my students, just as I had gotten within the patriarchal schools of my childhood and early teaching years. I expected them to respect me because of who I was, a man and their teacher, and I resented it when they challenged me. My middle school students—who had grown up with the understanding that their teacher should be a friend rather than someone they should fear—were not about to give me a respect I had not earned. Like most students, they quickly figured me out.

As I look back on that year now, I realize all the mistakes I made. I refused any offers of friendship from the students, refusing to be truly vulnerable—probably because I was unable to do so at that time in my life—and I refused to take the advice of a successful teacher who encouraged me to make friends with my students.

When my students became frustrated with a difficult lesson, rather than listening to them and trying to help them understand the grammar lesson, I threatened an entire eighth-grade class with failing grades if they didn't do their homework. They responded by lining up outside the assistant principal's office to complain about everything I was doing wrong, which resulted in the kind of conference no teacher wants to have, attended by my department chair and the assistant principal.

Worst of all, it became clear that I didn't really love this job—what I really wanted was a teaching position at one of the best high schools in the area. I was a short timer, operating under the assumption that I would easily snag a job at the school where I had done my student teaching once a position became available.

Today, I am astonished by the gentleness with which the school's administration treated me, although at the time, I failed to appreciate what they were offering me.

Despite all these issues, in May, the school offered me a chance to share my faith story, inviting me to lead an entire chapel service. I had just received a contract for another year, and I approached the task with an auteur's confidence. I decided to portray my year abroad as a faith journey with myself as the hero. I based it on the slideshow I had created for Rotary.

As I reflect on that moment now, thirty-five years later, I realize that that "film" was an early attempt to write a memoir. Unfortunately, I had not yet had time to process my past—in fact, I didn't even know I needed therapy. Worst of all, I didn't understand that a good memoir is self-aware, but not self-absorbed. The difference between the two is crucial.

To prepare for the presentation, I wrote a script, liberally drawing from the purple poetry I had shared in my newsletter. To produce my documentary "film," I cast my artistic friends as narrators on the soundtrack I recorded.

I used edgy pop music to create intervals.

My students were in middle school, and the last thing they wanted to see were photos of their teacher on a wild Rumspringa. I still have nightmares about that presentation—how long it went, the painful groan that went up as I changed slide carousels (There's more, folks!), and the dawning recognition that I had just made one of the worst mistakes in my life.

I have no idea how many parents called to complain, but by the following morning, I was in the principal's office. One of the kindest administrators I've ever worked with, he was clearly beyond frustrated. But he didn't get angry.

"Several of the teachers were talking with me after your presentation," he said, "and we believe this school might not be the right fit for you." His fingers toyed with his pen, not looking up at me as he spoke. "You could fight this, I suppose. You do have a contract for another year."

We sat for a moment in silence. The blood roared in my ears. I didn't know what to say. Humiliation vied with my sense of pride. If my colleagues thought I didn't fit in, why should I want to stay?

I immediately offered to resign, a move he accepted gratefully. We agreed I would finish out the year and move on. I told him I was thinking about graduate school, but privately, I thought I could still snare a job at Hoover High School, the top-ranked high school where I had really wanted to teach. I didn't consider that I might have to move home, or that I had so little cash on hand that I had had to request paycheck advances several times across the year.

I walked out of the office, relieved that I would not be returning. I knew my teaching mentor still admired my work, and I knew—based on conversations we had had—that a teaching position would become available in the fall at Hoover High School. I assumed my mentor would be able to get me the job there.

It didn't dawn on me that my resignation might hurt my chances of securing that position. And so, that night, relieved that I was leaving, I sat down at the typewriter and wrote a long resignation letter to my principal, detailing my reasons for leaving. The next morning, I turned it into the principal.

Only then did I call my mentor to tell him what I had done. Only after I heard the anger flash in his voice did the enormity of my mistake hit me. I didn't immediately know why, but I do now. My refusal to learn and adapt to my new school, my lack of strategy across the year, the fact that I didn't put the energy into getting to know my students, the fact that I had not been transparent with my mentor so that he could give me the advice I needed to succeed, culminating in my careless resignation when I still had a contract... all of this had ensured that I was now un-hirable, at least by Hoover High School. Top public schools like to steal good teachers, not hire a young teacher who has resigned from their first professional teaching position, no matter the reason.

And so, after finishing out the year, I returned to construction work. My boss offered me a solid salary if I would agree to commit to an entire year as a bricklayer. I hesitated, despondent. Working in the hot sun, doing work I had tried to escape by going to college, living at home again with my parents... I knew this wasn't what I wanted to do, but I had to survive financially.

It was then that one of my best friends urged me to apply to a range of schools looking for teachers, and in August, one of those schools gave me a call.

They paid even less than my previous school, but they were desperate for an English teacher, and they were happy to look past my resignation.

One interview later, I was hired.

I entered my new position at Steubenville Catholic Central with a sense of gratitude and humility, and the community welcomed me with open arms. I was just grateful for a teaching position, and best of all, I was teaching a very motivated class of juniors, whom I quickly bonded with. They had high academic goals, and they looked upon my experience in England with awe.

I discovered that I liked the Catholic community, which felt much more culturally like my experience in London. I had mostly cut ties with my home community, no longer having to interact with my family. I quickly began to make friends.

My students let me know how much better I was than my predecessor. I viewed this praise with a skeptical eye. In my previous school, I had at first been welcomed—until I wasn't any more. I feared my principal, who visited my classroom often, regularly leaving me corrective notes in my faculty mailbox— I darkly suspected my previous principal had given him a negative recommendation, but I had no proof. But ultimately, my new principal taught me that as a professional, the details matter. Later, I learned that he treated all his teachers this way.

But my failure as a teacher taught me a great deal. I had become more realistic in my view of myself. There was no guarantee of success, so I needed to work hard. I had learned the hard lesson that popularity can turn, and quickly. Relieved to be teaching students who appreciated me for who I was, I now drove to school each day happy to still be teaching.

In November, to my surprise, a prominent Mennonite minister from my previous school's community gave me a call. He wanted to meet for dinner and talk about my departure from Central Christian. The school board had asked him to meet with me because they were unhappy with the way my former principal had handled my departure and wanted to hear my side of the story.

It was a chance for me to hurt my former administrator, I suspect, but fortunately, I didn't do this. I wanted to put my previous school behind me. So, I assured the investigating pastor that I had left of my own accord, and that my former principal had done his best to work with me. This was mostly true. I was happy in my new teaching position at a Catholic school. My previous principal was not to blame.

The pastor's face showed a mixture of skepticism and relief, but he was glad to finish his investigation.

I was enthralled by this community of mostly second-generation European immigrants, probably because it contained some of the same elements of community I had enjoyed in my home community—many of them were related to each other, church was taken seriously, and I was welcomed warmly at any parish church I attended. Best of all, they didn't find the "sins" that had gotten me into trouble while abroad—drinking, dancing, theater—to be a problem. I was so impressed that I briefly joined the Roman Catholic Church, horrifying my parents.

Which was the point.

I stayed away from the church of my childhood whenever I returned home because I didn't want to be reminded of what I had left behind. Staying in Ohio and remaining only two hours from home, occasionally visiting friends and family on the weekend, was a compromise. I had fought free of my community's stifling embrace, but I missed my friends and worked hard to keep in touch with those who supported me. I also couldn't forget the community whose memories and perspective on faith still shaped how I viewed God.

I wanted to leave, but on some level, I was still tied to them. Unwilling to see a therapist, I had not yet processed what I had rejected and what I believed about God, about myself, about the world. In the back of my head, I still wondered whether my family might indeed be right.

Eventually, I was able to get a job at North Canton Hoover High School, where I had done my student teaching. It was a school that took pride in its academic success, the school of my dreams. I even bought a house less than a mile from the school.

While at North Canton, I started a summer program to earn my master's. In addition to all the new things I was learning and the new experiences in Vermont, I also found love.

Chapter 22: Two Dresses

I met Enyo during that third summer of study at the Bread Loaf School of English, a program Middlebury College provides during the summer for mostly English teachers. Within hours of arriving on campus, I'd caught a glimpse of her dark curly hair and willowy figure. She was alone on one of the famous chairs, reading a book and smoking a cigarette, and I was immediately drawn to her, struck by her poise and intensity.

Spotting her later at a keg party that night, I approached her, holding a craft beer in each hand. Pulling her long, black hair away from her face, she pushed aside the drink I offered her and took a sip from my own half-drunk pint. In her eyes I glimpsed a primal essence something that contrasted sharply with her flirty, little black dress.

It so happened we were taking the same two classes that summer, so, during our first break in our Page-to-Stage class, I dropped down beside her on a set of steps just outside the classroom. Without looking at me, she handed me a just-lit menthol cigarette.

In front of us, students clustered in small clumps on the bucolic grounds in front of us. I discovered she was a native of Minnesota, and she taught during the school year at a private school in Chicago. Enyo's acid observations kept me interested in talking with her because, in addition to being hot as Hell, she was incredibly intelligent. Too late, our break ended, students flowing past us. When I returned to class, she slipped into the empty seat beside me.

Where she proceeded to ignore me.

By now, I was in the prime of life. Having taught in the public schools for almost half-a-decade, I had begun to find my identity and assimilate into modern culture. Few people realized I came from an Amish-Mennonite background unless I told them.

The scars of several romances lay behind me, two of them serious, and I had begun to figure out what attracted women to me. I fancied myself an alpha male, and I thought women were attracted to my dominant personality—I was determined not to be like my father. I had also been directing drama now for several years, and I liked being in charge, not just in relationships, but also professionally. When I first approached Enyo, I sensed that a romantic relationship with her would look like other relationships I had had, what I called "spanking relationships."

Until then, most of the women who dated me were drawn to the fantasies

I had constructed out of the abuse I had experienced during my formative years. Now in my early thirties, I knew I was drawing upon my memories, but I did not realize that these fantasies were an attempt to exorcise the traumas of my past. Today, I know that the women I was dating were not part of the BDSM scene, so I was tapping into their own abuse histories, since most women from fundamentalist churches had experience with strict discipline. But I suspect their attraction was driven by their fascination with my past, and that they were willing to play because they loved me and wanted to make me happy.

I knew enough about the BDSM scene at that point—thanks to the internet—to know that the power dynamics I was playing with needed to be limited to the bedroom.

In fact, it was a point of pride with me that in real life, I considered myself a feminist. The idea that I would actually tell a woman what to do in the real world was horrifying to me. I believed my partners should have full autonomy. This was confusing to some of the girls I dated.

And so, I believed my need for control could be restricted to the bedroom. I believed I could control the games I was playing in the bedroom. I could turn off my need to dominate my partners after the fun was over. Whatever dominating impulse drove me to play would obediently trot back to the closet after the fun was over.

What bothered me most were the feelings of self-loathing I experienced after sex with my consenting partners. I understood perfectly the plight of the Beast in the Disney film, trapped within a body that disgusted him. Like the Beast, I didn't see any chance of escape.

But that summer at Bread Loaf, as Enyo's relationship with me turned intimate, I was shocked to discover that she understood exactly what was driving me.

Our first kiss surprised me.

At the end of the first week, our drama teacher randomly assigned Enyo and me to create an original scene together. Or perhaps it wasn't random—he may have seen that we were spending all of our breaks smoking together on the classroom steps. Perhaps he saw the electricity that was there between us.

By then, I had discovered that Enyo was a professional theater director, and her creative impulses were brilliant and fearless. In an empty classroom, we worked through the details of the scene's direction, arguing fiercely. But there was a moment when we both stopped talking. She looked up at me curiously for a long moment, and the kiss that followed was fierce. I wanted more.

Just before we made love for the first time—when I suggested she was a naughty girl who needed a spanking—she pulled me into a deep kiss and then refused my offer. "I've been through all that and have no interest in that kind of power dynamic with you," she said.

I was surprised. Usually, I read women more clearly. Seeing my disappointment, she reached out, took my face in both hands, and kissed me again.

"I've done that kind of relationship before," she said. "It was exciting… but ultimately, I didn't like the way it made me feel. I want more than that with you."

We spent the weekend at a small bed & breakfast, using the time to eat well at local restaurants, slept in and wandered the streets of the nearby town, looking through shops. I found myself able to relax with Enyo. By then, she had told me a bit about her history, a relationship from which she walked away at the first hint of domestic violence. Her courage and decisiveness impressed me.

One night after making love, she leaned on her pillow and stroked my face.

"I like you, a lot," she said. "But you haven't told me a lot about yourself. You seem to be fascinated by power dynamics—I see it in your stories about directing, your need to be in control. Where do you think that comes from?"

It was then I told her about my family, my community's belief in separation, the way women especially had to dress modestly, my reaction to this, and the way I fled the community at the age of twenty-five years old. She listened, utterly absorbed.

"Have you ever seen a therapist?" she asked, her eyes never leaving my face. "Perhaps to process what you've experienced?"

"I haven't," I admitted. "Do you think I should?"

"I think only you can answer that. But I've taken therapy to deal with the relationship I ended several years ago."

"What was it like?" I asked.

She studied me for a moment. "I think, based on what you've told me, that it would scare you… at first. Which is probably the reason you should go. You don't strike me as someone who's afraid of anything… not with the story you just told me about leaving."

Since Enyo and I were taking both of our classes together—we were both focused on theater classes that summer—we were able to spend all of class time together, working together on our classwork in our spare time.

When we weren't in class or studying, I was working in the campus theater program as the assistant director and actor. Since Enyo was a deeply committed thespian, she understood late-night rehearsals, often attending rehearsals as an observer. Afterward, she and her friends often joined me and other actors on the front porch of our cabin, where we would drink and smoke until late, talking theater.

Enyo was very good at asking questions, as well, and I found myself telling stories about my past, even to the porch group. As the semester wore on, I realized that rather than being repelled by my past, Enyo had begun to recognize the anger and bitterness toward my parents that lay at my core.

This was revealed when for the first time, I explored what I had been through in a five-minute scene, performed without dialogue. Costuming the three actors in Amish clothes, I set the scene in an attic. A young couple is caught making out in the young man's attic by his father. The young woman is sent away, the father grabs a stick, and he moves purposefully toward the young man, preparing to give him a beating. At that point, I froze the scene.

Writing and directing this fictionalized scene tapped into the abuse I had experienced as a child. As I watched the actors truthfully play out the emotions of the scene and then listened to my classmates discuss what they saw in the scene, objectively, for the first time, I felt the relief that comes with being vulnerable.

I had never been able to be this honest in any of the writing I had done before this, and it startled me that people discussed the scene with empathy and thoughtfulness. Most important to me, however, were Enyo's observations.

"How much of that was based on real life?" she asked.

I hesitated. "I had a father who *would* have spanked me, had he caught me doing that with a girl."

"That didn't look like a spanking," she said, pushing in close to me. "That father was about to *beat* his son."

My heart pounded as I looked at her, wordless.

I soon began to trust Enyo's empathetic nature. Although her personality could be explosive, especially when it came to dealing with artistic decisions, she was also inherently kind. I slowly began to realize that she was the kind of soulmate who might safeguard my heart.

For the first time, I began to have hope that I could find real romance.

One night over drinks on the front porch of my dorm, I told Enyo I was driving back to Ohio that weekend to attend my baby sister's wedding. By then, she knew all about my Amish-Mennonite family, and she quickly invited herself along because she was curious about my childhood world.

I considered the challenges ahead of us. Enyo was a strong believer in the theater, not in the Christian faith. She was an atheist. My sister's marriage would be a long church service, and the God my family worshipped was exactly the kind of God who would offend her intellectual sensibilities.

At that point, I wasn't sure what kind of faith I had, or if I had one at all. Enyo's approach to life and death—she was a committed atheist—made more and more sense. The people I knew from my past believed in an angry God who seemed eager to condemn people to Hell, rather than treat them as children He loved. In addition, the rigid, literalist approach to the Bible made no sense to me, the more I learned about textual analysis.

Enyo was passionately committed to using theater to explore the quest for justice and the search for truth, something that appealed to me deeply. Our mutual passion for the theater undergirded our relationship.

When I thought about my father's faith, I realized that he had completely misread what theater is all about. To him, actors were hypocrites because they played someone who wasn't themselves. I had long ago discovered that the best acting occurs when an actor reaches into themselves and finds a truthful response to any situation they find in the script.

In addition, knowing that Enyo was a strong feminist, I wondered how she would respond to my family's patriarchal culture.

But there was a deeper fear that lurked beneath my worries about introducing Enyo to my family. I wasn't sure I had yet put my family's culture behind me.

I worried that I might expose my patriarchal past, a world in which men casually assumed that their perspectives were superior to women. I worried that—surrounded by my family and community at the wedding—I might react in a way that proved to Enyo that at my core, I was *still* a conservative Mennonite boy dressed up in modern clothes. I worried that if she saw this, she might reject me. Letting Enyo get that close to me made me feel vulnerable, and that scared the Hell out of me.

But perhaps I just needed to trust her. Eventually, if we were going to survive, she needed to see my family at one point or another.

It might as well be now.

We left immediately after class on Friday and drove through the night to reach Ohio. We booked a hotel room in Canton, where we unpacked our wedding attire.

Enyo's favorite color was black. Over the last few weeks, I'd enjoyed watching her wear a series of little black dresses because they were invented for her. She had great legs and liked showing them off.

As we dressed for the wedding, she held up two dresses for me. One of her dresses was long and relatively modest; the other was one of her favorite little black dresses, fun and flirty, which barely grazed the middle of her tanned, toned thighs.

"Which one should I wear?" she asked. "You know your family."

It was here that I made my fatal error. At that point in time, I was desperate to prove to Enyo that I respected her right to make her own decisions. I had been telling her for several weeks about the control my family exercised, and I wanted to make sure she didn't think I was like them. This had become an obsession that blinded me.

Because of course, she knew that. What she was asking was the question any woman in love with a man would ask who was about to meet his family. She wanted to know what would make my family feel comfortable with her. She wanted to dress appropriately to show respect for his family's culture.

"I'm fine with either option," I said. "Which one makes you feel the most comfortable?"

I wanted to show that I could give my mate complete freedom outside the bedroom. Yet I was fooling myself, I realize now. All of my life back then had

215

to do with control—whether it was sex, or relationships, or religion. In the theater, I was drawn to directing because it gave me absolute control within a world I could create. While I told myself I was trying to give Enyo her freedom, that wasn't what I wanted in this situation.

What I wanted was to use Enyo to prove a point to my family and community. I wasn't thinking about Enyo's feelings or ensuring that she felt safe meeting my family for the first time. In fact, I wasn't thinking about her at all—I was thinking about myself. Instead of focusing on how I could make Enyo feel safe and happy—this woman who so clearly loved me—I was instead focused on proving to her that I was not like my family (which she already knew, or she wouldn't have been dating me). If that meant that my girlfriend would be dressed in a manner that showed disrespect for their culture, too bad.

What I never thought about was a foundational aspect of love—the fact that Enyo had feelings, that she might be humiliated by showing up without my having given her a cultural roadmap, that she would resent being used by me to put my finger in the face of my family. *I didn't care.* I was at war with my family, and if Enyo ended up becoming a casualty of that war, then so be it. She was a weapon to me, not a person that I loved, not someone that I should have protected from my family.

So today, I'm not surprised things unfolded the way they did.

"It's up to you," I said to her, smiling to hide my spike of concern. "It's your choice."

While I respected her right to choose—and encouraged her to do so because I would *not* be my father, dictating clothing choices to a spouse—I didn't realize that by not providing feedback, I was allowing her to walk into the lion's den that was my judgy community.

When we walked in the door of my childhood church for Heidi's wedding, I suddenly saw it through the eyes of my girlfriend. There was no stained glass, no statues, no elaborate, gilded crucifixes or gold-stitched altar cloth, no incense, and no organ. Just a plain, wooden table up front. Entering the sanctuary felt more like entering a filled lecture hall.

Having joined and left the Catholic church, having visited cathedrals all over the world, I saw how different my community's sanctuary now appeared to the outside world. It truly was a Plain community. I had always heard people from outside my world describe it that way, but until now, I hadn't felt what they had felt when they were visiting. Now, suddenly, I saw it through the eyes of a stranger.

In the sanctuary, there was row upon row of strict Amish-Mennonites. The men were buttoned tightly into dark Plain coats with not a tie in sight. The women wore starched, hand-stitched dresses draped modestly over their frames. Glancing at my girlfriend's little black dress, her arms and legs tanned in the midst of a crowd of fully covered women and men, jolted me, making me feel like we had been dropped into a medieval crowd, everyone staring at us with unfriendly eyes.

A solemn-faced usher led Enyo and me to a place of honor in the second row, as was customary for the bride's oldest brother. The rest of my siblings had already arrived, grouped together by family. Seeing the rest of the audience separated by gender—the men on the right, the women on the left—flashed me back to the services I had attended as a child. Nothing had changed.

What had changed was the deathly silence of the room, which felt more akin to a funeral than a wedding. This was not what I was used to when visiting our church in the past. People had always been welcoming, even to people who had left. It felt as if I had arrived in a completely different church where no one knew me. As I looked around, I realized that I knew almost no one. That was the moment when I realized how very few people of my community were attending this wedding. Most of them were from out of town, and based on what I saw, few of them knew me.

But my family still welcomed me. My older sisters greeted us with a smile, and my brother Dave reached around the child he was holding in his lap to shake my hand with a welcoming grin. "Glad you could make it, Steve."

To my surprise, my sister Elaine was already seated. It was the first time I had seen her since she had left at the age of twenty-one, and it was a relief to see her. She gave me an enthusiastic hug, and she also hugged Enyo, the only member of my family to do so. Now in her late thirties, Elaine still couldn't sit without wriggling restlessly. She glanced from Enyo to me, clearly proud of the fact that her "big brother" was dating such a beautiful and worldly woman. She wriggled her nose, suddenly, and I knew why. She had caught the scent of cigarette smoke.

Although I knew our community reacted strongly to smoking, considering it to be a sin, I had refused to tell Enyo that. This is who we were. If people didn't like it, too bad. And so, we had a smoke in the parking lot out at my car, just before we came in.

Now, Elaine leaned over, whispering with her trademark giggle, "I just want a cigarette."

I glanced at Enyo, wondering what she was thinking about our community. Her face was as expressionless as the rest of the church, but she gave me a brief smile before returning her attention to the front where the ministers had just taken their seats, wearing dark Plain coats with white cotton shirt collars showing at the top.

I glanced back at the rest of the church. Heidi had a lot of friends—my sister was a very outgoing person who made friends easily, as was her bridegroom—and it looked as if every friend they had was at the wedding. There were rows and rows of conservative Mennonite people, all dressed more or less in the same clothing style, packed into every bench, side by side.

217

Except for our bench. To the right of my sister Elaine, the bench stretched, bare and empty. Here we sat, the outcasts, plain as day. My community was consistent if nothing else. When someone sinned against anyone within the community—even themselves—it was a sin against all, and I was now that sinner. For the first time, I clearly felt the distance between myself and the community surrounding me.

Amish-Mennonite weddings, like courtships, are carefully planned affairs. I'd told Enyo about the two-hour wedding service, but two hours of preaching feels much longer than a two-hour play. Especially when you disagree with everything being said.

As with all Amish-Mennonite brides, my sister was immaculate in white, wearing a version of her modest dress she wore every Sunday. Pulled into a bun, her hair was hidden under a white bonnet. She wore dark hose and sensible shoes with not a speck of makeup. Her new church, even more conservative than my father's, didn't even allow her to carry flowers, yet, facing the minister, my sister's smile shone amid the solemnity.

At the beginning of the sermon, the ruddy-haired preacher rose, smiling.

My chest tightened when he began to preach. According to Brother Red, American culture had disintegrated, morals had slipped, values had declined because women had entered the workplace nearly a century before. Their vote destroyed the masculine goodness of our culture.

As I sat there listening, I realized how dramatically I had changed. In Phoenix, I'd have approved that sermon, perhaps even delivered it to the congregation on a Sunday evening. Now I believed the essence of being human was giving people autonomy, whether male or female. Limiting women to specific roles demeaned them, took away their autonomy, and destroyed their humanity.

Enyo sat rigid, staring straight ahead, and I sat restlessly beside her. I suspected this was all new to her, this soul-destroying belief system. I didn't know how much she knew about conservative Christianity. Enyo was brilliant, and she would know how flawed this pastor's argument was—even more so than I did. Would she get up, walk out in contempt? Perhaps interrupt with a colorful monologue?

But she didn't.

Enyo's silence should have been a clear indication to me of how much she cared about me. But she also understood when silence was important. She understood my community with a clarity I was years away from seeing. She instinctively knew when it was time to remain silent, and when it was time to talk.

Her growing love for me had given her the ability to reject the power games that my fetish would have demanded, which had ensured that our relationship remained on equal terms. But now, I wondered, was she worried that there were other ship-killing rocks buried beneath the placid waters of my family's culture?

Until then, all I'd experienced when visiting my home church had been warm smiles of welcome, even an eagerness to see me return. Now, as my sister and Enyo and I got up to leave—the two outcasts and one outsider—I faced something new—row upon row of the unfamiliar faces of my sister's new family and friends. To almost all of them, I was a stranger, an outsider.

During the return trip to Vermont, Enyo and I processed what we had seen.

"You told me how welcoming people are in your community. Yet no one talked to us. I mean, not a single person bothered to approach you," she said.

"I noticed that," I said. "I even asked Heidi about it when we were talking in line. She told me people are just shy."

"It might have helped if there had been anything to drink."

I laughed. I knew she wasn't talking about the non-alcoholic drinks they served.

"I think this is the first time I really felt like I was on the outside," I said. "People just... looked past us."

"Yeah," she said. "I saw that too."

It was an important moment. The tidal wave of distance we had felt between us and my sister's community had been startling. I had rejected my community years before—but this was the first time I finally realized how clearly my people had rejected me.

But Enyo hadn't yet gotten to what bothered her the most. The most obvious signal was what happened halfway through the trip home, when we stopped to rest at a motel. Before then, Enyo had never missed a chance to initiate passionate lovemaking; that night, however, she remained firmly on her side of the bed, her back to me.

Late the next day, as we crossed over the state line into Vermont, we had one of our most significant conversations, spurred on by a series of questions Enyo began asking me.

"What would you do if I told you I was pregnant? That I intended to have an abortion?"

I glanced at her, immediately worried that I was about to become a father.

She shook her head, impatiently. "I'm not pregnant. I'm just giving you a hypothetical."

Her suddenly stern manner made me feel like a schoolboy.

"I don't know," I said. "But I don't think it would be my decision. It would be your choice."

I don't remember what else she said, but I did sense her skepticism, and I understood why. She had just seen my home community, had seen how little agency the women had. But more to the point, Enyo was responding to the lack of conviction in articulating what I believed about something as basic as a woman's reproductive rights—which is key to a woman's agency. My uncertainty made her question what I did believe. Enyo needed a partner whose belief system was as clear as her own. She had rejected the world of religion and patriarchy, but she was not certain I had.

Well after midnight, several miles from the campus, Enyo picked up our earlier conversation, cutting to the heart of the matter. By then, she was driving the car.

"What was that conversation with your friend about?"

"What conversation?"

"The one between you and your friend after the wedding? While we were driving him to the reception?"

My heart dropped. I thought about the way we had laughed, about Enyo's silence as we talked.

"I think we were just amused at the way my family reacted to us."

Enyo didn't smile.

"I felt a bit like a weapon in that conversation, something you were using to get back at your family. By letting me wear that dress, you made sure of that. Didn't you?"

With a sinking heart, I realized she was right. But rather than admitting this, I went on the defensive.

"But what was I to do when you asked me what to wear? If I had told you what to wear, and then you'd heard that sermon, you would have thought I was exactly like my family, forcing the women to wear modest clothing."

She took a moment, then conceded.

"I understand. That makes sense. But Steven, if you really cared about me, wouldn't you have at least given me a warning, perhaps told me what the women would be wearing? Given me some context? It still would have been my choice that way."

"I didn't think about that," I admitted. "I just wanted to make sure you knew that I will never treat you like the men in our community treat their wives and daughters."

By then, we were pulling onto the campus. It was 2 AM, and the grounds were silent and still. She found a parking spot and we sat silently for a moment. Then she spoke, looking straight ahead.

"I think you have a lot of growing up to do, Steven. I'm going to need some time to think about... this. About us."

With that, she opened the door and grabbed her suitcase. I got out, but she was already heading in the direction of her sleeping quarters. She didn't look back.

No kiss, no hug, no goodbye.

It took a week before I had another conversation with Enyo. In class, she ignored me, and I gave her the space I thought she wanted. One evening, carrying a craft beer, she joined me as I hosted several friends on my dorm's front porch. She sat down beside me as if we were still a couple. She was intense and acerbic, as always. She made them laugh.

We were still a thing, I thought, relieved.

Afterward, she took me by the hand and led me to my room, undressing me as I stood beside the bed, uncertain. Afterwards, when we kissed in the dark, her tears stung my tongue.

But nothing had really been solved. I think Enyo knew that, although I was still too naïve to understand. We lasted until Christmas, at least by email, but the relationship had been forever changed, and eventually it fizzled out.

Today, as I reflect on that wedding, I realize that Enyo was rightfully pissed that I led her like a lamb to the slaughter—even if unintentionally. I had not given any thought to what was about to happen. I had not anticipated what my family would think of our relationship, nor did I apparently care. I had not considered the message I was sending by bringing someone who was blatantly outside of my family's world to my youngest sister's most special day of her life. I had not considered the ramifications of my actions.

Although I had thought I was ready for a serious relationship with a woman—one that was egalitarian in nature—in reality, I wasn't ready at all. I had no idea of what real love demanded, or of a marital affection that demanded I put my partner first. Instead, I had let my deep, abiding anger against my family rule my decisions. Worst of all, I didn't even realize why I was making those pain-bearing decisions.

I had refused to seek out therapeutic help, which would have helped me find healing for the trauma I was experiencing, because I didn't recognize the trauma within my body, nor the way my body had instinctively reacted to that trauma.

I had ignored Enyo's question about therapy early on in our relationship, once again assuming that I didn't need it because "I knew I wasn't insane," ignoring the danger signals that were now beginning to show. My unprocessed memories had begun to pound at the basement door. And so, rather than seeking therapy, once again, I had made bad choices that destroyed a romantic relationship with someone I cared about deeply.

In the relationships that followed, I returned to the familiar disciplinary play that I thought made my romantic relationships exciting. But I was slowly losing my soul, which became clear when one after another, my romances failed. And every time my lifeless eyes appeared in the mirror, I realized how unhappy I was.

I didn't understand romantic love. As a child, I had been told, again and again, that when my parents or teachers hurt me, they were expressing their love for me. Eventually, I had begun to believe them. Eventually, I had begun to believe that treating a woman as an object of pleasure was loving her. Eventually, I had become confused about what love and romance really meant.

Oh, yes, intellectually I could explain what love was when talking to others, even to the women I dated. But I didn't understand how to practice it, because to do that, you need to connect to your emotions, and I had blocked the emotional pain of the trauma just below the surface. To protect myself, I had rejected any shred of vulnerability.

But I still longed for love. And so, I chose the path of *dark* romance, which explored the painful elements of my past within sexual play, including abuse, trauma, and power dynamics. What resulted was traumatic repetition. And slowly but surely, my choices began to strip me of my humanity.

I needed to find a different path to true love.

Chapter 23: Dark Prince

The path that would eventually lead me to real romance appeared during a conversation with my boyhood friend Laban. During one of his visits, he told me about a girl he had begun seeing. "She's perfect for you," he told me, ironically.

They had been dating for a while, so I didn't think much about her, until Laban began to talk about the fact that he didn't think their relationship would survive. Despite his dire predictions about the relationship, they stayed together. I knew by now her name was Laura, and I couldn't forget that he thought we'd be perfect together. I became curious.

And then one day, Laban told me he had purchased a "fixer-upper" in Washington, D.C. He invited me to a Halloween party that was also supposed to be a housewarming...

My little Saturn coupe slowly crawled through the Columbia Heights neighborhood of Washington, D.C. I pulled over and parked. The mansion in front of me had seen better days, but, behind the cracked paint of the siding, and the occasionally broken window, lay the Victorian design of a top-flight architect.

In our conversation by phone the week before, Laban had warned me it wasn't the best neighborhood. That was a kind description. But the street was lined with well-apportioned automobiles, apparently guests to the party.

Making my way up the steps to the grand front door, I could hear a crowd inside. The door pushed open easily, and I entered.

Before me stretched a crowded hallway, leading to grand, sweeping steps with a battered, red runner leading up to the next floor. On the landing, a real-life Persephone, the nymph, stood, blonde ringlets cascading all the way to her waist. Her cream, form-fitting gown made her seem like the eternal girl, just on the cusp of womanhood.

My planet jolted to a stop.

As if in my dream, she moved toward me, taking a step down the stairs. Her startling blue eyes were fixed on me with more than casual interest. Her face was flawless, innocent.

My friend Laban appeared in a black tux. He grinned as they joined me at the bottom of the steps.

"Welcome, Steven. Meet Laura."

I suddenly remembered the ironic tone when Laban had described her, which I had dismissed as Laban just bragging about one more girl he had dated. But, he had called this one.

Damn right—she is perfect for me.

The thought was instinctive. I'd heard all my life about falling in love with someone I had been dating enough to know that you can't go by first impressions, but I tossed that logic to the winds. But then, an equally powerful thought slammed into my chest, right where my heart was located.

But he's still dating her.

In fact, they were living together. My heart sank to my black cowboy boots, but I stuck out my hand.

But instead of taking it, Laura reached for a flute of sparkling champagne from a passing waiter's tray. "May tonight change the future of your life," she said, taking me in as she handed me the flute.

My stomach did a slow flip. I knew she wasn't talking about us meeting—she was talking about her best friend Kami, whom Laban had told me she wanted me to meet—but as far as I was concerned, my future *had* just changed.

"Let's hope so," I grinned.

Turning toward Laban, Laura said, "Tell him about our game."

Laban grinned. "We've decided to let you find Kami." He stepped closer. "It'll be fun. She knows you're coming tonight—Laura's already given her the scoop on what you… like."

Laura smirked, and my face suddenly felt hot. In a moment of weakness, I had shared details of my fetish with Laban, which meant Laura knew as well. The fact that Laura knew what I liked added a certain amount of spice to our conversations, but now I was trying to assess her.

How does she feel about me?

During our last conversation, Laban had told me that one of her friends was into the scene, as well, and he'd promised to introduce us tonight. I was curious to meet Kami, yes, but the fact that Laura had agreed to introduce me to her best friend was a double-edged sword. It meant she approved, but it also might mean there was no chance with *us*.

Now that I'd met Laura and knew that her relationship with Laban had a termination date, my interest in Kami had dropped significantly. Was there a chance Laura would realize that she was indeed "perfect for me," as Laban had predicted?

Laban was starting to give me directions for the game. "This is the Great Room," Laban said. "There are five floors altogether. Start in the basement. It's an ancient speakeasy, which was popular during Prohibition."

Laura took over the assessment. "On the fourth floor, if you inspect the wall, you'll find bullet holes." She wrinkled her nose. "I can't believe Laban bought this place. They say a man was shot here about five years ago." She pointed to the ceiling. "We're calling the turret on the top floor The Dungeon. It's all about correction and punishment." She arched a brow.

"I thought dungeons are in the basement?" I bantered.

"Well," she glanced at Laban, her voice dripping with sarcasm. "You do the best you can with what you have. For tonight, he's dressed it up as the dungeon."

I knew Laban wasn't into the BDSM scene. He just had a knack for building loyal friendships with interesting people, and it was obvious—based on the art I saw—that he also loved collecting unique furniture. He loved garage sales and bargain shops because he could always find something that represented the various aspects of his personality. I wondered if Laura's interest in BDSM—which had inspired him to tell me about her—might have inspired him to create this little game.

I glanced around at the other guests, who were ignoring us, thankfully—I didn't usually talk about my fetish in front of others because the minute it was brought up, the conversation became all about that, and I went from being Steven to being the guy who likes to spank women.

I could see Laura was enjoying my discomfort. "Don't worry, Steven. Everyone else is playing the game too. They'll help you if you get lost."

"Or hand you a ruler," Laban said. "Didn't one of your teachers at our school wield one?"

"You told me it was a paddle," Laura challenged him. "One with holes, I think."

Tossing her long golden tresses, Laura turned to me. "Good luck finding Kami. She's dressed as a dominatrix. I think she even has a riding whip."

Laura curtsied. "Steven, I can't wait to hear what happens. From what Laban's told me, you and Kami ought to have plenty of dark secrets to share."

It was clear to me that Laban had told her a great deal about me—I was a little annoyed at him, but clearly, Laura and I were connecting... so maybe it wasn't all bad. I wondered about their relationship—I couldn't believe that he felt so comfortable talking about me in this way. And what was her history— how much was Laura into the same sort of disciplinary play that I was? I had been curious when I entered the house, but now... That was the moment I realized I was in deep trouble.

I'm falling for someone else's girl.

With a final, quick glance at me, Laura grabbed Laban's hand, and they headed toward the Great Room. The candlelight from the nearby sconces caught the gold of Laura's long tresses.

As I watched them disappear, I thought about my relationship with Laban—the way he always seemed to show up in my life at critical junctures. Publishing my first poem in high school. Pushing me to attend college just after I graduated. Showing up on my front doorstep in Steubenville, Ohio, where I was directing drama, and hanging out with me at poetry readings in Pittsburgh. Our latest moment of connection had been the previous summer at graduate school in Middlebury, when he had hung out with my friends and then teased me about the girl who was "perfect for me"… the girl he was currently dating.

She is perfect for me. Why does she have to be dating my close friend?

But I knew the answer to that. I would never have met her, otherwise. There was no sense in me pursuing her. I valued my friendship with Laban. But then I thought about her long blonde hair, her dancing blue eyes…

I had never wanted the wrong woman so much in all my life.

It was the one thought that governed the rest of my night. Oh, I met Kami, who, dressed in black leather, carrying a whip, had seemed interested at first, but there was no magic between us. I met several other interesting women, as well. But I was distracted and my conversational attempts faltered as I talked to the people I met. The entirety of my emotional bandwidth was dominated by one woman.

Laura.

The next morning, she was the only person on the planet, especially at the little hole-in-the-wall café where several of us went for a late brunch. The little black beanie Laura was wearing was cute. Especially the way she wore it, cocked to one side. And her long blonde ringlets were gone. Turns out they'd been extensions, leaving her with a pageboy haircut.

I said almost nothing to her. It was clear to me by then that she cared a great deal about Laban. They sat close, and kissed often over breakfast, with everyone treating that as a normal part of the meal. She barely looked at me, so it was clear that what I had thought was… interest in me… wasn't. But then, just as the party got up to go, she turned to me.

"So, what did you think of Kami?" she asked. Laban was talking to the waitress, credit card in hand.

"She's interesting," I said. "How do you know her?"

"We travel a lot," she said. "We went to Italy last summer. She's a perfect travel companion. Never boring," she said, lifting an eyebrow.

"I got her phone number," I said. "I think we're going to take in a play, when I come back to town."

"Really?" Laura said. "You must have really impressed her." She grabbed Laban's arm as he approached. "Darling, Steven thinks they might go out."

"Whoa… nice work, Steven," he said. He glanced down at Laura. "I didn't believe you when you said she *was* interested. Okay, in that case, perhaps the four of us should do something together."

"I'll figure it out with Kami," Laura said, excitedly. "I think there's an event at the National Press Club we could do… if you come in on New Year's. My boss just mentioned it."

Apparently, I had misread Kami—she *was* interested in me.

By December, Laura had secured us tickets. Laban called and suggested I get a tux—it was going to be a luxurious New Year's Eve Ball. I made plans to go. Kami and I had been exchanging emails by then, but I was still on the fence about her. She was attractive, and had a biting wit, which made me laugh, but I was still on the fence about whether or not that was going to work out.

What I found confusing was the fact that Laban kept confiding in me about the problems he was having with Laura.

"I'm not sure we're going to make it," he said. I couldn't tell over the line how he was feeling about this. "She's thinking about moving out," he said.

"But she's going with you to the Ball?"

"Oh, yes. Who knows when we'll break up," he said. "I'm just not sure."

I wasn't sure how to feel. I struggled between feelings of loyalty to Laban and my growing interest in Laura. In spite of the fact that several weeks had gone by, and that I hadn't talked to her, I still couldn't forget her.

The image of her in her beanie cap and pageboy haircut was seared on my mind. If she and Laban were to break up, maybe I could be the safe harbor she landed in.

I arrived in town for the weekend, having arranged ahead of time to go out with Kami. We would see *Uncle Vanya* together. She had gotten tickets and made reservations at a hip restaurant she thought I'd like, according to her email.

When I picked her up, she was dressed in a black leather skirt and red blouse with heels. She greeted me with a smile and took my hand as we went out to the car. After the show, we had dinner at the restaurant Kami had arranged, which turned out to be one of the top restaurants in D.C. The food and wine was delicious, which Kami seemed to enjoy, but I had to carry the conversation, asking questions to get her to talk. She didn't ask me a single question.

Does she know I'm interested in Laura?

It was, by far, the most expensive meal I'd ever paid for. Afterward, we drove in silence to her apartment. She didn't invite me in but said goodbye at the door.

I was confused. If Kami was interested in me, she had a strange way of showing it. She had not asked me a single question about myself. And then there was the extravagant cost of the meal, followed by a cold goodbye. Had she agreed to go out just to get a high-priced meal?

Or had she realized that I was really interested in her best friend?

But to my surprise, afterwards, when I arrived at Laban's home for the night, he came down alone to see me. Laura was already in bed, he told me. Over a nightcap, he told me that Kami had already checked in. She'd "had fun" with me and was looking forward to the ball.

I slept that night in the room with the bullet hole.

227

Knowing that I was in the same house as the girl I had been dreaming about for two months made it hard for me to go to sleep. I didn't know what to do about Kami—I suspected she had fed them the "fun" line because she didn't want me abandoning her before the ball. I was sure that we weren't compatible.

Years later, when I told Laura about that meal, she laughed. "Of course she would have taken you there," she said. "Clearly, she didn't like you as much as I thought she did."

Which meant my suspicions that night were correct.

By the time the four of us arrived the next evening for the black-tie event at the National Press Club, I was confused by the vibes I was getting. Kami seemed to be unhappy as she barely spoke to me, while Laban, who was supposedly on the outs with Laura, was playing the perfect host so that if I hadn't known, I wouldn't have expected that truth. And then there was Laura, dressed in a cream gown with fur, which set off her blue eyes and tanned skin exquisitely, the woman I wasn't sure I could win even if she and Laban broke up.

The four of us decided to have a cigar. This was back when it was okay to smoke inside public buildings. Shortly after we began smoking, Laban and Kami disappeared to get more drinks for all of us. Laura grew quiet. I wanted to talk to her about something other than the nice weather, but I probably couldn't have gotten even that out. But I had to try to say something because the silence was getting awkward.

"This is going to be a late night."

Laura didn't respond, only nodded absently, smoking her small aromatic cigar, and scanning the milling mob as if searching for a more interesting diversion.

I held my own cigar, glancing around, uncomfortable in my tux, which fit me no better than Kami, the sulky date I had brought. I couldn't figure out this mysterious creature beside me.

Maybe she just doesn't do small talk.

"I hope they return soon."

Laura eyed me, but, again, didn't respond.

I fell silent, watching the constant stream of older men accompanied by much younger women in sparkling cocktail dresses passing our booth. I was generally able to talk to anyone, but I didn't seem to be able to launch a conversation tonight with either of the two women who had come with us tonight to this ball. Then suddenly, Laura leaned forward, cigar in her hand.

"Laban told me some interesting facts about you. Like your strict religious background." Grinning, she took a sip of her bourbon.

I pulled on my cigar, then eyed her up and down, enjoying what I saw. It must have surprised her, because her blue eyes, already luminous in the dim light, widened. My entire body felt alive, suddenly fired with adrenaline.

228

Oh, she wanted to go there? Well, she was going to see that my religious background didn't preclude me from knowing how to flirt.

I reached over and brushed an imaginary piece of lint off her dress, then looked up directly into her eyes. I was close enough to kiss her, but Laban would soon return and while it was one thing to want his girlfriend, I did have enough sense of preserving our friendship that I wouldn't touch her—well, not if they were together. But if they broke up… All bets were off.

"Laban told me things about you, as well. That you have a dark side… that you enjoy attending scene parties."

Laura raised an eyebrow.

Have I finally gotten her attention?

"According to him, at night, you get… very little sleep," I said. "What do you do when you can't sleep… at night?"

Holding her cigar, Laura cocked her head. "I think," she said, "that Laban has told you *way* too much about me. You've probably been imagining all the various ways you think you can… mentor me?"

My mouth dropped open in surprise.

She flashed me another grin as she wrapped her bright red lips around her little cigar and sucked, hard. Then she let it all go, the smoke floating around her head. "And by the way, when I can't sleep, I write."

I didn't realize Laura was auditioning me that night.

As I would learn, she never made random decisions. She had the ability to analyze a battlefield like a chess player and choose every move carefully.

By then, she had already figured out that, despite my scandalous departure from my community, I was, at heart, a careful person. She was fascinated by my rebellion against my home community.

Laura, too, had left her family behind, reacting to a mother who had micromanaged her education (successfully), and had tried to control Laura's social life (unsuccessfully).

Laura also knew that, as a high school teacher, I had to undergo a criminal background check, and the only marks on my record were some tickets for speeding and moving violations.

But she also knew—because Laban had told her—that I was a Dominant who liked spanking the women I slept with, but also that I didn't attend scene parties, where players dressed up in fancy leather costumes in order to make a statement about their sexual preferences. In other words, boring on the outside, but, privately, I had a dark side.

What I didn't realize was *when* I had caught Laura's interest. It wasn't, as I thought, when Laban had revealed my secretive side, before the Halloween party. Instead, it happened on that New Year's weekend, when I drove in again to see Kami and stayed at their house again.

It happened a few hours before the New Year's Eve party, after I had showered and was getting ready to go out. In the bathroom upstairs, I was shaving at the mirror with the door open. At that point, Laura happened by, and she stopped to talk.

"I recall you getting ready for the New Year's Eve party," she told me years later. "You were standing in the bathroom, shaving. I was having a conversation with you, standing in the door. Your shirt was off, your body sculpted by the construction work you did each summer. You had just the right combination—a Shakespearean scholar with a construction worker's body."

I thought—after Laura admitted that to me—about the way life works, about how one thing leads to another. I was glad I had found the strength to leave my father's autobody shop, glad I had chosen to apprentice in construction work, giving Laura this body to appreciate.

After Laban and Kami returned, the evening continued as if nothing had happened, the conversation flowing naturally, with Laban telling stories, pulling me into some of them, and Laura adding a few of her own. Kami and I were saying little to each other—it was very clear that she and I were not feeling any vibes.

I studiously avoided looking at Laura, focusing on my date and on Laban. Laura talked comfortably to Laban and Kami, and gave no recognition that not long before, we had briefly flirted. It was also clear to me that Kami had figured out that I wasn't interested in her—she had certainly made no effort to cultivate my interest. I suspected by then she had told Laban she *really* didn't want to spend any more time with me.

I don't know if Laban had realized what was happening, but Laura was clearly paying attention to the tensions in the group. She has always been strong-willed, and she has always done what she wants. But I was about to find that out.

Shortly after midnight, after Kami gave me a kiss on the cheek when the ball dropped at midnight, the four of us made our way outside of the Press Club, where Laban hailed a cab, and the four of us crowded inside.

Laban crawled into the cab first, and before I knew it, Laura had guided Kami in to sit on his lap, then moved me in beside Laban. And in the next moment, Laura slipped onto my lap, pushing her firm hips up against my crotch. I could barely see in front of me, the fur coat brushing my face.

To my surprise, having landed on Laban's lap, Kami lit up, carrying on a wonky conversation with Laban about his government position. In contrast, I sat holding Laura, both of us silent. I was unable to focus on anything other than her warmth and scent of jasmine and lavender. Too soon, we reached Laban's ancient house.

When the taxi pulled up at the front steps, Laura climbed off my lap, then took Laban's hand, and they started into the house. Kami finally noticed me, asking me if she could slip past me back into the taxi. She never bothered to say goodbye.

Neither did I. She was definitely *not* the woman for me.

I headed upstairs and pulled my car keys out of my pocket—along with a bar napkin from the Press Club.

With Laura's telephone number and email address.

SyrtynChaos@aol.com

Her handle was a perfect description of how she saw herself, a wild child with out-of-control behaviors who needed my steady hand to tame her.

I was ready to do so.

So, when Laban and Laura broke up a week or so later, I did not waste time. Although I saw myself as loyal to my friends, I was not about to forego this chance. I had already fallen in love with Laura, and I suspected that I would never meet anyone else with her blend of talent and beauty who was exactly my type.

Laban would find another girl. He always did.

When the relationship ended officially, Laban called me, venting his feelings. It was clear they weren't right for each other. I was outwardly sympathetic, but I was delighted they had ended their relationship. They *weren't* right for each other. I knew this deep in my soul.

Laura was right for me.

Even though the breakup between Laban and Laura seemed consensual, I knew it was hard on both. I knew this because they both wrote to me about the same events, just from different points of view.

But I had no interest in being Laura's confidant or friend; I wanted to date her, wanted to be her dom. Although my friendship with Laban could be at risk because of what I was going to do, I had never felt this way about any woman I'd ever met, a raw need combined with a fascination for the way she thought.

She was a writer, she was beautiful, she had class. She knew how to dress, and she understood how to wear a mask. We both did—I wore the mask of a teacher at a conservative school district, she was a federal employee. We both knew the importance of keeping up public appearances. We both embraced cognitive dissonance.

Using the email Laura had provided me, I reached out to her. To my delight, she responded. Soon, we were instant messaging each night. It was far less expensive than long-distance telephone, and besides, Laura preferred to write rather than talk.

We soon began exploring questions about our past, and I found Laura was a good storyteller. Clearly, her grief for her and Laban's ended relationship didn't run too deep. The problem was, it was also clear that Laura didn't take me seriously as a partner either. I was the new plaything, and Laura wanted to play.

After several weeks of texting and emails, Laura and I agreed to meet in Cleveland for a weekend together. I would pick her up at the airport, and we would have plenty of time to be alone together.

I chose the Embassy Suite hotel. At Cleveland Hopkins Airport, Laura came through the gate, wearing a jean skirt, brown cowboy boots, and her blue beanie. My throat caught in my mouth.

During our time in that beautiful hotel, we played, we made love, we talked. I loved listening to her stories about her childhood and her love for reading. Her voice was restrained and cautious, her body submissive and yielding. She was as beautiful as I remembered.

She could also be spicy, her words cutting and decisive. No hothouse flower, she had grown up on the streets of Detroit, but her parents had sent her to a Catholic girls' school, where she had been one of her class's top students. But she had refused to play the academic game that the top students played. In high school, she'd refused to take the normal curriculum most AP students did, choosing World literature instead of British, for example. Like me, she had always played by her own rules.

Laura was a mixture of power and feminine wiles, and I quickly discovered I should not take her for granted. She walked with an air of confidence I had never seen in a woman, but she also knew how to make someone feel powerful. There wasn't a mask she didn't know how to wear.

She knew what she wanted, and she went after everything she wanted. By the end of that weekend, I wasn't sure she wanted me, but I *definitely* wanted her. For a lot longer than a weekend.

With every fiber of my being, I was in love.

But, in my initial flush of happiness, I didn't realize it takes time to move from one relationship to another. So, when, on Sunday evening, after Laura had returned to D.C. and she'd sent me a "I think we should keep things casual; I'm not ready for this" IM, her words cut my reality into tiny little bits.

I was no fool. I'd used that line myself. I didn't want to be just "friends," not with her, and I was a veteran of breakups. Laura loved cats, and I knew that, with a cat, you don't chase them. You let them come to you.

I let Laura go, feeling devastated, but letting her have her space. My strategy worked. Several weeks later, I was online when an Instant Message popped up. "Meow."

SyrtynChaos had returned.

One night after an extended session by IM, Laura asked me if I'd mind calling after we'd both gone to bed. Several minutes later, we were both connected, alone in our separate apartments. She lived in Alexandria, Virginia; I lived in suburban North Canton.

By then, she had told me a few of the stories of her own childhood, notably the conflicts with her mother, who seemed to have been unusually strict.

"But your dad—"

"Actually, he's not my biological dad."

I sat up. "I didn't know that—"

"How could you? But you should know, he's the only father I recognize."

"What do you mean?"

"My biological father abandoned me. Left my mother."

"They weren't married?"

"No. He left her. My mother raised me alone. Until she met my real dad."

"How old were you?"

"Three. Mom met him at a party. They were both strict Catholics. But he married her, even though she already had a child." A beat. "Me."

I waited, hoping she'd go on.

"He told me, first thing, that I was a pretty girl. I'll always love him for that reason alone."

"Because he said you were pretty?"

She giggled. "No, silly. Because he married my mom anyway. *Despite* me."

She sighed. "Oh, Steven."

For a moment, I imagined she was lying beside me again, warm, here in my bed, here in my arms. I wanted her in my life, living a life with her, not just seeing her on the occasional weekend.

"What was he like as a father? Strict?"

"My mother was the one who screamed at me. She'd be waiting for me when I came in late. Even a minute late, and she'd scream like a crazy woman. Him? A few times, he took the belt to me. Every time, my mom tried to get him to stop, so he only did it a few times. Usually, he just yelled at us when he got mad. Or swore." She imitated her dad's deep voice. "'Jesus Christ!'"

"My dad never swore." In my mind's eye, I saw him burst into the bedroom, me reading on the bed, his broad hand raising up above me. "But he sure as Hell knew how to beat us."

"Yeah, well, everyone swears in my family. It's part of the vocabulary. My dad's a blue-collar union man. A Democrat. The whole family is."

"But your parents wouldn't let you go to a public school?"

"No, public schools were horrible in Detroit. My mother wanted me to get a good education. I had to work hard, and the classwork was hard. The nuns were strict and demanding."

"Really?" Her education sounded a lot like my own, with teachers quick to correct. "It sounds a lot like the Catholic school where I once taught."

Her voice became breathy. "I wish you had been my teacher."

"Yeah? I'm glad I wasn't. There would have been trouble."

"I'll bet..."

"How would you have punished me?"

Usually, I wanted to play, but I didn't want to go down that trail tonight.

"Are you glad you received a Catholic education?"

233

"No." She sulked for a moment. But then, recognizing perhaps I wanted to actually talk, she went on. "I hated it. I hung out with the burnouts, the ones with tattoos and attitude issues. The way I dressed, our principal had no idea how well I was doing in class. She'd see me in the hall with my friends who, of course, weren't doing well, and glower at me." She laughed. "I wish you could have seen her face when I was called up on the platform at graduation to collect all the awards. She had no idea I was sixth in my huge class."

"It must have made your mother happy."

"Back then, I hated her. She was always afraid I'd end up like she did-- pregnant. If I came in a minute past curfew, she'd be waiting for me, yelling and screaming at me. At the time, I really thought she was crazy. Didn't appreciate what was driving her—that she loved me and wanted me to have the opportunities she didn't. So, I left home the summer after I graduated. And I stayed away. For a really long time."

I thought about my sister, Elaine, who had done the same thing. I wondered, as I often wondered, whether I might have been smarter to have done the same thing. Would my life have been the same?

"Why leave home?" I asked. "What really drove you?"

"I was determined to escape the world of my childhood."

"Like me." My voice was soft, but Laura heard it clearly.

"Yeah, like you. I thought *I* had a lot to escape from, but I think you had more."

We both lay in the dark, separated by hundreds of miles, worlds apart, but the moment had brought us together in a way that was new.

Although North Canton was only a short plane flight from D.C., it might as well have been two worlds apart. We were heading in two different directions.

I was a committed schoolteacher, a job which demanded ten months of the year committed to one zip code. My weekends were taken up with extra-curricular activities or grading, with only vacations allowing me to leave town.

Slowly, reality shaped our future, or the lack of it. Laura was never going to move to a little town like North Canton. Her government career took her around the globe, with long trips to the former Soviet Union and its satellites.

There was no chance we could sync up our lives. I was not about to move to D.C. Yet underneath her exotic stories, I sensed panic. Had I been wiser, had I paid more attention, I might have sensed what pulled us into each other's orbit.

But first I needed to cut myself loose from my small-town moorings.

Laura's vision of me was dark.

Having come out of a starkly religious world herself, she saw the anger I directed toward my father, supercharged by the fear of a literal, searing Hell. I was unable to differentiate between my view of an angry God and the fiercely literal community who'd invented Him.

Laura's insights frightened me. I tried not to think about the endearment she used to conclude our phone calls.

"Good night, Dark Prince."

Then in March 2000, about three years after we met, she called me.

"I've been offered a position in Moscow."

She announced this without drama, as if she was telling me that she was planning on buying a pizza tonight. I was still at school, grading papers, probably the only teacher here this late in the evening.

"Congratulations," I said, abruptly. *Once again, she's fleeing our relationship.* I didn't want to go down this route again. Every time she had to go somewhere for work, she'd disappear for months.

"Steven, are you there?"

"Yeah."

Clearly, this wasn't working out. We had so little time together. It seemed every time we did have a good weekend, she'd disappear for months. Now, she was heading across the globe again, and not looking to come back soon, and I had zero interest in wanting to learn Russian.

"You should take the position," I said.

Did I just break up with her?

I hadn't planned on saying that, and the shock hit me hard. Usually, she was the one who initiated our breakups. Perhaps I was more frustrated than I realized.

"Perhaps you could come see me at Christmas? You've never been to Russia, right?"

"Perhaps. No." It didn't take an astrophysicist to hear that I wasn't happy. I felt trapped. I had bought my house, thinking that it would free me from living with my parents, and then I had overspent, and added a second mortgage. I felt constrained.

"Why stay in North Canton, Steven?" Her voice was tight. "We talk about all the traveling we'd like to do, yet you never go anywhere."

"I spent last summer in Oxford."

And I had thoroughly enjoyed that time away from Ohio, living with other teachers who thought differently than I did, who taught all over the world in independent schools. They had a freedom that was a mystery to me, one that I would capture for a moment, but would then slip away from me.

"Why not other places? Why not the East? It can't be because you're afraid. I won't believe that."

I wondered about that. Was I afraid to leave? What was tying me to this community? Several years before, I had interviewed for a teaching position on St. Maarten. The principal I had interviewed told me how relaxing the schedule was... how he played golf every afternoon. But somehow I couldn't bring myself to take the job.

"I'm busy here."

"No more than anyone else. Steven, you realize how close you're living to your childhood community, right?"

It startled me. I hadn't thought of that, but she was right. I was teaching at the same school where I had done my student teaching, the semester before I left for London. But I didn't want to think about that right now.

"I'm teaching at one of the best schools in Ohio."

"Seven miles from your parents." We were talking past each other. "It's like there's an invisible umbilical cord tying you to your family—whom you can't stand, by the way."

It annoyed me, the way she could cut to the heart of any issue so clearly. She was right. I didn't like my family—when I was with my family, I felt restless, unable to just relax and enjoy being with them.

"I think we knew each other in a previous life, Steven. More than one. I think things keep going wrong for us because we're missing each other, and I think we're going to *keep* meeting each other until we figure it out."

"Groundhog Day. Of course."

I thought about the weatherman played by Bill Murray in the 1993 film *Groundhog Day*. It seemed we were repeating the same mistakes, having now broken up two previous times, and then gotten back together, without learning anything, it seemed. Or at least, *I* hadn't, according to her. Now it was about to happen again.

I heard her sigh.

"Good night, Steven."

I didn't answer because I didn't know what to say. There was nothing more I could do. I wasn't about to leave my job. I wasn't about to move to Russia for her… where I didn't know the language and didn't know if I could find a job. I felt paralyzed.

The phone went dead. I put it down, frustrated by the fact that once again, the relationship had ended. She was heading to Russia, and I was… what? Stuck here?

It would not occur to me until much later than she was not the one who had fled the relationship this time.

Chapter 24: The God Who Walks Among Us

I wasn't ready for marriage. But I did need to find a community where I could build friendships. By the time Laura left for Moscow, I had put down roots in North Canton—having purchased a house less than a mile from the school. My yearbook staff ran as smoothly as a Swiss watch, and my drama program was growing.

As director of the theater, I worked closely with the choir program, which was now led for the first time by a female director, Kim Melin. She was a talented musician, and we collaborated effectively. We became not only close professional colleagues, but great friends as well.

She and her husband Mike would often have me over for dinner in their home.

In August 2000, during my second class of the day, the classroom speaker crackled to life, calling all the choir members to an assembly. I found out what had happened an hour later when I got an email from Mike. His wife had been in a horrific car accident. The words leaped out at me.

Coma.

Death.

May never recover.

I left my classroom and walked out into the halls, trying to process what had happened. Students clustered in small groups hugging, crying, and talking. Faculty members exchanged glances, a tightness to their faces.

I struggled to breathe.

I couldn't fix her, I couldn't save her, and, sadly, I couldn't see her as her husband kept us from her. I understand that now, his decision to shield her from prying eyes and the interaction he'd have to have with her visitors, making him relive it over and over, but, at the time, it was one more thing out of my control. Me, who needed to be in control, had none.

Where was God now?

I didn't know how to answer that question.

I recall one Saturday night in particular. It was the darkest night of my life, the moment when the Sea of Faith retreated far down the shores of my spirit, leaving me to face a frozen beach of grief. In a nightmare come to life, the gaunt specter of Death tracked one of my closest friends.

The next morning, I didn't plan anything; I just operated on instinct. I got dressed in nice clothes and got into my car. I headed to church. Perhaps I needed answers, perhaps I needed to grieve. Perhaps I needed a community to wrap its arms around me, to shut out the pain.

I tried to understand Mike's decision to wall her off from the outside world. It left me hurt and frustrated, but... Mike was right, because there was nothing I could do there. Kim needed space inside her coma world, to fight for survival. She might never return, and I needed to accept that. For the moment, I couldn't see her, I couldn't touch her, I couldn't feel her presence. I was helpless to save my friend.

On that Sunday morning, as I headed to church, I was determined to do something. Having rejected the comforting culture of my childhood—and having seen no proof of His assistance in this awful, horrible scenario—I could no longer count on a patriarchal God who supposedly watched from the sky, a heavenly Father who would intervene to save His children. Random stuff happened to people, it was a fact of life; God was not an insurance agent. He didn't protect the most deserving.

I turned into the parking lot of the United Methodist Church some of my friends and colleagues and students attended. I slipped into the packed church, sitting toward the back.

Singing the hymns with the congregation felt familiar, some of the same hymns I had sung as a child. It comforted me, without reminding me of my home community. Hearing the pastor relate Jesus' words to world events in his sermon showed an awareness of a world gone wrong. It took me—and the rest of the congregation—from hearing about a lofty God, the one in the High Heaven— to a God who was here with us. It brought Him to earth for us—for me—in a way I hadn't considered before.

I thought about what my new pastor had said. In his sermon, he had brought Jesus to earth for me by relating him to worldly events affecting everyone.

How did God do this today?

Impressed by the sermon, I stayed behind to talk to the pastor. He was aware of Kim's accident. He had comforted many of his parishioners. Toward the end of our conversation, I felt safe enough to share what was really bothering me.

"I feel so helpless," I said.

"Neither of us has any control here," he said, empathy written into the lines of his face.

"Will she come out of the coma, do you think?" I needed to know.

"She might," he said. "If she does, she might never be the same. Victims of brain trauma are rarely the same. But that's not up to us."

"What does that mean? And don't tell me God's in control, because from where I'm sitting, I don't see it."

"That's the problem with being God," my pastor said gently. "You can't give humanity control, and then take it back whenever bad things happen. But He can comfort us."

"He seems pretty fucking distant to me right now."

My pastor didn't blink at my language.

"Look around. Perhaps you'll see Him."

It was only afterwards when I realized he was, perhaps without realizing it, talking about himself.

Over the next few Sundays, I returned to sing with the congregation and to listen to more of the pastor's sermons. He shared about people of faith who were fighting for justice, and in his words, I found understanding, rather than the sulfur-infused rants of old.

I kept going back, because... I had found a church community I could belong to. Those who attended believed in the old-fashioned idea that God is found within the strangers we meet, that when we serve others, we are the hands and feet of God—rather than evil.

It was this sense of community, and this community—specifically, made up of my students and their families and my work colleagues—that made me find my purpose because I needed to do something to help Kim. I might not be able to cure her, but there had to be something we, as a caring community, could do for her.

The answer came, as it had often done in my life, in the theater. We put together a show to benefit Kim, all proceeds going to her recovery. The drama and choir students embraced the idea of a benefit show enthusiastically.

I chose *It's a Wonderful Life* because it showed a small-town community, much like North Canton, where God chose to send the most incompetent angel available, but one who was able to help the hero see what the town would have been like had he not been there. Kim was someone who had made a dramatic impact on our town, as well.

One of the most important parts of staging *It's a Wonderful Life* required me to choose how I intended to portray the character of God.

Where should I place Him?

I decided that he needed to be a character on the stage and not an anonymous member of the town, upstage. Nor should he be the Almighty God in Heaven on a balcony behind the audience. My vision didn't see him in a box above the stage, waiting to respond to prayers, too far away to intervene to save George. Instead, he should be there, among the people, interacting, creating that sense of community.

Over the next few months, I began to realize that—like in the fictional story I was presenting on stage—I had encountered God again and again, walking among the people of my community.

239

I'd found God in Kim as she transformed the lives of her students. I'd spotted Him in other colleagues and students, who'd stood beside me in that church as we'd grieved our loss. I'd touched God when I had reached for comfort from my pastor and had gotten it. I'd recognized His hands at work when the firefighters had carefully extracted Kim's body from the smashed car, saving her life. He'd there among the community members as they had contributed to a Recovery Fund for Kim.

He walks among us.

On the night the show opened, an observant, grieving God moved among the other characters on stage, invisible to them, attentive to the pain they were undergoing, yet refusing to interfere in people's freedom of choice.

God was not an insurance agent; he was not a *deus ex machina*—that infernal machine in a Greek play; He was invisible to His creatures. But when people were attentive, when they stepped in to serve as God's hands and feet, He worked through them to change the world.

The impacts of Kim's accident reached farther than I realized—it touched my relationship with my parents. They *finally* attended one of my shows—the first of those I'd directed. They came because they loved the film. They came, they told me, because they wanted to show their support for me and my friend. Perhaps they came because, during that horrible, roiling tempest, they saw me endure, and they saw that my faith was real.

My parents had always had the answers when I was a child. Now, I saw them as human beings who owned an unshakeable faith in God but were still unable to explain to me or anyone else why this tragedy had occurred. But the fact that they took the time to attend Kim's benefit show told me how much they still loved me, no matter how confusing the tragedy was.

I still don't understand why Kim almost died. Why this had to happen to her. But today I recognize that life events are complex and interlocked, and lead to surprising results. Today, I recognize that if I went back in time and changed that one event, my world now would be a different place, as would Kim's. Today, I recognize that giving people autonomy, which makes us human, means God cannot control the events in our lives. He can only walk among us and can only grieve with us, when tragedy occurs.

Book VI: Depression

Will the Lord cast off forever? and will he be favourable no more?
Is his mercy clean gone forever? doth His promise fail for evermore?
Hath God forgotten to be gracious? Hath He in anger shut up
His tender mercies?... Thy way is in the sea, and thy path
in the great waters, and thy footsteps are not known.

~ Psalm 77: 7-9, 19, *The Holy Bible*, KJV, 1769

Interpolation VI: Tender Shepherds

There was no chance I could have realized, as I finished up my master's degree in English and theater, that my obsession with disciplinary role play within my romantic relationships was connected to my diagnosis of PTSD, which came out of the physical abuse I had suffered within our fundamentalist Mennonite community.

It's strange.

My childhood community sincerely tried to follow Jesus, who in Scripture is described as the Good Shepherd. The men in my community were conscientious objectors who refused to enter the military and believed that violence was always wrong. In the past, some of their ancestors had suffered rather than take up arms to protect themselves, their families, or their homeland. Yet that same community believed it was right to physically chastise children.

They chose to strike the most defenseless of human creatures.

Children like me.

It wasn't only my father who practiced such abuse in our community. In our Christian Day school, teachers were handed the paddle and expected to punish students who were defiant. Children were beaten for failing to do their homework on time, some of whom had special needs.

It is not an accident that this plague of abuse flooded my community of faith.

This happens in any community that teaches parents to take some of the contradictory commands in the Bible literally. I saw the results of this teaching, up close. I do not doubt the sincerity of my community's faith, but their practice of that faith was… complicated.

It took me years of education and research to realize that the physical abuse I endured as a child often happens when parents rely on the abusive example of their own parents: "My father whipped me a lot, and I turned out just fine." It happens within a world where people are suspicious of "higher education." It happens when parents attend a fundamentalist church where the Bible is taken literally, and where certain verses are cherry picked.

Poverty exacerbates the abuse. When adults struggle to survive financially, and are overwhelmed with financial stress, they tend to respond instinctively, treating their children the way they were treated when they were growing up. Thus, they continue the cycle of abuse, using Bible verses to prove that God commands them to abuse their own flesh and blood.

This was not the world described in my mother's favorite evensong, where sweet lambs could lift their frightened but trusting eyes to a "tender shepherd," who might use a friendly staff to guide the flock carefully through dangerous territory, or even reach out with the staff to pull a terrified lamb back from a steep drop off. No, this world was composed of pissed-off shepherds who—when frustrated—grabbed their staff with two large hands and beat the shit out of the lambs they were supposed to protect.

There was nothing safe about this world—not for the vulnerable children, not for those just trying to get by, and certainly not for a young man traumatized by the abuse he had suffered.

Chapter 25: A Scouting Trip

Grief is a powerful force, both for good and evil. I didn't realize at the turn of the millennium how deeply I had been impacted by my breakup with Laura, followed by the near-death of Kim—the two events following hard after each other. They devastated me.

Laura's utter passion for writing had allowed me to glimpse genius up close. Kim's artistic judgment showed me how to collaborate with talented artists. Their losses collided within me, two atoms in an explosion of grief. To my surprise, rather than destroying me, their losses fused and ignited my greatest passion. Telling stories.

Before that year, I saw myself as a director and a producer, drawing in talented artists and inspiring them to succeed. Although I dreamed of being a writer, I didn't think I had anything to say. I told other people's stories.

After Kim disappeared into a coma, stalked by Death, I turned inward. I searched for a way to tell the dark stories that suddenly hammered at my brain. The realities of loss and death taught me that we are given a limited time to make our mark.

My first story idea was triggered by my last conversation with Laura when she observed that we must have known each other in a previous life, and that we still had major issues to work out. The concept haunted me. So, after she left for Moscow, I began constructing my first screenplay.

I approached it as a director, thinking I could simply make my characters do what they wanted. My first draft was a disaster as I discovered how complex story structure is. The actors who read it were polite, but their feedback demolished my pride. I had work to do. I also learned that every screenwriting guru said the same thing—if you want to write screenplay, move to Los Angeles to learn the craft.

I began looking at this possibility, even applying for a teaching position at an L.A. independent school. But after the initial phone interview, I decided I wasn't ready. I began to plan out another year of teaching in North Canton.

Fate had other plans.

Several months later in July, I received an invitation from Marlin to visit him and his new love in San Francisco. She was an opera singer performing in *Carmen*. Did I want to tag along with him for a visit? When he wasn't with his girlfriend, we could catch up on each other's lives. Did I have the time?

I did.

In San Francisco, I enjoyed the time with Marlin and his girlfriend, working on my screenplay and having long conversations. But just before I was scheduled to fly back to Ohio, leaving Marlin in San Francisco, I realized something. I had an extra week to kill before I needed to return to Ohio. I was just a short plane flight from Los Angeles. Why not get a round-trip ticket and check out the City of Dreams?

I had never visited there. But Hazel, a friend I'd met on a writing conference two years back, lived there. When I shared my thoughts about moving to L.A. to try to become a screenwriter, she had assured me schools in L.A. were always looking for good English teachers and I'd have no problem getting a job. She mentioned that her school had an opening.

The seed was planted.

Now I reached out by phone. As we caught up, I mentioned I was barely a short flight from Los Angeles. When Hazel realized that I might visit, her voice warmed.

"Actually, Steven, there's a teaching position that's just opened here. We need a seventh-grade English teacher. Would you be interested in interviewing for the position?"

"I don't think so. I'm a high school teacher. This is just a scouting trip."

Hazel picked up on my uncertainty. "Perhaps you could consider it?"

I didn't say anything.

"Tell you what, Steven. If you agree to interview, Archer will cover the cost of one night's stay at your hotel."

I considered Hazel's offer. It *was* just an interview, after all. I didn't need to take the job if they offered it. I laughed. "Okay, I'll do it. I'm going to be in Los Angeles, anyway."

And so I flew into the city and visited my friend's school. The campus of The Archer School was gorgeous, the buildings surrounding a lovely courtyard. It was a former nursing home for the affluent and had been featured in the film *Chinatown*.

When I first stepped through the wide entrance doors, I surveyed the hallway. Above me, the ceiling arched like a museum and was darkly painted. Sunshine streamed through a porthole high above me, a pathway of light leading to the tiled roof.

Those tiles represented a world in transition.

Hispanic workers had built this structure almost a century ago, shaping the roof's clay tiles by slapping wet clay over their muscular thighs. They'd survived on minimal wages, but, due to an aggressive scholarship program, the descendants of those immigrants were being given an equal education alongside their famous, affluent peers, and all were required to wear simple uniforms— uniforms that breached the barriers of economic class.

This was exactly the sort of place I could appreciate, a place of equality, where every worthy student was given a chance at a better life.

246

That was the moment I bonded hard with The Archer School.

Thanks to Hazel's help, I toured the city and met one of her screenwriter friends at a cookout. While I waited for Hazel to arrange an interview at The Archer School, I strolled Venice Beach, taking in its unique artistic world, buying a set of roller blades, and spending hours sweeping along the sidewalks that stretched the entire beach.

I think that was when I fell in love with the city, the sunshine, and the people.

I wanted to live here.

But was it too much of a risk? I had a secure job in North Canton and was close to tenure. My entire year in theater was planned out. I had a house with two mortgages. The move would be practically impossible; why was I even thinking about doing this?

I recalled the words of my old mentor in London. "You're a pompous ass. You need to be dropped into a major city. You need to learn how to survive on your own, not depend on your community at home."

Originally, when Mr. Shaw had made that statement, I'd found that complete independence scared the Hell out of me. Instead, I'd chosen to spend a decade trying to find a way to become my own person while also reconciling with my family.

But it hadn't worked; I had *not* become my own person. Instead, living too close to my family had fostered my dependence on them. Mr. Shaw was right— if I wished to grow up, if I wished to assimilate into modern culture, I needed to finally come to terms with who I was.

I needed to leave home for good.

And here was my opportunity. I wanted to learn how to write screenplays. And only in Los Angeles could I find the help I needed. If I was serious about making it in The Business, I had move to L.A.

Archer had made me an attractive offer, even promising to reimburse my moving costs. To make the transition easier, the dean even offered to let me stay at his place for the first few weeks while I was looking for a place to live.

This was the chance I'd been waiting for. My dream was being handed to me on a plate. The promise of L.A. stretched before me.

Chapter 26: Sacrament of Fear

I finished packing and showering. I crossed to the ATM across the street and popped in my debit card. On the screen, three words appeared.

No funds available.

What? I stared at the ATM screen across the street from my hotel. What did they mean I didn't have money? I needed money to get back to the airport and only had a measly two dollars in my wallet. Why had I given Marlin that cash? Of course, *then*, I hadn't given it a second thought because I'd known I'd had money in my account—

The hotel bill. That was it. I'd charged it to my debit card; it must have hit this morning.

All right, I'd just take a cash advance on my credit card. I'd eat the extra fee they charged for peace of mind while traveling—

Except that was declined.

So was my second card.

What was going on? I should have more than enough money…

Oh. There were the meals I'd purchased. That set of expensive rollerblades that had given me such a sense of freedom as I explored Venice Beach. And now, the hotel bill.

I was flat broke.

How could I have been this stupid? What do I do now?

I did what I'd done before—I reached out to a friend, calling Hazel to borrow the money.

My new friend's shock hummed through the phone line just like…

Oh no, how could I have forgotten? Richard Cook. I'd asked him for help getting out of London.

I knew her answer even before she responded.

"Oh, Steven. I'm sorry. I can't lend you any money. Is there anyone else you can call? Perhaps from home?"

Just like with Richard, I'd screwed up another friendship in this town.

What kind of future would I have at Archer now if Hazel started to wonder if she'd made a mistake recommending me for the job?

"Don't worry, Hazel. I'll figure something out." And I would. I didn't know how I would, but I would. My dream was too close to jeopardize it now.

But while I might figure out how to get home, how was I going to survive on my own in the long run? How could I cut the umbilical cord to my community if my first instinct was to run back when something bad happened? And if I did manage to cut that cord, how would I be sure I wouldn't fail again at teaching middle school, just as I did over a decade ago at Central Christian School in Kidron, Ohio?

I gaped at myself in the mirror hanging above the desk. I might be thirty-seven years old, but I was still a child. I was still a boy.

Now, after the twelve-year detour I'd taken to avoid confronting what Mr. Shaw had recognized, I needed to figure this shit out.

I couldn't rely on anyone else.

I could no longer hide from the essential test of manhood.

I had come face-to-face with who I was. And I didn't like who I was seeing. I should have budgeted my money better, not spent so much on food, put money aside when I got my check every month… wait.

I was not without resources. I had Marlin's check because I'd given Marlin my last bit of cash just before I left because he'd needed it. He'd written a check to cover it, which I hadn't yet had the chance to cash.

I checked my watch. The bank across the street opened at 9 AM.

I was there at 8:59.

The teller looked at the check—*Banco Popular* sounded foreign, but the address said Chicago, Illinois—then sent me to the bank officer.

He peered at the check, looked at me, and asked if I had an account with them.

Of course I did not.

So, of course he wouldn't cash the check.

He did, however, mention another branch of the bank in the Koreatown section that would cash it.

I was desperate at this point. And annoyed at Marlin. Why had I ever offered to lend him that cash? I should have known better.

I considered the check, then opened my wallet one more time, hoping against hope that I had put what a friend in London had called "go to Hell money" in there. Money that my friend would take with her on a first date in case the guy was a loser, and she needed to get a cab home.

I had no GTH money.

I glanced at my watch. 9:20 AM. I had to leave the hotel by 11:00 to make the plane, and I still needed to stop by Archer to pick up my contract.

The clock was ticking, and I needed to get going.

But there was the added problem that I didn't have the cash or credit to pay for a cab to take me to that branch so I could cash the check—

Wait. A taxi wouldn't charge me until *after* I went to the bank, then returned to the hotel.

I eyed the Best Western hotel across the street, then broke into a run.

Once again, I was saved.

A few minutes later, a taxi pulled up to the hotel. The Mexican driver sang as he drove, harmonizing badly with the radio tunes... until we drove into the heart of Koreatown. Then, he quit singing and gawked as he drove.

His attitude wasn't making me feel like this was a good idea.

But what choice did I have?

When we pulled up in front of the branch, it had bars on the windows and guards with what appeared to be Uzis in their hands. This wasn't looking like a place that would be happy to give me money on a questionable bank's check that the last bank had refused to cash.

But I knew Marlin's check would go through. He had excellent credit and had never bounced a check in his life or overspent his limit. *He* was responsible with his money.

I glanced at the meter. It was already up to forty-four dollars. I had no choice now; I needed this check cashed.

I climbed out of the taxi, telling Happy Driver to wait while I cashed the check. He didn't seem to understand English, but he watched me as I climbed out into this world.

The door locks clicked behind me.

I couldn't blame him. Well, no choice now; I had to go forward.

I entered the door between two guards, then glanced around. I doubted if anyone spoke English, and I certainly didn't speak Korean, so this would be a test in and of itself.

I walked toward the nearest teller, who gave me a small smile of welcome. Thankfully, when I handed her the check and my driver's license, she went right to work. She considered the check, then stamped the back of it, her pen poised to fill in the details from my license.

I breathed a sigh of relief.

But then she glanced up at me. She turned the check over again and studied the signature.

I shifted my balance to my other foot.

She observed me with another small smile, then walked back to her boss, a taller woman standing ramrod straight in the center of the teller area.

Tall Teller accepted my check. She studied it as Young Teller chattered.

They both stared at me, a long moment of evaluation.

I suddenly realized how suspicious I looked. An out-of-town tourist trying to cash a large check that... oh no.

My heart dropped through my stomach. My mind flashed back to the moment with Marlin in the park as he sat on the bench, his checkbook on his knee, scribbling his signature.

Jesus, it looks forged.

Tall Teller picked up the phone, speaking in Korean—naturally—then put the check into a fax machine, before pushing some buttons.

251

They—and I—waited.

Every so often, Tall Teller spoke into the phone.

Time ticked by.

And there was nothing I could do but wait as my hopes of getting on that plane dimmed with each passing *tick*.

After what seemed like a half-hour of chitchat with what I presumed was *Banco Popular*'s main office, Tall Teller hung up the phone. She came toward me with the check in her hand and said in perfect English, "We can't cash this. So sorry. We just can't establish the accuracy of the signature. I'm sure you understand. Goodbye, and come see us again."

I gaped at her retreating back: what could I do?

I remembered those guards at the door.

I recalled the taxi driver and the running meter.

I was fucked.

I walked toward the door of the bank, considering my options. I could tell the driver I didn't have the money now—or I could wait until we arrived back at the hotel.

I needed to figure this out.

Moments later, I climbed back into the taxi and glanced at the meter. It had risen to $62. I didn't tell Happy Driver I lacked the funds to pay him. Feigning confidence, I told him to return to the hotel.

The taxi rolled away from the bank.

Come on, Steven! Surely you can think of something.

My mind raced over all the options I'd already considered. But now, not only did I not have the money to pay for the taxi to the airport, but I also had a taxi fare that kept increasing with every click of the meter.

It was time to give up on this business of figuring it out myself.

Any question I'd had about whether I should move to Los Angeles was settled. God had made his point, influenced, no doubt, by my father's prayers. I was done, no more risks for me. It was time to go home. I could read that memo, loud and clear.

But I still had to figure out a way to pay the driver.

I had to get practical.

The Best Western hotel loomed up ahead. Happy Driver pulled the taxi to a stop in front of the door, turning to look at me.

I stepped out, telling him to wait while I went in to get the money.

No problem. He turned up the music and danced away in his seat, the meter continuing to click.

People that happy shouldn't be allowed to drive cabs or collect money from me.

I shook my head. It was time to put my pride aside and call my brother Dave because, clearly, I *couldn't* handle this by myself.

I'd have him pay the hotel bill, promising to reimburse him as soon as I returned home. It shouldn't be a problem because Dave always had money. Then, the hotel could release the hold on my debit card, which would give me the needed cash to get out of Los Angeles.

And never return.

Enough of my dreams, I was going back home to teach in Ohio. Where I belonged.

But even that plan flopped.

The hotel needed a copy of Dave's card, but Dave couldn't get his fax machine to run the card through it.

I needed to leave for the airport in the next fifteen minutes if I wanted to stop at Archer and still have time to make my flight.

I asked Dave to try again, struggling to be patient. Back in Ohio, my brother fought to send a credit card through his industrial fax machine, but the damn thing wouldn't copy it.

Standing at the front desk, I wished one last time that I'd just told Marlin to go to another bank and get his own money. I didn't know what to do. I'd reached the utter limit of utter desperation.

"Dear God. Help me. I can't do this by myself."

A moment later, an older woman dressed in a dark business jacket and skirt entered the reception area from the back office. She scanned the room then exchanged a few words with the man who'd been working with me before heading my way. "How can I help you?"

Helen, as her name tag said, was clearly in charge if the deference the staff gave her was any indication. What did I have to lose?

I told her my story of my stupid plan to pay for the taxi with the money from the check, of the fact that no one would cash it, of my friend's carelessness in signing it in the park, of my drive to Koreatown and the dark bank...

And then my voice died away. I was done. Just... done.

Helen considered me for a long moment... and then she smiled. It transformed her face, and I was viewing someone genuine. A friendly neighbor.

"You know? I have no idea why I'm going to do this because I've never done it before in my life." She hit a button, and the cash register opened. "But I'm going to cash your check. How much do you need to pay for that taxi?"

I told her—it was over a hundred dollars by this point.

She took my check then gave me that hundred. "Go."

I ran out and Happy Driver was even happier when he left.

When I returned, Helen gave me the balance of the check in cash, making sure I signed for it.

My mind was spinning. What had happened? Five minutes ago, I'd been sure I shouldn't move here, but now this kindness...?

Putting the money in my billfold, I spent several minutes talking to the woman who had saved my life, trying to recover my balance.

Nothing made sense.

My rescuer put a warm hand on my arm, offering some advice.

"Listen," she said seriously. "If you love teaching back home, don't move here. The seasons here are so slight, the years blur by, you're barely aware of their passing until they do. Besides, people here tend to be superficial. I suspect they want different things than you do. You're a good person, honest and earnest. Stay home and make a good life for yourself in Ohio."

It was good advice, and the exact same decision I'd come to before she had come to my rescue. I *should* take it.

While I was still trying to figure it out, I did stop at Archer and sign the contract, accepting the position they offered me. I could always back out if I changed my mind when I got home.

And while I signed it with my own uncertainty, there was also this contractual uncertainty. It was an "at will" contract that gave me no guarantee or job security. But if I took the job and they fired me within the first year, I realized that I'd have no regrets because I would have at least fought to achieve my dreams.

I wouldn't spend the rest of my life wondering if I could have made it in Los Angeles.

As I reflect today on this experience, I want to be clear that being stranded in Los Angeles was not an accident, nor was I a victim. I was stranded at the Best Western Hotel, flat broke, because of *my* bad financial habits.

I had refused to discipline myself or budget my money. Although I'd been single and making a solid salary, an amount that allowed most of my teaching colleagues to raise families, I'd chosen to live above my means. I'd lived paycheck to paycheck, consistently running my credit cards past their limit— just like my father and grandfather had. It was only a matter of time before this would force a financial crisis.

It is true that I had grown up with a father who had a lot of children to feed and clothe and would shamelessly ask for financial help when he needed money. Due to the unselfish nature of our community, others often helped my father. This had been an agonizing experience for me as an adolescent, watching my father go hat-in-hand for help to the wealthier members of our community. Humiliated, I had criticized him. Yet, when I'd been faced with a crisis, I had followed his example to the letter, only, in my case, I'd asked strangers for help, figuring that it'd worked for my father, so it'd work for me.

In other words, I grew up believing such behavior was normal. I'd learned from my father that it was okay to pay your bills late, not realizing the impacts that poor credit had upon his options. He'd taught me to pray to God for help.

Although I'd understood that this was a poverty mindset, I'd followed his example, which had then limited my financial options as I'd tapped out my credit limits. When I faced a crisis, I'd had no resources to draw upon. As my own story shows, prayer works—but it might have been better had my poor financial habits *not* landed me in a place where I'd had to beg God for help.

Today, I'm living in a stable marriage with a wife who has helped teach me the basic financial skills that seem obvious to everyone else (for example, never making a late payment), but which had seemed foreign to me as I'd been struggling to assimilate into American society.

Today, I'm horrified by my past actions, realizing I'd created a lot of unnecessary drama because of my poor financial training. Today, I don't blame Marlin for the hurriedly-written check—the fact that my credit had been so poor that I'd had to cash his check at a bank that didn't know me was not Marlin's fault.

That fault had been my own.

But that didn't deter me from moving. The fact that I somehow managed to work with the community around me—to work hard to try and find help, to connect with the right person who cashed my check, to get to Archer on time to snag a teaching contract, and to make my plane on time—wasn't because I was a bold hero winning against all odds.

No, I won because I had the singular determination and courage to take a risk and trust that I would be able to work with those around me to accomplish something I thought would make the world a better place. I believed I needed to come to Los Angeles to get the coaching I needed to tell my stories.

I believed God was the one who walks among us, and that day, I met God in the woman across the desk at the Best Western. I found Him in the patient taxi driver who didn't seem worried when I needed extra time to pay my taxi fee. I even found Him in Hazel, who helped me find a job at Archer.

God didn't appear as a magician waving a wand to solve my problems. I had to collaborate with Him, fighting like Hell to show that I really wanted this thing. I needed to grow up and become a man, able to make decisions that were difficult. But still I found Him in Los Angeles, quietly guiding people around me to help when they could. That was my belief then, and it's my belief now.

Of *course* I didn't do it by myself.

Chapter 27: Creative License

My belief that I was doing the right thing was severely tested in the following weeks as I resigned from my position in North Canton. They hired a former student of mine to replace me, making my decision irrevocable. I needed every ounce of belief to sustain me as I packed up everything I owned, as I transported it across the continent in a U-Haul, and as I arrived in Los Angeles just in time to begin my duties at Archer.

I quickly grew to love Los Angeles, although it wasn't exactly the experience that I thought it would be. First, I couldn't locate a place to live on Venice Beach. The apartments there were beyond my price range. Thankfully, the dean allowed me to stay at his home until I found a place, and when our tech guy at Archer moved out of his rent-controlled apartment, I moved in, sharing the apartment with a motivated Persian woman who worked at her parents' business. The location allowed me to walk to school—a ten-minute walk, assuming I didn't stop at my favorite coffee shop on the way, which I usually did.

I soon found my tribe within the school, generally teachers from the Midwest. Having been asked to direct the student store, I quickly built a management system and recruited students. Seeing the way I empowered students, my headmistress threw her support behind me.

Students were eager to succeed, having gone through a rigorous application process to be selected. They welcomed me, often stopping at the end of each class to thank me for teaching.

It was all working out. Success was just ahead.

My hero was Quentin Tarantino, the video-store-clerk-turned-director who wrote and directed *Pulp Fiction* in 1994 and won an Academy Award for it. Like him, I believed I would write a screenplay and meet a famous producer. That producer would recognize my genius and insist I enter the glamorous world of directing.

Naturally, my first screenplay and film would transmogrify into a box-office hit. After that, I would mix with the Rich-and-Famous. I would have a riveting story about how a famous producer discovered his daughter's teacher, turning me into the hottest director in Hollywood.

But I didn't understand Hollywood, or even Los Angeles.

The city is a place where everyone is struggling to find their place, where they are trying to discover where their true genius lies. People take classes and seminars, and they find partners in bars and cafes. They are looking for the right connections that will allow them to scramble to the top of the heap. Most importantly, they are trying to find the perfect role.

In Hollywood, the movie industry loves to pigeonhole people. In addition to the many people who work below the line—doing lighting, makeup, sound, or stunts—there are also people who work above the line. Actors, for example, and Producers, and Directors. There are even hyphenates, like Actor-Directors, or Writer-Directors, or even Producer-Directors. It can all be confusing. So, it took me time to realize there are no Teacher-Directors.

Eventually, I realized that working at an independent school in Los Angeles—where some of the parents were power brokers—wasn't really like working in Hollywood.

Eventually, I realized that I wasn't part of the showbiz world.

Eventually, I realized that, although I taught the children of the Rich-and-Famous, *I* wasn't one of them.

I was The Help.

I remember standing in the Brentwood pharmacy, talking to Someone Important. She was a major donor and fundraiser for Archer who was connected to Powerful People. My headmistress had once introduced me to her, telling her I was one of Archer's outstanding teachers. The next time I ran into her at a local coffee shop, she remembered my name, to my surprise, taking the time to ask me questions about where I came from. Her curiosity about me seemed genuine; I was sure we were friends.

As we chatted comfortably there in the aisle of the pharmacy, I suddenly realized my opportunity. This woman was my friend; she could help me sell my screenplay.

Following my instincts, I began my pitch. "Did I mention that I'm writing a screenplay? It's about my Amish-Mennonite childhood." (I leaned into the word *Amish*.) "It's set in the Ohio Valley, and the protagonist is a lawyer who is dealing with the skeletons of his past—"

At that moment, she held up her hand. "Steven, I can't... listen to this."

I flushed with embarrassment, recalling too late that our headmistress had warned us teachers not to use our relationships with parents to break into the business. I had stumbled into an ethical conflict. The powerful woman I was facing was friends with my headmistress; what if she complained?

She must have sensed my worries because she smiled. "You'll need to get an agent if you have a screenplay," she said. "I'll be happy to recommend one for you."

"Thanks," I said, relieved by her kindness. "I would appreciate that."

She smiled again and moved toward the counter to make her purchase. I watched her go, then quickly made my escape.

As I slipped out the door, I quickly forgot my embarrassment. Of *course* she couldn't listen to my pitch, I rationalized to myself, but wasn't it nice that she would be recommending me to a top-flight agent? What a banner day! William Morris would soon be calling.

Eventually, as I reviewed our conversation in the cold light of the next morning, I realized she hadn't actually given me the name of an agent. She had said she *could* recommend me to someone, but I was so worried I'd get in trouble that I hadn't bothered to get a name from her.

And thus... no agent ever reached out to me, spurred on by the urgings of Someone Important.

It took my friend Steve, an old friend from graduate school who had also moved to Los Angeles, where he was now working as a writer-editor, to help me figure out Someone Important's true feelings.

"She's afraid she'll be sued," Steve said, laughing over his pancakes. We had met for breakfast at a local diner. "You're not a bullshit artist, like most people in Los Angeles, but you *are* full of shit. The thing about you, though, is that even when you're full of shit, you earnestly believe that you know what you're doing."

I stopped chewing my sausage, trying to figure out what he was really saying. "So, you're saying I should be less confident?"

"Understand that I admire this quality of resilience in you. You take failures in stride. I wish I had that same self-confidence."

"What's so admirable about that?"

He thought for a moment, then tapped the table decisively. "You're admirable because you give yourself the creative license to screw up."

I had grown up in a culture in which screwing up is classified as sin, which is why my teachers chose to beat their students when they cheated on spelling tests, or smoked cigarettes found along the road, or read comic books in school. Our teachers taught us that we should *never* risk screwing up.

But now, as my collaborator drizzled a stack of pancakes with butter and syrup, I realized he was right. I had embraced risk, so I also needed to accept the consequences when I screwed up.

Steve and I had become writing partners. A brilliant writer with a ready laugh and even sharper wit, Steve had been training as an improv actor, and he was hoping to make it in Hollywood—or at least enough so that he didn't have to wait tables to pay the bills. My screenplay wasn't going anywhere, so I had thought adding a comedic writer to the mix might be helpful.

One of the reasons our partnership worked was because Steve understood where I came from. He'd had his own brush with evangelical fundamentalism as a teen in a local church. But unlike me, he had little awe for authority. Now an agnostic, he questioned everything.

But he also recognized the deepest conflict in my life, which was holding me back as a writer and artist. Torn between my need for a close-knit community, yet highly reactive to controlling fundamentalism, I couldn't wrap my mind around the essential demand of creative work: the ideas need to be yours, and yours alone. Instead, I constantly looked for approval from others.

Steve was the first person to help me understand the way fundamentalist thinking stops people from learning. A fundamentalist believes that decisions are either right or wrong. There is no tolerance for those who disagree with you. Even though I had left my community, where everyone knew what was sinful and what was godly, I had not left behind the belief that there must be a right and a wrong in all situations, including in the choices I was making as a writer.

Thus, I found it difficult to go with my instincts, to lay it all out on the page, because what if my instincts were wrong? As Steve and I wrote together, we talked about the right brain (the creative instinct) and the left brain (the editorial instinct). Creative artists insist that you must shut down the judgmental part of your brain when you write the rough draft.

And thus, I found it difficult to break free of the judgmental part of my brain, desperately afraid I would make a mistake. I had inherited a mindset that fears sin and error rather than accepting the importance of mistakes within the creative process.

In Steve, I found a writing partner who had the ability to listen carefully to my most outrageous ideas without judgment, which created trust between us. I soon found myself confiding in him about my spanking obsession. He had a childlike curiosity, and he was always interested in hearing about my dating travails.

It was Steve who first told me I should write about the negative consequences of using corporal punishment on children. Although he distrusted religion, he trusted my reaction to fundamentalism. He knew that I reacted strongly when someone tried to tell me that their way was the only way—whether Christian, atheist, or progressive.

Chapter 28: The Cost of Control

One afternoon on Venice Beach, I was returning to my car after roller blading. As I crossed the parking lot, a random stranger approached me, saying he was a talent agent, and he thought I looked like the actor Ed Norton. He recommended I think about doing stand-in work for Norton.

I was flattered but didn't take him seriously. I wasn't interested in standing in for someone else—I wanted my *own* identity.

It was a bullshit reason, of course. I didn't realize the fear I had of giving up control. Here I was, in my early forties, living in Los Angeles, and yet, a massive confidence gap was blocking my ability to be successful in both art and love.

By now, I was beginning to understand that to be creative in my art, I needed to shut out the editor and lay out my ideas fearlessly, putting everything on the page, mistakes and all, and trusting that during the revision process, those mistakes could be cut. To create something authentic, I needed to give up control.

What I didn't understand is that true love demands the same courage.

My early trauma had materialized into my needing to be in control of my life and body. To do that, I found it satisfying to be in control of my partner's body and actions, so I became involved in the world of BDSM. This fulfilled my need for control, but… there were times when I tried to genuinely *not* feed my fetishism because on some level, I sensed that my obsession with spanking was blocking true love.

And so, when I became involved in a relationship where it was clear my partner wasn't interested in my obsession, I tried to set my obsession aside and develop a "vanilla" relationship. For a while, I would find satisfaction. At times, I even considered marriage.

But invariably, these "vanilla" relationships would fall apart because my need for control would roar to the surface. I'd lost that control as a child and had endured horrible, painful, humiliating experiences. Unable to forget, my subconscious couldn't let that go, no matter what my conscious mind decided was good for me.

My trauma was not unique to me—well, yes, the specifics might have been—but the fact is that most of us who want to leave, and most of us who do leave, experience profound isolation.

That isolation manifests in trauma.

261

This emerged for me first in 1994, shortly after I accepted a teaching position at North Canton, leasing an apartment just fifteen minutes away from my parents' home. Like an alcoholic in denial who returns to a familiar bar for "just one drink," I created an excuse to return to my home area: my parents were getting older, and my family needed me.

Shortly after I returned, the chest pains hit.

The first time, I freaked out and ran for the phone in the kitchen of my small apartment, trying to breathe and finding it impossible. I thought I was dying. Pressure was building in my chest. Frantically, I started to call 911, and then, suddenly, the chest pains just… disappeared, leaving me exhausted, sweaty and worried.

Chest pains… what had happened?

Was this the prelude to a heart attack?

How could my body fail me like this?

I knew my grandfather had had a heart attack in his forties. Did I have the same issue? But I was in my early thirties. I did construction work every summer. I was in great physical shape.

The next day, I talked to a colleague at school, who urgently recommended I seek medical help. Finding a colleague to cover for me, I left school early and went to see our family doctor in Hartville. She was new, whip-smart, and confident. She gave me an EKG, and then, worried by the results, she sent me straight to the hospital.

The technician who gave me a stress test didn't seem too worried by the results… but there had been that new doctor's reaction. Several days later, after stopping every afternoon at the local drug store to check my blood pressure (which always seemed fine), and after experiencing similar "chest pain" symptoms, I finally met with my heart specialist for his analysis. He answered my questions patiently, asked some of his own, and finally wrote me a referral for a therapist.

"You have PTSD," he said.

I looked at the referral. I didn't want to see a therapist—that's what "crazy people" did. I was desperate to find an easy way to solve the problem.

"Isn't there something else I can do for my chest pains?" I asked.

"You might find Tai Chi helpful," he said. "It will help reduce your stress load. Continuing with exercise is also good." A look of annoyance crossed his face: he was a practical soul. "But you don't have heart problems. You're healthy as a horse."

This is all in my head.

I left the building ten minutes later, walking into the bright Ohio sunshine. A load had lifted. I wasn't going to die after all. My heart was fine.

From now on, I just needed to ignore those chest pains because they *weren't* real.

Today I know that going to the doctor was the first step, a necessary one. What I didn't know at the time was that going to the doctor was *only* the first step. I needed to take the next one: admitting the problem and seeking therapeutic help.

In spite of the doctor's diagnosis, I refused to recognize the connection between the abuse I had been through, and the frightening manifestations of trauma I was now undergoing. Surely, I thought, there must be some way of solving this chest pain thing without taking the risk that people would think I was having "mental issues."

I just needed to "man up."

I was still fighting the cultural expectations I had been taught as a child within my fundamentalist community. I had no problem seeking medical help for any physical issue—for example, a bee sting, pneumonia, or a broken bone.

But trauma-induced PTSD?

To be fair, PTSD wasn't a recognized malady at the time in the general population. My demand for control wouldn't allow me to admit my shortcomings and failure, and to admit that I had been traumatized would have meant admitting my lack of control, as well.

So, I continued to ignore my panic attacks—they usually went away if I just waited. I marked them down to stress, finding relief in running each morning before school.

The chest pains got me to the doctor because my body was shouting to me, trying to make me see that I needed to begin doing the work that would help me heal. But I couldn't understand the message. I had not been taught to listen to my body.

I also didn't make the connection between my spanking obsession as a manifestation of this trauma—by then, I had simply accepted it as part of who I was. It was just how I thought about sex. And it sucked me into what promised to be the most exciting romance of my life... but was instead the most devastating.

As I settled into Los Angeles, I began actively looking for someone who was interested in a BDSM lifestyle. I was living in a large urban community, no one was looking over my shoulder, and I wasn't getting any younger. It was time to go after what I really wanted—a relationship with someone who shared my proclivities.

And sure enough, love came knocking.

I found it online in the form of Cecily, a brilliant and attractive woman in her thirties who lived in London and was undergoing a divorce. As we grew to know each other (virtually), she soon admitted that she too wanted the same type of romance I did. In fact, she was willing to move to Los Angeles. She could pursue her acting career while we got to know each other.

I eagerly agreed.

I didn't see the land mines strewn throughout our plans, the most lethal being that I had never physically shared space with a romantic partner before. I didn't realize how complex it was to learn how to live with an intimate partner. I didn't understand that living together in reality would be nothing like my fantasies.

It didn't take long for reality to hit.

By the next morning after she arrived, I had begun to get cold feet as I viewed Cecily's suitcase and personal effects strewn across my small bedroom. Somehow, I had failed to realize that living together meant I had to share my space. Usually, when I spent the night with a woman, we would split up the next morning, which gave me the time and space to order my space and assess the experience. Because she had moved in, that space had disappeared.

I didn't feel at all in control.

I also realized we were nothing alike. It turned out that I was reserved and private, and she was very dramatic. She was impossible to ignore, a diva used to constant attention who couldn't be turned off with the click of a mouse. I thought I had found a romantic partner who would fit into my well-ordered life, but when I had to negotiate the daily realities of living with her, I felt the same loss of control I'd experienced as a child. There was nothing rational about my feelings—I suddenly became desperate to escape, as I felt my autonomy slipping away.

I felt manipulated.

I realized with a sinking feeling that if someone was in control of this relationship, it wasn't... me. I had just fled a high-control religious community, and I didn't have the confidence to give up real control to anyone else—*especially someone who hadn't yet gotten a divorce*, I told myself self-righteously.

Generously, Cecily moved out and found her own place. We continued to see each other, but even after I reasserted control over my space, I felt uncomfortable.

Cecily was an experienced hand at long-term relationships, whereas I was a newcomer. She exuded vulnerability, and she knew that I needed to open up to her if we wished to connect emotionally. She wanted to understand the ghosts in my life that shaped me. Fascinated by my unique childhood, by the abuse I had suffered, she wanted to connect the dots leading to my need for control.

In contrast, I was an experienced hand at blocking real intimacy. Surviving inside and outside my Amish-Mennonite community had taught me how to build emotional barriers. So, when Cecily questioned me about my childhood, or about my relationship with my mother and father, I gave her vague answers. I stonewalled, agreeing when I didn't agree, promising but not following through. I wasn't ready to face who I was.

As Cecily continued to push, I found myself treating her with contempt. She found this confusing, and so did I. Until then, I had treated my romantic partners politely (and of course, distantly). But Cecily wanted inside my head, and I wasn't about to give her that kind of control.

The cost seemed too high.

The reality was, I thought I had found someone whose fetish matched mine perfectly, which meant all my fantasies could now become reality. I thought I only wanted to dominate her during sex—to which Cecily had given her enthusiastic consent—but in reality, I wanted absolute control in every area of *my* life. I wasn't ready for a committed relationship in which I had to be vulnerable, nor with a woman whose stubbornness matched my own.

A true BDSM relationship is far more than a fantasy. It can be healthy when the relationship is consensual with clearly defined boundaries, and when the Dominant understands that control is a gift from the submissive so the Dominant can provide her with security and pleasure, not because the Dominant is afraid of giving up control, as I was.

I only wanted the fantasy.

I only wanted absolute control.

I couldn't have articulated this—in fact, I would have denied it at the time—and thus my decision to step back was instinctive. But as I retreated, the vulnerability we had so treasured online disappeared.

Had I understood what I was going through, I might have ended the relationship more quickly. But no. Cecily was sure our relationship could work. She had done her homework, she knew what I needed to fulfill my fantasies, and she had become precisely that.

She refused to give me up.

Which put her in control, I slowly realized. I had entered the relationship thinking her offer was absolute control—only to discover I had no control at all where it mattered.

Somehow our relationship limped along for two years, following a cycle of breakups and makeups. Sometimes we both dated others, but we would always return to each other. Eventually, I determined to end it, no matter what. And so, one night, we broke up for good, and she left.

I was taking back control of my life.

It was summer vacation. The next morning, I was home alone when Cecily dropped by, working on a screenplay. She was having second thoughts, but I was determined not to let her manipulate me into returning. I turned away as we argued, but she moved in, reaching for my shoulders.

I froze. Quietly, I asked her to leave.

She wouldn't.

To escape, I moved to the kitchen.

This time, she begged me.

"Steven, what have I done wrong? I've done everything you've asked me to do. Why can't you figure out what you want?"

Usually, words like this gained my sympathy. Now, however, I saw it all as manipulation, and I snapped. Standing in the center of the living room, I shouted at her, telling her to… "Just. Go. Away." My voice echoed in the room.

Cecily stared at me, but finally turned and opened the front door,

I could see beyond her. Several neighbors clustered together outside, eyeing us worriedly. The apartment wasn't insulated or soundproofed, but I was beyond caring. The relationship, which was causing me so much pain, had to end.

"Just go, Cecily!" I was screaming. "Go!"

When she finally pushed past the onlookers, I sank onto the nearby couch, overwhelmed. My friends came inside.

"Are you okay?" one of them asked.

I wasn't.

I returned to my desktop computer. The page was unintelligible gibberish. I hated myself, hated the control she exerted over me, hated the way guilt flooded over me because of my unkind words.

The scene played over and over in my head.

Late that night, I called Cecily and apologized. Relieved, she told me it was her fault. She suggested slyly that she should be punished for her behavior. And so, we made up, and so, the cycle began again.

My vacillation, my inability to decide, was indicative of the psychological damage I was still managing. Yes, I hated the guilt, but Cecily's crawling back to me also empowered me. The need it fulfilled in my psyche went well beyond sexual satisfaction. Although I felt guilty about the rhythm of our cycle, the entire process gave me a high as I took control.

I still didn't understand its true cost.

Although Cecily and I made up afterwards, our public fight was the breaking point. Shortly afterwards, Cecily moved on with her life. She was done, and so was I.

I was forty-one then, in the prime of life. I began seeing other women. Occasionally, I heard about her from my friends, who saw her at parties. And eventually, my roommate, who was still friends with both of us, told me Cecily had returned to London.

It was only years afterward that I realized I was never in control.

Cecily's "submission" was a tool she had used to develop trust in our relationship. She had cared about me, perhaps even loved me, and if playing the submissive was the cost of my love, she was happy to pay it. Talented and smart, Cecily had always been the one in control.

I just hadn't realized it.

Because, to me, control had always been the person with the upper hand— literally. My father, swatting down. My teacher, wielding the paddle. Now, me, spanking my partner. Those were the ones in control, so, therefore, by performing the same actions, I was also in control.

I hadn't understood the psychological components at play here. Sex adds layers of control and submission, which Cecily played perfectly. The crux of the whole matter was that, in facing her manipulation of my issues, I had to admit that I'd never been in control.

Yet again.

Just like when I'd been a hurt child, when I ran home for comfort from my mother. Yes, the rules were strict, but at least I understood the rules and consequences.

It was trust I longed for most. The true cost of control was my inability to depend on anyone else, my inability to become vulnerable, my inability to trust that the person I loved most was in my corner. My obsession had blinded me.

The kind of life partner I needed—which I hadn't known I was looking for—was a powerful woman who could match me, someone who would be a friend and partner, someone I could trust enough to give up control.

But before I could find her, I needed to submit to the healing process.

Chapter 29: Breaking It All Down

They say the bad stuff, the things that matter about your life, the nightmares that force you to write, don't emerge until you've reached your forties and feel safe from your past. In that case, I was right on schedule. By the time I was staring forty in the face, the summer before my third year at Archer, I was using exercise to quell panic attacks.

It worked, but only a little.

During the summer of 2003, I began writing a novel. I set it in a small imaginary valley along the Ohio River, creating a world that looked like my childhood. The protagonist was a corporate lawyer in his mid-thirties who had fled his Amish-Mennonite background. The antagonist was a preacher who beat little kids for sexual pleasure, all the while claiming he was acting for God.

My main character was seriously fucked up, and I decided he needed therapy. But how was I to write about therapy? I'd never gone myself.

Well, that was easily remedied. Thanks to good health insurance, I would do research as any writer does and go to therapy. That way, I could return to my novel with real-life experience under my belt.

I jumped online and found Dr. Thea Kiran, who was able to see me that day. I was careful to assure Dr. Kiran I didn't need therapy; I was just doing research for a screenplay.

"Half of my clients are writing a screenplay."

Turns out, *every*one in L.A. is writing a screenplay, but I didn't accuse her of lying—because I'd also been lying.

To myself.

"So, what brought you here?"

"Oh, the character in my novel—"

"Yes, I heard you, but let's talk about you, not your art. What's going on in your life? Why are you here?"

I shifted in my seat.

My therapist chuckled. "Lots of people take therapy. May I call you Steven?"

"Sure."

The idea that this therapist thought I might have a real reason for being here worried me. If I told her what I was really like, what it was like to be me inside my tightly controlled mind, especially if I admitted my sexual fetish, I was sure she would treat me... well, like the very strange person I knew I was.

"I'm curious to see how this works."

"What do you want to know?" Her vibe was relaxed, confident. She threw up her hands. "You're in charge, so I'm happy to listen. Your insurance company pays me either way."

I hadn't considered that I would be in control. I'd been having problems moving forward in my novel, but with her statement, I glimpsed a new world in which that type of problem melted away. With that simple, "You're in charge," she had given *me* control, something I hadn't felt in a while as I struggled to fit my book's characters into the plot.

"So why do most people take therapy?" I asked. "I mean, I'm just wondering since I'm trying to figure out how to get my main character into therapy. He's pretty fucked up, since he was abused as a child. What kind of techniques would you suggest?"

"Well, it depends on the person. You mentioned that your character is a lawyer and writer, right? Since this is L.A., I help a lot of screenwriters and actors. Artists like this often have something in their past that drives their writing, but at one point, it just becomes overwhelming. Some suffer panic attacks, and we manage that with a combination of techniques, including medication and lifestyle adjustments."

I was still back on the term *panic attacks*.

"Can you actually cure panic attacks? I mean... since I think my character suffers from them."

My therapist studied me for a moment.

"I do use Cognitive Behavioral Therapy with my patients. It helps modify negative thought patterns. Does this sound helpful?"

I nodded, quickly, my breathing tight.

"We also use breathing exercises and mindfulness techniques. But since you're a writer, we might consider narrative therapy." She paused, thinking. "But perhaps... let's talk about you. Are you having panic attacks?"

"I don't know," I said. "Perhaps."

"Can you describe what you are experiencing?"

"It's like a pressure in the chest. My heart starts pounding. I'll wake up in the mornings, and I can hardly breathe."

"What happens then?" She had begun taking notes. "Have you ever called 911?"

"No. I just wait it out." I took a deep breath. "I know it's not a heart attack because my heart specialist told me my heart is fine. He said it was just Post-Traumatic... something like that."

"Post-Traumatic Stress Disorder?" On my nod, she frowned. "That's a serious diagnosis. Tell me more."

I told her about my panic attacks and the heart specialist's diagnosis.

"He recommended therapy... but I didn't think I needed it."

"*You* didn't think you needed therapy?"

"I didn't think I was insane."

"Who told you that therapy is only for the insane?"

"My family. They tell others to trust God instead. But prayer didn't help my panic attacks."

My therapist made a note on her pad. "Did your doctor diagnose *why* you had PTSD?"

"He said it was probably from trauma I experienced."

"You mean the trauma of leaving a strict, religious community, and being told you're going to Hell for it?"

My mouth dropped open and it took me a few seconds to be able to form my next question because... religion caused trauma? "Well... I *have* always been told that people who leave experience guilt because they left for a life of sin."

"That's very common for people in these situations; however, the reality is that there are two parts to trauma. First, there are the acts that typically happen to children within these closed communities—abuse. Sexual molestation. Physical harm."

"My father called it *spanking*," I said.

She didn't bat an eye, just nodded. "I'm sure he did. The second part is the body's reaction. It can happen years after the original abuse. Suddenly, that child, now fully grown and in their forties, begins to have panic attacks. Nightmares. Does this sound familiar?"

I nodded.

"What you are going through is not uncommon, although it must feel that way. I treat a lot of Jewish clients who have left strict Orthodox and Hasidic Jewish communities, and they experience the same symptoms you are."

"So... this means I'm not crazy?"

"You're not. Doing therapy doesn't mean you're crazy; it means you want to get whole again."

"What does that mean, getting whole?"

"I think there's a reason you came to see me, Steven, and I don't think it's because you're writing a book." She waited for a second, as if expecting me to argue with her, but I didn't. I was hanging on to her every word.

"I think you're writing a book because you've been instinctively using narrative therapy to try to recover from whatever hurt you. It's clear something traumatized you. We just don't know what."

"What is narrative therapy?" I asked.

"It's a form of storytelling," she said. "The patient writes about their memories and tries to figure out what it means." She glanced at the clock. "Perhaps we can talk about that next time."

Luckily, I didn't have to go broke to attend therapy since my insurance would cover the cost of the sessions. Which was good news.

I had just begun to realize that I might be able to get more from these sessions than just research for my novel. As I reflected on our first session, I realized that my therapist had figured out sooner than I had that I wasn't there to talk about my character's panic attacks—I was there to talk about my own. And my therapist had respected that. She made it clear I wasn't crazy. My heart warmed as I realized how safe I had felt during that session.

Perhaps she was right. Perhaps I needed to be honest... perhaps I was fighting with trauma from my past. How deep did the damage go? I didn't know why I was traumatized, but I did trust my therapist to begin to deal with it.

I thought about what my community might say if they knew I was taking therapy. And then I realized I didn't care. I had left that world for a reason.

Maybe this outside world would be able to fix what my community had damaged.

Within several sessions, I had found a rhythm with my therapist. I would talk about the week, any pressures or issues I was facing. Occasionally, she'd ask a question that prompted a story from my past—she always knew exactly the right kind to ask to get the best stories.

After several weeks, I realized my panic attacks had subsided. This gave me the courage to ask tougher questions.

One of the most startling conversations occurred as we began to talk about Dad's extreme discipline. For example, across my childhood, Dad had laid down the rule that we must all be in bed by 8:15 PM, but my brothers and I repeatedly ignored it. Usually, the reminder was delivered and then Dad would get distracted.

One night, Dad snapped. Using a two-foot length of rubber hose, about half-an-inch thick, with us in only our pajama bottoms, he spanked us so hard that the house resounded with our cries of pain.

My therapist listened to my story, occasionally wiping her eyes. When I finished, we sat there for a moment, then she asked, "Why do you keep using the word *spank*? A spanking is several slaps on the bottom with the hand to get the child's attention. What you endured is more accurately described as a beating."

I shook my head, struggling against the cognitive dissonance.

"Wait," I said. "I thought beatings were extreme corporal punishment. A spanking is *reasonable*."

"So how would you define reasonable?" she asked. The question hit me hard as I began to process it, as I tried to answer it.

"I think with the hand," I said. I shook my head again, trying to process it. "But my parents used... switches, tree branches. They kept them on top of the refrigerator. Dad sometimes used flat sticks..." My voice died away as I began to realize what I was saying.

I began having difficulty catching my breath, looking down at the floor. I felt her hand on my arm.

"You're all right, Steven. It's okay." Her face was concerned. "These are memories."

I took a deep breath, trying to relax. My breathing steadied.

"This is called doing the work," she said. "How did you feel as you talked about that?"

"Confused... Corporal punishment was part of our culture. Most everyone I knew was spanked. If you misbehaved, or didn't do your homework, you got paddled."

"How do you feel about that now?"

"It makes me really angry, but there was nothing I could do about it. That's just the way things worked."

"You had no control."

"No. It's probably why I quit doing my homework in middle school. Why I failed eighth grade. But my teacher, the one who saved me... never paddled kids. But if beating is hitting kids with something other than your hand, then..."

I let the words hang there. I was struggling to deal with the dissonance.

"And how do you differentiate between *extreme* corporal punishment and reasonable?" my therapist asked. I didn't answer. "It's almost impossible. Today, we don't call it spanking. As a teacher in a secular school, I suspect you know this, but you probably never applied it to your own situation. Today it's called—"

"Physical abuse," I finished her thought. I shivered, even though the room was warm. I realized I was exhausted. "Do you think it's possible that my PTSD comes from... that?"

"It's possible."

As I walked home that afternoon in the California sunshine, I realized it was the first time I had used the term "physical abuse" in connection to my childhood. Was it possible? Had I had been physically abused?

My father had beaten my siblings and me without our consent, and I was quickly beginning to realize it had most likely caused the trauma I was now dealing with.

Had my father abused me?

It was the first time I had considered that possibility. I knew by then that the severe discipline I had received as a child had probably caused my spanking fetish. Now, as I thought about the spanking relationships I had had with my female partners, I wondered.

Had they too been abused?

As my therapist and I continued to work, I began to connect what we were discussing with a term that I had heard during conversations in private chatrooms for people who shared a spanking fetish: *traumatic repetition*. It referred to the victim's attempt to repeat the abuse in an attempt to exorcise that trauma.

Almost every player I knew could point back to a time when spanking first aroused them, and it was often due to a time when they had been spanked. They often joked about going through traumatic repetition.

I shared this with my therapist. It was the first time I had talked about my fetish within a clinical setting, and I worried that she might judge me, but she didn't.

"I'm aware of BDSM," she said. "I would hesitate to judge anyone who wants to fly their freak flag."

"How does it work?" I asked my therapist. "Can it be helpful? Can it relieve the trauma?"

"It depends," she said. "Repetition can be helpful in rewiring the brain after trauma through a process called neuroplasticity."

"What is neuroplasticity?"

"It's the brain's ability to reorganize itself by forming new neural connections throughout your life. If you've known someone with traumatic brain injury, they probably used neuroplasticity to help recover."

"So, it's not all bad."

"No. But traumatic repetition—sometimes they call it repetition compulsion—can actually exacerbate the trauma. It's something you might want to think about."

"You think my spanking fetish, replaying what I went through as a child, is actually exacerbating my need for control?"

"I don't know. That's only something you can answer. I do know the research indicates that repeatedly experiencing or re-enacting traumatic events can reinforce neural pathways and potentially worsen the impact of the trauma."

During another session, she asked me a question about my family that I couldn't get out of my head for days. "How do you think your family is going to feel about you telling the family secrets?"

"I don't know," I said. "I haven't really thought about that. This is confidential, right?"

"It is," she assured me. "But that's not the point. Do you feel at all guilty?"

"Sometimes," I said. "I worry about how this might hurt my parents' feelings, or my siblings'."

"But you're willing to do it anyway," she said. "That shows you're finally beginning to experience healing."

"What do you mean?"

"You need to know as we move forward that the number one rule in families like yours—in fundamentalist families that use punishment and fear of Hell to keep people in line—is that you can't spill the family secrets. What goes on behind closed doors should never be told. Here, with me, you're choosing to share these secrets. This means they're losing control over you. You're taking charge of your narrative. That's very powerful."

It was a transformative moment. For the first time, I saw a way to take back control of my life from my family, from my community… and to rewrite my story based on what I was learning in narrative therapy. Dr. Kiran had given it back to me by helping me shift the way I saw myself and my family. Most importantly, I had the right to my own voice and my own story. A surge of energy coursed through me as I walked home that afternoon, with writing ideas racing through my head.

As I reflect back on that moment, I realize it was then that the seed was first planted—that I could write specifically about the world of my hometown and my family. Not a novel that fictionalized everything about my past, but instead, a memoir that would explore why I had become who I was.

Chapter 30: Reconnecting

Dr. Kiran's words—that proclamation of my own power—changed me in subtle ways. While I wasn't suddenly the All-Powerful Man, I began to look at interactions with others—specifically my family members—in a new way.

Several months later, my brother Richard and his wife showed up to visit. I spent time with his family, showing them around some of the touristy sites. Before they left, Richard and I ended up taking a drive together, just us two brothers, enjoying the Malibu highway. We stopped to explore a rocky area and ended up enjoying the sunset there. Our silent reflection on that scene led to a conversation that was deeper—more real and honest—than any I'd ever had with him before as I tested out my newfound power of autonomy that my therapy sessions was helping to grow. I told Richard that I had filed for bankruptcy the previous year. Now, Richard was very good with money, and I was worried he'd condemn me, but this newfound autonomy gave me the courage to share this difficulty with him. I told him about the tough time I'd had selling my house in Ohio before leaving for Los Angeles, and about the credit card debts that had been piling up.

To my surprise—and as testament to Dr. Kiran's assurance that I was permitted to make mistakes in learning—Richard didn't condemn me. He listened... and it was almost with respect. As if me being vulnerable had touched him.

"I think most of us know you've been going through some tough times out here," he said. "I know you've struggled with debt. But I appreciate the way you continue to pay off the money I've loaned you... and the interest you paid on that debt."

"There was no way I was not going to pay you," I said. "You're my brother."

"And that's why I helped you. I wasn't even sure you'd ever pay me back, but you're my brother. I care about you."

We sat there for a few more minutes. I suddenly realized that Richard was more than just a brother. He was also my friend.

I had also reconnected with my cousin Jean, who was living in Pennsylvania. She had been my favorite cousin on my dad's side of the family. With a voice like an angel, she had starred in all the Christmas pageants at her high school. She had always been my ally when our family went to visit Dad's family in Lancaster. She had admired my book smarts and had hung out with me during family reunions. After high school, she had married a farmer and had become a nurse. I hadn't seen her in years.

Now she reached out to me. She was coming to Los Angeles and wanted to meet. When she arrived, I accompanied her as she checked out the popular sites in Los Angeles. When she heard I was writing a book based on my childhood, she was fascinated. She told me about how judgmental my father had been with her mother.

One evening over dinner and drinks, she told me about her success as a Mary Kay salesperson (she had earned her pink Cadillac), and I finally opened up about my own struggles with finances. She had been through therapy, as well, and as I shared with her about what I was discovering about myself and the abuse I had experienced, she affirmed what I was discovering.

"I could never understand the strict culture you guys had," she told me. "When your sisters would visit, they would beg to wear our 'worldly' clothes."

"My parents let that happen?" I asked.

"No way. We kept it a secret. But I found your dad to be so frustrating. Every time he visited, he would preach to my mother about her worldly clothes."

"Yes, I'm sorry about that. I loved your parents. I'll never forget that one Christmas we celebrated at your place. You sang 'Oh, Holy Night' in church. You looked like the Virgin Mary."

She giggled, once more a teenager. "It was ridiculous, the rules your church had about musical instruments. Do you remember the way your dad immediately went to the piano the minute he arrived for Christmas reunions? He belonged to that church that didn't allow instruments, yet the minute he got a chance, he played them at our place. It was all so hypocritical."

When I shared with Jean about the physical abuse I had experienced, she listened sympathetically. Her parents, who had been pastors of a more conservative church, had never put her through the severe discipline I had experienced, but she had paid attention to what my siblings had gone through.

"I can't imagine what you've been through," she said.

I took a deep breath. I hadn't realized how tense this conversation had made me.

"Have you read Brene Brown?" she asked. "I've been reading her book. She talks about the power of shame, the way it's connected to control. I know the way the men in your church try to control their wives… do you think you're struggling with that?"

Before she left, Jean gave me a hug.

"You're on the right path, Steven," she said. "Let's keep talking."

For the first time in years, I was beginning to have real conversations with my family.

The following week, when I questioned Dr. Kiran about when I needed to talk to my other siblings. Dr. Kiran didn't give me an answer.

"This is your choice," she said. "You're in charge of how much you want to tell your family."

"What does that mean?" I asked.

"You're trying to figure out the difference between privacy and secrets," she said. "You are trying to decide how much to tell your family about what happened to you... and to them."

"Do you think my siblings had the same experience with my father?"

"Look how long it took *you* to come see me, to begin talking about the trauma you experienced. Do you think you're the only one in a family of eight children to go through what you have? To experience the trauma of having been abused?"

"But none of them admit it."

"Have you asked them?"

"Not yet," I said. "But they don't seem to be traumatized."

She nodded, not surprised.

"One day, one of your other siblings is going to go through the same thing you have, and they'll probably want to talk to you about it. That will give you a chance to do something important for them—to confirm what they've been through."

Until then, I had never realized what should have been completely obvious. Until then, I had not considered the impact my father's stern discipline might have had upon my other siblings. Until then, I had believed that I was on this journey all by myself. Did I want to help them? Did I want to take on the trauma they had gone through as well as my own, or was my own difficult enough? I wasn't sure.

For a moment, my therapist remained silent.

"You may not be ready for this yet. That's okay. But I think you're going to face this eventually, and when you do, you should know that one of the most powerful tools in therapy is called 'Bearing Witness.'" Seeing my confusion, she clarified. "It refers to the therapist's role in actively listening to and acknowledging a client's experiences, particularly in trauma therapy."

"I don't know if that's ever going to happen," I said. "My family thinks I'm living on the 'Left Coast'—no one takes me seriously because I'm no longer part of the faith."

My therapist smiled. "Yes, that's true. That's what they say now. But when they face a crisis, when they suddenly wake up with panic attacks, and they know your story, they will eventually come to you. Bearing witness is the heart of narrative therapy. It's what I do in here with you. By doing this, I am creating a safe space for you to share your stories without judgment. I offer empathy and validate your feelings. It's part of the healing journey."

"And you think the conversations I am having might take my family on this journey?"

"Perhaps," she said. "Although your family members may not be willing to take therapy, you might be able to bear witness for your family members when they finally decide to trust you and tell you what they've been through."

"You're saying I need to share more with them?"

She raised her hand. "No, *you* are not required to do anything. Anything you share in here can remain here. You have the right to keep things private. But there are things you will need to share with someone. If you don't tell someone those dreadful secrets, your body will drive you to do something to relieve itself of the poison within."

"Panic attacks. You're saying I get panic attacks because the secrets want out?"

"Yes. Think of a monster down in the dark basement. That's what secrets are. The pounding you hear, that's the panic attack you feel. The monster wants out, and until you throw open the door and deal with the monster, the panic attacks won't stop."

"And when I do that…"

"You see the monster for what it is. Sometimes it's small, sometimes it's large. But either way, the monster quits pounding. You get rid of the fear."

"But my family doesn't want me to do that," I said.

"No. They fear that you might tell the world about what you experienced, about that monster—they're just as afraid of it. When you no longer fear that monster, they have no control over you anymore."

"And I do this by spilling the family secrets?"

"Yes. But only when you're ready."

In my mind's eyes, I saw my father, his broad hand smashing down. I saw him playing "Mary Had a Little Lamb" on the saw to our youth group. I saw the way his grandchildren loved crowding around him. They had never seen his rage, never had to fear him.

"My family believes when someone does something wrong, you just need to forgive and forget."

"Even if it leaves the abuser the freedom to keep abusing?" my therapist said. "Victims suffer trauma because no one has had the courage to spill the secrets. You aren't the only one your father abused. Imagine the trauma they are experiencing."

"None of my brothers and sisters are going to go see a therapist," I said.

She shook her head, angry.

"Steven, it will never be okay for you to tell your family stories if you play by their rules. They want you to forgive without holding your abuser responsible."

She was right, but if I went there… My siblings admired my parents, as far as I knew. How could I be the one to destroy that admiration—or worse, what if they didn't believe me?

Every so often, I was able to take a break when my panic attacks subsided, but Dr. Kiran was there for me when I faced a new problem and wanted to return—*needed* to return—to therapy.

Laura had re-entered my life.

I had not been able to get over Laura. And what was more, I kept comparing every woman I met to her.

Laura was an impossible dream—*my* impossible dream. We'd kept in touch via emails and letters after she moved to Moscow, but I had moved on with my life, having seen several different women since I'd arrived in Los Angeles. But then Laura had reached out with news. She'd gotten married, and... oh yeah, she'd written a novel, and could I give her feedback?

Feedback for her *story*? I couldn't get beyond the fact that she'd gotten married. I had hoped—believed—that we would eventually get back together, but her marriage had killed that possibility. We really *were* over.

"And how did you feel about that?" Dr. Kiran asked.

There was the $10,000 question. "I realized how stupid I was to let her go."

"So, did you agree to help her with her novel?"

Did I help Laura? Of course, I had. Hell, she'd become all I could think about. I had read her novel through—twice—and hadn't been able to keep from allegorizing the two men who fought over the heroine, wondering which one had been based on me. Finally, I'd written back, politely congratulating her on her marriage, and yes, if she wanted developmental feedback, I'd be happy to help.

"And that's where I ran into problems," I admitted. "I gave her a lot of feedback. Then we began talking by IM—she was still in Moscow and her husband was back in the States. And then our conversation turned... sexual." I cleared my throat. "And he discovered our conversations."

"And then what happened?"

The thing with a good therapist is that there's no judgment; they just ask questions that help you make your own conclusions—something I hadn't been able to... or been willing to do... on my own.

"Well, her husband was angry, but Laura insisted that she and I need to keep working together because she needs and values my feedback."

"How did he take *that* news?"

"If you know Laura, you know she gets her way. She's pretty determined. So, he finally agreed to let us work together as long as he had access to all our conversations, and complete access to Laura's email and texts. And, of course, no sexting. She agreed."

"How do you feel about that?" Dr. Kiran asked

"I'm not so sure. It's like I have no control in the situation. I feel torn about it. I also feel used. But Laura needs me... and I believe in her."

"So, you've chosen to remain in a relationship in which you have no control? That shows progress, Steven."

"Well, it's not really a romantic relationship, just a friendship," I said, but I blushed.

Dr. Kiran chuckled. "Is that what you're going to tell yourself?"

That was the turning point for me in my work together with Dr. Kiran. For the first time, I had come to grips with a romance in which I suddenly had no control. In the past, with Laura, I had always been in control… when she walked away, I let her go, and she had been the one to return to me.

Now she had somehow taken control, both with her husband and with me.

This went against the pattern I had always followed in any romance. If this had happened before, I would have walked away, demonstrating to her that I was the one who called the shots, forcing her to either come back to me on my terms, or not at all.

That's what had happened when Laura invited me to go to Moscow with her. Since I didn't know Russian, it would have made me too vulnerable, and so I had walked away, and the relationship had ended. But something had happened to me since then.

I realized that I cared enough about Laura that I was willing to let her take control in order to keep the relationship. I couldn't believe it. I had never stayed in a relationship where the woman was in control.

But I had been in therapy for several years now, and Dr. Kiran and I had been able to analyze and break down why I felt the need for such control. During the last session together, we had even analyzed my history with Laura. Now, a week later, my therapist was able to help me come to a compromise in which *both* of us would have to cede some control.

"You still care about her? You think there's still something there?"

"Perhaps… It feels awkward, admitting that."

"Because she's married?"

"Yes." I couldn't believe I was saying that, but Dr. Kiran didn't seem shocked.

"Is there something you can do to make her husband feel safe so that you can work together? Is there a way for both of you to compromise, with neither of you in complete control?"

I eyed her, uncertain about the idea I was about to drop.

"Okay," I said. "How about this—it's a ridiculous idea, but maybe… Maybe I could *charge* her for my time?"

"Is that a ridiculous idea? I don't think so. As an experienced writer, you have earned the right to charge writers who want to work with you, and Laura's a writer who wants your guidance. And you would meet your goal—it would make her husband feel safe because you're not going to mess around with a paycheck. Charging her would create a professional boundary he could respect. It's actually a good solution to everyone's dilemma."

To my surprise, the boundaries we established worked. I was now working with Laura as a writing colleague. Charging her ensured that our relationship remained professional since I recorded the hours that I spent working with her, billed her for the time, and received her payments. As a result, it changed the nature of our relationship.

For the first time, I had been able to give up control with someone for whom I still had feelings. I told myself this was because she was no longer an ex-girlfriend, but a client. Any romance between us was definitely locked away in the past. She was merely a professional colleague. Yet I had never ceded control before, especially with an *ex*-girlfriend. But to my surprise, my decision paid off.

The boundaries Laura and I set allowed us to develop a genuine friendship. It developed into a relationship I had never had with anyone before—Laura became a friend I was able to not only respect but also trust implicitly.

This shift would dramatically alter my life. But I had no idea how difficult that shift would be, spinning me around and pushing me off in a powerful new direction that would be more painful than anything I had yet experienced.

Book VII: Acceptance

There is a river, the streams whereof shall make glad the city of God,
the holy place of the tabernacles of the most High.

~ Psalm 46: 3-4, *The Holy Bible,* KJV, 1769

Interpolation VII: Patriarchs of Abuse

As I was growing up, the late evangelical influencer James Dobson was one of the most influential writers on the topic of spanking children. Dare to Discipline (Tyndale, 1977), his breakout book, argues that corporal punishment is necessary to ensure a happy home.

Dobson was reacting to the theories of Dr. Benjamin McLane Spock, who in 1946 published the gold standard on child-rearing, The Common Sense Book of Baby and Child Care (Duell, Sloan and Pearce, 1946), It argued against the use of corporal punishment. With his book, Dobson changed the national conversation.

He was followed by an even more extreme writer, evangelical pastor Roy Lessin, who published a disciplinary guide for parents, Spanking: Why, When, How (Bethany, 1979). I recall seeing the book in my parents' library. The book gives such ritualized directions—even encouraging bare-bottom spankings— that it has been compared to a BDSM manual. The book was revised, but you can still buy the original version online.

In an open letter online, How Spanking Changed My Life (2010), Bethany A. Fenimore bravely writes about the severe psychological damage she experienced under her father, one of Lessin's followers. She reports suffering from IBS and PTSD, and describes her punishments explicitly, along with her decade-long struggle "to find a healthy sexuality outside the memories I have of the Roy Lessin spankings."

In the past ten years, an Exvangelical movement of deconstruction has arisen in reaction to patriarchs like these, first inspired by a former evangelical-pastor-turned-podcaster, Blake Chastain, whose memoir Exvangelical & Beyond (Tarcher Perigee, 2024) reports on his own deconstruction. Like the Exvangelicals who followed him, Chastain reports being driven away by the abuse he saw in the church. Some wrote memoirs trying to understand their abuse.

The best of these include Linda Kay Klein's Pure: Inside the Evangelical Movement That Shamed a Generation of Young Women and How I Broke Free (Atria, 2018), Tia Levings' A Well-Trained Wife (St. Martin's, 2024), and Jocelyn R. Zichterman's I Fired God (St. Martin's, 2025). NPR reporter Sarah McCammon also analyzes evangelical purity culture in The Exvangelicals (St. Martin's, 2024). All report on their childhood experiences with severe corporal punishment. Some admit, to their shame, that as adults they used it on their own children before recognizing and breaking the cycle of abuse.

Steven Denlinger

The Exvangelical movement was inevitable. The Apostle Paul advised fathers not to "provoke" their "children to wrath," and thanks to the abuse taught by these patriarchs of abuse, that wrath is now shaking up the evangelical community. Because as victims of this community have deconstructed their faith—finding support from an ever-widening Exvangelical community—they find it impossible to remain.

Torn asunder by their integrity, they have rejected both the abuse and their faith.

Chapter 31: Torching the Wall

At the age of 46, as September 2009 rolled down the calendar, my world crashed down around me with a single phone call. I put down the cell phone.

Mom died on the operating table, but they brought her back to life.

According to my older sister, Mom was still in danger due to complications of heart failure and diverticulitis. Using my cell phone and my Facebook account, which, by then, had thousands of readers due to my writing on *HuffPost,* I began to post about my mother, giving daily updates.

A year previous, I had left Archer. After spending six years teaching there, I had decided I needed to focus exclusively on my writing if I was ever going to publish my novel, which I had started years before.

I have better things waiting for me.

To make the rent in the months that followed, I tried being an insurance agent, but it turned out that I was better at teaching fellow agents how to sell insurance than do it myself. So, I gave up on that and tried writing my novel full time, using my 401K savings to live. Writing a blog for *HuffPost* (thanks to Archer parent, Arianna Huffington), publishing snippets of my life growing up in my Amish-Mennonite community, I fully expected to get an agent and sell my upcoming novel, but that didn't work out either.

And then my mom had a heart attack.

My mother's crisis began to reconnect me to my family. My family and friends saw that, although on *HuffPost* I had been highly critical of my parents and family, I also loved them. Perhaps they understood what I did not—the opposite of love is not hatred, but indifference, and I was anything but indifferent to the woman who had birthed me, who had given me freedom to attend school a year early, who had wept as I'd struggled to break away from my community, and who was now one of my closest friends—and fighting for her life.

In October, my oldest sister, Marcia, called me.

"I don't think she wanted to come back."

"Why do you think that?"

"Steven, she died on the operating table. I think she wishes she'd been able to... remain gone, you know?"

I didn't. I didn't know what to say because I hadn't been there in eight years for any length of time.

"Maybe you could come home? For a while? You're not teaching at

Archer anymore. This might be a good time for you to spend time with Mom and Dad. I mean, you're teaching online, right? Couldn't you teach from Ohio?"

"I..." Nothing was working in Los Angeles, financially. I had gotten no traction in my search for an agent. The long hours alone at the computer, away from people, drained me. I needed to be around people to thrive. Which was why I had returned to teaching adults, teaching both online and on-ground for the University of Phoenix.

Plus, I was my mother's firstborn son... and she was dying.

"I'll be there."

Today, the impracticalities of that trip astonish me. How I thought I could take a road trip in the winter, as broke as I was, makes little sense. But, like my plan to go to therapy to accurately portray a character in my novel—when what I needed was therapy—I had a gift for being able to fool myself into doing the right thing.

I started the journey east, driving the same plum-colored 1994 Saturn in which I had arrived over eight years earlier. It was ironic, nothing had changed. Was it God in control this time or was I at the mercy of a capricious Fate? I had arrived in Los Angeles with the winds of hope at my back, the help of a perfect stranger causing me to believe that the Almighty was guiding me. Believing this, I had taken a massive chance and thrown away a tenure-track job in North Canton. Now I was heading home again, dead broke, with barely enough money to pay for gas.

Once again, I had to ask for help, just like my father. A close friend and supporter of my writing, who would have admired my father for being humble enough to ask for help, sent me gas money. She lived on the edge herself, in a small town in Tennessee, helping those writers she admired, and she didn't hold much with banks. She trusted Walmart, though, so she had me collect the money at a local outlet.

Maybe I was too hard on my father.

The tired drive across the blazing desert was silent, the red and purple rays of the sun setting behind me.

I didn't want to leave California.

My first stop was Phoenix where I stayed for the night with Glendon. After I had moved to Los Angeles, I had reconnected with him, our friendship just as strong as ever, but with both of us having undergone changes. He too had left the conservative Mennonites, but he was still politically conservative. We had accepted our differences and listened to each other. He was fascinated by my writing goals. His spacious home, a hushed oasis in the Arizona heat, was a relief to my shattered sensibilities, a vivid contrast from the past few weeks. I spent the evening with his family, and in the morning, I pushed on.

Several nights later, I stopped in Fountain, Colorado, and spent the evening with old friends from my home community. They had moved out here after leaving the conservative Mennonites, as well. Like Glendon, their evangelical faith was strong, and they were also politically conservative.

They welcomed me as if I were family. They had been following my writing in *HuffPost*, and they approved. They invited their extended family to join us for dinner, and afterwards, as the family sat talking, the grief and stress of the last few weeks overcame me. I fell asleep amidst that company.

Before I headed to the guest bedroom, my hosts asked if they could pray for me.

I agreed where I sat, half-asleep.

I expected a quick prayer. Instead, they all gathered around, children and adults, laying their hands on me. The children's intensity, their parents' tenderness toward them, made me remember the nights when my family would gather around the couch, listening as my mother's gentle voice led us in an evening prayer.

I felt a rush of familiar warmth, the feeling of acceptance, the feeling of unconditional love I always experienced during those moments.

The voices of the children praying for me were high and trusting.

"Dear God, please help our friend as he goes home to his family."

There was an innocence in these prayers, a confidence in God that couldn't be fake.

When I awoke the next morning, my friend served me a homemade breakfast of scrambled eggs and crispy bacon and thick toast with real butter as I listened to her story. I knew she had changed—she no longer wore the homemade clothes and white bonnet that my sisters and mother still wore.

They had left our faith community a decade previous, she told me, rejecting the spiritual abuse they saw practiced on their friends. God had spoken to her, and her husband had listened to what she had to say. They had moved to this community and joined other families of former Mennonites, all of whom had rejected the abuse, all of whom were hoping to discover God's will for their lives.

"God led us the entire way. I'm a different person, my husband says."

"How?"

"I'm not afraid to speak my mind. God speaks through me, the same as he does through the men. We left all that behind us in Ohio. My family doesn't really understand our decision to leave."

Neither does mine. And now I'm going back there.

Around us, my friend's children played and studied in their home school. Her personal narrative told me how far she had come after she'd left her childhood community with her husband, and it revealed a strength of character I hadn't seen when I had last known her. During our final cup of coffee, she pushed a hundred dollars in cash toward me.

"Let us help you with your expenses on the way home."

I tried not to gape, tried not to show the relief that flooded over me. "I haven't told you anything about my financial struggles."

She smiled, refusing to judge. "God is going to do great things for you and your family."

I shook my head. "Your confidence is reassuring," I said, doubt laced through my words. I started to move toward the door, out to where my car was warming up. "I wish I could believe the way you believe. Right now, my life seems to be a total wreck."

"I know that's what you think now, but it's not," she reassured me. "There is a reason you're going home to your family. You are following the path God intended you to follow. I promise you."

"How do you know?" I asked.

"I just do."

I drove off into the glaring white, considering what I had seen during that brief visit.

I was glad to have spent time with them. I didn't know the person she'd become over the past twenty-five years, but the one I'd met during this visit renewed my faith in faith.

While I was financially strapped, people had reached out to help me, stepping in to serve as God's hands and feet. I was ashamed of the way I had judged my father in the past for his "poor financial choices." What had started out as a road trip driven by a son's guilt and intent to see his mother before she died had now become my own journey back to my faith.

God had laid out the path before me and I'd chosen to follow it.

I arrived at Marcia's farm in Seymour, Missouri, late at night. After we chatted, Marcia led me up the creaking stairs, where I would sleep in the guest bedroom. The next morning as we talked, she made her signature dish, a mouth-watering breakfast roll drizzled with syrup, the mouth-feel chewy and melting and sweet, the richness of the caramel balanced and perfect against the bitter perfection of the coffee.

The buttery softness of the roll brought up all sorts of memories of eating around the breakfast table when we were both kids—the memories were coming at me, fast and furious, now that I was with someone who'd once shared my home.

Those memories came spilling out when she asked me to read to her from my memoir. Marcia, like me, was a writer—she'd published hundreds of short stories in church magazines, so we talk the same language. She listened to the chapter I chose, at first ironing and folding clothes as she listened. But finally, she stopped, sitting down silently, as I read to her about the abuse I'd suffered at our father's hands.

"Dad was so much harder on you boys."

For the first time, I had found a witness to my past, someone to affirm what had happened during those crushing years. Marcia did not accuse me of dreaming up the abuse; she saw the truth of my memories, the pain that forged my torment… and she accepted her role as a witness. It was real—I didn't just make it up.

All of which meant that my anger, my iron wall of bitterness—icy and black—had been forged authentically.

Her words stood there, alone in the silence, then moved through me, my body relaxing into the truth of the moment. I felt valued in her acknowledgment. For the first time, someone who had been there had affirmed my writing.

I didn't believe at the time that grace had the power to torch that wall. Perhaps I didn't think about it, or perhaps I didn't *want* to think about it. But it was impossible to ignore what I was feeling. The anger had begun to dissolve.

Abuse is a complex thing, and it must first be fully grasped, fully comprehended, its scar tissue debrided, before the healing process can commence. A child cannot discover the truth of their abuse while dancing barefoot on a red-hot griddle.

One must first escape.

I *had* escaped, I was no longer a child, and I had found my own path.

Chapter 32: An Infusion of Grace

My sister Marcia's witness to the truth of my abuse had finally cracked the wall of isolation. For years, I had kept my father's abuse a dark secret, believing that no one would understand what I was feeling. That moment with my sister was a moment of vulnerability I could not have achieved before I entered therapy.

Until I began therapy, I had refused to talk about these shameful secrets. But as my therapist eventually explained to me, hiding secrets destroys your ability to be vulnerable—we cannot choose which emotions to feel. Vulnerability is a requirement for love within all our relationships, including those within my family.

I shouldn't have been shocked when my youngest sister Heidi reacted to my revelations on *HuffPost* by telling me, "We didn't like what you were saying, but at least we finally knew what you were thinking."

But I had to return home from Los Angeles to discover that. Until that journey, which launched my mid-life crisis, I had believed, along with Simon and Garfunkel, that I was an island. The writing I had published on *HuffPost* during my last year there had centered around this theme, positioning me as a man standing alone.

Yet the stories of my life proved the exact opposite. During every turn in my climb up the ladder of ambition, I found friends and strangers who supported me. A hotel manager who gave me a break and cashed my check when I was flat broke. A famous parent who insisted I publish my work on her nascent online newspaper. Several friends who lent me thousands of dollars to keep writing during my last year in Los Angeles. And at the end, friends who stored my belongings and pushed cash into my hands for gas and lodging when I left.

I still hadn't connected the pieces. To do that, I would have to push through the lowest level of the dark valley I had begun to cross. But my sister's rock-solid affirmation of my memories—something I did not expect—became an infusion of grace that permitted me to return and view my family through different eyes.

On the night of my arrival in Ohio, as I pulled into the driveway of my parents' home where most of my siblings and their children had gathered to welcome me, I wasn't looking forward to the reunion. I dreaded my father's disapproval—I was dead broke, dependent upon modest payments from online teaching, and being barraged by calls from creditors.

I was desperate.

Living a life of affluence in Los Angeles, I had publicly blamed our family's poverty on my father, casting extreme judgment. But as I opened the car door to greet my family, I realized our positions had been reversed. Thanks to my youngest brother Richard's advice, my father was debt free, unlike me. Dad was finally on a budget with a steady income, unlike me.

Yet as he welcomed me, my father refused to criticize or judge. Like the father in the Parable of the Prodigal Son, he had generously prepared a feast, and his enthusiastic greeting was equally uninhibited.

Downstairs, he offered me a bedroom and bathroom on one side. There was internet access, so I could teach online. I was welcome to stay as long as I wished—it was my home. I felt the financial worries weighing me down begin to lift. I had no intention of taking advantage of my parents—I knew I'd be able to find some way to support myself—but knowing that I had a place to stay while I got back on my feet was a relief.

Over the next week, I settled in. When I had left Los Angeles, I had told my readers that my visit home would just be one stop on a quixotic road trip around the country, during which I would finish my novel. Fascinated by my work on *HuffPost,* almost forty friends and relatives had invited me to visit, but by the time I arrived home in November 2009, having faced brutal weather on the way, I knew my road trip was a pipe dream.

I wondered whether my parents would give me a list of restrictions while living with them. But the next day, as my father and I looked over my mother's brown and lifeless garden, he turned to me.

"You're a man now. Your decisions are your own."

It slowly dawned on me. For the first time, my father had recognized my autonomy. His demeanor was respectful. I choked up but didn't say anything. I had always wondered what my father thought of me. Yes, he had always supported my teaching, but he had never given my writing career his formal blessing. Now here he was, telling me that I was a man, and that he would not interfere with the way I lived my life.

Most importantly, I realized my father was giving me a choice, something I desperately needed. Without realizing it, I had spent the last two decades fighting to establish myself as a man, yet because my father had refused to recognize my freedom, I had never lost the sense of being a juvenile. I had not realized how much I craved his blessing.

Standing there in the grey of an Ohio winter with my father, I experienced a moment of healing.

This realization was affirmed early the next morning. As I booted up my computer, I glanced over to see my father. The sun was coming through the window, and it lit him up as he was kneeling. His head was bowed. Before him on the chair lay a sheet of paper, which I eventually discovered held the names of over 400 people for whom he prayed. The light captured the now-ancient lines of his face, the red beard turning gray, and the hair on his head that was thinner than I had ever seen it. It was like glimpsing a painting of him.

I caught my breath.

As a child and adolescent, I'd seen my father rise early every morning for a time of meditation and prayer. He had never missed it, except when sick. Even when the wolf was scratching at the door, even when he had very little money for food, my father took the time to pray.

I had endured financial setbacks over the last two years, and rather than strengthening my faith, they had caused me to lose hope. Watching my father still practicing his faith impressed me, because for the first time, I realized something.

My father's financial struggles were due to illness and a lack of education, which would have helped him gain a professional position with healthcare and sick days. Far from being lazy, my father had lived his life with discipline and perseverance, which extended even to the way he practiced his faith.

For the first time, it dawned on me that my visit home might have a purpose. Perhaps I could learn from my father. He had finally learned how to handle his money properly in his late 60s by taking direction from his *youngest* son, my brother Richard. Rather than being proud, he had followed the road of humility.

Perhaps this is why I found the image of him at prayer to be so beautiful. Far from grasping for control, my father had given it up in order to secure a better future. True, I didn't see God the same way, but what mattered is that my father had a clear conception of who he was as a man in the presence of his God.

I was determined not to take advantage of my parents' generosity, so during the first few weeks before I found work, I found things to do around the house. It was bitterly cold, with a light sprinkle of snow on the ground. One of my brothers had cut down several trees on the property, and logs and branches littered the back yard like a collection of skeletons from my past.

Something needed to be done. Borrowing my brother's equipment, I tackled the yard. With the chainsaw roaring, I tore through the trees and brush, the oily smoke circling my body. As always, I found solace in hard work.

I didn't see a way forward, or a way to return to the life I had left behind. I was in despair, my heart exposed and bleeding. I picked up the axe, beginning to split the logs.

Chop.

Perhaps I should give up on my dreams.

Chop.

Perhaps I should return to our church—they'll have to forgive me.

Chop.

Was my life journey—which had allowed me to flee my community and assimilate into the world—simply an exercise in futility, fueled by my pride?

I felt entirely alone.

Desperate to make financial headway, I signed up to be a substitute teacher at my previous school district. But as I waited for work to be offered, my brothers—seeing my determination and work ethic—began to employ me regularly as a bricklayer, my earlier experience finally paying off.

By the time substitute job offers began to come in, I realized that working with my brothers earned me more money, while allowing me to teach online in the evenings. Right now, my primary focus was getting out of debt as quickly as possible and starting a savings account. Working in construction was also putting me in the best physical shape I'd enjoyed since my twenties. The heavy labor settled my mind and quieted my soul.

These were moments that touched me with grace.

Being home, surrounded by my deeply spiritual family, I found myself questioning my choices. Over the past few years, I had lost the habit of going to church, but now I was starting to feel that expectation.

To my parents' sheer delight, I attended church with them, trying to show appreciation for their help. I recognized most of the congregation. The boldest challenged me about what I had written in *HuffPost*, but most conversations were simply tinged with the flavor of betrayal.

This is no place for me.

The realization was startling, because somewhere in my mind, I had imagined I could always come home. But as I interacted with people about town, I realized there were too many rumors attached to my name. In Los Angeles, I had been able to remain anonymous. Here, the gossips were having a field day. Everyone knew my family, and when I ran into someone, they felt comfortable speculating about me to my face.

I needed to find my own tribe.

Each month, my brother Richard met with my father to guide his expenses. As I watched them interact, I realized my younger brother had picked up the frugality my mother modeled, while I had followed my father's example of overspending. So, I also began turning to my youngest brother for advice, hoping to learn from him.

He was employing me more than Dave, probably because over the past several years, Richard had regularly called me for my advice and approval when making decisions about my parents' retirement. Always, I had supported his decisions as he had planned and built a new house for Mom and Dad. We shared a great deal of trust.

Now, I told him the truth about my financial straits. We were in the midst of the Great Recession, and work was hard to find, but Richard was a savvy businessman, and he believed in me. He respected my willingness to take risks, knowing that sometimes you fail. Seeing my determination to get out of debt, he offered me a proposition.

"I'm thinking about flipping a foreclosure property," he said. "I'll front the investment. My real estate broker knows how to price things, even in this market. I can give you as much work as you want, paying you per hour, and if we make money, we'll split the profits. What do you think?"

I knew he had done this before, so I agreed. Our partnership began, with Richard making the choices as I followed his directions. Within four months, we restored the house completely and it sold immediately. There were no profits, but the sale paid for our time.

My financial quest gained momentum. In addition to helping my parents with groceries and yard improvements, I put every spare dollar toward paying down debt.

Across that year, one of the deepest relationships I rebuilt was with a buddy I had known since first grade. Dave Miller and I had played basketball together and sung in The Harvesters.

Shortly after I arrived home, Dave invited me out for ice cream. As he and his wife Joanne arrived in a light snowstorm, my mother fussed over me at the door, providing a warm pair of gloves, and slipping me some cash. "Buy ice cream and coffee," she urged. My heart warmed. She knew I was struggling, and she was on my side.

At an ancient ice cream parlor in Canton, we slipped into high-backed booths and settled into conversation. It was as if I hadn't left. They both knew all the gossip and filled me in. But unlike the community, they admired my work on *HuffPost*, glad that I was speaking my truth.

Reassured, I asked them about their new remodeling business. In the midst of the recession, it was flourishing, due to their mission of helping people bring their dreams to life. Their passion was inspiring, helping me believe I too might achieve my dreams. My friends still believed in me.

"When will your book come out?" Dave asked.

"I've been struggling," I said, awkwardly. "I think I'm going to be here... awhile." I changed the subject. "I'm just trying to figure out if there's a church in the area I like."

"You might try ours," Joanne said.

"Why?" I asked. I knew they had left our church years before I did, and I was curious how they were surviving. With enthusiasm, they told me about Maple Grove, their "liberal" Mennonite church. "I think you'd like the pastor," Dave said. "You'd fit in a whole lot better than at your parents' church."

The next Sunday, I showed up. I was skeptical, but when I stepped into the sanctuary, I was welcomed by people I didn't know but who seemed familiar. When I sat down in a pew, an older woman with weathered skin and hair pulled up in a bun turned around.

"Hello, Steve. Glad you found us. Your mother told me you might be coming."

My face broke into a smile. I knew her. She was one of the "liberal" Mennonite friends Mom had made years before while working at the Hartville Kitchen cleaning pots and pans.

Standing at the front, Dave and Joanne led the worship band. The sanctuary was decorated with flowers, and musical lyrics hovered above them on PowerPoint slides. People were dressed in modern clothes, with nary a white bonnet or Plain Coat in sight. Later, at a Sunday School session with people our age, their thoughtful questions pulled me into the discussion.

Here was a community where people didn't care about my recent past, a place where I could explore my faith and find a new path to my future.

I'd found a haven that suited me.

Going to church with Dave allowed me to deepen our relationship. During late evenings sitting by the fire, our conversations circled around questions of faith. I had been shaken by my mother's near death and had been surprised by the way people cared for me. I had begun to see the hand of God in my experiences, although I didn't know why I had ended up back home.

One evening, as we sipped bourbon and watched the flames crackle, I disclosed how bad things had gotten. Dave's warm brown eyes never left my face. Having lost my idealistic dreams, I told him, I was struggling to discover the meaning of the last year. My friends were at the peak of their careers, and I had reached the bottom.

"What's the purpose?" I asked. "How did I end up back here?"

Dave, in his spiritual wisdom, resolved my conundrum.

"I think you're trying to find your way home."

Dave was right. I needed to dig down to my soul's core before I could find my life's purpose and return to the fight. Unless I did that, I was fated to repeat the cycle, spinning through my own personal Groundhog Day again and again.

Several months later, this conversation echoed in my mind as Richard and I were driving home. Our reconstruction project was going well, but as always, my youngest brother was thinking ahead. He knew my passion didn't lie in construction.

"Have you thought about returning to teaching?" he asked.

"Perhaps." I knew he had something on his mind.

"You put a lot of money into your education," he mused. "And I know you're a good teacher. I've seen your former students' comments on Facebook. I'm just wondering when you're going to start looking for another full-time teaching job."

In fact, I had been looking. Several local colleges had expressed interest, but nothing had come of those. I was pretty sure I could find another position in a local high school, but if I did, I would be forced to stay in the area, and I didn't belong here. So, I was uncertain about the next step.

After that conversation with Richard, I tried to figure out why I loved teaching high school. I had begun to realize that I needed to do more than lecture college students. What motivated me most was building a community of young people looking for something meaningful to do, whether it was theater, a student store, or journalism. The students who joined me created an alternate family that provided them the support they needed to thrive and sometimes heal.

Watching this happen gave meaning to my life.

But the greatest infusion of grace I received that year involved my father, whom I was now beginning to see as a man, not simply as my father. I was ambivalent about him, and wasn't sure we'd ever be friends, now that I understood what his physical abuse had done to me. But I was becoming aware that something about my father had changed.

Dad had finally discovered a way to fulfill his greatest passion. Thanks to the church's reversal of the ban on musical instruments, my father was now able to play instruments publicly. This had allowed him to land the job of entertainment director at a local nursing home.

I stopped by one day, and as I watched him lead the residents in song with his guitar, I was impressed by his presence. Relaxed and joyful, he displayed no judgment. Music seemed to transport him. My new pastor had spoken with admiration about Dad's ability to play music at the bedsides of the dying, with their families now requesting his soothing presence.

It was a stark contrast to my formative memories. When I had left for Los Angeles, I had seen my father as rigid and unforgiving, but now I was beginning to see about him an aura of grace and compassion. Had my father evolved since I had left? Would he eventually recognize that he had abused me, and that his abuse had had a profound impact on my mental health? Was I ready to have that conversation with him?

I wasn't.

In spite of this torment churning through my mind, I was also able to realize for the first time something about his relationship with my mother that I had somehow missed.

As a child, I had respected the way Dad put on an apron and washed dishes with my mother. Letting my mother sleep in, he got up early in the mornings to make breakfast (although his pasty oatmeal made me hate the dish for years). I realized now he had never made a significant decision without her approval. His greatest joke—"I'm the Man of the House, and I have my wife's permission to say so!"—was funny because it described their relationship perfectly.

Yet in my teens, as I visited my friends' homes, I decided these were not normal practices for men. My father's deference to my mother's wishes proved that he had no spine. Across the decades, this perception remained frozen within the amber of my formative memories. Even as I received my education, even as I began to believe that relationships between men and women needed to be equal, I failed to rethink my childhood perspective. I still believed my father was weak. I couldn't see that my father's egalitarian relationship with my mother proved that he was incredibly strong.

Now home from Los Angeles, applying the principles of narrative therapy, I began to rethink these memories. As I watched my parents interact with each other—the two of them playing Scrabble late at night, my father washing the dishes after my mother made the meal, my mother expressing her opinions to him about how money should be spent—I realized the truth.

Set against a patriarchal society, my father was unusual in the way he interacted with my mother. He never used authority with her as a method of getting his way—instead, he treated her respectfully as an equal.

This helped me reflect on my own relationships with women. Until then, I had been unable to achieve the type of egalitarian relationship my parents enjoyed. Perhaps, in spite of what my father had put me through, he had something to teach me. Perhaps, moving forward, I could learn to give up control to someone I loved... or even be vulnerable with her... thanks to my father's example.

Although I didn't realize it at the time, the year I spent with my father helped me break my extreme need for control. It allowed me to cut the umbilical cord that had withered but still tied me emotionally to his fundamentalist community. This final separation granted me a powerful infusion of grace.

I did not realize how dramatically this would change my future.

Chapter 33: Your One True Love

When I reflect on my lifelong relationship with Laura, which began when I met her on Halloween in October 1997, I believe the most important moment occurred in early 2008 while Laura was in Moscow.

Not that I realized it at the time.

I was in Los Angeles, and we had been working together for almost four years, giving feedback to each other's writing. One day, out of the blue, she called me. I was working in my studio apartment, trying to develop a screenplay for a producer who had expressed interest in helping me write and direct a short film.

I got up from my laptop and paced the apartment, becoming more and more worried as she talked. It was the middle of the day, which meant it was late at night for her. She told me she was worried—someone was threatening her life, and her husband was out of reach, perhaps on a plane between D.C. and Washington State, where he lived. At least, he wasn't getting back to her.

That moment broke down a wall we had erected between us. Over the next few months, we talked several times by phone. Technically, it was against the rules her husband had set for our working relationship, but Laura was in danger, and I suddenly didn't care about any rules. More than anything, I sensed that Laura needed to know I was there for her.

That moment turned out to be a crucial moment in our relationship. It wasn't about romance, I thought at the time, it was about trust. Little did I realize at the time that for Laura, those two terms are synonymous.

When Laura made the decision to return to the States, moving to join her husband in Pasco, WA, I was relieved. More than anything, I wanted to make sure she was safe. I had given up on any romantic feelings I had for her by then.

But during those conversations, she shared with me something that I sensed was important to her. It felt larger than anything we had ever discussed before.

"I've always known that if I were trapped in a burning house, and I couldn't come out, you would come in to rescue me, no matter what—no matter what the danger."

Although I didn't know it at the time, it was the most romantic thing she had ever said to me until then.

Now, almost a year later, I was stranded in Ohio. I had no hopes when it came to Laura, but I did know that I was unhappy about my romantic prospects.

Since Laura and I had broken up in 2001, I hadn't been able to forget her. I knew I had made a mistake, letting her go. In fact, I had even taken the time to collect all the emails we had exchanged since the day we had met, creating an epistolary novel I would sometimes read and reread, trying to figure out why our relationship had failed. If only…

It was useless, I knew.

There was no chance now. I knew Laura was happily married to her husband. It was one rule I had—I didn't do affairs with married women. So, I had left Laura far behind me. The problem was—as several former romantic prospects would tell me years later—when beginning to date someone attractive, I would invariably compare them to Laura without realizing it in conversations. Perhaps that's why I was still far from finding the right marriage partner.

Now in Ohio, the problem had been exacerbated by the fact that women in Ohio didn't tend to have the same goals I did. Most of the people in my social circle now were conservative, and many were Mennonite. And although I tried to blend in, I no longer fit into the culture of this world. I was growing more and more frustrated as I realized how little in common I shared with the available women who seemed attracted to me.

I remember clearly a prayer I offered God one night.

The prayer might have come after I realized that the woman I had begun to date casually was someone my parents liked but who wasn't right for me. The prayer might have come while scrolling Facebook after grading essays online until the wee hours of the morning and suddenly seeing how well everyone else was doing in Los Angeles, while I was stranded in Ohio. The prayer might have come after going out with friends, seeing how successful their lives had become in the late stages of their career, and realizing that my path didn't fit into any life I saw here.

I had almost given up on trying to find love. I was forty-six years old. I had gone through one relationship after another. The women I liked were never women my family would appreciate. The only woman who would satisfy my family would be conservative Mennonite, exactly the type of woman I was *not* going to marry.

What kind of woman would marry me, knowing that?

To be clear, until then, I had claimed not to care about my family's opinion. But as I considered my dating history, I knew that I did. I had flinched too many times when facing the real or imagined judgment of my family. It was an impossible situation. My family would never understand my world, and since the type of women I love would come from that world, they would never understand her.

I needed to accept the inevitable. If I wanted to marry the type of woman who fit into my life, I needed to give up on the dream that my family would approve of her.

One night, coming home late, I prepared for bed. I didn't usually kneel to pray—I was more of a talk-to-God-as-I-did-other-things type of guy, but, that night, I did. My words were halting. Sometimes it's hard to put what you want into words.

Dear God, I don't know what to do, I don't understand how to find love. You know my situation—it's impossible. I'm tired of being in relationships that don't work out. Help me to find the right person, someone who can love me in spite of everything. And my family, oh God. It's impossible. You know who I am, how complex I am. Dear God, help me.

I am sometimes surprised by God's ability to answer impossible prayers because He helped me find the one woman who was perfect for me. Or perhaps I should say, he helped me realize that the perfect woman for me was my writing collaborator.

I knew Laura was happily married. I had served as one of her writing mentors and had written her recommendation to get into an MFA program in commercial fiction at the Stonecoast MFA program at the University of Southern Maine, and she had completed several romance novels, and her agent was shopping them to publishing companies. But we hadn't connected in a while.

She was not on my radar, romantically.

Several weeks after that prayer, that radar exploded when she called me. That in and of itself was surprising because of the rules she and her husband had worked out. So, I knew something had happened when her name popped up on my cell phone.

"I have two important pieces of news for you," was her opening volley.

"Tell me." I stopped typing.

"My agent just called me to let me know she's sold my second book. Two books, Steven. She sold two books in just thirty days."

A feeling of pride and exultation rushed over me.

"Oh my God, Laura. That is so exciting. You totally deserve it. You've worked so hard."

I had barely taken that in when she dropped the second piece of news. Her marriage had failed, which meant she was free to talk to me.

I had a difficult time breathing, trying to process her words. She was free. For seven years, we had been forced to maintain a platonic relationship. Now she was free. Did she still have the same feelings for me? Seven years is a long time, and we had studiously maintained our professional relationship.

Of course, I didn't say any of this to her. Instead, I murmured sympathetic sounds. Of course, I was sorry her marriage had failed. Of course, I felt bad for the way things had gone.

305

Of course, I was lying.

But I wasn't going to say anything until I was sure of her feelings. Suddenly, the stakes in our relationship had risen dramatically. What was a secure friendship had suddenly become a card game, and I knew from our history that Laura knew her way around the betting tables. She wasn't about to reveal her cards until she was sure of how I felt.

"I wasn't about to start dating again," she told me later. "But I didn't count on the fact that you'd be lying in wait for me, ready to pounce."

We soon found reasons to begin instant messaging more frequently. I was playing it safe, or so I thought. Laura became impatient, wanting to know my intentions. And so, several weeks later, in a late-night conversation, she admitted that things had not been going well for a while in the marriage.

It was she who had finally taken the initiative to end it.

On another night, as we were discussing the details of her divorce, she dropped a bomb into our conversation, telling me about her last conversation with her ex.

"He told me something that surprised me. He said that he thought *you* have always been my true love."

Her cursor blinked. My mind was spinning as I tried to take in her ex's honesty. I didn't trust him, and surely, he didn't intend to hand me this ace of hearts. Perhaps he didn't say it. Perhaps Laura was simply trying to tell me something, trying to tell me how she felt.

I had no reason to doubt her, and it was late at night, and we were talking by Instant Message on AOL, and it's the way we've always communicated most honestly, and then suddenly, before I could say anything, Laura beat me to it.

"I don't know what to do with that, Steven."

She was lying, no question about it. I knew she respected my intelligence. I knew the way she thought, and I knew she would count on me figuring out that she was lying. Anyway, it didn't matter—whether he said it was beside the point. She wanted me to know she loved me, and she'd just given me a clear invitation to act.

I'd better not screw this one up.

The next day in a burst of clarity, I called my friend Dave and told him we were meeting at our favorite ice cream parlor. That evening, sitting in a high wooden booth, I told him the story of Laura—how I had met and fallen in love with her over twelve years before, how we had broken up and gotten back together three times, and how the relationship had failed. I told him I'd been in love with her from the start. Then I told him about our conversation the night before.

Dave usually gave me good advice, having been in a successful but-not-always-easy marriage for over twenty years. But, this time, he raised his eyebrows, quizzically.

In that moment, I realized that I had been given the chance to take control of my life. Would my parents or family approve of her? She was divorced, so I knew they would disapprove, and in that moment with a rush of joy, I realized I didn't care what they thought. The only one whose vote mattered in this decision was mine. I needed to believe in what I was doing, and in this case, I absolutely did.

I had spent the last nine years since we broke up wandering a romantic desert, unable to find anyone who matched what Laura offered me. Time and time again, meeting attractive women who seemed perfect for me, I had compared them to Laura and found them wanting. She was the other half of my soul who understood me better than anyone else, and she still loved me.

With sudden confidence, I decided. "I'm going to put a ring on her finger this time."

Dave's grin split his face, perhaps reflecting my happiness.

"I can't wait to meet her," he said.

"Will you be my best man?" I asked.

Laura was still living in Pasco, Washington, and traveled a lot so we had to build our romantic relationship via texting and phone calls, until we finally met up for the first time in ten years at a writer's conference in Columbus, Ohio. While we enjoyed the same level of sexual intensity we'd had when we first met, something more was layered into it.

Over the years that we had worked together professionally, we'd built up a strong partnership working together as writers, both online and by telephone. We respected each other, but there was more. Over the past decade, amid everything and despite the restraints—or perhaps because they forced us to focus on our partnership rather than our romance—Laura had become my best friend.

This shone through most clearly in the abiding presence of laughter in our relationship, which undergirded the happiness we felt when we were together. Perhaps it was a mark of the confidence we had in our relationship, our ability to trust each other and let loose. Perhaps it was the fact that we'd both gone through tough times and had gained some humility, ensuring that we didn't take ourselves quite so seriously. Whatever it was, we could now laugh together.

Even Laura's Siberian cats, whom Laura called *bears* because of their large paws, sensed this. When Laura first invited me to visit her in Eastern Washington and showed me her house and her precious bears, I found Pandora, her alpha cat, very interesting.

For Pandora, it seemed that it was love at first sight.

When Laura returned from taking me to the airport at the end of the weekend, Pandora met her at the door. But Pandora ignored Laura, peering around her for someone else.

Me.

With that, Laura told me much later, she knew she'd made the right decision. Or, as my goddaughter once put it, "The cats always know."

It didn't take a cat's approval for me to decide to close the deal. Our conversations by phone were becoming longer and more intense. But I worried. I knew the failure of her marriage, which I didn't completely understand, had made her gun-shy. She seemed hesitant about committing to me.

During our conversations, she would add qualifiers to her declarations of love. "I really think I love you" or "I'm sure I love you" or "I don't think I've ever loved anyone more." I needed more than that, but I also knew that patience had paid off in the past with her. More than anything, based on what I knew of her previous relationships, she needed to feel safe with me. But I also knew how to follow my instincts. And so, when the moment presented itself, I laid down my cards.

I was talking to Laura as I walked on my parents' lawn, taking a break from mowing and fertilizing it. She'd just returned from Europe, and we were planning her trip to Ohio. "I think we'd better make this relationship more permanent."

There was a long silence on the other end of the phone.

"Laura?"

I barely heard her response, but then she repeated it.

"I think you might be right."

It didn't take long after that conversation for us to decide that, when she flew in to meet my family, we would make our engagement official.

Taking no chances, I planned out the engagement meal with great deliberation. I knew she enjoyed good wines, so when one of my former students recommended Gervasi Vineyard in North Canton, I googled it. Rustic architecture, fine wines, five-star meals. Who would have imagined there would be an Italian-villa-styled vineyard and restaurant not ten miles from my parents' place?

Although we had both agreed this would be our engagement weekend, Laura had no idea I had made any special plans. I'd taken advantage of my heritage, letting her think no self-respecting, Amish-Mennonite lad would bother with a ring.

When we arrived at the villa, we ordered drinks at the bar. Glasses in hand, I suggested a stroll through the grounds. Outside, the patio was packed with guests. I guided Laura across the lawn to the empty pavilion, lit only by the moon.

And then, suddenly, the immortal music of Lionel Ritchie's "Lady," was playing over the pavilion speakers.

I knelt before her. "Laura, will you marry me?"

Laura's hands went to her mouth.

I asked her again. I had never done this before, putting my life in the hands of someone I loved, committing to love someone for the rest of my life.

The next moment remains frozen in my mind.

I was kneeling in the pavilion, holding up the most beautiful piece of jewelry I had ever given anyone.

Laura was gazing at me, speechless. She was wearing heels and a black cocktail dress, standing in the late Ohio summer evening with a full moon shimmering on the nearby lake.

Finally, she blurted out her answer. "God, yes. Oh, Steven. Of course, yes!"

My heart skipped a beat, and I stood to my feet, pulling her face in for a kiss. Tumultuous joy rushed over me, as we wrapped our arms around each other and held on tight.

At that moment, on the lake beside the pavilion, two swans swam up. It felt surreal, but it matched the flood of gratitude that overcame me, the realization that God had answered my prayer in a way that I could not have predicted.

On Saturday morning, after having breakfast together and sending out media posts to all our friends on Facebook, with a rush of joyous responses, I drove Laura out to my parents' home to meet them. Marcia had chosen that weekend to visit, and after I introduced Laura to my mother and father, I went to the kitchen to get Laura a soda to drink, leaving her with my mother.

As I poured the drink, I glanced into the living room, and the sight mesmerized me. My mother was explaining something, I couldn't hear what, and Laura was leaning toward my mother, eyes intent upon my mother. My mother laughed, and Laura laughed with her. She glanced over at me, her blue eyes sparkling, before she and Mom turned to look at the garden I had planted, my mother gesturing toward it with pride.

That's when the shock hit me as I realized the truth. I had been sure my mother would disapprove, but I was wrong. When Laura told me on the way back to the hotel about how much she enjoyed meeting my mother, I knew for sure that I was right. For the first time, I knew my mother approved of Laura.

Things didn't go as well with the rest of my family, however, whom we would meet during a visit to my parents' church that Sunday night. She was fascinated by my past and wanted to see what my culture was like. I was genuinely worried about how things would go. I had seen my sisters, especially, respond in a passive-aggressive manner to past girlfriends, asking them questions about what they were wearing, or asking them about the details of their conversation. I had no desire to put Laura through the same inquisition, so I didn't mince words when preparing my sisters to meet her.

"Please don't ask questions about what she is wearing, and please don't try to evangelize her," I told Ann. "Laura was raised Catholic, and I want her to feel comfortable with our family." They agreed, but I could tell they were skeptical. I didn't care. More than anything, I wanted to protect Laura from being attacked by my family.

Over the next month, Laura and I made plans. We decided to move in together as we made plans for our wedding. Laura's divorce had been finalized, and after considering four cities where we could set up a home, we settled on Seattle. She had left the federal government and was working for a contractor.

Several weeks later, on a business trip to Seattle, Laura signed a lease for a beautiful, vintage 1950s house overlooking Lake Washington. Laura thought she could move there by late October, and I planned to join her in early November. I called the friend of mine who was storing my household goods in eastern Los Angeles and arranged for him to transport them to our new home.

But it began to dawn on me that I was taking a risk by choosing to move in with Laura before we got married. I heard it in the offhand remarks family members made at family dinners. My mother spoke to me. Although I didn't attend my family's church, I began to hear about the prayers and concerns my family members were sharing about me. At one point, my sister Marcia pulled me aside at a family gathering and began to ask me about my fiancée's relationship with God.

"Does Laura love Jesus?" she asked me.

I didn't know how to answer that. It was the type of question that Evangelicals ask because, unlike mainstream denominations, the most important thing about your faith is the personal relationship you have with Christ. Laura had grown up in a Catholic parish where she would have been encouraged to develop a personal relationship with Jesus' mother.

Marcia was waiting patiently for my answer, her brown eyes intent. I shrugged.

"Of course she does," I answered. "All Christians love Jesus."

She looked unconvinced.

Although I knew that my pending marriage would cause great conflict with my family, I was determined to push through with my decision. I had left home before and survived. I knew how to ignore telephone calls or letters.

But planning a marriage is a different proposition. A wedding is a community event in which friends and relatives gather to support the happy couple. I had seen many weddings but had never understood the politics that go on behind the scenes. I assumed that my family would eventually fall in line. After all, other people had left our church and when they got married, their families showed up.

I also took my father's word seriously when he had told me that I was now a man, and that he respected my right to make my own decisions. What I didn't take seriously was that "shacking up" with a woman before we got married wasn't something he felt any man had the right to do. I was challenging my home community's belief system in choosing someone I didn't think they'd approve of.

My decision was huge, and yet I chose to imagine that I had the right to make my own decision without suffering any negative consequences within a world in which all decisions are judged by the entire community.

The Amish and Mennonite communities have used the powerful weapon of cancel culture for centuries. It helps keep members of the church in line, knowing that if they cross the community, they can be forced to stand up and confess what they have done publicly. If they refuse to do that, they can be excommunicated. The Amish refuse to eat with someone who has been disciplined by the church. And yet here I was, the descendant of both Amish and Mennonite families, and somehow, I had come to believe I could do whatever I wanted without any real consequences.

I was naïve.

But I also knew the woman I was marrying. Laura was a planner. I was financially strapped, and Laura had just paid for a divorce. We both knew it would take time to plan a wedding, and to pay for one. And so, we made the fateful decision to put off the wedding until we were ready. I was committed to joining Laura in Seattle.

Working extra hours, I began to save money to prepare for the move. In a telephone interview, I secured a part-time teaching position at a University of Phoenix campus in Seattle, and I could also continue teaching online. Things would be tight until I got a full-time, high school teaching position, but until then, I thought we could survive.

But then, a week before I was to leave, my mother had a second heart attack.

Book VIII: Integration

"For they that say such things declare plainly that they seek a country. And truly, if they had been mindful of that country from whence they came out, they might have had opportunity to have returned. But now they desire a better country, that is, an heavenly: wherefore God is not ashamed to be called their God: for he hath prepared for them a city."

~ Hebrews 11: 14-16, *The Holy Bible,* KJV, 1769

Interpolation VIII: Disrupting the Cycle

During those critical formative years, I should have known corporal punishment was wrong—except that every religious authority taught us that my parents and teachers had the God-given right to physically abuse us.

I couldn't hear what my body was saying to me. The anger I felt about the beatings. The way I acted out "spankings" with my playmate as a pre-teen. The sexual effects that were connected. The resulting shame associated with my fetishism.

I kept all these feelings a secret.

That should have been the red flag. But I didn't know how to talk about my truth. I knew of no one who could discuss my abuse and emerging trauma with me. In fact, I didn't even know that I needed to. And so, my anger and bitterness toward my father continued to grow, year by year.

One of the most credible exposés written on the issue of abuse within the Amish and conservative Mennonite communities is a six-part story, published on May 20, 2019, in the Pittsburgh Post-Gazette *in the article "Coverings: Mennonites, Amish face growing recognition of widespread sexual abuse in their communities." Written by Peter Smith and Shelly Bradbury, and photographed by Stephanie Strasburg, the story connects corporal punishment to sexual abuse within local Amish and Mennonite communities. A major goal of those who came forward was to stop the "chains of this generational abuse."*

The problem has never been that leaders don't know about the abuse. Instead, they fear exposing it because they believe that airing the church's dirty laundry will hurt the cause of Christ. In reality, protecting abusers has driven a generation away from Christ, as they see the corruption of religious leaders whose only goal seems to be protecting their own power.

It was so in our community, as well.

Our religious leaders tolerated the rasp of the farmer's voice in church as he angrily mansplained the scriptures. They had to be aware that he was physically abusing his children, beating at least one of them with a two-by-four. They sat silent when an outspoken father in our church waxed eloquent about the Bible, and they ignored what they must have known about his abusive behavior toward his son, one of my best friends, who after being beaten by this father, was left with bloody stripes across his back, enraged and helpless. And in a more conservative church not far away, the bishop solemnly listened to sermons by one of his preachers who beat his children with steel coat hangers.

315

Our spiritual leaders' tolerance of physical abuse sent a clear message to us victims about whose side they would take when physical abuse was reported. When a young woman in our church reported being sexually molested, she soon faced a visiting preacher who chastised her verbally for her "rebellious attitude" and for spreading rumors about her molester.

Their refusal to condemn abuse and their choice to silence victims who did speak up—humiliating them through victim-blaming—ensured that our abusers would continue hurting the most vulnerable among us.

I do not remember a single religious leader who spoke out against physical abuse.

I long for the day when the community I left begins to offer tools of empowerment to those who are suffering. Anyone can report abuse to the police or to social services, initiating an investigation, allowing the authorities to protect and defend victims, whose privacy will be protected by law, even during a public trial. Professionals in health care and education are Mandatory Reporters who are required to report to the authorities even the suspicion of abuse. For those victims who wish to go public, they can out their abusers on social media.

Abuse is an infection that surges through families, begetting more abuse. But it doesn't have to. As "Coverings" demonstrates, it's possible to disrupt this cycle of abuse.

Chapter 34: Just Us Siblings

My plans to leave for Seattle got put on hold when my mother was admitted to the hospital again. The heart attack was severe, and this time there didn't seem to be any hope. My father was distraught and not in the state of mind to make any decisions on her behalf.

That left it up to the eight of us.

We were sitting in a conference room not far away from Mom's hospital room, where nurses and doctors fought to save her life. For the first time in no-one-could-remember, we were all gathered, but at an event none of us wanted to be at. The doctors were asking us to decide between stopping all measures or sending her home on hospice because surgery wasn't an option; she wasn't strong enough to survive it.

It was just us siblings. We had to figure out not only what we thought was best for our mother, but what she would want. Ann told us what had happened that last time in the hospital when they'd resuscitated her. We had to decide within the next hour.

The last time we had all been together in a room like this was—well, actually, it had never happened before. There was always a reason for one or the other of us to be missing. Elaine was on the other side of the country. Or I was in Los Angeles, or London. Now we were all together.

Ironically, none of us wanted to be here.

The doctor answered our questions as best he could. There was no guarantee Mom would live. Did we want to resuscitate her if her heart stopped again? Did we want to bring her home, put her into hospice care? This meant we were writing a living will for her. Since she was on heavy drugs that made it impossible for her to communicate with us, we had to decide.

We talked about it. What would Mom want?

Ann told us Mom's reaction when the doctors had brought her back. Her first response when her eyes blinked open had been deep distress. Ann had come to her side immediately.

"Don't do that again," Mom had snapped.

I then told them about my observation last winter when I'd first returned, those moments when she had stared into space, and the strong sense I'd had that she didn't want to be here, that she'd wished she were gone.

What should we do?

It was a hard decision but, eventually, we all, collectively and unanimously, chose hospice. Mom would be brought home with the order not to resuscitate. She would eat good food, not sterile hospital meals, and we would care for her there. If she died, she would die surrounded by her family's love.

We fully expected her to be gone within a week.

But then something surprising occurred. After the life support was removed and the powerful medications were discontinued, she began to recover. By 2 AM, she was awake and having cookies and milk with my brother Dave.

The next day, at home, she was able to watch me work in the garden from the hospital bed in the living room.

Within days, she was back on her feet, puttering about the kitchen, even creating suet for the wildlife outside her window. The birds gathered around the porch, fluttering and chirping, as she worked. Squirrels raced across the deck, and across the railings. The whole experience felt like a miracle.

Seeing her come back to life again gave me hope for the future. Here, once again, God had given me the gift of time with my mother.

I had left because of my community's practices, but in my heart, I still believed in the goodness and possibility of God. In my darkest moments, I had felt the gentle touch of the Holy Spirit, even when I knew I didn't deserve God's grace.

Now I had found my own direction, which I believed came from God. And even though I was departing, I was leaving Mom happy, surrounded by all her friends and family. I had no illusions. I knew she might die at any time. But I also knew she might survive for years.

More and more, my mind was turning to my new life in Seattle, where I had a fiancée waiting for me. She would soon be my wife. My mother could no longer hold priority in my life. Other family members could care for her better than I.

But I also doubted what I should do.

Would I be able to leave my family behind again, but this time, retain the relationships I'd just spent the last year rebuilding? More importantly, would Laura and I work out as a couple? She'd survived a decade of marriage, but I had spent my entire life as a single man, unable to form any real attachments or create my own family.

Yet it was time to follow the path God had laid down for me.

I'd been willing to make what had been the biggest leap of my life by leaving home for Los Angeles—and now it was time to take another leap. And while leaving before hadn't quite worked out the way I'd wanted, I was putting my faith in my love for Laura.

As always, all I could do was trust my instincts.

Chapter 35: The Boat That Floated

By Thanksgiving 2010, Laura and I had unpacked and settled into the vintage 1950s house she had rented in North Seattle. In the mornings, I awoke to look out over Lake Washington to a stunning view of Mount Rainier, its glorious peak hovering above the skyline of the city.

I had never lived successfully with someone I loved romantically, not long-term. I quickly found spending a weekend with someone was much different than living with them day-to-day. One night shortly after I arrived, I became especially worried about the expenses I was facing, and my inability to find a full-time teaching position. Sleepless, I went out to the living room, regarding the lake stretching out before me. "How did my father do it all those years?" I questioned.

The cold darkness refused to answer.

I reflected on the year I'd spent with my parents. For the first time, I realized what I had received. Without realizing it, I had seen my father model what it meant to love a woman.

It had long been known among all my relatives that my father knew how to take care of my mother. My Uncle Ed had once put it to me bluntly during my teen years. "Your mother has told me more than once that your father is a good lover."

I'd stared at him in shock. It wasn't exactly the thing you expected to hear from your Mennonite uncle. But, by then, nothing Uncle Ed said surprised me too much because he was a man of the world.

"I've not always agreed with your father on everything," he confided. "I certainly think he could have done some things better, but, in this area, I give him credit."

I had agreed with my uncle because I knew how openly affectionate my mother and father had been while we were children. There were no puritanical ideas in our home. He would pull her into his lap to snuggle her, and he would kiss my mother passionately before going to work as she wrapped her arms around his neck. The words "I love you" were often spoken.

But that wasn't all I learned from my father that year. Living closely with my parents had allowed me to see why my father was such an expert at loving his wife. Any time he'd get a chance, my father chose to spend time with her. This meant that, when he wasn't working at the nursing home, he came home to have lunch with her. This had always been the case as I was growing up, but I'd simply never noticed it before.

He had also loved helping her around the house and did so with enthusiasm. He had continued to do the dishes on Sundays so my mother could have time off. In the evenings, they had played board games together, and the laughter coming from the kitchen made them sound like a couple that had just fallen in love. Most importantly, my father had always put my mother's wishes first. When I was younger, this had caused me to blame my mother for my father's debts since, due to her wishes, he had often spent money on things he didn't need.

What an advantage that had given him. Politeness, kindness, patience, attention—all of these were skills my father had used to strengthen his marriage. It was my father's secret sauce, keeping his marriage healthy and happy, even in the worst of times. And now, thanks to my father, that secret sauce was mine and I would use it to make sure my marriage was equally as strong.

By September the following year, I'd replaced my battered Saturn with a brand-new Subaru Forester. With dependable transportation, I was slowly beginning to pay down my student loans and tax debt because, while still teaching for the University of Phoenix in Western Washington, I'd also secured a part-time job teaching English and debate at a local high school. Now we both felt comfortable moving ahead with our plans to get married.

Laura's excitement as she planned a large Mennonite wedding was all over her Facebook page for her friends and fans to read. She wrote all about my large, rambling family of tens of cousins and uncles and nephews and nieces, and she envisioned a massive gathering of my extended family in Hartville.

Part of this sprang from her own experience with her family. Her birth father had abandoned her mother before she was born, and her adoptive father had had only one child with her mother, Laura's half-sister. This theme of abandonment—what we casually called her *daddy issues*—still haunted Laura. It was at the center of every romance novel she had written until then. Her childhood pain made her envy my large family.

We began to make plans to hold the wedding in Ohio at Maple Grove Mennonite Church, in the sanctuary where my parents were married in 1954. The church was only nine-tenths of a mile from my parents' home in Hartville. This was the church I'd attended there the year I'd lived with my parents and had grown to love the pastor.

He agreed to marry us, enthusiastic about our choice. We would honor my family, observe the traditions of my Mennonite past I still appreciated, and celebrate our love in front of my home community.

I should have known better.

My father fired the first shot a year after we'd moved in together—and eight months before the wedding. Laura and I were preparing dinner in our kitchen in Seattle, talking by speakerphone to him back in Ohio.

"Mom just told me she's excited about the wedding. Are you?"

There was a funereal moment of silence.

Then on the speakerphone, came a long, dramatic sigh. "Well, I don't know. You've… you're living together in sin… you aren't married."

Something began pounding inside my head. I was well aware of the fact that Laura was divorced, and I knew my father didn't agree with divorce, but I didn't think it would keep my family from coming to my wedding. I cast about for a convincing argument.

"But Dad, we're getting married. We're addressing *the problem*. We thought you'd be happy about that."

Silence.

Then another sigh from my father.

"I can't come, Steve. You know how I feel about divorce and remarriage."

My stomach turned ice cold.

"Are you saying your belief system is more important than your love for your firstborn son?"

Beside me, Laura turned her face away. Was she crying? Infuriated? I didn't know.

"Dad." I tried to stop this train wreck. "We'll be having the wedding less than a mile from your house. I don't understand. Are you sure?"

He remained silent… and quite sure.

Laura quietly left the kitchen, not glancing back.

In reality, my father's mind was made up. Our public flaunting of my family's beliefs had crystalized his decision. Not even Mom, who told me by phone that she supported our wedding but couldn't come because her health didn't allow her to travel, could coax Dad to amend his decision. And so, in short order, my family lined up behind my father's decision, one by one. Not a single one of my siblings would agree to come.

I was shocked; I'd just spent a year with my family, trying to rebuild bridges, and had thought I'd succeeded. But my family saw it differently. When I'd returned from Los Angeles, they hadn't seen a son worried about his mother. They'd seen me as the Prodigal Son returned, driven home by the Hedge of Thorns, broken and repentant. When I'd moved to Seattle a year later to join Laura, my family had taken that as a return to the Fields of Sin. Perhaps I'd simply *faked* repentance. They felt used.

For me, this was the last straw. My family was disloyal. They were rejecting the woman I'd loved more than anyone else in the world. Once again, I was facing the same conflict I'd faced twenty-three years before when I'd chosen to leave my childhood community.

But, this time, it was worse. Back then, only *I'd* been hurt. This time, they had chosen to insult and manipulate my future wife, the person I was determined to protect.

I remember trying to talk to my sister Heidi by phone. She was the gentle sister I'd always seen as a laughing Roo. Now, I was feeling her claws.

"I'll talk about it with my husband."

"What's there to talk about?" I asked. "When you wanted me to travel from Vermont for your wedding, I never *talked about* it; I just came, never mind the travel difficulties."

"Well, you're living together." She seemed to be choosing her words carefully. "By coming to your wedding, we would be showing approval for your actions. We don't approve."

My mind flashed back to the rows of blank faces at her wedding, to how I'd felt facing them. Anger crashed over me.

"Heidi, I came to your wedding."

I didn't know if she was crying, and I didn't care.

"Even though I completely disagreed with your belief system, I brought a girlfriend all the way from Middlebury, Vermont to attend, driving through the night to make it on time. Your husband's people were unfriendly to us during your wedding, but I stayed. Now you're telling me you can't come to mine?"

The silence on the other end of the line told me this conversation was useless.

I realized my family was attempting to push away a woman I loved. However, this time was different. Laura was my bride, already married to me, as far as I was concerned. She was part of me, and their actions told me they had rejected her, regardless of the fact that their mouths said they loved us.

I realized for the first time in my life that I would have to decide about my family. I considered trying to help Laura understand them, using the old saying, "We don't choose our families." But then I realized something—nothing about that was true.

My family had chosen to value a biblical interpretation about divorce—on which even respected scholars within the Anabaptist faith disagree—more than they valued their relationship with me or the possibility of a relationship with my wife.

In the past, their disapproval would have given me pause, and most likely brought me to heel. But over the past year, as I had lived with them and seen clearly the love they had for each other and for me, but also the unbearable hypocrisy that had ruled the decisions made by their communities.

Thus, when I faced my family's disapproval, I understood what they were trying to do, and I rejected it completely. This time, I felt no uncertainty, nor was I tempted to pause. My family's judgment failed to work on me or inspire guilt.

Instead, righteous fury empowered my spirit. It forged a new lens through which I could now clearly view my family's fundamentalist approach to faith. Nothing in the rulebook had changed; it was the same approach other fundamentalist faiths took whether they were Mormon, Jehovah's Witness, Hasidic Jew, or Muslim. If you disagreed, you were excluded.

There was a reason I had left my community, and it was staring me right in the face. I had decided to reject fundamentalism, choosing instead to honor diversity and open-mindedness. I had decided to create an inclusive family in which fundamentalism would have no sway.

As I reflect on that time today, I realize how significant my decision was. I had broken my family's grip on my spirit. I had become a man, making a life-changing decision, and I now owned that decision proudly.

It would change my life forever.

We would not hold the wedding in Hartville. But if not there, where?

The answer to our dilemma emerged as clean and clear as the Seattle skyline as I drove downtown, heading from North Seattle to Vashon Island on a cold February morning, talking on the phone with Gerald Mast, an old friend who had recently undertaken his own marital journey.

"Gerald, my family's intolerance was why I left my childhood community in the first place. Why did I ever try to go back?"

Gerald laughed. "I don't know. You're the one who decided to spend a year at home." He sighed, the laughter suddenly gone. "Look, Steve, you need to have your wedding among the friends who stand up with you, among the community that's committed to you. Your family is no longer part of that community."

Those words helped Laura and me cut into the bitter truth. Why plan a wedding in Hartville when my family and childhood friends might not attend? Laura and I were already building a new community here in Seattle and on Vashon Island, where I had begun to teach school. Those who really loved us would be happy to join us here in Seattle. People traveled all the time to attend weddings. We needed to invite the guests who were part of our *family*—those who had stuck beside us.

And so, we decided to go with a small wedding in our home on the shores of Lake Washington. But I couldn't fool my own body. Several days later, I had the first panic attack I'd had in months. My inside core was still vibrating with anger.

I decided to call my Los Angeles therapist, Dr. Kiran.

Several days later, I found myself sitting in my car in the parking lot of Vashon High School, unloading my bitterness and anger to my therapist on the phone. "A person's family should support them when everyone else in the world turns against them, not the other way around."

I could feel my face flush with anger.

"Something as important as marriage shouldn't be based on whether you follow their religious code. It's manipulative. And wrong. My family has fought me every step of the way—and now this drama." I sucked in a breath to calm down. "You know? One of my friends suggested I write a letter divorcing my family—and I've already written it in my head."

"I'd love to hear it." Dr. Kiran chuckled.

I recited it.

Dear Family,
Today, I am getting married. I now have a new family with Laura.
You are no longer my family. You've made your choice. I've made
mine.

Dr. Kiran took her time responding. "Laura must feel very supported by the way you're reacting to your family and taking her side. I wish more men did the same thing. I have two Jewish clients right now who feel insecure because their husbands refuse to take their side against domineering parents. One of them took her fiancée to her rabbi. He told the bridegroom that Torah commands him to take the side of his wife over the wishes of his parents."

"He's right."

"He is. But just because the rabbi said it was so doesn't make it easier for him to go against his parents. What about you, Steven? If you could send that letter now, can you handle the drama it will cause?"

"No."

"Then why not wait until the wedding is over? See if you still need to send it then. This is *your* time, not theirs. Let them figure it out on their own."

After a few more minutes, we hung up, and I sat in silence.

I remembered Laura's reaction to my father when he first told us he wouldn't be coming to the wedding, the way she slipped from the kitchen, unwilling to engage with someone who had rejected her. I remembered the anger that brimmed over when my sister Heidi explained to me why they wouldn't be attending. I remembered my sister Marcia's judgmental question asking whether Laura loved Jesus. I was unwilling to remain within a community that used judgment to manipulate people. I would instead choose to live within communities that offered people the freedom to believe what they wished.

In a few minutes, I was due in class. But in that moment as I sat there holding the cell phone in my lap, the smell of springtime filling my parked Subaru, I realized that I was at peace. I recognized the path God had provided. And the next stopping point on that path was my wedding.

Several months later, I was cutting vegetables with a sharp knife, when Laura drifted into the kitchen, carrying a glass of red wine. She stopped to watch me work.

She had something on her mind.

"You know, Steven, had you not defended me against your family... had you just tried to explain that this is who your family is, I don't think I could have trusted you again." She leaned in to kiss me. "Yes, their attitude bothered me, but only because they were rejecting you. I knew how much you cared."

"You aren't hurt by them?"

"How can I be? I barely know them. They barely know me. It's obvious their rejection isn't directed toward me. They barely met me when we visited them over our engagement weekend. I am The Woman Steven Is Living With." She glanced at me, her eyes misty. "It's you they're trying to manipulate."

After she left, I leaned against the kitchen cabinet, thinking. For all my family's talk about their concern for people, when it came down to it, they saw Laura only as an object, something they could use to teach me another moral lesson. They didn't recognize her as a human being with feelings. It all felt unkind and unloving.

I shook my head. I refused to let them shape our story. My siblings and my father would not be at our wedding, and they would not have a chance to sink their claws of judgment into the woman I loved most. There was a reason we had chosen to move back out West, to live this far from my community. I had almost made the mistake of trying to assimilate her into their world. I had forgotten that my original goal was to leave that community. That was the path God had showed me in the first place.

I picked up my knife. We had a wedding to plan.

A week before the wedding, two of my two closest friends—Ami Wagner, who had worked with me for years in the theater, and John Fohner, whom I considered my fourth brother—arrived to help prepare the house for our wedding. Laura's father soon joined us. We spent the week prepping the house for the event.

Then to my shock, I got a phone call. My brother Dave had decided to attend the wedding after all. He would fly in the night before the wedding. I hung up the phone, my heart dropping into my stomach. I should have been happy.

But I wasn't.

My closest friends were nothing but suspicious when they heard Dave would attend, worrying he'd preach an impromptu sermon—he'd done it before. John said he'd watch Dave like a hawk. I had no doubt he would. John's the kind of bulldog anyone would want around when a pesky brother comes preaching.

By the time Dave arrived, Laura and I had retired to bed, but I put on a robe and went out to greet him. His large frame engulfed me in a massive hug. After chatting with him for a few minutes, I got him settled on the couch in the Great Room, and we agreed to have breakfast the next morning, together. Sure enough, by 7 AM, we were enjoying coffee and pastries at a local coffee shop.

When I asked the obvious question, Dave tried to explain. "I don't approve of you and Laura living together."

"So why did you decide to come?"

"Jan told me I should."

"Your *wife* said that?"

"She reminded me that when I got married, you flew all the way across the country to Alberta, Canada to be my best man. I owed it to you."

"Even though you disapprove of us?"

"Yes. Family is family."

I wasn't sure I agreed. He was the only one who supported me, out of my entire immediate family. But as we drank coffee and told stories, I realized something—I loved my brother. Having him here was special, no matter how much we disagreed about religion.

As I was reflecting on this, I suddenly realized that my friend John had joined us, a cup of coffee in his hand. He was in a cheerful mood. But my brother Dave was in no mood to shut up. He was in the mood to talk.

"So, I have a story for you."

"Go ahead." After all, he had flown across the country to see me.

"Do you remember the boat you built when we were young?"

"I don't," I said.

"Well, I do." He turned to John, deciding to tell him the story.

"He spent a lot of time on that boat. I was impressed. I believed in my big brother Steve. In fact, until then, I'd idolized my brother. And since he was enthusiastic about that boat, I was, too. When we pulled it out of the car and carried it to Uncle Ed's pond for its maiden voyage, I was excited. I couldn't wait."

John laughed. "I know exactly what you mean."

"So, Steve jumped into the boat and grabbed the oars," Dave reported. I could tell he was winding up for the climax. And now I did remember the moment. "My father and I pushed it into the water. Steve began to row, hard." My brother paused, dramatically, glancing first at John and then at me. "That boat sank like a stone."

John roared with laughter. I didn't. I was trying to figure out what Dave was trying to say.

"I was shocked," Dave said. "It had never occurred to me that my big brother's boat might not float. He'd had such confidence that I couldn't understand why it didn't float. For the first time, I realized my brother Steve might not know everything."

By now, I was beginning to wish my brother had just stayed home. But Dave wasn't done.

"But that's my brother. He's not afraid to take a risk. And I'm so glad he took a risk on Laura, because she fits him perfectly. I knew that when I met her when she came to Ohio, when they got engaged."

Dave turned to me.

"I don't approve of you two living together, but I'm glad you are getting married. She's perfect for you."

Dave got up to go get another cup of coffee, and John and I watched admiringly as he began to chat up the waitress.

"Wow, your brother isn't afraid to talk to anyone," John said. "He's friendlier than you are, and that's saying something."

I was still trying to wrap my head around Dave's story.

John gave me a sympathetic glance. "You don't know what he meant, do you?"

"Not really. Was he being insulting?"

"Not at all," John said. "I think everyone has had their own 'boat moment' with you."

"Okay, you're going to have explain that."

"Okay, the reason his boat story worked is because we all know you. We've all seen you jump into new projects, filled with utter confidence that what you are about to do will work. Some of your projects succeed brilliantly, but some also fail just as spectacularly."

"I disagree," I said, sardonically. "*All* of my projects fail."

John laughed again, then went on. "No, seriously, he was paying you a compliment. What's different about you is that failure doesn't seem to faze you. You don't get discouraged and quit. You don't become more tentative. You just step back and figure out how to do it differently, or you start over with another project. And you attack that project with the same amount of enthusiasm. When you fail, you just build another boat."

"So, Dave is saying that Laura is my latest boat?"

John laughed, even more loudly this time.

"You really don't get it, do you?" He took a long swig of his coffee, then turned to me. He was a teacher, and I was the student, too dull to get his point.

"Dave admires you a great deal. What he was trying to say—and I completely agree with him—is that you have a certain tenacity that all of us wish we had. No matter the challenges, you keep moving forward. You pick yourself up by the bootstraps, as it were, and you carry on. Your attempt to build a boat is a metaphor for how you work. The boat sinks? You build another boat."

My brother was finishing his conversation with the girl behind the counter, who seemed to hang on his every word. This was the way my brother interacted with the world—he had a natural charisma that drew people to him.

"Your brother believes in your marriage," John said softly. "The fact that he came to your wedding… He may not agree with you two living together before you got married, but he's all in on the two of you. I mean, let's be honest, you've built and sunk a lot of relationship boats"—my friend gave me a lopsided grin at this point— "but you just kept building another boat, one after another; you never gave up. I think he was trying to say, however awkwardly, that he believes you'll bring the same determination to your marriage."

The epiphany began during the last few minutes before our pastor and I led the wedding party onto the front lawn, where Laura and I would exchange ancient vows that came straight out of *The English Common Book of Prayer*, for which we had a deep affection, due to the formal language of prayer found within it.

With this ring I thee wed
This gold and silver I thee give
With my body I thee worship

As I waited for my cue to enter, I stood just inside the doorway. I smelled the earthy wetness of the rain outside, which had just stopped falling. The sun had entered, just in time for the ceremony, its warm rays shining on our celebration. It was as if God Himself were smiling down on us.

Behind me, at the back of the line of chattering bridesmaids and groomsmen dressed in green dresses and powder gray summer tuxedos, Laura stood alone in her white dress with a sage green sash. In front of me, just outside our front door, was a white tent on our green lawn. Gathered around it were earthen beds of shrubs, rocks and flowers, their bold colors of purple, red and white helping to create a sacramental space.

Within the tent sat over seventy of our close friends and colleagues, dressed in flowery summer skirts and casual sports coats. Some had traveled a great distance to join us—one of Laura's friends had flown all the way from Japan to be with us—unlike my own family, who refused to take what would have been for them a far shorter journey. Their deliberate snub had hurt me, but I was determined to focus on the family I had chosen, those who were now surrounding us. Their love and support and affection, revealed through their smiling faces, served as a balm for my hurt feelings, filling my entire body with a powerful feeling of well-being.

Here in the sun-drenched doorway of our home, as I stood waiting for the processional to begin, when Laura would walk down the aisle to join me on a new journey together, I realized I was as happy as I'd ever felt in my life. I'd been searching for love for so many years, not thinking I'd find someone who truly understood me. Yet I had. Laura had made me whole.

It had taken all the years between now and Halloween 1997 to bring me to this moment—Laura was right; for years, we'd been too busy staring into the mirror to notice each other. I'd spent nine years without her, going through one relationship after another. The women I'd dated weren't the problem; the real problem was that none of them was Laura. I'd been in love with her ever since the moment her blue eyes had met mine on the landing of that ancient house in Washington, D.C. It had taken me nearly a decade of living in an emotional desert to realize the truth: Without Laura, my life would never be complete.

But I hadn't been able to come to that conclusion until I'd broken free of my family's judgment. When I'd asked Laura to marry me, I'd finally made my own choice. No matter what my family believed, this—*she*—was the right decision for me.

And this time, the boat floated.

Chapter 36: The Last Time

My mother gave me my love for reading and writing, and she allowed me to begin school early. In the evenings, since our family didn't have a television or radio, our life centered around books. Mom often read to us the stories she loved. Having seen my profound love for books and stories, she knew I was going to be a writer and teacher long before I had a clue.

I was a stubborn child, and I often struggled against my mother, who usually won through a combination of a winsome personality and quiet persistence. I learned from watching her, and I've tried to use the same blend of personality traits to achieve my goals.

My wife has my mother's brilliance and determination, but as a professional diplomat, she has bargaining skills I simply can't match. However, I rarely give up, even if my methods lack her subtlety. During the rare moments when I've been able to hold my own, my wife has sometimes resorted to a wry observation about my childhood: "Your mother must have had a time raising you; I've never met anyone more stubborn." I have learned to keep my mouth shut when she makes this observation.

I think I learned that trait from my mother.

This trait allowed my mother to manage my father across the fifty-eight years of their marriage, a relationship that was healthy and loving and sometimes combative. It also allowed her to face down Death across the operating table when she knew her mission was not yet done.

And as she approached her second meeting with Him, she carried the same brilliance and persistence that she used to face Him the first time. Clear-eyed and fearless, guided by a rock-solid faith in her Redeemer, she was determined to meet him and cross over to the Other Side on her own terms.

About six months after our wedding, Mom began to lose the energy that pulled people to her, and, on the evening of February 12, 2013, Ann called to tell me that Mom's end was near.

I purchased a ticket, took time off from school, and flew home. For a week, I spent every morning with my mother. Sometimes, my father led in devotions and prayer. Sometimes, my mother asked me to share my stories, and she'd listen closely, impatient when my father interrupted. She wanted to hear me read.

One of my last memories of Mom is connected to a photo of her and Dad in the living room. It was the last time I had morning devotions with my parents.

In the photo, as my father reads from the Scriptures, my mother sits in her maroon dress, hunched over her large Bible. Her eyes are focused on the page before her.

When my father finished reading the Scriptures and made his comments, my mother once again started our family song, her voice now quavering, with my father's stronger voice supporting hers as we sang.

> *Jesus, Tender Shepherd, hear me,*
> *Bless thy little lamb tonight.*

When we finished, a bird chirped just outside the kitchen window. My mother lifted her head, her face temporarily relaxing into a small smile.

The tension in her face... she's holding in so much pain.

Mom never complained. But I realized in that moment the depth of pain Mom was living with. For a moment, hearing the bird's chirp, she had forgotten it. The bird's chirp signaled springtime, which brought with it a promise of new life, a promise embedded in my mother's deep faith.

That faith sustained my mother. Her favorite song, found in Handel's Messiah, was "I Know That My Redeemer Liveth," and she was confident that when her spirit shrugged off her body, she would find the springtime of new life. She knew this because she had almost accomplished that, four years before on the operating table, just before she was yanked back into the pain of this world by the electric shocks that brought her back to life. The chirp of the bird had reminded her that new life was ahead. It had given her hope.

In that moment, I realized something else.

Mom's return to life, which led to my return from Los Angeles, had given me the space to discover what really mattered to me. Coming home to Ohio, I had arrived at a crossroads in my life. I had been forced to confront who I was, dig down to my core, and decide who I intended to be. I had only spent a year there, in retreat from the world, but that time had been transformational.

To be clear, I don't believe God struck my mother with congestive heart failure to force me to come home. My mother's return mission encompassed far more than me—but I was part of it. Her trip to the Other World was the initiating incident that allowed me to discover a new path for my life, taking me away from bitterness and toward healing.

Over the year I spent with Mom, having seen her life up close, I realized that my mother no longer feared Death. She had just faced off against Him, the two of them hovering in the gray light of eternity above the operating table. I would like to imagine that—faced by my mother's determined love for her firstborn son—Death granted her several more years to complete her life's mission. Now Mom sensed that her mission was complete, and her time was short. Death was returning to meet her.

She would greet him as a familiar friend.

I flew back to Seattle, back to my life as a teacher and husband to Laura. With our time being so short, each conversation I had with my mother took on more meaning. One morning in May, talking by phone, Mom told me her hospice team had said her health was going backward. It was time to put her house in order.

"Is there anything we still need to talk about?" she asked. "Do you still feel angry about your childhood?"

I thought about the way she had supported me as I'd fought to start first grade early; the way she had stood helplessly by, trying to find a way to help my father and me reconcile; the difficulties when I'd been in London, trying to find my own way; the tentative years following in which we'd recovered and built a real friendship; the vulnerability she'd shown in her conversations with me as I'd lived in Los Angeles; the way she had taken me in when I'd returned; and the way she had quietly shown approval for my marriage to Laura, even when my father had encouraged my siblings not to attend our wedding by refusing to attend himself or give us his blessing.

I thought about her pride in my work as a writer; the way she'd insisted that my sister and father "Be quiet!" so she could hear me read. I thought about Laura's wry remarks about what I must have put my mother through as a child, thanks to my bullheadedness; and how much Mom had loved me. I realized now that, although she had made her mistakes, she'd been *with* me the entire time. No mother could have loved her firstborn son more.

All my anger was gone. "There's nothing to worry about here, Mom."

My mother sighed, perhaps in relief, and then there was a moment of silence between us. It spoke to our comfort level. Then her thoughts turned back to the practicalities of living.

"I'm planning a little garden this spring." Mom's love for the earth infused every word. "Last year, I planted tomatoes, and I had way too many plants, at least fourteen. They just took over the entire garden. This year, I need to plant less."

I smiled. For the first time, I recognized that I had changed in that year I spent with them as my mother passed on to me this deep, lifelong love, her ability to tend the earth and help plants thrive. I recognized something else I'd missed as well, that now when I worked in my own garden, my mother's spirit guided my choices. I would always have that, no matter where my mother was, and so I would have her with me, no matter where I was.

A month later, as I worked in the early morning in my kitchen, my father called me.

"Steve, you don't have a mother anymore. I don't have a wife."

My father's words were harsh, perhaps reflective of his lifelong approach to life and death. But behind his awkward expression, I sensed he could barely get the words out, devastated by the loss of the one person who truly understood him.

I listened to the details of her death, then put down the phone. I ascended the stairs to the master bedroom, where my wife was getting ready to go to work. We stood, facing each other, as I told her the news.

But beneath the flat delivery of information, I was dumbstruck. I was unprepared for my father's harsh delivery of the news, which had left me distraught. To become vulnerable in this moment, even with the woman I trusted more than anyone, would have been to lose control. The worst had happened, and if I gave up that control, I would have lost everything.

Yet I also recognized the finality—I would never see Mom again, not in this life. Yes, I was happy that Mom wasn't in pain anymore, that the suffering that she had held within her body was now gone, but... what could I do now?

Unable to process, I shut down, maintaining my emotional control. I didn't know what my face showed, but I knew Laura understood me better than anyone else. I didn't have to say anything. She knew my rhythms, knew how my emotions worked.

She put her arms around me, kissed my forehead, and held me tight.

Bad weather caused us to miss a flight connection, and so we arrived late for my mother's viewing in Ohio. In the church parking lot, a quiet line of simply dressed adults and children waited patiently.

We entered the sanctuary where my siblings were lined up on either side of my mother's white coffin, to receive guests. We were led to the front of the receiving line, where every member of the family welcomed Laura warmly, honoring us as a married couple for the first time.

I relaxed into the moment because, at all Mennonite and Amish wakes, religious differences are set aside. The drama of the past year and my siblings' resistance to our marriage faded like the morning mist.

But they hadn't been forgotten, not really. This was just a truce.

My siblings and my wife stepped back to give me time alone with my mother. Her body lay on her right side in the coffin, her body permanently set. Mom had died in her sleep and the undertaker had not been able to change her position.

"Hi, Mom," I said silently to her. "I'm so glad the pain is gone. I'm so glad we got to talk before you left. I'm so glad you are finally at peace. Oh, God." I thought about our morning conversations. "Why did this have to happen now, when we had finally begun to understand each other?"

More than anyone else, my mother's fascination with true stories, and her love for the written word, had inspired me to write. More than anyone else in my family, my mother had loved and respected my writing. Even her concern about the controversial poem depicting me allegedly wandering the streets of London, drunk, came out of her deep love for my writing—she hated gratuitous language and the careless use of words. She read constantly, and she knew more about our family's history than anyone else.

At that moment, standing beside her casket, uncertain of how to grieve, unable to cry, I realized that just because a mother has passed on doesn't mean she's gone. My mother's love for words had helped make me a reader and a writer. The inspiration she provided has never left me.

After the service, our rental car followed the hearse across town, with the entire line of vehicles moving smoothly up the hill to the Walnut Grove Cemetery, next to the abandoned Amish church my mother had attended as a girl. Our family joined us, Laura walking beside me through the grass to the middle of the graveyard, wearing her white trench coat over a blue dress.

Before us, my mother's coffin was perched above the grave.

"Ashes to ashes, dust to dust."

As we all watched, the coffin descended into the grave. As is tradition, people had the opportunity to throw shovels of dirt over the coffin, their last connection to the body that had once housed my mother.

Men and women passed the shovels to each other, the dirt showering down onto the casket. Solemn men in shirtsleeves moved among the grandchildren and children and friends, offering us roses. Each in our own time, we tossed them onto her coffin.

Because Laura hadn't been raised in our community, she has always communicated differently with other beings who have passed. Laura had connected deeply with my mother during the one time she'd met her in the living room of my father's new house, during the weekend we had become engaged.

Laura and I had entered the house together, and soon my older sister had pulled me aside for a question. While trying to listen to her, I glanced over to see Laura and Mom talking by the window. The moment seemed dreamlike, since I couldn't hear their words. My mother's face was lively and curious as she listened to my fiancée, and Laura in turn was intently focused on my mother.

I realized, perhaps because I read my mother so well, that she was treating Laura with profound respect, more so than with any woman I had ever introduced her to. It was then I made the connection between these two women I loved so much. I had a strong and brilliant mother who loved words and wished she had gotten an education in history to perhaps become a history professor or a writer, but she didn't have that choice. Now I was marrying a strong and brilliant woman who also loved words and had gotten several masters' degrees, all involving history and English, having had the opportunities my mother had never had. My wife and mother were more alike than I had ever imagined.

Now, as my mother's casket was lowered into the ground, Laura relayed to me later, she saw Mom's spirit there beside us, listening carefully.

"I told your mother that I've got you. That she doesn't need to worry. That I'll take care of her firstborn son.'"

Hearing Laura's words, realizing that although my mother had passed, I had a wife and best friend who truly *got* me, who truly understood me, who had not only promised to love me on my wedding day, but who had also promised my mother to care for me… that's when I really cried. I had been blessed with the gift of a meaningful life, thanks to these two women.

Four years before, my mother had faced off with Death in order to return, in order to be there in Ohio as I returned, searching for a path forward. Rather than telling me what to do, she had given me a safe space—created out of her pure love and acceptance and confidence—where I could plan a new future. She had understood what I needed.

Thanks to that safe space, I had found the time to read, to reflect on the purpose of my life with close friends… and then to rebuild my relationship with Laura. When I had introduced Mom to my fiancée, Mom had welcomed her and believed in my choice. Although my mother didn't agree with my choice to live with Laura before we got married, she had believed in *us*. She had verbally supported our marriage—even when my father had not.

Most importantly, Mom had known and believed in my life's mission, which I was slowly discovering. She had respected my work as a writer, insisting I read my memoir to her, insisting I share *my* truth, not the truth others wanted me to offer. Even my mother's last words—"Is there anything we need to talk about?"—had showed respect and deference for the central struggle within my life and work.

Now, even though her physical body was gone, I knew my mother was with me in spirit, guiding me. My mother had known I needed to find peace with my past in order to build my future. And now, as Laura and I returned to Seattle, I faced the greatest quest of my life.

I would need all of my mother's wisdom and support to do it.

Book IX: Healing

For if ye forgive men their trespasses, your heavenly Father will also forgive you: but if you forgive not men their trespasses, neither will your Father forgive your trespasses.

Matthew 6: 14-15, *The Holy Bible,* KJV, 1769

Interpolation IX: The Paradox of Forgiveness

It has taken me years to understand the paradox of forgiveness—how to forgive an abuser when the abuser refuses to take responsibility for their actions or continues to abuse their victims—and even longer to realize that I am not the only one who has faced this paradox. In Amish and Mennonite communities today, religious authorities put pressure on victims *to forgive and forget their abusers. Multiple victims have shared their stories with me about ministers requiring this.*

I saw this as a child when two young women stood in front of our congregation, forced to confess to sexual sin. Their reputations were permanently damaged, while their partners were allowed to escape without bearing responsibility.

Even as a child, I knew this was wrong.

Unfortunately, as shown in a slew of memoirs from abuse victims, this is still common in conservative evangelical churches around the world. Religious leaders have historically chosen to believe and protect those in power rather than expose abuse.

This is strongly condemned by Jesus himself in Luke 17: 1-2.

It is impossible but that offences will come: but woe unto him, through whom they come! It were better for him that a millstone were hanged about his neck, and he cast into the sea, than that he should offend one of these little ones.

Ironically, religious leaders have often misread these words, using this verse to describe the victim as the offender—for example, young woman who are "dressed immodestly"—rather than recognizing that each person is responsible for their actions, especially youth leaders and ministers.

Thus, policies must be set in place to protect the victims by requiring that all teachers, ministers, and youth leaders become mandatory reporters of physical abuse both to church leaders and to secular authorities. Victims must be given an iron-clad assurance of confidentiality.

No one has the right to demand that a victim forgive and forget their abuser. Religious leaders have used the Lord's Prayer—in which we are forgiven our own sins only to the extent we have forgiven others—to pressure victims of abuse to shut up, essentially re-traumatizing them. This is wrong, which becomes clear when you examine God's pattern of forgiveness.

According to the Scriptures, God himself cannot forgive a sinner until the offender repents by fully owning up to the offense. Therefore, if we are to follow His example, it is up to the abuse victim to judge whether or not the abuser is truly repentant, not religious leaders or the allies of the abuser. Assuming the abuser can convince the victim to listen, it is the victim's right to decide whether or not to forgive.

Nor should a victim be encouraged to forget the offense that has happened—the truth must be spoken aloud for a victim to heal. Requiring that the victim remain silent about the abuse, which allows the abuser to strike again, only deepens the victim's trauma and makes them feel unsafe.

Secrets lead to trauma, and trauma expresses itself in PTSD. God might be able to forget our transgressions, he might have "removed our transgressions" from His memory, but I am not God.

I'm human.

Chapter 37: Remnants of Anger

The death of my mother in June 2013 created a huge gap. During family gatherings we felt her absence keenly. She had always been a balm for me, and an advocate for me in my relationship with my father, softening the sharp edges between us.

I was at peace with my mother's death. I now saw her gentle question during our last conversation—asking if *we* were all right, and if I was still angry about my childhood—as a plea for forgiveness. That morning, I had reassured her that things were okay. Any remnants of anger I might have felt toward her had disappeared, like soap bubbles blown by children, their airy lightness exploding in a single pop.

But now, as I reflected on the humility and grace Mom had extended to me, I began to recognize the difference between my relationship with her, and the one I had with my father. I struggled to understand what had gone wrong between us. I didn't know how to talk to him because I failed to see that his church had taught a theology of abuse during my formative years.

Thus, I could not understand how to find reconciliation between us.

In the next few years, after my mother passed, I struggled to find healing. As I reflected on my relationship with my father, I was haunted by my memories of a moment when my father tried unsuccessfully to bridge the gap between us.

It occurred in July 2005, several years before I returned to Ohio for my year with my parents. I had flown home from Los Angeles to help my family celebrate our parents' fiftieth wedding anniversary. Toward the end of a potluck dinner after church, I found myself standing amidst a small group of men, listening to my father tell one of his favorite jokes. After he delivered the punchline, the other men drifted away, leaving us alone.

"When do you fly out?" he asked.

"Tomorrow morning," I said. "But I'm heading out now… I'm meeting someone in Akron." As always when dealing with my family, I had arranged ahead of time to meet a friend as a way to escape with minimal drama.

The disappointment on his face told me he wished I would stay, but my body was already buzzing with the residue of adolescent memories flooding my body. I needed to shake off the feeling of helplessness that clung to me like a miasma whenever I spent any significant amount of time with my father. I was no longer afraid of him, but I could never entirely relax in his presence.

Others saw my father as a gentle raconteur with sparkling blue eyes telling jokes and stories in his gray suit and neatly trimmed beard. But my vision of him was clouded by the past—memories of him as a raging disciplinarian with his hand raised, memories of him screaming at me when I screwed up a task in his cluttered body shop, memories of his powerful voice shouting as he encountered the messy project I had left strewn all over the basement, my mother's soft voice soothing his anger—all of these memories left me mentally exhausted, my sense of control shattered.

It overwhelmed me. I needed to leave, needed to retreat back to the safe anonymity of Los Angeles, where I could lock these memories down, where I could re-establish my dominance and reassert the control I needed to push forward with my career. Vaguely, I wondered if this was something I should process with my therapist.

What I didn't know at the time was that I desperately needed healing. What I *did* know was that my father desperately wanted reconciliation—and I didn't have what it took to cross the chasm between us. My entire being resisted that journey. I wasn't ready to begin the healing process, which would require the kind of honesty I couldn't yet summon up. Right now, I just wanted to escape this all-too-familiar world so that I could scrub away the residue of memories that clung to me like barnacles on a wind-beaten craft.

"I'll see you later," I muttered.

But as I turned to leave, my father reached out to give me a hug, catching me off guard. I let his arms engulf me, let him pull me into him. I didn't know how to respond. I stood there lifeless… frozen… unable to respond.

"I love you, son," he said, joy and love coming through in his voice. He clearly wasn't sensing my reactions. It all felt so distant, as if my body was on another planet, and this was my avatar receiving my father's affection and listening to his words.

I turned and stumbled away, leaving the room in a daze.

I know now what I was fighting, and I wish I had been able to articulate this to him back then. But I had years of work in front of me. I didn't yet understand how deeply he had been affected by the theology of abuse that he had lived under within our community.

I had read into that hug a desire for my forgiveness, which I too desperately wanted to give him. Perhaps I even wanted to be friends. But before that could happen, we both needed to understand what had happened. My father needed to unlock his own memories.

He needed to show me what he had gone through.

Two years after my mother's death, I found myself still haunted by the memory of my father's attempt to hug me, nine years previous. It lingered in my memory, a nightmare frozen in amber, and it disturbed me.

I couldn't forget it.

I replayed the memory in my mind, sharpening the reality of our relationship. I thought my father had released me, given me my freedom… even offering me his blessing. But his refusal to bless our wedding—in spite of my pleas, in spite of my mother's wishes—had proved that his rigid approach to me had not really changed. When I contrasted this with the humility shown to me by my mother before her death, I realized I did not understand my father.

We were not okay.

Thinking about this forced my issues with control into the foreground. My father showed no awareness—in spite of the conversations I'd had with him—that he had done anything wrong.

In the next year, as I worked with my students, took them to New York City for a journalism conference, and nurtured my large garden, I reflected on my relationship with my father. This could not go on. Was I finally ready to confront my father?

As my students and I went on winter break in December 2015, I began to make plans to visit my father and encourage him to tell me his life story. Perhaps he had experienced abuse, perhaps he too was suffering from PTSD. I was armed with empathy, ready to hear his life story and try to understand the man who was my father. Perhaps we could finally reach across the great divide.

A week later, I discovered he had cancer.

Chapter 38: The Great Divide

When my father called me several days after Christmas, to tell me he had been diagnosed with pancreatic cancer, stage 4, my heart sank.

At my mother's funeral, I had confidently predicted to my wife that my father would probably find another wife and move on with his life. His parents had both lived to be ninety-six years old, and he was in his early eighties. My wife didn't say much, just glanced at the fragile shell of my father sitting in his wheelchair beside my mother's grave, his blue eyes rheumy and distant.

Now as I discussed the phone call with my wife, I realized that my father and I might never be able to cross the great divide of our shared history... because time had run out.

Or had it?

I decided I should fly back to Ohio after New Year's Day to spend time with him. The timing seemed reasonable; it was doubtful my father would go in only three weeks, notwithstanding his doctor's ominous claims.

I was determined to finally *talk* to my father when I went. It was time. I would seize the chance to hear him tell me his stories. Perhaps I could break through and find the soft-hearted father I'd loved as a child before the abuse had begun.

The flight into the Midwest from Seattle on Monday, January 11 was icy and rough. During several connecting flights, I watched—twitching with nerves—as workmen, like crawling ants, de-iced the planes.

Just before leaving, I had learned on WhatsApp that I had underestimated my father's timeline. Dad's condition had nosedived, and he was already in the hospital, fatally enmeshed in a web of tubes and wires. On WhatsApp, my sister Ann had scheduled time for each of us to stand vigil each night, watching over Dad.

He would not be left alone.

After my plane touched down at the Akron-Canton airport, I made my way alone to baggage claim. Pacing, I waited for my bags. Every five minutes, I glanced anxiously at my watch. I needed to get to Mercy Hospital.

Now I have to wait for my fucking bags?

An hour later, I edged into the hospital room, nose wrinkling against the acidic assault of bleach and urine, ears filling with the hum of machines set to monitor my father's every breath. The room was dark, my father's emaciated form covered by a white sheet on the hospital bed.

My brother Dave's powerful body uncurled from the visitor's couch. He was guarding my father tonight; my turn would come later. Dave reached for me, enveloping me in a hug. He seemed half-asleep, but he was gripping his study Bible like a shipwreck victim clutches a life preserver.

"Welcome, brother," he said softly.

He enveloped me in a hug, and I held him close for a moment, then let go and turned to my father. His eyes were open, curious in the dim light. I knelt by his bed.

"It's Steven, Dad."

"Oh, Steve." Even now, my father's welcoming chuckle warmed me.

My brother slapped my shoulder. "I'm going to head down for a cup of coffee," he whispered. "You'll be here?"

"I'll be here."

My father's massive hands enveloped mine. They were weaker now, no longer the threat they had posed to me as a child. I felt them relax into mine.

He was dying.

Dying.

I knelt beside my father's bed, the memories washing over me. The years, the miles, the choices that distanced us, starting with that long-ago year I'd spent in London, ostensibly studying at Richmond College—doing what I knew he disapproved of—drinking, smoking, dancing, theater; acts he considered evil. Then, the years I'd spent in Los Angeles, teaching the children of celebrities, enmeshed in the coils of a sinful world. I knew his high hopes for me, that I would become a minister of the Gospel. I knew I had disappointed him.

Even at this moment in time, safely married and living a more-or-less conventional life on a rural island near Seattle as a high school English teacher, I knew that I, his firstborn son, would never be able to satisfy him. I would never return to his traditional Amish-Mennonite world, in which television, worldly clothes. and jewelry were considered tools of Satan. I'd never return to his community, the one that set hard rules for dress and conduct, each one as harsh and unyielding as the concrete footer my brother had poured that day.

I would never return to his God. That was what wounded him the most. He wanted me to live by Brother Roman's stern beliefs, beliefs my father so admired, especially the belief that Christians must remain cloistered, separating themselves from the outside world.

I thought about London, about the tears I'd caused my mother when she discovered I'd begun to drink, and the long difficult years as I'd tried and failed, then tried again, to lay my own foundation on which to build my life. The memories of my careless words struck me like a gut punch to the stomach, and suddenly, the sorrow washed over me then, heightened by the knowledge that soon, my father would leave me.

I found myself crying.

"Daddy, I'm so sorry I caused you so much pain. I wish I hadn't gone... left you... disappointed you—"

Above me, my father suddenly groaned, as if in pain. I stumbled to my feet, looking down at my father. His eyes were shut. Around me, the monitors beeped, the lights of the heart monitor blinked steadily. My father wasn't conscious. He was in no state, really, to grant the absolution I craved.

I sat down on a chair beside the bed, staring at my father, who lay quietly under the sheets. I needed to take stock of what had just happened. It had been years since I'd cried in my father's presence. I tried to understand the tsunami of guilt that crashed over me.

Suddenly, I remembered a letter he'd written me, back when I'd still lived in Steubenville, Ohio, having barely escaped from the fold. I was teaching at a Catholic school and preparing to join the Roman Catholic church. Working among Catholic young people, I had realized how wrong my church had been— Steubenville's warm immigrant community of Catholic believers was composed of fervent believers who practiced their faith with the same sincerity as I had found in my home community, and they had welcomed me with open arms. No one was interested in burning heretics anymore, no matter what my father had told me.

But as I read the letter, I realized that my father was using a far more subtle approach to coax me to return. He was still telling me I was on the wrong path, but he was blaming himself, perhaps hoping to arouse my sympathy along with my guilt.

Dear Steve, I'm writing to apologize to you for my failures as your father. I'm sorry my example drew you away from the One True Church. My love for musical instruments and performing somehow made you love theater.

I understood Dad's conundrum. Although he loved performing Gospel music and *a cappella* hymns, he believed popular music and the music of Broadway musicals were sinful art forms because they didn't literally glorify God.

In one area, Dad was right. My love of the arts came from him. I had decided long ago that I gotten my love of words from my mother, but I had inherited my father's artistic personality. Dad couldn't hide his passion, as his open mic performance of "The House Across the Hedge" provided during my childhood. So, when I finally discovered what theater really was, under Professor Michael Richard's mentorship in London, there was no chance I would ever put on the Plain coat again.

How I hated my father's hypocrisy as a child, seeing the way the church's rules were stifling him. How I hated the way he dragged our family up in front of church to perform Gospel music for them. How I hated the way his passion for the arts was choked off by the church's rigid belief that art should only show the good, and never the evil.

I thought about the rest of the letter—Dad had done everything in his power to win me back to the church. He must have spent hours trying to write it. At the end, he made a direct appeal to my conscience, reminding me of the vows I had made "on bended knee." I had been twelve and an emotionally distraught child when I joined the church, promising to obey the rules of our church community "until death."

Standing in my little basement apartment at my desk, I read the words of that letter, typed on the back of a recycled telephone invoice. On one hand, it felt good to declare my independence from my home church by joining Rome. On the other hand, my stomach roiled as I considered what would happen—the literal Hell that awaited me—if Dad was right.

Dad had reached back to the Reformation to remind me of the evils of the Catholic church, "the church that martyred so many of your forefathers. They gave their lives for the Truth of the Gospel," my father had reminded me. At the end of his letter, he had pleaded with me to "turn back to the One True Church," ending with the statement I had heard him deliver again and again across my teen years. "There's only one way to Heaven!"

The letter had left me deeply frustrated. I had torn it up afterwards. The idea that our little conservative Mennonite church was the only true faith had seemed arrogant and ignorant. My father's attitude was the reason I was allergic to fundamentalism, the idea that anyone could be sure they were the only ones right, whether they were Christian or Atheist.

But now, facing the reality of my father's impending death, I found myself wiping away tears. I had slowly come to realize that the reason he could arouse such anger in me was because I cared so deeply about what he thought. My intense grief also came from the knowledge that my father and I would never… ever… agree when it came to our beliefs about God.

My strongest beliefs had been formed in high school under the guidance of an English teacher who encouraged me to ask difficult questions, rather than chiding me for fulfilling my childhood nickname, Question Box. While I was in London, making friends with Jews and Muslims at my international college, I had come to realize that they too had grown up in a faith community that believed they were the only ones right about God.

It was a shock—but it had confirmed my thinking about faith. It had also immunized me to friends of mine who rejected faith entirely—those who chose either agnosticism or atheism. Because the reality is, I believed, you can't rationalize your way to the truth about the mystery of faith. Ultimately, you have to come to it on your own terms, and most importantly, you have to be okay with others doing the same thing. People who differed with my faith weren't a threat to my own.

This was the heart of our great divide.

My father believed that his literalist faith—which had led to the physical abuse that had caused such trauma in my life—was the only true faith.

I was never going to change his mind.

Once again, I found myself scrubbing tears from my cheeks. I wasn't sure I was going to make it through the week that loomed ahead of me. My father hadn't changed a bit—hadn't softened one scintilla—in the fifty-two years we'd shared this planet. I still couldn't talk to him, even as he lay dying.

I heard my brother's footsteps.

"You okay, Steve?"

I stumbled to my feet to stand, looking down at my father on his deathbed. His blue eyes blinked up at me in confusion, barely awake.

"No." The word tore at my throat. "I'm not okay."

My brother scratched his head. "It's the drugs they have him on. To let him sleep," Dave said. "Um… did you want to stay?"

There was nothing I could do here. Not now. Might as well let Dad get his rest.

"I think I'm going to head up to Akron." I wiped my eyes and pulled myself together. "I'm staying with a friend."

"Okay, hope you get some sleep. It's nice to see you again." Dave drifted back to his vigil on the couch as I left the hospital room.

My father lingered for days, and I returned to his bedside, again and again. People from my family's church visited, often singing for him. I recognized most of the music, but there were new songs I didn't recognize. And of course, all of the music at my father's bedside was sung *a cappella*, without musical instruments.

My home community still did not believe musical instruments should be used in worship. Growing up, I was taught that instrumental music was part of the Old Testament worship experience, whereas simple and Plain hymns should be sung within the New Testament church. In the same way people dressed Plain, the singing during worship services was also Plain—without any musical instruments—with human voices harmonizing cleanly and simply. It matched the church's belief that holiness is found in simplicity and Plainness.

My father had loved *a cappella* music, but he had also loved playing musical instruments. About a decade before, the church had changed the rules, and now musical instruments were no longer forbidden, as long as you played them outside of worship services, where they were still forbidden. For years, my father had respected the church's sanction of musical instruments, except playing his harmonica around home or during visits to his family in Pennsylvania, where no one would be offended. In the last decade of his life, he had been able to enjoy playing music without fearing that he would offend others in our church.

347

Now, as he lay dying, the people of our church visited regularly, and almost always they sang for him, *a cappella*, whether or not he was conscious. It was a delight for me. It brought back memories of my singing in the choir, singing with my family, and singing with our high school quartet.

As members of his congregation sang, my father drifted in and out of consciousness. At times, when he was alert, he would sing with them. One Sunday afternoon, when a group of church friends stayed too long, my father's patience snapped, gesturing to his three visitors. "Tell them to sing a song and then leave," he instructed my sister and me, impatiently. As they droned through a hymn about "how beautiful Heaven must be," he sang each verse with them, without missing a word. Then he closed his eyes as my sister ushered his visitors out the door, their faces mired in confusion.

I tried not to laugh, but afterwards, as I repeated the story to my siblings, they broke into giggles of merriment. Dad had finally had it with virtue-signaling visitors who were there to make themselves feel good, rather than being sensitive to his family's feelings. It was the one moment during the deathwatch when his irrepressible humor broke through.

During the last week, he lapsed into a coma. People continued to visit and sing, but by now Dad was so heavily medicated with morphine that he was barely aware of us. However, I knew what my family believed—that even a comatose body can hear what people are saying, and that the Gospel hymns and songs Dad had sung all his life were comforting to him as he prepared to face Death, the last struggle before he was admitted to Heaven.

I continued to struggle with guilt over not having had the chance to reconcile with my father. I had wanted to ask him about his life, had wanted to talk frankly about the bitterness I still felt toward him. But it was too late for that. We had had a lifetime together, that conversation had never happened, so perhaps I needed to accept that it was an impossibility.

I suddenly came out of my reverie as my sisters rose to gather around Dad. I realized his breathing had stopped. Then the beeper flatlined.

"He's gone," one of my sisters murmured.

Ann reached to hold Dad, pull him toward her, and I suddenly realized she was speaking to him, almost wild with excitement.

"Do you see her? Do you see Mom?" It was as if she were hoping to see the joy Dad must be feeling as he saw Mom for the first time, with Jesus standing just behind her.

Both Ann and Marcia gazed into Dad's yellowing face eagerly, as if looking for some sign of life in his eyes, perhaps hoping to see my mother's sweet face mirrored in them, like images reflected in Agent Smith's sunglasses during *The Matrix* movie. I watched silently, knowing that my sister was hoping my father would give some indication of the joy he must be feeling now in the presence of Christ, having just entered Heaven. For a moment, I wondered whether or not Dad would respond, but I knew better. His body was lifeless, the light gone out of his eyes.

Dad was gone.

I watched my sister, hoping against hope that Dad would give her what she wanted, but at the same time convinced that Dad would be unable to send her a final message from across the great chasm of death. I knew her hope was based on the legends surrounding death that my people subscribed to—a bird tapping on a window outside the room where a person has just passed, a ray of light appearing on the lawn just as the soul passes, a butterfly the dead person had always loved landing suddenly on the window ledge outside the room.

My sister, whose faith was powerful and strong, was hoping my father had seen Mom's face just before he died, and would let her know with a parting smile, letting us know that he had passed safely out of this world that had caused him so much pain in the last month of his life.

But no, the rictus of death had frozen his face into a mask. My oldest sister reached out and closed my father's eyes for the last time. Then the two of them held each other, tears streaming down their cheeks. They reached for me, pulling me into a group hug as they wept.

Dad was gone.

I felt their sobs but was unable to cry. I looked at the husk of my father's body, defeat flooding my senses. I had waited too long to ask him the questions I wanted to know about his own life. Perhaps if I had, we could have mended our relationship. I stood there, my emotions locked up somewhere inside me. I wanted to feel sorrow, wanted to cry with my sisters. But I felt nothing, only the need to begin the practical steps of planning the funeral and writing the obituary and preparing the eulogy.

Why didn't I feel grief the same way others did?

I remembered the words of a close friend: "Everyone experiences grief differently. Don't try to decide ahead of time how you should react." Remembering that advice kept me calm.

I don't need to feel everything all at once. Perhaps I'll cry later.

Quietly slipping out of the room, I left my sisters to the traditional task our women do when someone has died: cleaning and preparing my father's body for the burial.

In the next few hours, as my wife purchased airline tickets and made plans to join me, I met with the lead pastor, planning the funeral and obituary. I knew him well. His hands were steady, and he spoke to me with the respect reserved for any firstborn son. I was surprised by the way he took direction from me. I should have remembered the iron-clad tradition within Amish and Mennonite communities—when it comes to death, all grievances and disagreements are set aside in honor of the person who has passed.

Later that afternoon, I slipped away from my grieving family and returned to where I was staying to write my father's eulogy. I needed to compartmentalize my emotions so that I could assume my father's role as the family patriarch, now thrust upon me by my childhood community. As such, certain tasks fell to me, including the eulogy. I had dreaded writing it. What could I say that my people would believe? How could I—a son who never had closure and didn't know how to grieve his father's death—encapsulate the devout life my father had lived that my siblings and his congregation wanted... no, deserved to hear?

Alone now in the bedroom, seated at the giant wooden desk in front of my laptop, I stared at the blank page. I thought about my anger, I thought about our differences, and I thought about the great divide between us. There was a lot about my father I needed to process. But now was not the time. There were many people who loved my father, who spoke fondly of him, who needed to know that I, his oldest son, had the grace to recognize what he had given to their community. Now was the time to celebrate what made my father so unique. Now was not the time to air my differences, but I also knew I needed to be as authentic as my father was.

I remembered telling him while I was in Ohio that I had been writing a memoir, and that a lot of it dealt with him, with us. He had looked at me calmly, unafraid, and then told me something I didn't expect.

"You have my permission to write anything you wish about me," he said. "We have had our differences. Just be honest in whatever you write about me," he said. "That's all I ask."

Recalling that gave me the freedom I needed. And so, setting aside whatever emotions I might have, I focused on the job at hand.

What did I appreciate most about my father?

There was nothing my father loved more than music. It was the great passion of his life, but also the great wound. We were only allowed to sing *a cappella* music during church services, due to a twisted interpretation of Scripture—it didn't allow him to play musical instruments during worship services. And because he was brilliant at playing instruments, and because his voice was unexceptional, his chance to fulfill himself by performing as a soloist during worship services became limited, cutting him off from his greatest joy. Only in the last few years of his life did the church relent and bless his use of musical instruments.

But my father knew that in Heaven, there would be golden harps on golden streets. Musical instruments were part of the heavenly culture, according to the Bible. There was also a heavenly choir, and my father would finally have a perfect voice. He could be the Elvis of Heaven, a superstar musician.

I didn't say that in my eulogy—but I wanted to, because I knew it was true.

But he wouldn't want to be Elvis—he'd want to be B.B. King or Muddy Waters, blues musicians who really knew how to play. I was on a roll now, thinking about the happiness my father must be feeling, trying out his new golden harp... no, his gold-plated guitar. Perhaps they handed one to him when he first entered Heaven. I imagined the joy that would flood his body as the angels put such a treasured instrument into my father's hands.

And then the words came quickly.

Online, I found an old radio show my father loved, and I used its basic concept to paint a picture of my father leaving this life by way of a supersonic airplane that would carry him to Heaven. I worked late into the night, half-asleep, using stream of consciousness to lay out the eulogy. Then I got up, made a cup of coffee, and revised and polished it deep into the night.

Eventually, I captured the best aspects of the father I knew, tapping the emotions in my piece and weaving them into a narrative. And then to my surprise, when I stopped and reread my piece, the tears came.

The next morning, standing before the silent throng of our family's supporters in the sanctuary of my old church, I described my father's tormented love for instrumental music, his profound commitment to prayer, and his deep love for my mother.

I struggled to keep the tears back, realizing as I spoke that for the first time, my words had allowed me to slip past the wall of bitterness and anger that had dominated my feelings about my father for so long.

As I looked out at my father's community and saw the sorrow my family was experiencing, a deep sense of grief welled up in my heart. For the first time since I had left, the powerful connection I had once shared with my community crackled to life.

It was then that the truth hit me.

I had feared I was a bad son, that I didn't feel grief for my father's passing, yet my deep sorrow had been there the whole time. It just came out differently, using words on the page, rather than the warm, emotional language relied upon by my family.

Perhaps this was because of the complicated relationship I had with my father. Perhaps this was because I had been grieving my departure from my community for so long—the profound loss I felt in losing a network of irreplaceable friendships. Perhaps this was because my eulogy was the culmination of a grieving process that had begun the day I left home—sitting alone on that hard wooden bench immediately after returning from London.

I had feared this day for so long, the day when I would have to deal with who my father was, who I had become, and—more significantly—how our thorny history had shaped me as a man. Writing my father's eulogy had perhaps softened the edges of the great divide between us, but it had also made something very clear to me.

The divide still existed.

In that moment, I saw the path before me. My quest for authenticity—a painful gift passed on to me from my father—demanded that I come to terms with my lack of forgiveness toward him. The process of writing that eulogy had revealed the truth.

I was allowed to *not* forgive him.

I was allowed to be angry.

I was also allowed to deliver a beautiful eulogy.

Doing all these three things at the same time wasn't being insincere. It was being gracious. Because, really, was I going to get up there and air our family's dirty laundry and have a public therapy session in the painful aftermath of my father's death?

No, of course not.

Granted, my father wasn't the dad I wanted, but he was someone people knew and loved and respected. How would it look if I went up and denounced him? In the long run, who would that benefit? And so, I crafted a eulogy that would help my siblings deal with his death, and one that would allow me—privately—to come to terms with his passing.

I didn't know if I'd ever be able to forgive my father or release the anger I felt toward him. But the writing of my father's eulogy, and the emotions that had flooded me as I had delivered it, had also shown me something important, something I hadn't realized before.

I loved my father.

Could my refusal to forgive his abuse co-exist with my love for him?

That was the question I needed to answer.

Chapter 39: A Place of Rest

In the years that followed my father's death, I tried to understand how I felt about my father, about his actions, and about what he believed. His death and the aftermath had helped me understand a lot about our relationship. For example, my sister Marcia, sitting with me at my father's deathbed, had shared with me "how proud Dad was" of me.

So, if Dad was proud of me, he loved me.

But if he loved me, I rationalized, why wasn't he able to own up to what he had done?

I had spent years in therapy, trying to understand the way I'd been damaged. I had tried to wrap my head around this one truth: that the way I was raised was not *normal*. It had taken me years to truly believe this.

With my father gone, I finally descended to the chasmic depths of my memory's basement, digging through the rubble with a ferocity I couldn't previously muster. It was there, in the yawning darkness, that I finally owned up to the truth. It wasn't just *physical* abuse that had initiated my PTSD (which had presented as chest pains) at the age of thirty-one.

The most damaging abuse was *spiritual*.

As a child, I had sat riveted, imagination ablaze, under dozens of preachers who manipulated their audiences with their most powerful threat—eternity spent in a howling, fiery Hell. In sermon after sermon, they described it as a literal place of eternally conscious torment.

Since we were all born in sin, we were all headed there.

Turning the screws even tighter, these evangelists had preached that if I *resisted* God's call, if I quenched the pleading of the Holy Spirit, I would be committing The Unpardonable Sin—for which there was *no* forgiveness, no matter how long or how often I begged for God's forgiveness. But if I submitted to their patriarchal demands and said the magic words—"God be merciful to me a sinner"—Christ would be my Savior, Bob would be my uncle, and all fear would disappear. They were telling me about The Wizard of Oz, not the God Who Walks Beside Us.

Because as often as I prayed, as often as I tried to submit to their God, that fear never left me. How could it, with an imagination like mine? I finally realized this after I stumbled down the aisle, repeatedly, to "accept Jesus"— only to discover, repeatedly, that the next day I was back to square one—still convinced that I was a sinner, and *still* convinced that I was going to Hell. Somehow, the magic words refused to work for me.

Again and again, this raw fire hose of fear was leveled at me. And because I was an intelligent child, and because I had a vivid imagination combined with exceptional empathy, and because my father taught me that the Bible must be read literally, I took all this shit seriously.

It was telling that when I began to write screenplays, and chose horror as my genre, I began writing satanic horror. Writers of horror, to be effective, must tap into their greatest fears, and I couldn't imagine anything more frightening than Satan himself.

Is it any wonder I suffered PTSD?

By the time I was nine, even after I had "accepted Jesus into my heart" multiple times, I still found myself running into the kitchen, my chest tightening as I found it difficult to breathe, screaming in fear: "I'm dying, I'm dying." On a trip to my father's community in Lancaster, PA, my parents finally took the advice of his college-educated sister. We went to see a "liberal" Mennonite pediatrician, a kindly man, who after giving me a thorough examination with my parents in the room, confirmed that God loved me, that I was a strong healthy boy, and that I would live a long life.

Somehow, I believed him, and the panic attacks subsided.

Several years ago, I began reading memoirs written by prominent Ex-vangelicals. These thought leaders have chosen to deconstruct their faith, and many have left Evangelicalism, which is a movement stretching across mostly Protestant churches. Evangelicals can be Presbyterians, Baptists, Methodists, Mennonites. Many evangelical churches are independent and not associated with any of the major Christian denominations.

Like the preachers of my childhood, Evangelicals believe that true conversion occurs during a Damascus Road experience when you undergo a personal encounter with God. The result is an intimate relationship with Jesus, one in which you are—as the Christian rock singer Keith Green put it—"bananas for Jesus." To be an Evangelical, you must believe that every word of the Bible is literally true, and you must embrace the patriarchal order found in the New Testament in which women are not permitted to serve in major leadership roles in the church. For the youth, there is an emphasis on purity culture, with young women expected to embrace femininity and dress modestly in order to avoid tempting a young man. The greatest gift a young woman can give her newlywed husband is her virginity.

As I read the stories of the survivors of this movement, I finally began to understand what I had faced. It wasn't only the physical abuse that caused my PTSD—it was also the emotional pounding I had taken as a child, when preachers threatened me with a literal, burning Hell.

In my reading, I also learned the official diagnosis for what I'd worked through over a decade before with my therapist: Religious Trauma Syndrome.

Perhaps the term hadn't existed at the time, but in our sessions, Dr. Thea Kiran had clearly described the symptoms and the cause to a T.

Reading them gave me a profound sense of relief as I realized that *I was not the only one*. Many others in spiritual communities like mine have experienced the same symptoms. In fact, my experience was so common that the medical field had to create a clinical name for it. There's a ton of relief in knowing what your illness is.

As I understood the connection, understanding flooded over me. Those moments when my heart galloped in my chest, when the pressure in my chest felt like I was about to explode, when fear leaped into the driver's seat and hammered the throttle of my instincts to the floor… those were not random incidents. They were a direct result of years of physical and spiritual abuse—actions taken by adults who should have protected me, actions taken by adults who chose to use fear as a weapon, actions taken by adults to manipulate me into staying.

Several months before my father's death, at a family gathering, I gathered my courage. In a quiet conversation with my father, I asked him why he disciplined me with such severity.

"I choose to obey God rather than men," my father said simply. His eyes, rheumy now with age, showed his stolid determination. I didn't argue with him. I had spent my teen years doing that, and I had never convinced him. He believed that following the Bible's commands, literally, was the path to Heaven. Nothing I said now, as he stood gazing into the Valley of the Shadow of Death, would change his mind.

After my father passed, I reflected again and again on that conversation. It came up frequently in conversations with my wife, as I strove to put to rest the anger I felt at his refusal to accept or make amends for what he had done. My father had refused to see the impact that his actions had caused.

This was hard to accept.

As I reflect today on the impacts of my father's discipline within my family, I am despondent. A lifetime of working with children has taught me how very wrong my father was. You cannot learn when your body is frozen by fear. You cannot love someone you fear—no matter how often the literalist tells you that "the fear of God is the beginning of wisdom," and that this godly fear is inculcated within us when parents use "the rod" on their children.

A parent's natural—instinctual, biological—instinct is to *not* harm their children. In fact, we are genetically programmed to protect our young. Otherwise, our species would die out. The lack of this parental instinct in my father spoke to a darkness I am loathe to contemplate. What if my father had hit me too many times? What if I had moved, and he had bashed in my temple and killed me, or broken my bones?

Such things have happened.

It was only by getting an education and leaving my community that I avoided the worst of these impacts—the fact that those who are abused physically as children tend to replicate the abuse when *they* become parents. As I began to understand the abnormality of my father's discipline in college, I changed the direction of my life, rejecting the patriarchal thinking I had been taught. I left the Christian school system—which encouraged the use of corporal punishment—choosing to teach within schools which forbade it.

As I began to understand the resulting trauma that I had experienced, I avoided marriage. And then, in my forties, after therapy helped me begin to heal and I found the love of my life, I decided I didn't trust myself to have children. The chance that the indoctrination that attracted my father might lie coiled within *my* psyche—that I might feel the need to beat my *own* children—frightened me.

How does one react to this understanding? How does one honor a parent who made such appalling choices? How does a firstborn son—for the sake of his health and sanity—find a way to forgive his father?

I had been taught that we are to forgive as God forgives—by forgiving *and* forgetting. "As far as the East is from the West," Psalm 103:12 says, "so far has He removed our transgressions from us." According to the Lord's Prayer (Matthew 6:9-13), God can only "forgive us our trespasses as we forgive those who trespass against us." We are to forgive others, even if they hurt us "seventy times seven" (Matthew 18:22).

But did that mean I had to forget the actions of a man who told me he didn't believe he had done anything wrong? How could my mind forget—as God does so majestically—when my very human *body* refused to forget?

In my thirties, I tried to put my past behind me, but my body decided otherwise, the PTSD forcing traumatic memories up and out of the basement of my subconscious—memories I had until then subverted—my body commandeering my nervous system with terrifying chest pains, my imagination attempting to release trauma through my art. Only under the skilled guidance of my therapist was I able to get past the shame and unpack my childhood experiences, finally admitting to Dr. Kiran what had gone wrong in my family.

Thanks to her, I confronted the truth of my father's abuse. The work we did together allowed me to see what had gone wrong in my family, which led to the healing I needed. I finally realized that whether or not I wished to forgive my father was my choice.

And I had no desire to forgive my father.

Forgiveness isn't something that pops out of a vending machine when the right words are inserted. Forgiveness cannot come until the abuser recognizes and owns what they did, asks the victim for forgiveness, and gives them *the freedom to reject that apology*. Until this happens, there is no chance of real reconciliation, much less friendship.

My father chose to beat me, regularly, and even worse, to send me to a Christian school where men with muscles hardened by construction work regularly worked over their students with wooden paddles, some of them riddled with holes to ensure maximum pain.

Why did he embrace such severity? Who taught him that beating his children was in any way okay? Certainly not his mother or father. The level of severity used by my father didn't come from his home—because none of my Denlinger cousins has reported similar experiences.

It appears that his beliefs came from my mother's side of the family. Across the years, I've heard multiple stories about the beatings my Overholt cousins experienced. I have wondered about the childhood discipline tales that they now find amusing, and the current abuse that still goes on because "the Bible teaches" that "children need that kind of discipline."

According to the stories I have heard, the Overholt men in our extended family who used the severest discipline were considered the most respected and the most spiritual. Knowing what I know about how such abuse destroys relationships, I find this kind of spirituality horrifying.

I have heard extended family members report on the bitterness that destroyed their relationships with their parents, and the violence that erupted when they decided they had had enough of the beatings. I have heard from women within our communities whose sexual libidos were deeply affected by their experiences with abusive fathers and church leaders.

This is what occurs when adults abuse helpless children in the name of God.

For decades, medical science has supported what the Apostle Paul says when he advises fathers not to "provoke your children to anger" and bitterness (Ephesians 6:4), which is why teachers in public schools are required to report any suspicions of domestic abuse.

Why did my father—who was known for his gentle spirit and kind approach to others—take exactly the opposite approach to his own children? Could it be that by attending family reunions and seeing how other male patriarchs practiced discipline, my father concluded that such abuse was godly? If so, my father's choice to abuse his children makes sense.

Patriarchal culture had poisoned his mind.

I have spent the last decade trying to understand my father's motivations.

And I recognize that most of all, my father was driven by fear, which was planted within him by our patriarchal society. Fear is a powerful thing. My father believed that to avoid Hell, he needed to follow scrupulously God's every command—even if that meant obeying the Bible's literal commands to beat his children.

He could not have foreseen the impact it would have on me.

Please understand, I do not believe that his choices were in any way okay.

But recognizing that my father believed he was obeying God, and recognizing the influence of my community's patriarchal culture, helped me understand that my father was also a victim to a systemic system of belief that used fear to get my father to toe the party line.

Knowing this allowed me to make the conscious choice to confront my feelings of resentment, anger, desire for revenge—and to let them go.

How did I release them?

I'm not entirely sure. Perhaps I released them as I told stories about my father to my students, retelling the jokes he loved so. Perhaps I released them by leaning into the qualities of kindness and gentleness my father modeled for me in his earlier years, before the dark years of my adolescence. Perhaps I released them by seeing the way my father treated my mother during that year I was home, and following his example, making my wife the center of my world as my father made my mother the center of his.

It has helped me build a marriage that enriches my life each day.

Whatever the reason, I made the decision to forgive my father because I realized that *not* forgiving him would sentence me to a life trudging through the world with a backpack of emotional dynamite strapped to my aching shoulders. If I didn't shed that backpack, it would eventually explode, destroying me and everyone I loved.

It bears repeating. Forgiving my father doesn't mean I have forgotten or excused his behavior. It doesn't mean the harms he caused didn't occur. It doesn't mean the trauma I experienced was *not* real.

Forgiving my father demanded a series of choices. I had to forgive him, again and again, as I processed the trauma. I wrote and rewrote our story together. I tried to see things from my father's perspective.

And then eventually, I didn't have to make that choice anymore because the anger was suddenly… gone.

Is this forgiveness?

I think it is.

Thirty-seven years before, as I left my family's community, I believed my faith to be a fragile thing. Conditioned by my father, I feared the world would destroy it.

But I underestimated the depth of God's love for me.

And then, in the darkest moment of my life, amidst the howling chaos of my friend Kim's near death, I discovered The God Who Walks Among Us was pacing beside me. I should have seen Him earlier—within my sociology professor at Malone University, within my theater professor in London, within the hotel manager on Venice Beach, within the thoughtful guidance of my therapist, and even within my former student in Colorado.

They all recognized my quest.

The people I bonded with—outliers who barely fit into their own communities—understood this intuitively. They welcomed me without judgement, rejecting the weapons of guilt and fear and providing me with a lens that allowed me to see the world differently.

By so doing, they gave me—a Cowardly Lion—the kind of courage that allowed me to face down the mighty Wizard who demanded my submission. By so doing, they helped me see The God Who Walks Beside Us. By so doing, they helped me determine how to accomplish my purpose in the world.

They offered my anxious soul a place of rest.

The End

Afterword

My life has been a series of decisions with unintended consequences. I went into therapy because I believed it would help me write a novel. As I healed, I began to look ahead to a brighter future. But as I began to teach what I was learning, I realized I had stumbled on something—the fact that writing about traumatic events can reframe the way you see your past.

I have embraced my dual role as a writer and teacher.

Recognizing that writing memoir can help you transform, I made the decision to use my writing to show others the way out. My editor, Judi Fennell, recognized and bonded with me over this mission, encouraging me to keep focused on it in every scene, paragraph, line, and word.

"You've made that promise in writing—within these very pages," she once told me. "So, you MUST deliver on it. Always ask 'How does this serve the purpose of the chapter and, therefore, the book?'"

I am deeply grateful for Judi's editorial guidance.

But I cannot just write—I am compelled to teach what I learn. And so, it is no surprise that as I began practicing these concepts in my writing, I began to teach my students how to tell their stories, as well—whether I was teaching high school seniors how to write their college application essays or showing college freshmen how to write memoir.

Thus, my writing and teaching became recursive. My mission expanded beyond narrative therapy into my teaching others how to heal through writing. And what I kept learning inspired me to keep nugging away at this memoir.

My writing journey has been long, lasting almost two decades. What drove me forward was my belief that narrative therapy—the telling and retelling of my story to understand my past—would allow me to heal, releasing the trauma from my body, one cell at a time.

Some of the most powerful moments in my writing process have occurred when I've read or told part of my story to someone and heard their response turn inward, reflecting on their own life. In fact, that has become a test for me. When I read something to someone, and they respond by discussing the details of *my* story, I know it isn't yet working. When they respond to my writing by talking to me about their own experiences, I know I have shown the truth in my narrative.

I found healing in my journey, thanks to those who recognized the importance of my mission—a caring therapist who pointed me toward narrative therapy, theater communities who performed my dreams and nightmares without judgment, the editor who signed on to steer this manuscript all the way to publishing, and most of all, the love of my life (who is now my wife, lover, travel companion, alpha reader, and business partner), all of them helping me to exorcise the demon of anger and bitterness that threatened to destroy my life.

By processing this story, and forgiving my father, I reclaimed my emotional energy, rather than letting his actions continue to cause me suffering, decades after the abuse ended. Learning how to reframe the most difficult memories was a gift of grace that allowed me to trace my journey out of darkness and into the light.

Steven L. Denlinger
Alexandria, Virginia
September 5, 2025

Acknowledgments

In the end, it took a community of friends and readers to produce this book, and I dedicate my writing to them, especially those students who encouraged me to read chapters of my memoir aloud to them and then pushed me forward. "You need to publish your memoir, Mr. Denlinger," they kept telling me.

To Judi Fennell, whose insightful developmental and line editing inspired an entire rewrite of the book. Thank you for not letting me slip by with easy answers. Your questions infuriated me, forced me to rewrite again and again, and ultimately, helped me get to where I needed to go.

To Erinn Cawthon, whose legal advice I deeply value, who translated the law into practical and insightful advice, and who read and reread earlier versions of this book and commented on them. Thanks for your gift of friendship.

To Arianna Huffington, who allowed me to teach her daughters and invited me to write for *HuffPost* after I left Archer—thank you for your notes of encouragement, both spoken and emailed. Thank you for giving me a national audience to begin talking about my past.

To my therapist, Dr. Thea Kiran, who listened to my stories—thank you for guiding me through RTS and PTSD with a wise and insightful ear, introducing me to narrative therapy to use my writing to heal. Thank you for reassuring me that people would want to read my story.

To my lifelong friend, Verne Dagenais, who, while helping to save my life in middle school, was dealing with his own trauma. I'd like to think that I could have helped you in the same way, but we were both just trying to survive. It's our lasting friendship that has helped heal those wounds.

To my friend, Ami Wagner, who helped me understand my father, who offered a big-picture perspective and a cultural education, who refused to judge my past, who provided booming laughter and generous hugs, who offered a useful collection of swear words, and who encouraged me to keep going when the book seemed nothing but a vanity project. How many chapters have I read aloud to you on the phone over the years?

To Kara Fohner, a seriously talented journalist and poet, who repeatedly spent hours on the phone with me talking honestly about the latest draft, who believed in the project, and whose comment—"I think you're grieving the loss of your community"—inspired me to construct the story upon the stages of grief.

To Taylor Ross, whose supportive friendship I appreciate, and whose conversations about our writing always inspire me, and whose beta reader feedback to both my writing and my wife's is deeply appreciated.

To Steven Huey, who was the first to give me real feedback to my writing, who taught me that rewriting a story again and again is like marinating good whiskey, and who, after reading the first draft, wondered how I had managed to write a memoir while leaving myself out of it. You know how to make me laugh, Steven.

To Dylan Struzan, whose own experience with "religion" within a Jehovah's Witness community helped her recognize my own faith journey, and especially my mother's love for me. Thanks for proposing the original title, "How To Tie a Necktie," when the original blog came out on *HuffPost*.

To Mike Langworthy, who read and reread drafts of the original memoir, and whose most memorable advice occurred when I objected to watching *Breaking Bad* because I couldn't handle the darkness of a teacher gone wrong: "You just need to get over yourself and watch the show," he told me. Wisdom, it was.

To Regina "Just-K" Dillard, whose initial encouragement, financial help during the dark days, always supportive ear, and personal stories were the inspiration that kept me going. You knew from the start that my love for "The Laura" was real. I'm glad we each found the love of our life at almost the same time.

To Candace Mount, who still helps me remember my Ohio roots, who has read draft after draft repeatedly, offering developmental advice, and who has always helped me see my story from my home community's perspective.

To Mary Jo Fohner, whose lifelong friendship and support I value deeply, and whose candid readings and blunt assessments and ability to spot problems with the details led to her work as my copy editor.

To John Fohner, my fourth brother, whose lifelong friendship was there for me always as I left my home community, who always offers valuable bits of advice through the eyes of Eeyore (his spirit animal), and who impatiently told me for years that I just needed a deadline to make this memoir work. See Hollywood Steve's comments about whiskey, John.

To Marlin Miller, my oldest and closest friend, who helped me dream of the outside world as a teenager, whose own path to the outside world always encouraged me, whose financial resources helped me survive the darkest days in Los Angeles, who helped me balance my teaching and writing careers, and whose friendship I treasure.

To Theresa Ann Aleshire Williams, writer of *The Secret of Hurricanes,* who mentored me while I was in Los Angeles, and believed in me.

To the late Alice Aspen March, who believed in this project from the first day, who understood my father, and who told me, "It's never about the money."

To Gerald Mast, who read one of my first drafts and took it seriously. Here's to his insistence that I shouldn't write a *Bildungsroman* but instead offer it to my community as a sprawling biblical narrative. Thank you for helping me to understand how reading the Bible requires more than a literal lens. Thanks also for agreeing to write your insightful foreword.

To Halvor Undem, who read my unpublished memoir piece, *Driving with Joe Overholt*, and loved it; who introduced me to Francis Thompson's poem "The Hound of Heaven" and the accompanying series of paintings by R.H. Ives Gammell; and who helped found our Hound of Heaven Bible Study, offering frequent analogies to film and literature during our discussions.

To all my original readers of *HuffPost*, whose enthusiasm for my initial column sent me on this journey. Your interest and notes helped me believe I could do this.

To my family, who have been listening to me talk about this book for two decades, who have given candid feedback as I shared it with them, and who have supported me with their love across my journey. Thanks for believing in me, even when you disagreed with my perspective.

To my mother, whose love for words and great memoirs eventually soaked into my consciousness, and whose abiding love and trust in who I am gave me the strength to write my own story. How often did you read the book *First We Have Coffee* (Here's Life, 1982) to us?

To my father who gave me the freedom to write our story, and thus find healing… hopefully, also, for you. We didn't understand each other while we lived, but perhaps we do now.

To my brother Dave, a true friend who listened again and again to my chapters, who always had memories to share that helped me understand my story, and who helped me see what was working. Perhaps you too will write your own version of our family story.

To my wife, Laura. Your love and patience have brought stability to my life. You refrained from calling me self-absorbed as I wrote and rewrote this story, and you carefully read draft after draft. Your careful wordsmith's eye has taught me what it means to write and edit, and your ability to polish with rhetorical devices show me how to find my voice. Most importantly, my dearest of darlings, thank you for your pragmatic perspective on life… and romance. How I love thee.

Just one more thing.

This lengthy collection of acknowledgements is inspired by my astonishing friend Sloane Davidson, whom I met while she was working in the Development Office at The Archer School, and who has found her destiny by helping her immigrant neighbors in Pittsburgh. She once told me over a glass of wine that she always reads the Acknowledgments section of a book first, just to see how grateful a person the writer is. Sloane, if you ever get around to reading this book, I just thought you should know I didn't forget that comment.

About the Author

Steven L. Denlinger
Memoir Instructor & Community Builder

Steven L. Denlinger is a memoirist, journalism teacher and college instructor whose stories center around themes of community, repression, and redemption.

Using education as a ladder of escape from fundamentalism, Steven was the first in his sprawling family ever to attend college, majoring in English and history at Malone University in Canton, Ohio. He clinched his escape from home by winning a Rotary Ambassadorial Scholarship to study in London. By the end of that year, the Berlin Wall had fallen, and Steven had abandoned the Mennonite world, alienated his community, but gained his B.A. and his hard-won freedom. (His blogs in *HuffPost* focus on these formative years.)

After leaving, Steven studied at Oxford University while working on his M.A. in English from Middlebury College. In 2021, Steven returned to school to earn his Leadership Endorsement at Longwood University. He has applied those skills by partnering with Laura Navarre—an Amazon bestselling author—as the CEO of Ascendant Press, their boutique independent publishing firm.

Steven has taught high school in Ohio, California, and Washington State. He is now advising the yearbook staff and teaching first-generation college students at Justice High School and Northern Virginia Community College.

Steven's recent awards include being honored as Teacher of the Month at Justice High School and being awarded Special Recognition Adviser by Columbia Scholastic Press Association in 2021. His lit mag, newspaper, and yearbook staffs from North Canton, Vashon Island, Stafford, and Justice have earned top rankings, and his yearbook staffs have snared two Pacemaker nominations from the National Scholastic Press Association. He earned an All-American award as editor-in-chief of his college newspaper.

Steven and his wife Laura currently live with Puddin' and Lannister, their two Siberian Neva Masquerade cats, in Northern Virginia.

THANK YOU!

If you enjoyed this memoir, I invite you to follow me on Substack—Unicorn in the Church Pew.

To help other readers like you find this book, please leave a review on your favorite bookseller site.

Follow me on Facebook, Linkedin, YouTube and Instagram, or reach out to me at StevenDenlinger@substack.com.